D0202834

The New Canadian Political Economy

The revival of political economy as an important area of research in Canada began in the early 1970s with the publication of Kari Levitt's *Silent Surrender*. In 1976 it was launched in earnest by the first session on Canadian political economy at the meetings of the Canadian Learned Societies in Quebec City. While many academics now classify themselves as political economists, until *The New Canadian Political Economy* there has not been any attempt to systematically survey, review, and assess the scores of books and articles which can now be classified as belonging in this field.

Wallace Clement and Glen Williams have ensured that all areas of the field are discussed, with chapters on the state, resources, industrialization, provinces and regions, labour, gender, Quebec culture, race and ethnicity, the legal system, capital formation, and Canada's position in international political economy. The editors' introduction defines the field of political economy in the 1980s by comparing it to traditional studies of Innis and others and evaluates the strengths and weaknesses of the new approach.

Clement and Williams believe that studies in political economy are now at a crossroads. *The New Canadian Political Economy* suggests important new directions for continued study.

WALLACE CLEMENT is a member of the Department of Sociology and Anthropology, Carleton University.

GLEN WILLIAMS is a member of the Department of Political Science, Carleton University.

The New Canadian Political Economy

Edited by
Wallace Clement and Glen Williams

McGill-Queen's University Press
Kingston, Montreal, London

© McGill-Queen's University Press 1989
ISBN 0-7735-0672-1 (cloth)
ISBN 0-7735-0681-0 (paper)

Legal deposit first quarter 1989
Bibliothèque nationale du Québec

Printed in Canada on acid-free paper

Canadian Cataloguing in Publication Data

Main entry under title:
The New Canadian political economy

Includes index.
Bibliography: p.
ISBN 0-7735-0672-1 (bound). –
ISBN 0-7735-0681-0 (pbk.)

1. Canada – Economic conditions – 1971–
I. Clement, Wallace II. Williams, Glen, 1947–

HB121.A2N49 1989   330.971   C88-090450-X

Contents

Acknowledgments

The editors wish most of all to acknowledge the contributors to this volume. This book developed out of our desire to consolidate the new Canadian political economy so that it can move ahead. In undertaking this task, we consciously approached a diverse cross-section of contributors. This strategy proved particularly effective at a writers' workshop that we organized early in this project, where each contributor outlined his or her chapter and received comments and suggestions from the others. This book is stronger because of that process of supportive cross-fertilization. We readily acknowledge that we have not covered everything: we claim only a significant step in the right direction.

We wish to thank Philip Cercone of McGill-Queen's University Press for his enthusiastic support for this project. We also acknowledge the helpful editorial assistance of John Parry.

Wallace Clement and Glen Williams
Ottawa

Contributors

Frances Abele
School of Public Administration
Carleton University

Gregory Albo
Department of Political Science
Carleton University •

Isabella Bakker
Department of Political Science
York University

Amy Bartholomew
Department of Law
Carleton University

Susan Boyd
Department of Law
Carleton University

Neil Bradford
Department of Political Science
Carleton University

Janine Brodie
Department of Political Science
York University

Wallace Clement
Department of Sociology and
    Anthropology
Carleton University

William D. Coleman
Department of Political Science
McMaster University

Jane Jenson
Department of Political Science
Carleton University

Ted Magder
Department of Political Science
Wilfrid Laurier University

Paul Phillips
Department of Economics
University of Manitoba

Daiva Stasiulis
Department of Sociology and
    Anthropology
Carleton University

Mel Watkins
Department of Economics
University of Toronto

Glen Williams
Department of Political Science
Carleton University

The New Canadian Political Economy

Introduction

The pioneering of political economy approaches gave some of Canada's leading social scientists international recognition for their contributions to world scholarship during the period from the 1920s to the 1950s. After being all but abandoned during the next two decades, a *new* Canadian political economy can be dated from the popularization of nationalist issues identified in the 1968 report of a federal government task force on foreign ownership in Canadian industry, known commonly as "The Watkins Report," and the 1970 publication of Kari Levitt's *Silent Surrender: The Multinational Corporation in Canada.*[1] The revived tradition was launched in earnest by the first Canadian Political Economy sessions in 1976 at the Learned Society meetings in Quebec City, organized by Daniel Drache. These sessions thereafter became a regular feature of the annual "Learneds."

Central to the first decade of the new Canadian political economy were three collections of articles: *Close the 49th Parallel Etc.: The Americanization of Canada*, edited by Ian Lumsden in 1970; *Capitalism and the National Question in Canada*, edited by Gary Teeple in 1972; and *The Canadian State: Political Economy and Political Power*, edited by Leo Panitch in 1977.[2] Intellectual work proceeded rapidly enough for Wallace Clement and Daniel Drache to compile *A Practical Guide to Canadian Political Economy* in 1978, drawing together an eclectic set of readings from a variety of disciplines relevant to the revived political economy tradition.[3] Of continuing importance was the 1979 creation of the learned journal *Studies in Political Economy: A Socialist Review* (twenty-six issues had appeared by the summer of 1988). Through the 1980s, the revival was not only under way, it was flourishing. The wealth of published research it produced was documented in 1985 by Daniel Drache and Wallace Clement's *The New Practical Guide to Canadian Political Economy.*[4] This time the *Guide* required a host of contributors and twenty-five sub-fields to introduce the subject. This exten-

sive output by a new generation drawing on an older tradition revealed that
the new Canadian political economy had come of age.[5]

But, as we look toward the 1990s, this tradition is at another crossroads.
A generation of scholars has established the new Canadian political economy on a solid foundation, but it is now time for reflection and rejuvenation.
This volume seeks to stimulate fresh directions by connecting the past with
the future. It draws on the emerging talents and directions of the new
political Canadian economy by bridging the generations with contributors
who have both helped create the revival and developed within it.

This collection marks the first publication of a comprehensive and systematic review of the new Canadian political economy. Each chapter makes
links between the classics of Canadian political economy, the current state
of the art, and its projected future. Chapter topics were selected both to
reflect the traditional strengths of Canadian political economy and to capture its more recently defined, rapidly developing, intellectual fields – gender,
law, race and ethnicity, and culture and communications. Although without
their own chapter contributions to this volume, still other fields currently in
embryonic form in Canada will, we hope, soon be robust enough to make
their contributions to the wider body of political economy research – the
environment, peace, popular discourse, and the eclipse of social democracy
and the welfare state.

POLITICAL ECONOMY: ROOTS AND MEANING

Political economy has held different meanings over time, and, more important, political economy has been incorporated into both liberal and Marxist
world views. 'Classical' European political economy is associated with
Adam Smith and David Ricardo, British economists who wrote as capitalism blossomed around the turn of the nineteenth century. Their focus was on
the development of commodity markets and the relations of production
made manifest by the labour theory of value. Commodities are goods (or
services) produced for exchange rather than for direct consumption by the
producer. They imply and require the existence of a competitive market
where buying and selling can take place. The labour theory of value contends that the basis of a commodity's value depends on the human labour
expended or consumed in its production.

Smith founded the study of political economy in its modern sense as the
application of scientific methods of analysis to human society. "Science," he
wrote, is "the great antidote to the poison of enthusiasm and superstition,"
and political economy was based on scientific inquiry into "the nature and
causes of the wealth of nations."[6] Smith proposed an economic theory of
history based on human desires for betterment and acquisitiveness as well as
people's capacities for co-operation and exchange of commodities. These

characteristics provided the basis for the division of labour and, as a direct result, human progress, through four qualitatively distinct stages of economic development, each displaying its own social and political structures.

Especially interesting to Smith was the transition from farming to commerce. The social and economic inefficiencies of feudal agriculture were gradually broken down by the rise of the towns and the accompanying development of industrial capitalism through the unconscious operation of the "invisible hand" of the market: "A revolution of the greatest importance to the public happiness, was in this manner brought about by two different orders of people, who had not the least intention to serve the public. To gratify the most childish vanity was the sole motive of the great proprietors. The merchants and artificers, much less ridiculous, acted merely from a view to their own interest, and in pursuit of their own pedlar principle of turning a penny wherever a penny was to be got. Neither of them had knowledge or foresight of that great revolution which the folly of one, and the industry of the other was gradually bringing about."[7]

From this vision of an "invisible hand" that shapes socially beneficial ends from the chaos of individuals seeking to promote their own selfish purposes, Smith derived his theory of the minimal state. He believed, that government intervention in the market, no matter how well intentioned, could serve in the end only to distort the social benefits that would flow from the free competition of industry and capital. The minimal state, Smith argued, would prevent the state from returning to the role it had taken on in previous economic eras as a line of defence for the rich against the poor.[8]

Political economy became a popular label widely employed in nineteenth-century studies of liberal economics and society. There was considerable debate about its exact meaning, but most definitions were compatible in a general fashion with Smith's search for scientific insight into the mechanisms of socially organized production. John Stuart Mill, for example, believed that "writers on Political Economy profess to teach, or to investigate, the nature of Wealth, and the laws of its production and distribution: including, directly or remotely, the operation of all the causes by which the condition of mankind, or any society of human beings, in respect to this universal object of human desire, is made prosperous or the reverse. Not that any treatise on Political Economy can discuss or even enumerate all these causes; but it undertakes to set forth as much as is known of the laws and principles according to which they operate."[9]

Karl Marx, also writing in the nineteenth century, developed his political economy in critique of the dominant liberal or bourgeois political economy that had grown from the work of Smith and Ricardo. Their analysis of markets and profits within capitalism was the orthodoxy against which Marx raged. Smith and Ricardo were the theoreticians of capitalism against feudalism, whereas Marx's task was to expose the internal contradictions of capitalism in seeking the release of new relations of production. Nevertheless, at a macro level, Marx's analysis shared important similarities with Smithian political economy, including a stress on "scientific" social analysis, a stage theory of economic development, the centrality of labour in creating value, and a view of the state as alien and repressive. At the core of Marx's political economy was a notion most fully elaborated by Ricardo – the labour theory of value – but for Marx the commodity "labour" had a dual quality. Not only does labour produce more than its cost of reproduction (surplus value), and so provide the basis for capitalist exploitation and economic growth, but labour has consciousness, an ability to act politically to transform the conditions of its sale. Exploitation and struggle are the hallmarks of Marx's political economy.

In the *Grundrisse: Introduction to the Critique of Political Economy*, written in 1857, Marx outlines "The Method of Political Economy," saying: "When we consider a given country politico-economically, we begin with its population, its distribution among classes, town, country, the coast, the different branches of production, export and import, annual production and consumption, commodity prices, etc. . . . The population is an abstraction if I leave out, for example, the classes of which it is composed. These classes in turn are an empty phrase if I am not familiar with the elements on which they rest, e.g. wage labour, capital, etc. These latter in turn presuppose exchange, division of labour, prices, etc. For example, capital is nothing without wage labour, without value, money, price, etc."[10]

Marx's political economy has come to be known as "historical materialist." It is materialist in the sense that it focuses on the processes whereby material requirements are satisfied. It is historical in its concern for social processes that transform societies. A historical materialist approach seeks to understand the dynamic of change in the transformation of production and reproduction with particular attention given to the tensions, struggles, and contradictions within societies and between them. Political institutions were given an important place by Marx in the regulation of social conflict. As Bob Jessop has argued so persuasively, Marx's historical materialist analysis of the state and politics had its "discontinuities and disjunctions" but offered an open richness that has spurred a "wide range" of state theories.[11] Derived from Marx, these state theories focus generally on the mechanisms through which government social and economic policies help to stabilize the dynamic process of capitalist accumulation.

To summarize, while political economy is based on a tradition that investigates the relationship between the economy and politics as they affect the social and cultural life of societies, within political economy there have been divergent tendencies. Broadly, the liberal political economy tradition has placed determinate weight on the political system and markets, while the Marxist tradition grants primacy to the economic system and classes. Such facile statements, however, underplay the complexity of positions within each tradition. Political economy at its strongest has focused on processes whereby social change is located in the historical interaction of the economic, political, cultural, and ideological moments of social life, with the dynamic rooted in socio-economic conflict. The best of political economy has avoided "economism," which attributes all explanations to the laws of motion of capitalism, instead impregnating materialism with "human agency," whereby the decisions and actions of people are integral to explaining the course of history.

While the contributors to this volume are all working in the political economy tradition, all do not share an identical world view. Such eclecticism reflects the variety of world views associated with Canadian political economy. All do share, however, the strength of the new political economy, which is the incorporation of the political and cultural/ideological within a materialist understanding. As Clement has written elsewhere, "While the economic provides the context, it is the political and the cultural/ideological that write the text of history, the particularities of each nation, and the possibilities for the future. The script is one in which human actors have significant freedom of action."[12] We will return later in this introduction to the question of common ground in the scope and method of the new Canadian political economy.

FROM CLASSICS TO CONTEMPORARIES: INNIS

Through their pioneering of the staples approach to understanding Canadian economic development, Harold Adams Innis (1894-1952) and W. A. Mackintosh (1895-1970) became the founders of the political economy tradition in Canada. Although they at first appeared to proceed from shared assumptions, their conclusions began to diverge markedly with the passage of time.[13] Whereas Mackintosh's message could be absorbed (and eventually obscured) within orthodox neo-classical economics. Innis's analysis was so forcefully original that his commanding presence has been evident throughout the history of the tradition. Innis has stood sometimes as inspiration, sometimes as foil, for those who have worked to create the new Canadian political economy.

As testimony to his staying power, aspects of Innis's staples thesis are recounted in virtually all the chapters. Its essence is that Canada was developed to exploit a series of raw materials for more industrially advanced metropolitan nations. Canada's reliance on resource exports led to a failure to capture the benefits of the "linkages" associated with the inputs into production and processing of the raw materials, thereby locking it into a spiral of dependent relations. Apparent similarities between Innis's staples thesis and later Latin American dependency theories led the founders of the new Canadian political economy to proclaim Innis a forerunner of their own application of *dependencia* analysis to Canada. Glen Williams's chapter argues that although this link was key in relaunching the tradition, it was a product more of wishful imagination than of careful analysis. Unlike dependency theory, the staples approach was not rooted in neo-Marxist models of socio-regional exploitation.

But Innis was much more than a staples theorist, contributing to a wide range of issues like regionalism, culture, and communications still central to the study of contemporary Canadian life. He also remained relevant because, like those in the new political economy, he worked outside the mainstream of neo-classical doctrine. Innis's critique of neo-classical political economy was, however, derived not from Marx but from his reading of Adam Smith and the radical heretic of US economics in the early twentieth century, Thorstein Veblen. Innis recorded that Veblen was "the first to attempt a general stocktaking of general tendencies in a dynamic society saddled with machine industry, just as Adam Smith was the first to present a general stocktaking before machine industry came in."[14]

In a revealing tribute to Veblen, Innis recorded many features of Veblen's work that characterized his own method. In contrast to ahistorical and static neo-classical analysis, Veblen's approach was "dynamic," Innis wrote, since it focused on "the study of processes of growth and decay" of economic institutions.[15] Also in contrast to neo-classical orthodoxy, Veblen's humanistic interdisciplinary perspective was grounded in the premiss that economic man "is not simply a bundle of desires that are to be saturated by being placed in the path of the forces of the environment, but rather a coherent structure of propensities and habits which seeks realization and expression in an unfolding activity."[16] Another important area of agreement between Innis and Veblen was their stress on the significance of understanding the relationship between machine technology and the character of human activity.[17] This was to become an especially important theme in Innis's later work on culture and communications. Finally, Innis admired what he perceived to be Veblen's detached, unbiased, apolitical, scientific approach, "protecting him from absorption into the partialities of modern movements. His anxiety has always been to detect trends and escape their effects." Veblen, like Innis, was an "individualist . . . in revolt" against mass society.[18]

FURTHER LINKS WITH THE PAST: PENTLAND AND MACPHERSON

Innis provided the new Canadian political economy with a non-Marxist alternative to the neo-classical models that today still dominate the training of professional economists. Pentland and Macpherson, as we shall see, provided a Marxist-influenced basis for the rejection of the dominant liberal models of social analysis.

H. Clare Pentland (1914–1978) has been an important, if somewhat underground, figure in both the rediscovery and the revitalization of Canadian political economy. Pentland's work asked central questions about the making of Canadian labour, in terms of both labour market and class formation, within an immigrant society undergoing industrialization and resource exploitation. Pentland became widely known through a few seminal journal articles, but close followers have always referred to his doctoral thesis, defended in 1961, and a major report prepared for the Task Force on Labour Relations in 1968. Not until 1981 was his thesis, *Labour and Capital in Canada 1650–1860*, finally published under the editorship of Paul Phillips.[19] While Pentland's main work was produced in the 1960s and was not published until the 1980s, its major influence for the revival of Canadian political economy was in the 1970s. Significant critiques of Pentland's work have now begun to appear,[20] testament to both the continuing importance of his contribution and also the more scrutinizing gaze of the new political economy's ever stronger foundation of empirical research, a point emphasized in the chapter by Abele and Stasiulis in this volume.

Crawford Brough Macpherson, better known as "C.B." (1911–1987), also continues to have a major impact on Canadian political economy. His justly famous *Democracy in Alberta: Social Credit and the Party System* was first published in 1953, and he went on to build a world-wide following as a political theorist, culminating in 1985 with *The Rise and Fall of Economic Justice*.[21] Macpherson's greatest contribution to the new political economy has been through his extensive writings on theories of property, on democracy, and on the development of a theory of rights.

In their own ways, both Pentland and Macpherson fostered and influenced the growth of a strong neo-Marxist presence within Canadian political economy. However, Canadian neo-Marxism has owed its vigour also to a post-1960s resurgence, centred in western Europe, of left intellectual analysis. Not surprisingly, controversies marking the new Canadian political economy in the 1980s have centred on the respective contributions of Innis and Marx. Debate was sparked by a special issue of *Studies in Political Economy*, where David McNally, Leo Panitch, and Ray Schmidt critiqued "Innisian-inspired" dependency perspectives, especially the weakness of class analysis within the Canadian dependency school.[22] This critique initiated energetic responses by Ian Parker, Daniel Drache, and Mel Watkins defending the relevance of Innis.[23]

At issue has never been whether Innis was a Marxist – of course, he was not – but whether there was a common ground of mutual relevance between the class and dependency/Innisian perspectives within contemporary Cana-

dian political economy. Clement has argued, using the case of mining, that
Innis's massive empirical contribution can enrich class analysis. Such an
undertaking is informed by Innis's insights, but the more powerful explanation is Marxist.[24] For the most part, the tension between the two approaches
has been creative for the new political economy. The challenge continues to
be to produce fresh paradigms that build on the insights of traditional ones.

SCOPE AND METHOD IN
CANADIAN POLITICAL ECONOMY

Despite their work being complementary, we have seen that classical and
contemporary, liberal and neo-Marxist, class and dependency political
economists have proceeded largely from radically different premises. At
the risk of overgeneralizing, we will now explore, through consideration of
scope and method, how these distinct strands can be woven back together
into the fabric of Canadian political economy.

The object of political economy research is typically macro-level description and/or explanation of material practices. The subject of this research
knows no boundaries, as long as the analysis develops the subject's reciprocal linkages to related subjects and fields of inquiry. Consequently, political
economy analysis is interdisciplinary, bridging such organized disciplines as
history, economics, geography, philosophy, anthropology, literature, communications, psychology, political science, and sociology. At its best, political
economy makes the connection between the economic, political, and cul-
tural/ideological moments of social life in a holistic way. As well, researchers typically use a historical developmental approach in order to
locate their subject in time, hence the focus on social change and transformation. Finally, research is frequently spatially sensitive: that is, the subject
is defined territorially through a relational linkage with other domestic and
international territories.

While founded in an era of nationalism, the new Canadian political economy has always been outward-looking: both concerned about the impact of
international forces on Canada and open to incorporating international theoretical movements into its research. In the late 1960s, the dependency
literature, drawn from the experience of Africa, Latin America, and the
Caribbean, stimulated debate. As it matured, however, the new political
economy has become more integrated within a wider international political
economy centred in western Europe. Increasingly, it has become more truly
comparative in its methodology, moving away from the classical political
economists' universe, centred in Great Britain and the United States, toward
developing comparisons with other smaller, late-industrializing countries in
Scandinavia and Australasia.

Some have mistakenly attributed economic determinism to Canadian political economy, but it has focused primarily on human agency – choices and decisions made by political, economic, and social actors and their effects. These choices are defined both historically and territorially and are mediated through cultural and ideological factors on the one hand and forms of social organization and/or technology on the other. Where liberal political economists might emphasize culture and technology, neo-Marxists would stress ideology and social organization. The concept of agency is employed here to convey the sense that social outcomes are not predetermined. However, the "definition" and "mediation" of these choices indicate that social and material boundaries extensively structure decision-making. Canadian political economy's different theoretical perspectives often hotly debate the different weights they ascribe to "agency" and "structure" in determining outcomes.

Political economy's methodological insight is to study the effects of totalities from a materialist perspective. Social relations are located within the context of the economic, political, and ideological/cultural dimensions on the one hand and within the dimensions of time and space on the other. To understand the forces of change, political economy requires a broad base. In Innis's terms, this means that political economy is concerned with linkages, but these linkages are conceptual as well as material. Relations within political economy are not static forces. To the contrary, political economy seeks to discover tensions within society as it produces struggle and resistance. To know how societies are, and can be, transformed is the primary goal of political economy. Frequently this means challenging conventional wisdoms and ideological structures in the popular, academic, and political domains.

As the following chapters will make abundantly clear, Canadian political economy covers a great deal of ground! Its current sub-fields are represented in the following twelve chapters. The reader will soon discover that these sub-fields are indeed linked in a common tradition, but it is an eclectic tradition in terms of subject, ideology, and specific approach. It does not lay exclusive claim to any special research techniques, nor does it promote a homogeneous "line". Political economy in Canada prides itself on its openness, its willingness to engage in disputes over theoretical paradigms, and its eagerness to incorporate new discoveries. Its vibrancy comes from the prolific research of its practioners and the engagement of its followers.

OVERVIEW OF THE VOLUME

Mel Watkins, whose published work is widely acknowledged to link the old and new Canadian political economies, poses an enduring question within both traditions: under the shadow of imperial powers, what has marked the specific character of Canada's pattern of economic development? Canadian growth, he answers, has persistently been structured around staples production and its linkages. This has led to a unique pattern of capital and class formation which establishes Canada's place in the world and gives meaning to its internal growth patterns.

Wallace Clement follows by giving specific attention to resource production. Outlining the contribution of Innis's staples approach, he focuses as well on the class and feminist critiques of that classical tradition. While Clement documents the continuing importance of resources for Canada's international trade and as a basis of regionalism, he also explores how staples extraction affects employment, the labour movement, and the social relations of production.

Neil Bradford and Glen Williams address the peculiar historical trajectory of Canadian industrialization. By building on Innis, they locate Canadian industrialization in the staples tradition of resource dependency and technological dependency on more advanced nations. Rather than being satisfied with Innis's answers, however, they recount how the literature has posed important new questions that arise from the concern of many in the new political economy with social processes and political struggles that have shaped state industrial policies.

Like Bradford and Williams, Paul Phillips identifies key approaches within the new Canadian political economy, this time in relation to labour. While evaluating critically Innis's relative silence on labour, Phillips recounts the work of the institutionalists, the pioneer new political economists, the class culture historians, the labour process analysts, and the radical economists. Phillips then builds toward a synthesis that encompasses culture, class, and the economy in an understanding of labour. This includes segmented labour markets, workplace control structures, and state policies.

Feminism challenges political economy, Isabella Bakker argues, in a way whereby both can gain, since each locates its fundamental understanding of power within historical materialism. Feminist political economy means, for her, the articulation of class and gender struggles. In Canada, Bakker contends, an indigenous feminist analysis that reformulates the categories of political economy is beginning to unfold. She notes particularly differences in gender relations within English-speaking Canada and Quebec. The politics of feminism plays an important part in her chapter, including an extension of the meaning of politics through feminist insights into social reproduction and the economic crisis.

Canada in the world system is Glen Williams's subject, one of the thorniest for the new Canadian political economy but one that clearly links it with its classical tradition. He is critical of the dependency approach which marked the first period of political economy's revival and also surveys the three perspectives on this question that succeeded dependency. Williams advocates a position that returns partially to Innis's notion of Canada in the world system – as a lesser region within the centre (namely, the United States). Continentalism maintains its hegemony through popular culture and political institutions as much as through economics, he argues.

Regionalism, Janine Brodie demonstrates, has been and remains a profound feature of Canadian society and a central axis of conflict in the experience of Canadian economic, political, and cultural life. She emphasizes the spatial dimension to the classical contributions by Innis and Fowke as a place to build the new political economy. She encourages us to consider regions relationally, as an outcome of human agency that makes them political products, and historically, so that uneven spatial development becomes the central focus. Within this framework Brodie locates federal-provincial relations and provincial development strategies in what she calls "the political creation of regions."

William D. Coleman explains that classic political economy in Quebec had origins distinct from those in English-speaking Canada. Coleman shows how these distinct origins were linked to the emergence of a new Quebec political economy in which analysts saw an identity between class and nation and tended to stress the primacy of national/ethnic questions over class struggles. Contradictions at the heart of this analysis have in recent years propelled class and gender to centre stage. Coleman argues persuasively that the uniquely comprehensive treatment of federal, regional economic, class, and gender conflict in Quebec's political economy allows it to offer a great deal to scholars examining other parts of Canada.

Gregory Albo and Jane Jenson explore the premiss of the relative autonomy of the state as a way of cutting into the new Canadian political economy literature. Outlining the place of the state in the work of the classical political economists, including Innis, they also focus on transitional figures such as Macpherson, Pentland, and Ryerson. The next era, they contend, marks a key break within political economy over the issue of a peripheral Canadian state in the face of dependency. They examine, as well, both the instrumentalist and structuralist positions within the new political economy and extend their review to socialist-feminist contributions.

A political economy approach to the legal system, according to Amy Bartholomew and Susan Boyd, is still in an "embryonic" stage of development in Canada. Their chapter greatly advances our thinking on this subject by drawing together a diverse literature that speaks to the discourse and practice of law through the state apparatus. Giving their subject a firm theoretical grounding in class and feminist analysis, Bartholomew and Boyd address the twin questions of how social forces may "determine" the content of laws and the structure of the legal system, and, equally important, how the discourse of law may "overdetermine" social relations and social conflict.

Arguing that race and ethnicity are integral to understanding the relationships between ideology, culture, and politics in the unfolding of the economic order, Frances Abele and Daiva Stasiulis present a critique of classical political economy and engage the new Canadian political economy with a challenge. They contend that the popular application of the designation of "white settler colony" to Canada has tended to "white-wash" the subordination of racial and ethnic minorities that was fundamental to Canada's development. It is against the invisibility of race and ethnicity within political economy that they protest. Also prominent in their chapter is the experience of gender, which is given analytical significance along with the concept of resistance, in the sense of struggles that define social experience.

Finally, Ted Magder also takes the new Canadian political economy to task – for not sustaining an inquiry into the production, distribution, and consumption of cultural practices. A political economy of culture brings us up against US hegemony in Canada's cultural communication and the process by which this dependency has been secured. It also leads us to investigate the "contradictory dynamics" of both state and commercial cultural initiatives in Canada in the face of this hegemony. In setting out a model of "dependent cultural development," Magder seeks to create distance between a sophisticated political economy of Canadian culture and communications and simple cultural nationalism. "Democratic alternatives" to current structures must be sought, he believes.

At the end of this collection, the reader will find an extensive bibliography of all works mentioned in the text. The bibliography gives full references for materials appearing in the notes at the end of each chapter. We hope that the reader enjoys (and learns from) this book as much as we did preparing it.

NOTES

1 Canada, Privy Council Office, *Foreign Ownership and Canadian Industry*; Levitt, *Silent Surrender*.
2 Lumsden, ed., *Close the 49th Parallel Etc: The Americanization of Canada*; Teeple, ed., *Capitalism and the National Question in Canada*; Panitch, ed., *The Canadian State*.
3 Clement and Drache, *A Practical Guide to Canadian Political Economy*.
4 Drache and Clement, eds., *The New Practical Guide to Canadian Political Economy*.
5 Another mid-1980s bibliographical compilation of the extensive research record of the new Canadian political economy can be found in Marchak, "Canadian Political Economy." She suggests that "political economy is the study of power derived from or contingent upon a system of property rights; the historical development of power relationships; and the cultural and social embodiments of them. It is also an academic community in Canada, sharing a history, a paradigm, a so-

cial network, and a general perspective on both its subject matter and the engagement of academics in Canadian political life" (p. 673).

6 Smith, *An Inquiry*, Book IV, p. 200, Book V, p. 318.

7 Ibid., Book III, p. 440.

8 Ibid., Book IV, pp. 208, 477–478; Book V, p. 236.

9 Mill, *Principles of Political Economy*, 1. See also Mill's "On the Definition of Political Economy."

10 Marx, *Grundrisse*, 100.

11 Jessop, *The Capitalist State: Marxist Theories and Methods*, 1.

12 Clement, "Canadian Political Economy," 456.

13 Glen Williams, *Not for Export*, chap. 7.

14 Innis, "The Work of Thorstein Veblen," 25.

15 Ibid., 24–6.

16 Veblen, "Why Is Economics Not an Evolutionary Science?" 233.

17 See, for example, Veblen, "The Discipline of the Machine."

18 Innis, "Veblen," 25.

19 Pentland, *Labour and Capital in Canada 1650–1860*; Canada, Privy Council Office, Report of the Task Force on Labour Relations, *Industrial Relations*.

20 Greer, "Wage Labour."

21 Macpherson, *Democracy in Alberta*.

22 McNally, "Staple Theory as Commodity Fetishism"; Panitch, "Dependency and Class in Canadian Political Economy"; Schmidt, "Canadian Political Economy: A Critique."

23 Drache, "Harold Innis and Canadian Capitalist Development"; Watkins, "The Innis Tradition"; Parker, " 'Commodity Fetishism' and 'Vulgar Marxism' "; Drache, "The Crisis of Canadian Political Economy."

24 Clement, "Transformations in Mining."

CHAPTER ONE

The Political Economy of Growth

Mel Watkins

Canada is a rich country, unambiguously so by global standards (which does not mean that there are no poor people in Canada, for there are many – indeed, indefensibly so, given that overall level of affluence). How did it get that way? Canada is noted for the abundance of its natural resources, or staples, and its reliance on their export. Has that situation given a particular character, or specificity, to the economy, while providing an important clue as to how growth has taken place, at least initially and perhaps even down to the present day? Canada is an industrialized country – its prime minister is allowed to attend the prestigious annual economic summit of the seven leading industrial nations of the non-Communist world. But does it in fact have a rounded industrial structure, or instead one that is – in the language of the Science Council of Canada – truncated?

The means of production in Canada are predominantly in private hands: Canada is a capitalist country, and its capitalist, or business, class is dominant. But what is the nature of that capitalist class? Is it predominantly commercial or industrial? Independent or dependent?

Canada happens to be located next door to the United States, which has long been bigger and more dynamic and is now a superpower and great imperial centre. What effect has that had on Canada's economic growth? (John Kenneth Galbraith said recently: "Canadian and Polish situations are similar: they're both major errors of location.")

These are surely enough questions for one essay – though it is hardly an exhaustive list of issues that could be probed under the rubric of the political economy of growth. This particular set of questions happens to have been of central concern to Canadian political economists, past and present, who, in the process of answering these questions, have made important advances in theorizing the Canadian case.

The old school of political economy, which was at its peak in the period between the two world wars, left as its legacy the so-called staple approach of Harold Innis and W.A. Mackintosh: the engine of growth of the Canadian economy had been from the outset staple exports to more advanced industrialized economies, and different staples had left their distinctive stamp on the Canadian social formation. The new school of political economy, which has emerged in the past two decades, has likewise produced one "big idea," the so-called Naylor-Clement thesis (after its two main formulators, R.T. Naylor and Wallace Clement) about the commercial, rather than industrial, bias of the Canadian capitalist class and the dependent branch-plant industrialization that flows from an unequal alliance with American monopoly capital.

There are many links between the old and the new schools. Donald Creighton, as well as Innis, wrote of commercialism, or the reign of merchant capital, as characteristic of Canada; Clement writes extensively on resources (including in this volume); and Mel Watkins and Daniel Drache have updated the staples approach in the light of the findings of the new political economy. Eric Kierans reminded us powerfully of the economic rent or surplus that inheres in resource production but has not necessarily been put to productive use within Canada. Kari Levitt's seminal work on foreign ownership referred back to Innis while in some respects anticipating Naylor and Clement, whose starting point was also why so much of the Canadian economy was foreign owned. Glen Williams sees industrialization as a strategy of the Canadian business class to use tariffs to replace imports with domestic production, but all within the context of an economy where the domestic market grew as a by-product of the spread effects of staple exports. Jorge Niosi writes of a Canadian bourgeoisie with a new confidence to control the resource industries and operate continentally but still reluctant to be serious industrialists able to compete internationally. Rianne Mahon ties the story of the contemporary restructuring of the Canadian textile industry to the traditional structure of power in a staples economy; Michael Asch has theorized about modes of production in his writing on the fur trade and aboriginal people; and Philip Ehrensaft and Warwick Armstrong have generalized the concept of a staples economy applied to Canada to that of "Dominion capitalism," which they then apply as well to Australia, New Zealand, Argentina, and Uruguay. In her recently published book, *A Staple State: Canadian Industrial Resources in Cold War*, Melissa Clark-Jones shows how the Canadian state translates the American strategic interest and the continental corporate interest into the Canadian "national" interest. And so on.[1]

This paper seeks to further the merger of the old and the new political economies, the better to answer our questions. It can be seen, on the one hand, as modifying the staple approach to allow for the phenomenon of foreign ownership as elucidated by the Naylor-Clement thesis and, on the other hand, as modifying the Naylor-Clement thesis by allowing for the centrality of staples.

THE STAPLES THESIS

Canada was founded in the modern period of history as an offshoot of Europe; the aboriginal people were already present, of course, but their rights were respected only to the extent that imperial and, in the long run, settler interests were served. Though initially merely an impediment on the route to the rumoured riches of Cathay, Canada soon came to be valued in its own right for its resources (fish, fur, etc), which were exported to the mother country, first France and then Britain; an industrializing Britain, for its part, was able to vent its surpluses of manufactures, capital, and people. These self-evident truths are the building blocks of a staple theory of economic growth relevant to Canada (and to other new countries, notably the American colonies, Australia, and New Zealand, and, with modifications, to South Africa, the Caribbean, and Latin America).

Economic growth is a process by which one thing leads to another – or fails to do so.[2] The export of a staple has potential spread effects or linkages to other sectors at home (at the margin) or abroad (at the metropolitan centre). The staple can be subjected to further processing or manufacturing, such as fur into hats or wheat into flour; this is a forward linkage. Inputs can be produced for use by the staple sector. This backward linkage can be further subdivided into infrastructure linkage (railways to move wheat) and capital goods linkage (mining machinery). The building of infrastructure in its turn can then have further and powerful spread effects, potentially exceeding the original linkage from the staple itself and leading to pervasive industrialization; the central importance of Canadian railways for both staple production and industrialization has long been understood.[3]

The disposition of the incomes generated in the export sector creates final demand linkage. It too can be further subdivided, into consumption linkage (spending on a range of consumer goods from cotton textiles to colour television sets) and fiscal linkage (the appropriation by the state of economic rent or surplus generated in the resource sector – over and above all costs, including a normal return to capital – and *its* disposition). Eric Kierans's estimates of the massive rents generated by metal mining in Manitoba – captured mostly by foreign owners rather than by the provincial state – and the contrasting reality of the Alberta Heritage Fund accumulated from OPEC-assisted rents in oil and gas show the extraordinary potential of this fiscal linkage to seed further linkages. The softwood lumber imbroglio between Canada and the United States in the mid-1980s resulted in part from the failure of provincial and federal governments in Canada to capture rents, with the consequence that prices were lower – in effect, American consumers got the rents – and US producers were able to claim unfair competition. Faced with the threat of a US tax, with the US government getting the rents, Canadian governments finally put on their own tax. As well, the failure of the state to capture rents may simply mean that private capital becomes sloppy and inefficient and fails to generate them.[4]

Opportunities will vary from one staple to another. Growth of a more diversified character around the export base will be facilitated by the availability of labour via immigration and capital via borrowing. Demand for the staple sets the pace, but the extent to which economic growth takes place around it depends as well on supply responses, both institutional and technological. Alexander Dow, after detailed research on the metal mining industry, discovers "Canadian entrepreneurship and innovation without which the industry would not, most likely, have succeeded as it did." John Fogarty, drawing on the historical experiences of Argentina and Australia as well as Canada, likewise argues against the demand-bias of the staple theory, insisting that it is entrepreneurship, private and public, that really counts. Carl Solberg's careful comparison of the wheat economies of Canada and Argentina demonstrates that it is public entrepreneurship – government policies with respect to agricultural research and education, rail transportation, and the grading, storing, and marketing of wheat – that enabled Canada to reap the larger benefits in the long run.[5]

This serves to remind us that in all cases – and not only with respect to fiscal linkage – responses can be the result not only of the operation of markets but also of state policies, both at the margin and at the centre, which can help or hurt. These state policies in their turn can be powerfully conditioned by the specific social formations that emanate from the exploitation of specific staples. Hence the family farm on the Canadian prairies – itself a consequence of homestead policy – facilitated the co-operative movement and the agrarian protest politics that then pushed the government in positive ways.

Conceptually, what is here being described is centrally a Keynesian model of growth, with exports rather than domestic investment as the leading sector driving the economy via multiplier-accelerator spread effects; so, too, it is exports that are the leading source of instability. Mackintosh grasped this point early, and by grafting the staple theory on to Keynesian theory provided the rationale for Canada's post–Second World War strategy of economic growth based on large-scale exports of resources to the United States, with inflows of American capital providing funds to expand staple sectors and with markets secured by foreign ownership ties. So it was that Keynesianism, the greatest innovation in economic theory and practice in this century, fraught with apparent potential to lead to greater emphasis on the domestic market as the prime source of growth, actually led to no alteration in the staples bias of Canadian economic policy.[6]

It is helpful to be more explicit about the spatial dimension in two senses, namely, whether linkages are reaped at home or abroad and whether by domestic or foreign capital. The first issue is: how much production takes place locally, at the periphery, around the export-base? The second issue is: of that local production, how much is under the control of local capitalists and how much under the control of external capitalists? The first issue is about the quantity of production and the extent of growth; the second is about the extent of indigenous ownership and control, that is, the independence and maturity of the resulting capitalist development.[7]

Take forward linkage: resources can be processed at the point either of production or of consumption (or even at somewhere in between, as in the case of bauxite, which is processed where electric power is cheap). Encouragement to process within Canada has been called "the manufacturing condition"; it has been consciously pursued by provincial governments, from Ontario's "little National Policy" in the late 19th and early 20th centuries to Alberta's "province-building" in the post-war years.[8] A recurring theme in the Canadian literature is the limited nature of forward linkages. There is a persistent tendency to export relatively unprocessed resources and certainly no ability to make a quantum leap from supplying a range of critical inputs for industrialization to having an advanced industrial structure.[9]

It seems reasonable to infer that foreign ownership of the resource industry will exacerbate the tendency of forward linkages to be weak, particularly when the foreign owner is a vertically integrated corporation using the resource as an input into its metropolitan operations. A case in point is the ownership of Labrador iron ore by US steel interests; one of the "linkages" of this is that it enabled Mr Mulroney to apprentice in serving foreign capital, acquiring skills that he could later use as prime minister. Perhaps the most striking example of weak and ineffectual linkage – actually of all linkages – is Sudbury, long the site of some of the the world's richest nickel-lead mines but now dependent for jobs on a government decision to locate the processing of tax returns there.

Backward linkage and, above all, consumption linkage define a range of market demands. In the nature of things (meaning mostly transport costs), from the outset, some, even many, of these opportunities will lead to home production in the new country. But also in the nature of things – the newness of the hinterland, the politics of the imperial connection favouring industry at the centre over that at the margin – there will be substantial reliance on imports at the outset, for manufactures in general and for more sophisticated goods like machinery in particular. The greater the leakage into imports, the less the growth locally around the export base.

The propensity to import capital goods may persist indefinitely. The reliance on substantial imports of machinery down to the present day, even in the mining sector, where Canada has been a world-class producer for a century, brands Canada's industrial structure as not fully developed (see Clement's paper in this volume).

Within the broader manufacturing sector, the process of import-substitution tends to proceed inexorably as local producers try to pre-empt markets defined by imports; this switch to domestic sourcing may actually have been facilitated by the import houses themselves.[10] It is to be expected that manufacturers will further attempt to aid and abet that process by resort to protection. The resulting tariff is no aberration and, notwithstanding orthodox economic theorizing, has its benefits. Consumption linkage is enhanced, and, with supplies of labour and capital available from abroad, the overall growth of the economy accelerates. Historically, the tariff not only had this protectionist effect, it also generated increased revenues during periods such as the export boom in the early 20th century as significant volumes of imports continued; these revenues were then used to build more railways, leading to further rounds of linkage effects. The tariff, then, also contributes to growth via fiscal linkage and infrastructure linkage. (There really was no end to the process: railways built through solid rock in outlandish places in northern Ontario led to discoveries of minerals faster than would otherwise have been the case, unleashing yet further linkages.)[11]

There was yet one further consequence of the tariff that links our two spatial dimensions. Unable to export to Canada, some foreign producers, particularly from the United States, jumped the high tariff wall after 1879 and set up branch plants in Canada. To that extent, while Canada got industrial production – beyond that which it already had from the 1850s on – it did not get it under the control of indigenous Canadian capital; it got its own industry but not, to the same extent, its own industrial capitalists; it industrialized, but dependently and incompletely.

It would be wrong, however, to attribute this incomplete, dependent industrialization simply to the tariff. The tariff made it more attractive for foreign capital to move to Canada, but it can hardly be credited with creating the fresh expansionist urges of foreign capital. The time has come (by appeal to the writings of Naylor and Clement) to meld this aspect of capitalist development into the story of staples growth, to see how a staples economy comes to be characterized by dependent industrialization.

THE NAYLOR-CLEMENT THESIS

Begin with a general argument about early industrialization that has been made with respect to Britain and to continental Europe, notably by the Marxist historian Maurice Dobb.[12] There are, it is said, two paths to industrialization: one that emerges out of artisanal beginnings in the hands of new capitalists, and one based on the extension of pre-existing merchant capital into the new industrial sphere. The first is the strong path, which leads to a mature industrial structure; the second is a weak path, where industrial capital never comes fully to dominate financial capital.

Can this line of reasoning be applied to Canada? There are two problems in doing so. First, Canada's economy was dominated in its pre-industrial phase not simply by commerce and finance but specifically by trade in staples. Second, Canada is industrializing later, after capitalism has transformed itself from a competitive mode to a monopoly mode as a result of the rise of the large corporation, including its multinational variant.

Naylor and Clement[13] agree that Canada ends up on the weak path. Naylor sees merchant-cum-financial capital remaining dominant and tolerating, indeed inviting in, foreign industrial capital to give a weak path of dependent industrialization. Canadian financial capital is antagonistic toward indigenous industrial capital. Clement subtly amends. The critical point for him is the rise of the American industrial corporation; it is born multinational and as the agent of foreign monopoly capital creates barriers to entry for smaller indigenous industrial firms. Previously the techniques of the more advanced United States next door had moved to Canada (or British North America) via the migration of individual American businessmen who then became permanent residents, even founders of great Canadian families like the Masseys; now it came in institutional corporate form. The result was to stifle indigenous Canadian development, which, emulating the United States, had been proceeding with a lag along the strong path. Canada was shunted on to the weak path. The villain of the piece becomes American industrial capital – though Canadian capital can be seen as complicit, in Naylor's sense.

The path of dependent industrialization was, for reasons we have already seen, one of import substitution, of producing for the protected domestic market rather than taking on world markets in manufactures. That can be seen as second best (as Naylor does) but Williams properly insists that Canadian capital pioneered the import-substitution industrialization model – it is in fact known elsewhere, particularly in Latin America, as the "Canadian model" – and that, in conjunction with the large domestic market associated with a succession of staple exports, Canada has done remarkably well out of it.

The result is not an alliance within Canada between indigenous financial and industrial capital (creating, in Hilferding's term, finance capital), with industrial capitalists as the dominant or hegemonic fraction within the capitalist class. Rather, there is an alliance between Canadian financial capital and American industrial capital. Because of the size and power of the United States, the resulting alliance is, in Clement's phrase, an unequal alliance, with Canadian capital a junior partner to American capital. Within Canada, the hegemonic fraction remains financial capital.

This analysis is almost, but not quite, right. Canada being a staple economy, a distinction should be made within industrial capital between staple industries, or primary manufacturing, and secondary manufacturing proper. The former can be, and in fact are, more powerful than the latter. The hegemonic fraction is financial capital and staple capital, foreign and domestic, which are in alliance with American industrial capital; this fraction is disproportionately represented within the structures of the state.[14] As a consequence, the manufacturing interest is weak in Canada, and it is difficult to work out an industrial strategy proper. Though Canada is industrialized, industry is in important respects immature and the country remains a staples economy – a pattern that Drache calls "advanced resource capitalism."

Canadian capital has accepted a division of labour both sectorally and geographically. Historically, it has been able to dominate in commerce and finance, including infrastructure and real estate, but not in industry proper. In the staple sector, the story is mixed, with the majority of resource industries remaining under foreign control down into the post-war period. Recently, however, there has been increasing Canadian ownership within this resource sector, too, as Canadian capital has been attracted by the large rents that can be appropriated. This shows some maturing of Canadian capital, but toward more efficiency as rentier capital than as industrial capital proper.

Consider the case of Edper Investments, owned by the Toronto Bronfmans, whose fortunes originated in the previous generation of the family in the liquor business (one of the more interesting forward linkages – from grain). Its president, Trevor Eyton, was interviewed in 1986: "According to Mr. Eyton, the group tries to balance its real-estate interests – the field in which the brothers had initial experience – with natural resources – a must for a Canadian company in their view – and financial services." Resources are a "must," while manufacturing is not mentioned.[15]

In those sectors where capital is able to dominate at home, it will have a base to try to become world class and operate abroad. This is true in Canada, but the division of labour that constrains Canadian capital is its tendency to see only the American market, not the whole world, as its oyster. It may even be that in recent years Canadian capital has become more confident in its dealings with American capital, albeit as the latter struggles to maintain its international hegemony vis-à-vis Japanese and European capital. The increasing Canadian control in the resource sector in the past two decades has been relative mostly to American capital, but this is Canada as a base for continental capital rather than for global capital proper.[16]

There remains one critical shortcoming to this story from the perspective of the new political economy, with its Marxist cast: what about the rest of the Canadian class formation and its inherent conflicts, which are presumed to generate change? Just as the staples bias affects the capitalist class, so it affects the rest of the class structure. A distinction must be made between the earlier staples – trades – and the later staples – industries.[17] The direct producers in the staple trades are not a proletariat proper but independent commodity producers, varying from Indian bands in the days of the fur trade to family farmers producing wheat. Conflict takes place around the terms of the exchange of the staple for trade-goods and interest paid on debts incurred by the direct producers; surplus is appropriated by capital via mechanisms of unequal exchange. The protest movements of western grain farmers are ample evidence of the reality and intensity of these conflicts from which flowed important political and economic effects. In contrast, the staple industries, such as mining and newsprint production, are industries proper, with workers who are paid a wage over which they typically bargain collectively through a union, with surplus being appropriated in the customary Marxist manner. From these conflicts emerge important consequences for wage structures and hence for living standards and for technological change; for example, high wages create a larger domestic market for consumer goods while encouraging labour-saving innovation and (frequently) the import of capital goods.

Whether the staple activity is a trade or an industry, capitalism makes the struggle of the direct producers with capital unequal. Not surprisingly, if Canadian capital has been unable to formulate a full-fledged industrial strategy, neither Canadian farmers nor Canadian workers, separately or together, have been able to assume that task in its stead.[18] The project becomes truly daunting when allowance is made for the divisiveness of the intense regionalism characteristic of the Canadian economy; that regionalism seems to inhere in the strung-out, bicultural Canadian economy and is further exacerbated by the uneven development associated with specialization in staples. This situation has typically divided people, or popular forces, more than it has divided capital.

THE CRITICS

I am attempting in this chapter to generalize and extend the staples thesis by joining the Naylor-Clement thesis to it. Each of these theses is controversial in its own right; combining them risks compounding a felony. Let us look at some of the critiques that have been made of each and what we can learn from them.

Take first the criticisms of the staples approach, both by orthodox scholars under the influence of neo-classical economic thinking and by political economists who take their Marxism literally, even dogmatically. Liberal orthodoxy says that by focusing on the resource-export sector, staple theorists miss out far too much by way of the sources of growth in what has long been a more complex economy. Marxist orthodoxy says that the staples school is guilty of a deterministic and reductionist commodity fetishism. Both see the staples approach as too narrow.[19]

No methodology is without its limits and its flaws, but these criticisms seem wide of the mark and distinctly unhelpful. Certainly, it is difficult to see how anyone could read such a broad-ranging writer as Innis and conclude that he was a narrow determinist. Rather, for him what is now called the staple approach was a focus on a specific activity as a unifying theme around which to organize a vast array of experience. The editor of the series in which Innis's *The Cod Fisheries* was published wrote in his foreword to the volume, "The author keeps his eye on the fish"; Innis also (forgive the pun) cast his net widely. Following Innis, we should see staples as "background": things can happen independently of them but are influenced thereby. (A powerful example of this mode of thinking comes from Thatcher's Britain, about which Perry Anderson – a Marxist it should be noted – has written: "North Sea [oil and gas] revenues have throughout been the background condition of the whole Thatcherite experience. . . . Without this windfall, the political economy of Thatcherism would have been unsustainable.")[20]

If so much of the early history of Canada can be told around fish and fur, why cannot large amounts of contemporary history likewise be written around such staples as oil and gas, forest products, and minerals – or even, since the Innisian technique need not be confined to staples proper, around such other important export industries as automobiles, arms, and tourism? Indeed, we already have such excellent staple studies: for example, Larry Pratt and John Richards on the prairies' transition from wheat to petroleum and potash, Patricia Marchak on BC forestry, and Solberg on wheat in Canada and Argentina. Though eschewing the staples approach, the emerging publications of Paul Craven and Tom Traves on the myriad effects of railways in Canada seem very much in the Innis tradition of studying the impact of technology writ large. We would have more such works if writers on specific industries were willing to think more imaginatively and were not constrained by, for instance, the blinders of orthodox economics or orthodox historiography.

Consider, in fact, the automotive industry. It, and the associated trade with the United States under the Autopact, are of such importance to Ontario that Premier David Peterson recently spoke of the Autopact itself as "the most important document we have in this province – indeed, in this country – in terms of generating wealth." Peterson, being a politician, is presumably prone to the hyperbolic. But Canada is one of the world's major automobile manufacturers, with an output now almost a half greater than Britain, which has double the population, and based on a high level of exports to, and imports from, the United States. Perhaps the ultimate accolade is that Hugh Hood's most recent novel, set in post-war Canada, is titled *The Motor Boys in Ottawa*. (Not all reviewers have been sympathetic; William French of the *Globe and Mail* criticized "the ludicrous prominence given to the signing and implementation of the Canada-U.S. auto pact in 1965," insisting that "Balzac would have had trouble making a novel with *that* as one of its central features.")

The neo-classicists want us to abandon a concrete and specific model for one that, despite all its abstract niceties, has not made any sense anywhere of the main thrust of historical change. They regularly reinvent a wheel that turns out in practice to be a pile of disconnected spokes labelled "investment," "technology," "quality of the labour force," and so on, which can be assembled by the economic theorist but not by the economic historian. So many things can matter that no one thing can ever really matter; this imparts a certain nihilistic tone to the theorists' output. They are wont to point to the *Cambridge Economic History of Europe*, volume VII, part I. In the introduction, Robert Solow and Peter Temin write on the inputs for growth; the volume then degenerates into chapters on capital here and labour there, with only the loosest of reference to the introduction; Solow has since warned that economic theory that pretends to be true for all times and places corrupts, rather than enriches, economic history, which is necessarily concerned with the specific.[21] Still, to the extent that historians of this persuasion stay close to the detailed terrain, they can convince: Douglass McCalla's work on Upper Canadian development shows that we should not overstate the importance of exports of either wheat or square timber.[22]

Albert Hirschman notes that Marxists can supplement and deepen their work at the macro level on the capitalist mode of production by work at the micro level on the relationship between specific activities and social formations. This is exactly what Innis did, though clearly not as a Marxist. It is what a contemporary scholar like Clement is doing in Marxist terms in his studies on nickel mining and the fisheries. From this perspective, the virulence with which David McNally dismisses Innis makes no sense; it may even contribute to his curious inability in two articles in *Studies in Political Economy* to generate a single fresh insight about Canadian economic development while failing to acquaint himself with Hirschman's point.[23] In general, the refusal of even the best of the orthodox Marxists writers on Canada, from Stanley Ryerson to Leo Panitch, to build on Innis's staple studies rather than critiquing them is ironic and unfortunate; it has almost certainly inhibited the development of an alternative grand thesis in the new political economy of comparable insight to that of Naylor and Clement.

What of the criticisms of the Naylor-Clement thesis? Can we benefit from them? There has been a lot by way of attack, with somewhat more against

Naylor's overly robust version (antagonism between commercial and industrial capital within Canada) than Clement's more moderate position (commercial dominance inside Canada in the wider context of American
industrial hegemony). Naylor writes as an economic historian, combining
economics and history; Clement as a sociologist. Both economics and history are very ideological disciplines, dominated by the orthodox who are
resolved to maintain their respective monopolies of knowledge; sociology is
a notoriously pluralistic paradigm, within which Marxist scholarship is seen
as legitimate.

Rather too much of the criticism of the Naylor-Clement thesis has hinged
on superficial assertions. Since Marx classified all infrastructure like railways as "industrial," they must be so classified unambiguously in Canada –
even if built to transport wheat – and once we do that, the industrial character of Canadian capitalism is thereby confirmed. Or Canadian capitalists
behaved rationally and did as well as they could, so any implication that the
capitalism they built is less than fully mature is unfair. Or, insofar as Canadian capitalists of whatever sectoral persuasion tended to consort with each
other, sitting on each other's boards of directors as well as on the boards of
foreign-controlled subsidiaries, Canadian capitalism was firmly in the hands
of Canadian capitalists.

Nevertheless, a great deal of impressive research has been done in the
past few years by political economists on the nature of the Canadian capitalist class. We must take it into account. It requires us to amend the pristine
Naylor-Clement thesis but not, in my view, to discard it or the modified
staples model that I am endeavouring to set forth here. Two leading exponents are Jorge Niosi and William Carroll. Both emphasize the considerable
decrease in foreign (meaning mostly American) ownership of the Canadian
economy since 1970 and the offsetting emergence of new centres of indigenous corporate power – an occurrence for which the political economy
literature on foreign ownership, from myself and Levitt to Naylor and Clement, hardly prepared us. The Canadian capitalist class is now – and perhaps
long has been? – more impressive than some of us thought.

But that turns out to be only half the story. For both writers tell us (as I
read them) other things as well. The Canadian economy remains staples-
biased and semi-industrial. The Canadian bourgeoisie has flexed its muscle
much more in the resources sector, lured on by economic rents, than in
manufacturing. Canadian business has secured its position (what Niosi calls
its "niche") mostly within the continental North American economy and
mostly within traditional sectors – real estate development being the outstanding example – and has done so at a time when American competitive-
ness is increasingly in doubt in a global context. Overall Canada is as
dependent as ever – note now its unprecedented trade ties with the United
States – and, though definitely an advanced capitalist country, is different

from the others, in the extent of its Americanization (and all that follows therefrom) in matters economic, political, social, cultural, and military. All this is, surely, consistent with the central thrust of the staples theory and the Naylor-Clement thesis, rethought to accommodate events to the mid-1980s.

Research on Canadian class structure in a comparative context bears out these findings. Canada's industrial and occupational composition – with fewer workers in manufacturing and a larger resource proletariat than the average industrialized country – bears the imprint of truncated development consistent with the claims of Clement and others. But Canada has also incorporated distinctively American practices for the organization of capitalist production, deploying a disproportionate amount of labour power in control and surveillance of other workers, particularly in sectors traditionally dominated by American capital.[24]

Finally, note must be taken of an ambitious attempt by Gordon Laxer to construct a fresh analysis of Canadian political economy premised neither on staples and Naylor-Clement nor on orthodox Marxism, but rather on Alexander Gerschenkron's model for the comparative study of economic backwardness. I cannot do justice here to the breadth of his argument. He emphasizes factors lost in the recent shuffle of debate, such as (incredibly for a left-leaning political economy) the role of popular-democratic forces in pushing, so far ineffectually, for more diversified growth from below, and factors long ignored, such as the role of military spending. But in explaining the sense in which Canada is "backward," he frequently cites Naylor: on imported technology via licensing arrangements, on American control from the outset over the leading sectors of the second Industrial Revolution in Canada, on the short-term-loans bias of the Canadian banking system, on the mania for railway building. Laxer did not generate his findings within the framework that is the concern of this chapter – and that is an important point about creativity that I do not wish to push aside – but his findings (like those of Niosi and Carroll) can to a surprising degree be accommodated within that framework.[25]

THE AMERICAN CONNECTION

From the beginning, the United States has cast its shadow over the northern half of North America. By and large, its greater dynamism has tended both to facilitate Canadian growth *and* to constrain it. The "aggressive commercialism" (Innis's phrase) of New England that emerged around its fishery – climate favoured its winter fishery, and location favoured its trade with the West Indies – confined Nova Scotia and Newfoundland. With American independence, Nova Scotia's prospects improved within the British Empire, but those of the United States improved even more outside the empire. The fur trade for a while made it possible for France to imagine that it could control the continent from the St Lawrence River, but everywhere the fur trade retreated in the face of settlement, and Canada became the portion of the continent less suitable for settlement and the economic diversification that results.

American technique, the wonder of the world by the early 19th century, moved easily to British North America, and later to Canada, via American emigrants, individual and corporate; dissatisfied Canadians, seeking greater political freedom or more economic opportunities, just as easily went south. This was one of myriad ways in which the Canadian-American relationship both enhanced and limited Canadian growth. W.A. Mackintosh argued that, in formulating national policies on transportation, settlement, and tariffs, Canadians emulated the American model with a lag. Canada could never catch up, not only because the United States refused to stand still, but also because an increasingly successful America increasingly established its hegemony around the globe, particularly over its northern neighbour, in ways that precluded others from going down the same road of economic independence. The United States built an independent industrial structure with its own companies behind its tariff walls. When Canada quite consciously copied the high American tariffs, it built, aided by those American companies, a dependent industrial structure. Laxer asks, "If the oldest and most developed settler colony was able to generate an independent and mature industrial economy, why was the second oldest and second most developed colony not able to do the same?,"[26] and implies that there is no obvious answer. He thereby opens himself to the charge of naïveté about the nature of American imperial power.

Canada has never known any experience except that of a dependency, first of France, then of Britain, now of the United States. It may have greater room for manouevre, creating at least the illusion of freedom, when it can operate, as it did in the days of the North Atlantic triangle, in the interstices of two empires and hope on occasion to play one off against the other. Otherwise, it would seem that the best it can hope for, as a hinterland, is to be treated benignly by the metropole and be granted preferential treatment and special status within the empire. But, in the nature of power, these benefits are likely to be attainable only at the cost of vowing loyally to live within imperial confines.

Canada's trade pattern has from the outset been one of importing manufactured goods in return for the export of staples. Throughout this century, the United States has been the main source of imports of manufactured goods, increasingly so over time. Between the wars, the United States also replaced Britain as the major market for Canadian exports, and this, too, has become increasingly the case. The result is today's overwhelming trade dependence on the United States and vast uncertainties should the United States at any point waver in its commitment to an open economy.

In the past half-century, the final break-up of the British Empire has left Canada solely within the American empire. The long period from 1945 to approximately 1970 was fundamentally one of prosperity for both the United States and Canada in the context of a generalized boom in the world economy under American hegemony. Nevertheless, the tightness of the American embrace of Canada created episodic costs for Canada which required special arrangements. In the 1960s, the United States had, in order to prevent panic in Canadian financial markets, to grant special exemptions to Canada from the Interest Equalization Tax and from balance-of-payments directives to American companies operating abroad. The Defence Production Sharing Agreement (DPSA) of 1958 and the Autopact of 1965 gave Canada (often meaning American subsidiaries in Canada) preferred access to American markets for arms and autos, thereby creating needed jobs in Canada – so that Canada could pay for the arms and autos that the United States wanted to continue to sell it. Both agreements entrenched the technological and managerial dependence of the Canadian industry on its American counterpart, while the Autopact resulted in a quantum leap in the level of automotive trade between the two countries that must be seen as increasing the political dependence of the smaller country.

This period, dubbed the era of "exemptionalism" by R.D. Cuff and J.L. Granatstein, the leading historians of post-war Canadian-American relations,[27] ended by unilateral American fiat in the early 1970s. This coincided with the beginning of a period of generalized economic crisis and waning American hegemony globally that has persisted to the present. In 1971, in the face of a weak American dollar, the United States imposed an across-the-board surcharge on imports and refused to exempt Canada even when asked. In 1972, President Nixon tried to keep his mind off the looming Watergate crisis by visiting Canada and unilaterally declaring it independent – Washington would grant to Canada no more exemptions and permit no more special arrangements.

Existing arrangements, like the DPSA and the Autopact, stayed in place, cushioning the adverse effect on Canada. Canada responded by adopting more independent policies of its own, such as creation of the Canada Development Corporation and Petrocan as major new crown corporations and of the Foreign Investment Review Agency (FIRA) to monitor takeovers by foreign corporations. Canadian capital moved to occupy any room opened up by less efficient American capital and a more supportive Canadian state. But the so-called Third Option in the Trudeau government's foreign policy, of lessening economic integration with the United States, failed miserably: ominously, Canada's trade dependence on that country actually grew yet further in the 1970s.

As the decade closed, Canada took the most vigorous of its steps in the direction of lessening economic dependence with the National Energy Program. It was most badly timed. Simultaneously, the United States switched from dealing with its declining hegemony by Nixon and Carter's policies of détente – which left a bit more space for the rest of the world, including Canada – to becoming aggressive and truculent, trying, under Reagan in the 1980s, to make other countries solve *its* economic policies. In Stephen Clarkson's felicitous phrase, Canada was cast in the role of the exemplary client state and did its best to oblige.[28] Canadian policy went into reverse gear. The National Energy Program was scrapped and has been supplanted by an explicitly continental energy policy. FIRA was gutted and renamed Investment Canada, the better to shill for foreign capital. Bilateral free trade discussions with the United States were initiated by Trudeau and formal negotiations leading toward a comprehensive treaty proceeded under Mulroney, with the overwhelming support of the Canadian business community.

CONCLUSION

The moral of this paper can be simply put. Canada is a prosperous First World country, sharing with the United States not only a continent but also its standard of living. The economy, however, is staples-biased; the industrial structure is truncated and dependent; the Canadian bourgeoisie is continentalist to the core; the society is pervasively Americanized. These factors combine to create a circle that narrowly constrains Canada.

This has long been true of Canada – but I do not pretend to know what will happen next. There is nothing in economics, orthodox or Marxist, dismal sciences though they be, that is wholly deterministic. The academic mind is overly inclined to want to explain everything, but the careful student will have noted that it is most successful in doing that for things that have already happened, and even then there is much disagreement. There is always some room to manoeuvre in the hope of improving our lot; the trick is to find it and use it. The point of the study of political economy – of growth and of other things – should be to help us do that.

EPILOGUE

In 1988, matters economic and political are in a rare state of flux in Canada, making these interesting but uncertain times to ponder Canada's economic prospects.

First, a sweeping trade deal negotiated by the Mulroney government with the Reagan administration awaits legislative approval in both countries. There has been nothing like this since the United States offered Canada reciprocity in 1911 and Canada turned it down (a decision that Canada survived, it should be noted – as our subsequent prosperity shows). The interests of the staple industries figure prominently in the agreement. The

Canadian government wanted an agreement in the hope of limiting American protectionist measures that have been targeted against Canadian resource exports such as softwood lumber, potash, and fish. (In fact, the binational disputes resolution that would be set up under the deal seems ineffectual). The Americans wanted even more access than they already have to Canadian resources, notably energy; significantly, there is a continental energy deal imbedded in the trade agreement. Opposition within the United States to the deal is minimal and has come mostly from American resource interests fearful of Canadian competition.

It seems likely that free trade between Canada and the United States would, in the long run, exacerbate the staples bias of the Canadian economy. The removal of barriers to trade would permit each country to pursue more fully its comparative advantage. Canada's surplus in resource trade with the United States would grow, while deficits in manufactures and services would likewise increase. The volume of two-way trade would take a quantum leap upward, thereby integrating the Canadian economy decisively into the American; Canada's increased economic dependence would increase its political and cultural dependence.

Second, the federal New Democratic Party has had, for the first time ever, a strong, even leading, position in the public opinion polls. The possibility exists that it might form at least a minority government. Yet more incredibly for what has always been, since its origins as the Co-operative Commonwealth Federation (CCF), an English-Canadian party, it has a strong position even in Quebec, thereby transcending the long-standing separateness, even antagonism, of popular forces in Quebec and the rest of Canada. As well – and perhaps aiding the NDP's new-found strength – the long reign of the international unions, with their great and deleterious effect on the NDP, has ended in the past decade. For the first time Canada has a sovereign labour movement, able to be more explicitly nationalist and socialist and to push the NDP in those directions.

Imagine (orthodox economists say "assume," but political economists are more poetic) that the NDP is elected. It is clear that this would create an unprecedented opportunity to alter the dependent staples base of the Canadian economy. If a free trade deal has been implemented, the first tasks would be to deliver on the NDP's commitment to abrogate that and then to work out and implement national policies. Political economy teaches us that to do such things would require very considerable mobilization and commitment – to an extent difficult for a parliamentary formation to sustain – given the power of capital, nationally and internationally, to oppose, frustrate, and subvert and given what Creighton once called "the embarrassments peculiar to a staples-producing country." There would be great potential for an NDP government to foster economic growth in Canada, but it would be wrong to pretend that there are not many pitfalls and large risks.

Third, there was the crash of October 1987, the likes of which we have not heard since 1929. In the latter's aftermath came the Depression and all the horrors of the dirty thirties, in which the world remained mired until the Second World War. We can hope for better this time – and the lowering of interest rates by the world's central banks immediately after Black Monday was a heartening sign – but there is not much doubt that the prospects for growth in Canada and elsewhere, which were not all that good before the crash, are now worse.

The American economy, the victim of years of Reaganomics, is particularly beleaguered; cuts, perhaps severe, in the American standard of living seem probable. Given Canada's extraordinary trade ties with the United States (even without the free trade agreement), it is hard to see how Canada can avoid paying the price as well. Certainly, the case can be made, on the one hand, for not doing anything that would increase the ties (as the free trade deal will) and, on the other hand, for electing a government (like the NDP) that might be prepared to do something to steady and restore the economy.

NOTES

1 This literature is cited in Drache and Clement, eds., *The New Practical Guide to Canadian Political Economy.*
2 See my "A Staple Theory of Economic Growth."
3 The concepts of forward and backward linkage were first put forward by Hirschman in his *Strategy of Economic Development*. He updated these concepts – identifying infrastructure linkage, plus others noted below – in "A Generalized Linkage Approach." On the dual contribution of railways to Canadian economic development, see in particular Pentland, *Labour and Capital in Canada 1650–1860.*
4 The distinction between consumption and fiscal linkages is made by Hirschman in "Approach." For Kierans's work, see his Report on Natural Resource Policy in Manitoba, done for the NDP government and, regrettably, now out of print. The failure of rents even to be generated in the absence of a proper tax-and-royalty régime is a point made by Thomas Gunton, resource economist at Simon Fraser University and sometime assistant deputy minister of Energy and mines, Policy Planning and Project Development, Manitoba; see his "Manitoba's Nickel Industry."
5 I played down this supply-side dimension in my "A Staple Theory." Dow has been diligent in correcting this omission in his writing on metal mining. For the quote, see his "Prometheus in Canada: The Expansion of Metal Mining, 1900–1950," 227. See also Fogarty, "Staples, Super-Staples and the Limits of Staple Theory," and Solberg, *The Prairies and the Pampas.*

6 See Mackintosh, "Canadian Economic Policy from 1945 to 1957 – Origins and Influences." Mackintosh's role in bringing Keynes's ideas to Canada has been emphasized by David Wolfe in his writings on the politics of post-war Canadian economic development, and most recently by Richards, "The Staple Debates."

7 In "Approach," Hirschman makes a different distinction between inside linkage (further activity undertaken by those already in the original activity) and outside linkage (by newcomers or those outside the existing activity).

8 See Nelles, *The Politics of Development*, and Pratt, "The State and Province-Building."

9 See research done under the auspices of the Science Council of Canada, notably Bourgault, *Innovation and the Structure of Canadian Industry*.

10 This neglected point is made by Traves in "The Staple Model."

11 Hirschman ("Approach") refers to the tariff in the export-led economy as indirect fiscal linkage. Of contemporary writers, Naylor has been particularly conscious of the revenue effects of the National Policy tariffs; in the past, so were Mackintosh and Innis.

12 Dobb, *Studies in the Development of Capitalism*.

13 Of the voluminous writings of each of these authors, see in particular Naylor, *The History of Canadian Business*, 2 vols., and Clement, *Continental Corporate Power*.

14 For elaboration of this latter point, see Mahon, *The Politics of Industrial Restructuring*, 7–12.

15 *International Herald Tribune*, 12 Nov. 1986. However, Peter and Edward Bronfman also control Brascan and have retained its long-time subsidiary John Labatt – a diversified manufacturer – and have acquired controlling interest in American-based Scott Paper Co.; see Carroll, *Corporate Power and Canadian Capitalism*, 178.

16 The rentier and continental cast of contemporary Canadian capitalism is powerfully argued in Niosi, "The Canadian Bourgeoisie."

17 The importance of this distinction has recently been made by Phillips, "Staples, Surplus, and Exchange."

18 For an analysis of such problems associated with the tariff in the earlier period, see Craven and Traves, "Class Politics of the National Policy 1872–1933." In general, see the work of Gordon Laxer (discussed below; cited note 25).

19 For recent examples of each see, respectively, McCalla and George, "Measurement, Myth and Reality," and McNally, "Staple Theory as Commodity Fetishism."

20 Perry Anderson, "The Figures of Descent," 71.

21 See Solow and Temin, "Introduction: The Inputs for Growth," and Solow, "Economic History and Economics."

22 McCalla, "The Wheat Staple" and "Forest Products." But on wheat see also McCallum, *Unequal Beginnings*, where much the same quantitative evidence is fitted into a "modified staples approach." Innis, in the preface to *The Cod Fisheries*, mentions wheat being "the basis for independent growth."

23 The first is "Staple Theory as Commodity Fetishism." The second is "Technological Determinism."
24 This paragraph is a précis, mostly in the authors' words, of Black and Myles,
   "Dependent Industrialization."
25 Gordon Laxer, "The Political Economy of Aborted Development" and "Foreign
   Ownership and Myths."
26 Gordon Laxer, "Foreign Ownership," 315.
27 Cuff and Granatstein, *Ties That Bind*, chap. 8.
28 Clarkson, *Canada and the Reagan Challenge*.

CHAPTER TWO

Debates and Directions:
A Political Economy of Resources
Wallace Clement

Why has Canadian political economy devoted so much attention to resources? The answer is not self-evident, since it appears that a declining share of the labour force is working in the resource sector. The primary justification for the attention is the integral role of resources in Canadian society. Resources established the formative forces that have left their scars on Canada's economic and social life; moreover, they remain the cornerstone of Canada's export-dependent economy and the life blood for a multitude of resource-dependent communities spread across the country. Rex Lucas's classic study of single-resource industries, *Minetown, Milltown, Railtown*,[1] could cover as well fish-packing communities, grain-handling ports, hydroelectric stations, and petroleum towns, but it nonetheless captures the essential resource-character of Canada outside the industrial corridor from Montreal through Toronto to Windsor.

Resource dependence includes not only the immediate extraction of natural products but also their processing and transportation. To resource extraction may be added pulp and paper-making and fish-packing and the operation of railways, pipelines, and ports designed to move the resources. Thunder Bay, Ontario, for example, with over 100,000 residents, is a resource-dependent community, even though it does not directly produce resources. Located in the centre of the country at the lakehead of the St Lawrence Seaway, this port's volume is exceeded only by Vancouver and Montreal. Canada's largest grain-handling port also connects rail lines and docks for the transfer of coal, ore, and forest products from the resource hinterlands in exchange for manufactured products destined to be consumed in the west. The community began as a fur trade linchpin under the name Fort William, serving as the focal point for the North West Co. and suffering with its decline. Currently the community is hurt by a bust in the international grain market, reflected in massive layoffs for grain-handlers.

Thunder Bay is one reason why the new Canadian political economy continues to focus on resources.

Traditional Canadian political economy cut its teeth on the study of resource exploitation. The corpus of Harold Innis's work in particular has come to be identified as the classic staples approach and is the logical point of departure for any understanding of Canadian resources. New political economy has also placed resources in a central place within its understanding of Canada's formation, typically beginning its analysis with a critique of Innis. This chapter explores the traditions of political economy both analytically and substantively, evaluating critically the classic tradition of staples using both class and feminist perspectives. In so doing, it highlights particular features of Canada's economy and social structure. It seeks to integrate several levels of analysis, from the immediate labour process experienced by resource workers to the broader demand for labour in Canada. This requires us to locate Canada's place in the world system, a task admirably initiated within Innis's classic staples approach but calling out for revision.

THE STAPLES TRADITION

Staples are natural resource products that have undergone minimal processing and that are exploited for the purpose of export to other areas where they are manufactured into end products. When staples are the leading sector of the economy they set the pace for economic growth and lead to a resource-intensive strategy of national development based on international markets for that product. The staples tradition describes the backward linkages (inputs to production), forward linkages (refining output), and final demand linkages (consumer goods) associated with resource production. The argument of the classical staples tradition revolves around these linkages, contending that there are leakages from the benefits connected with resource development and associated distortions caused by unequal international power relations entered into by recently developing countries. Such distortions in marginal societies follow from concentration on the extraction of natural resources for centre markets.

Moreover, the unfoldings of the staples are themselves related. For Innis in particular, the character of the staple determines the necessary techniques of its exploitation. Capital structure, types of labour required, transportation techniques, and production methods follow from the character of the staple. Each staple's trajectory is determined by external market forces. Because of the distorted nature of staple development geared to external control, the principal benefits of development accrue to centre nations at the expense of marginal ones. The pace of economic growth is determined externally, and its contours are distorted toward an unending quest to extract natural resources without capturing the beneficial linkages associated with their development. This predicament Innis referred to as the "staple trap."

The following passage is Innis's clearest statement on the history of staples and the essentials of his argument. It comes from his 1930 study, *The Fur Trade in Canada: An Introduction to Canadian Economic History*:

The most promising source of early trade was found in the abundance of *fish*, especially cod, to be caught off the Grand Banks of Newfoundland and in the territory adjacent to the Gulf of St. Lawrence. The abundance of cod led the peoples concerned to direct all their available energy to the prosecution of the fishing industry which developed extensively. In the interior, trade with the Indians offered the largest returns in the commodity which was available on a large scale and which yielded substantial profits, namely *furs* and especially beaver. With the disappearance of beaver in more accessible territory, *lumber* became the product which brought the largest returns. In British Columbia *gold* became the product following the fur trade but eventually lumber and fish came into prominence. The lumber industry has been supplemented by the development of the *pulp and paper* industry with its chief reliance on spruce. *Agriculture* products – as in the case of wheat – and later minerals – gold, nickel, and other metals – have followed the inroads of machine industry.

The economic history of Canada has been dominated by the discrepancy between the *centre* and the *margin* of western civilization. Energy has been directed toward the exploitation of staple products and the tendency has been cumulative. *The raw material supplied to the mother country stimulated manufactures of the finished product and also of the products which were in demand in the colony.* . . . Agriculture, industry, transportation, trade, finance, and governmental activities tend to become *subordinate to the production of the staple* for a more highly specialized manufacturing community.[2]

In the drive for economic returns directed from the centre, major externally induced requirements were created in the margin, hence distorting the margin's development.

In subsequent work, especially *Empire and Communication* published twenty years later, Innis focused on the cyclonic nature of the transition between staples: "Each staple in its turn left its stamp, and the shift to new staples invariably produced periods of crisis in which adjustments in the old structure were painfully made and a new pattern created in relation to a new staple."[3]

A good deal of confusion has surrounded the staple approach as articulated by Innis and those who followed, particularly in terms of the claims made by those who have adopted elements from that approach. As Mel Watkins said in his first article on the staples approach, it is not "a general theory of economic growth, nor even a general theory about the growth of export-oriented economies, but rather as applicable to the atypical case of the new country."[4] The staples approach is a description of specific empirical matters and a statement about the origins and trajectories of resource-intensive exports and their linkages within new countries. When Watkins later changed his paradigm from neo-classical economics to Marxism, he continued to use the staples tradition, arguing that Innis was "a liberal with a difference, who saw the dark underside and the gross contradictions and this makes him susceptible to an approach that specializes in such matters."[5] Readers of the previous chapter will be familiar with Watkins's current views.

THE CLASS CRITIQUE

Resources have occupied a justifiably central place in Canadian political economy.[6] The staple tradition of Innis was constructed on a systematic and detailed account of staples exploitation, transportation, and market demands. The new political economy has also paid special attention to staples but has approached them more in terms of the labour processes and living conditions they engender, each located within the context of Canada as an exporter of raw resources (and importer of finished goods). Staples are no longer the explanation but the object of investigation.

The new tradition focuses on the social relations of production. New political economists have not adopted Innis's work wholesale, because of weaknesses in his formulation of problems and the limitations of his historical observations for contemporary practices. The staples tradition is actually a set of observations about *trade* and hence is limited to particular social relations. As Watkins observed in a more recent formulation, "Mineral production (including petroleum) is an industry not a trade, and it needs both rights to the use of land and people who will work for a wage."[7] Consequently, industrial staples (unlike their commercial forbears) are produced directly through systems of wage labour (or their equivalent) under the command of capital, not through relations of exchange. Employment relations involving industrial staples tend to be less conventional than typical manufacturing, often involving systems of bonus (mining), piece work (forestry), or prices that are proxies for wages (fishing). Nevertheless, the tendency in all these cases is clearly to proletarianization, from formal to real subordination of labour.

The staples tradition is about the distribution of economic surplus among nations; the new political economy adds the distribution of surplus among classes and power distribution in class terms to explain that distribution. Thus both national power and class power are cornerstones in the revisionist tradition.

In "Transformations in Mining: A Critique of H.A. Innis," I argue against entirely rejecting the staples tradition and urge drawing on its empirical insights within a class explanation. Such an explanation focuses on the forces of production (capitalization, markets, technology) as conditioned by the social and political relations of production, hence reversing Innis's logic, which holds that "each staple has its own peculiar developments and its peculiar relations with other staples."[8] It substitutes instead the Marxist contradiction "between the material development of production and its social form".[9] Such an analysis introduces a different dimension – labour as a conscious commodity with the capacity to respond to and shape the forces that act on it.

In a word, the difference between the "old" and "new" staples traditions is class. Class is a relation that necessarily involves the dynamic between capital and labour as a source of social change and labour as an active force in history. What the traditions have in common is the location of Canada within a world system and a recognition of the centrality of resource exports (and manufacturing imports) as a distorting feature of Canadian society. This is manifest in not only the effects of branch plant structures but also the constraints of the particular patterns of trade that Canada has nurtured. As argued, the classic staples were characteristically commercial (trade or exchange relations), whereas wage labour prevails in industrial staple production. The transport of staples continues to pervade issues involving transportation systems: railways, ports, docks, canals, and pipelines continue to be major capital projects sponsored by the state. Canada continues its export-orientation, including heavy branch plant control as well as concentrated market control, and is captured in the logic of technological dependence through the import of manufactures which are both capital goods for production and consumer goods. While it may have been possible initially to criticize new political economists for their fixation on the capitalist class,[10] such is no longer the case.[11]

The most innovative recent contributions have challenged the "assumptions of uniqueness and inevitability" dominant in the staples tradition.[12] Gord Laxer has called for a more open view of the social relations associated with resource economies: "The point is that the internal social structure and politics of a staples-based economy had an effect on its course of development. 'Staples traps' do not flow inevitably from external and geographic factors."[13] Laxer agrees that "Canada still pays its way in the world by massive exports of resources"[14] and acknowledges the high foreign ownership in Canadian resources and manufacturing, the domination of patents issued to foreigners, and the market control exercised when the exports go to highly organized and concentrated industrial firms. The focus of his analysis, however, is on a reinterpretation of pre-Second World War developments wherein he argues that Canada was a "late-follower" country (like Italy, Japan, the Soviet Union, and Sweden) and not like the "settler dominions" (Argentina, Australia, and New Zealand). Laxer's critique is less about where Canada is now within the world system than about how it got there, asserting a greater place for political agency within the explanation than the traditional staples approach allows.

The strength of the staples approach is also its weakness; nearly exclusive analytical weight was given to international dynamics with scant attention paid to the explanatory power of internal social relations. Internal "factors," such as geography or the characteristics of the staple itself, are identified mostly as constraints or limits, not the social relations of production (class) and the power relations of the political actors (class and state). Obviously it is no longer adequate (nor was it ever) to characterize Canada simply according to its staples. The point has been the disproportionate place that raw material exports have in Canada's economy, social structure, and state policy. Staples have been relied upon as the "engine of growth" by the state and as a prime secure source of resources by US industrialists and have organized the lives of countless Canadians.

THE FEMINIST CRITIQUE

Many of those affected by the dominance of staples are women, a fact about which most classical political economists have been silent. The most exciting challenges to traditional approaches have overlapped the class-based critique of traditional staples analysis with the gender-based critique of feminism. The influence of this emerging tendency has been impressive and its output prolific. Around the fur trade, for example, the historical work of Jennifer Brown and Sylvia Van Kirk gave attention to the role of women, while the research of Ron Bourgeault has linked the analysis of class and patriarchy in a challenging understanding of gender, development, and race.[15] By focusing on women in what has traditionally been understood as "a man's world" (women are not mentioned in the index to Innis's *The Fur Trade in Canada*), these authors are compelled to offer new understandings and are rewarded with fresh insights.

Suzanne Mackenzie provides some sense of the analytical difference attention to gender makes when she says, "Socialist-feminist analysis focuses not primarily on production, not primarily on reproduction, but on the relations between the two. The nature of this intersection is seen to define gender relations."[16] Similarly, Bettina Bradbury, in her review of the relationship between women and working-class history as written in Canada, stresses the importance of "family" as a subject of analysis. "Family," she argues, bridges the history of women and the working class and can "tell us much about working-class survival, class reproduction, and the social construction of gender." Developing her claim in terms germane to the present discussion, Bradbury observes:

In the mining, lumber, and other resource towns, for instance, which have been so important in the staples sectors of Canada's economy, virtually no wage labour existed for women. Why then consider them? Because it is relevant and important to consider whether the workers in such towns were single males, perhaps living in company-run bunkhouses, or married men with families in the town. Strategies of resistance and struggle, and the ability to withstand long strikes, would be different in each case. The support of women and children for industrial action – whether they turned out for parades and rallies, ran active auxiliaries, staffed picket lines, or stretched strike pay could be crucial – as could their lack of support.[17]

Whereas Bradbury directs our attention toward the writing of working-class history, Marilyn Porter has posed the challenge of a dialogue between political economy and feminism in the context of writing about the Atlantic region.[18] Porter observes that much greater attention has been given to the capture of fish, where men are prominent, compared to processing, where women are located. This imbalance has been rectified somewhat as more feminists have become engaged in fisheries-related research, where women's economic practices, including the key relationship between domestic and paid work, are studied.[19] The work of Connelly and MacDonald, for example, emphasizes the importance of "*family* employment patterns," especially in resource communities, and "life cycle considerations" for households, including child and parent care demands. Women in fisheries-dependent communities, they argue, tend to be called on to bear the heaviest burden of seasonal work, subsistence preparations, and labour-force restructuring through market fluctuations and technological change.[20]

Although fishing has been especially noteworthy for feminists' research on resource-based communities, it is not alone. Meg Luxton's path-breaking study, *More Than a Labour of Love*, set in the mining town of Flin Flon, Manitoba, has often been cited as a model for feminists. Luxton's follow-up study documents a restructuring of paid employment within this resource town that has drawn women into the paid labour force. She documents, however, the persistence of a gendered division of labour that has resulted in a crisis within domestic lives. Women joined the labour force but did so in jobs paying drastically less than their husbands, who tended to work directly with resource extraction. This diminishes the "bread winner power" of the women even when they work outside the home and weakens the impact such work might have for restructuring domestic labour.[21] Luxton has also examined labour struggles and women's mobilization within resource communities, using the examples of the 1978–9 strike in Sudbury at Inco and the 1981 Cape Breton coal strike. Both provide instances of "wives' committees" being formed within the communities and offering challenges to the union movement.[22] Studies such as these meet Bradbury's call for understanding the interaction between gender and working-class movements within resource-based communities.

Table 1
International Trade Comparisons (% of GNP), 1984

	Canada	Australia	United States
Exports	26.8	15.3	6.7
Imports	22.8	15.1	9.9

Source: OECD Economic Surveys 1984/1985: Canada (Paris: Organization for Economic Co-operation and Development 1985), 69ff.

Generally the challenge of feminism within resource studies has enriched the understanding of social relations and broadened the explanatory power of the new political economy. It would be misleading, however, to deny that most research has been gender-blind. Only recent investigations have included women both as subjects and as part of the explanation.

CANADA'S TRADE PATTERNS AND THEIR IMPLICATIONS

Canada remains a nation where trade is the cornerstone of the economy. The most recent figures confirm a long-standing pattern: exports account for 27 per cent of Canada's gross national product (76 per cent of those exports going to the United States), imports 23 per cent (72 per cent coming from the United States).[23] Table 1 locates the dimensions of this trade, comparing Australia and the United States.

Half of the Canadian GNP is attributed to trade, compared to 30 per cent for Australia and only 17 per cent for the United States. While the volume of trade is important, its content is more significant. Canada continues, in classic fashion, to export raw materials that have undergone only limited processing and to import finished goods.[24]

While the patterns may have been established before the Second World War, the essential structures for transferring commercial staples to industrial staples were not constructed until after the war. One of the critical architects was the 1952 Paley Report on *Resources for Freedom*, produced by a US presidential commission, which flagged as ingredients essential for US hegemony 13 of 22 "key" materials in Canada: asbestos, copper, iron ore, lead, nickel, sulphur and zinc, all listed in Table 4, plus aluminum, cobalt, natural gas, newsprint, petroleum, and titanium. During this era crucial changes occurred in the pattern of US ownership and control over Canada's mining and smelting. The level of US control rose from 38 per cent in 1946 to 57 per cent in 1953 and finally to 70 per cent by 1957.[25] Moreover, the proportion of processing in Canada declined, thus leading to cruder exports of natural resources. The volume of Canada's exports was increasing but their quality declining, as US-controlled branch plants took the dominant place in organizing resource production.

The importance of US interests for mineral extraction was not lost on the commissioner of Yukon, who in 1955 told the Royal Commission on Canada's Economic Prospects that "the Paley Report published in the United States in 1952 . . . foresees for the decades immediately ahead an expansion in world demand for metals and other minerals even more remarkable than the growth that this demand has undergone in years past. . . . This increasing demand is bound in the long run to have significant consequences for the Yukon."[26] He might have added for Canada as a whole.

Melissa Clarke has provided a detailed analysis of what she calls Canada's "addiction to staples exports" during this period.[27] Unlike the classic staples approach, she focuses on both state policies and the implications for labour:

State policies set during the formative stages of mining, forest, and energy resources development had inherent in them four characteristics: the facilitation of capital concentration and the continuation of reliance on external market and capital dependency; the subsidization of resource development by all levels of state; increasingly centralized decision-making involving industry-state cooperation; and a decreasing emphasis on both large-scale employment and the manufacturing condition.[28]

The dynamic relations between class and state animate her analysis (and critique of Innis). She has not been alone. Glen Williams, in his aptly titled *Not for Export*, focused on Canada's "arrested industrialization," arguing that a long-term industrial strategy has been consistently sacrificed to the politically expedient altars of the immediate stimulation promised by branch plant manufacture and resource exports. This pattern, he contends, has been especially prevalent for the provinces that spend much effort competing with one another for branch plants and intensifying resource extraction.[29]

Basic to resource policy in Canada is the fact that "resources" fall under provincial jurisdiction – forestry, mining, and energy being key examples. However, trade (interprovincial or international) brings resource products under federal jurisdiction. When the trade is primarily interprovincial, as in energy, conflict occurs between provinces, with the interests of energy users being opposed to those of energy producers. This problem is even further confounded by Canada's "triangular" petroleum trade (Canada exports western oil to the United States but imports a virtually equal amount to the east from international sources), again dominated by foreign-controlled multinational corporations.

I have argued that Canada's uneven internal development is conditioned by its place in the world system. External patterns of dependence have not caused regionalism in Canada but have contributed to its shaping. Particu-

Table 2
Unemployment by Region (%)

	1974	1980	1984
Atlantic provinces	8.3	11.1	15.4
Quebec	6.6	9.8	12.8
Ontario	4.4	6.8	9.1
Manitoba	3.6	5.5	8.3
Saskatchewan	2.8	4.4	8.0
Alberta	3.5	3.7	11.2
British Columbia	6.2	6.8	14.7
National	5.3	7.5	11.3

Source: As Table 1.

Note: OECD cautions the "unemployment" figures of 1,399,000 for 1984 by noting that there were in addition 167,000 discouraged workers plus 508,000 involuntary part-time workers and 112,000 short-time workers (p. 29).

larly important has been the mediation between external forces and uneven internal development.[30] It can be documented, for example, that unemployment in Canada has been consistently higher than in Europe or the United States and responds more severely to booms and busts.[31] Within Canada it is clear that all "regions" (province being a crude indicator of region) are not equally affected by economic crisis. Those areas most closely associated with resource production experience the wildest fluctuations in the demand for labour (see Table 2).

Despite provincial jurisdiction over resources and over most labour issues, the federal government has been active in its intervention concerning resource workers because of the crucial role they are deemed to have in "the national interest." A federally sponsored review of such activities notes: "Federal involvement with labour disputes is inextricably interwoven with the development of labour relations in the mineral industry." One can note the examples of coal in British Columbia at the turn of the century, the Conciliation Act, 1900, and the Industrial Disputes Investigation Act, 1907. "In considerable measure, the history of labour in Canada is the history of labour in the mineral system."[32] While this is an overstatement, the federal state has been willing to intervene in resource disputes, thus setting the tone for often-repressive labour practices and hostile industrial relations within the resource sector.

Noteworthy has been the presence of "international" unions (US-based unions that operate in Canada), especially in Canada's resource industries. The proportion of international union members decreased from 46 per cent in 1980 to 36 per cent by 1986, because of moves for autonomy by the

United Autoworkers (1985) and the Energy and Chemical Workers (1980), unionization of state-sector workers in Canadian unions, and the decline of employment in manufacturing, mining, and construction, all sectors where international unions predominate. Over the past five years, half the decline in numbers of international members can be attributed to breakaways and half to layoffs. This change has altered significantly the composition of the Canadian Labour Congress from 56 per cent international members in 1980 to 35 per cent in 1985.[33]

I have argued elsewhere that Canadian workers have been doubly exposed to both fluctuations in the international demand for resource products and the increasing substitution of imported equipment for local labour.[34] As the labour process within the resource sector becomes increasingly mechanized, thus substituting direct labour for the labour stored in equipment, foreign labour has captured much more of the value added through the use of imported machinery. When resources were labour-intensive, Canadian labour had to be applied directly to securing the resource, but, as will be seen, foreign-made equipment is displacing Canadian resource workers, thus exporting the jobs contained in building the equipment used to obtain the resource. Capital resists labour by displacing direct workers with machinery, partially in response to the capital/labour dynamic of struggle and partially in response to competition from other capital. Both inter- and intra-class forces affect resource exploitation in Canada, displacing resource workers at the same time that resources occupy an increasingly significant place in the economy.

SOME CASES OF RESOURCE EXPORTS

This section reviews the contemporary location of some key staples within the export market and notes, in particular, the nature of the labour process characteristic of these staples. While grain and fish represent traditional staples, the organization of production for these commodities has also been subject to change since the Second World War. Agriculture continues to be organized largely in family farms, now highly mechanized. Actual control over production, however, is governed by the banks, railways, grain merchants, and equipment suppliers; farmers organize only their immediate labour process. Similarly, fishers persist in a world of individual ownership alongside corporate control. Fishing has become capital-intensive, highly regulated, and dominated by giant processing companies.[35] The other cases of minerals and forestry products reviewed here represent industrial staples that have been transformed in their production relations from formal to real control over the labour process.[27] In both, struggles by labour have significantly affected the unfolding of the industries.

The prominence of resource companies among top exporters in Table 3 is

Table 3
Canada's Top Exporters, 1985

Company	Exports ($Millions)	Exports as % of Sales	Ownership
Canadian Wheat Board (w)*	3,610	88	Federal gov't
Canadian Pacific (m)	2,682	18	21% foreign
Alcan Aluminium (m)	1,710	22	54% foreign
MacMillan Bloedel (f)	1,326	57	Noranda 49%
Alberta & Southern Gas (e)	1,300	83	100% foreign
Shell Canada (e)	1,244	21	72% foreign
Mitsui & Co. (Canada) (e)	1,028	57	100% foreign
Inco (m)	1,010	50	65% foreign
Mitsubishi Canada (e)	980	77	100% foreign
Imperial Oil (e)	966	11	75% foreign
IBM Canada	922	29	100% foreign
PetroCanada (e)	903	17	Federal gov't
Mobil Oil (e)	898	48	100% foreign
Noranda (m,f)	860	25	Brascan 43%
Nova Corporation (e)	852	26	5% foreign
TransCanada PipeLine (e)	827	18	Bell 48%
B.C. Resources (e,f)	818	78	Canada

Source: The Financial Post 500, "Tops in Exporting" (Summer 1986): 111.

Note: Table excludes the big three US automobile companies (General Motors, Ford, and Chrysler), which operate under the Automotive Products Trade Agreement (AutoPact). These companies are required to produce a vehicle in Canada for each one sold there, although component or part purchases are fixed at only 60 per cent of sales.

*Code: e = energy; f = forestry; m = minerals; w = wheat.

outstanding. Canadian Pacific is deceptive: its exports are primarily from its subsidiary Cominco (a mining company); otherwise, only IBM Canada on the list is not associated with resources. Well over half the companies listed are foreign-controlled. Grains are prominent (Cargill Grains, the US subsidiary, did not appear in 1985 because of the slump in world demand), as are forest products, minerals, and energy companies (gas, oil, and coal). Except in the petroleum companies, which have a major Canadian market, exports dominate total sales.

A great deal has been made about Canadianization of the energy field in the 1980s, but foreign firms still dominate the sector. The top three firms, Imperial Oil, Shell, and Mobil, are all foreign-owned. The fourth largest, Gulf Canada, was purchased in 1985 by the Reichmann brothers (Olympia and York, which also purchased Abitibi-Price in 1986), and the fifth, Petro-Canada, is owned by the federal government. Little research has been undertaken on the labour process within this sector, except concerning the effect of offshore energy exploration on east coast communities and, of course, the effect of pipeline construction in the north. The industry is labour-intensive during exploration and construction, yet highly capital-intensive during production.

As the recent decline in the world price of petroleum has once again reinforced, workers in this industry ride the waves of boom and bust that have come to be a feature of resources. Politics dominate production. The price is established within the world system, by the politics of the Organization of Petroleum Exporting Countries and the economics of multinational corporations, and Canada's cost of production is high, making sales suitable largely for domestic markets.

The foundation on which exports are built profoundly affects producers. The export dependence of wheat producers leaves them subject to the fluctuations of the world market. The actual cost of production is about $200 a tonne.[37] Wheat prices dropped by 19 per cent from 1985 ($165 a tonne) to 1986 ($130), the lowest in seven years. This resulted in a decline of over $1 billion in farm incomes for the next season, increasing farm foreclosures. Agriculture, especially simple commodity producers, no longer dominates among staple producers.

Fishing, however, is still significant among export companies, with Canada being the world's largest exporter. It remains a classic staple, since 80 per cent of Canada's products are for export. Moreover, "the degree of upgrading of Atlantic coast fish products has been declining since 1976," according to the Task Force on Atlantic Fisheries.[38] The giant exporter Fisheries Products International makes two-thirds of its output into ground-fish frozen blocks, which are processed into finished products in the United States.[39] While the fish-buying end of the industry is doing less processing and shipping rawer resources, the catching end is becoming more capital-intensive, thus requiring less direct labour. In its place is being substituted foreign equipment, as Canada imports 70 per cent of its fishing gear and vessel hardware and virtually all its marine electronics, some $80 million worth a year.[40]

While wheat and, to a lesser extent, fish can be seen as classic staples, most contemporary staples serve as industrial raw materials. Neither farmers nor fishers have command over their markets, and the state sustains production through direct market intervention. Wheat is a raw material serving as the basis for flour; fish, especially from Atlantic Canada, is sold in industrial blocks to be further processed. Neither, however, experiences the additional degree of industrial transformation that occurs with minerals following its export.

Prominent among Canada's exports are minerals. Table 4 provides a particularly revealing view of Canada's mineral exports to the United States

Table 4
Canadian Minerals and US Supply Patterns
1982–5 averages

Commodity	Canada's Exports to US as % of Canada's Production	Imports from Canada as % of US Imports	Imports from Canada as % of US Consumption
Asbestos	22	91	81
Copper	21	27	7
Gypsum	75	74	27
Iron Ore	34	54	35
Lead	28	49	8
Nickel	36	35	28
Potash	56	81	65
Silver	94	29	24
Sulphur	17	64	12
Zinc	34	54	35

Source: Prepared by Energy, Mines and Resources Canada, Ottawa, 27 March 1986. Thanks to Diana Pilsworth.

and the relative importance of these minerals for US imports and consumption. Three-quarters of Canada's total gypsum production, for example, is exported to the United States, and Canada supplies nearly three-quarters of all gypsum imports and over a quarter of all US gypsum consumption. Overall, more than four-fifths of Canada's mineral production is exported.[41] Iron, nickel, and copper account for 45 per cent of crude mineral exports, followed by zinc, coal, asbestos and potash; together they account for 80 per cent of mineral exports.

Minerals are a central element in Canada's economy. They "constitute about 60 per cent of all railway freight (by weight), one half of all cargoes loaded at Canadian seaports and about one half of Seaway and Great Lakes shipping traffic."[42] How effective has Canada been at capturing linkages from minerals? Not very. In 1980, the mining industry paid $1.2 billion for equipment, machines, and parts and imported $640 million of that, some 53 per cent of purchases. Moreover, the direction is reverting: "By 1978 Canadian-made equipment, as a ratio of total equipment purchased, had *shrunk to a mere 27 per cent*, from almost 50 per cent in 1965."[43] As the mining industry becomes increasingly capital-intensive it relies more heavily on imported equipment, cutting Canadian workers out of jobs, particularly the more highly skilled and better-paying work in machine design and manufacture.

To take an example, Inco's labour force has shrunk from 21,000 to

13,200 since 1982, but its metal production has increased by 70 per cent. Three out of five jobs at Inco have disappeared since 1980.[44] It will not be possible here to develop fully the implications of such developments for communities, environment, health and safety of workers, and skill levels.[45] The effects, however, are dramatic. Inco, for instance, planned to bury in June 1988 the town of Creighton (population 450) which had 12,000 people in the 1920s, 2,200 in 1940. There were 76 company and 46 privately owned homes remaining, 40 already having been demolished. Inco wishes to escape the "landlord" business. Once it needed the town to secure available labour, but now workers can commute from Sudbury.[46]

Inco's strategies have been conditioned by international demand for minerals but have also been directly influenced by industrial relations. During the late 1960s, when nickel was in great demand and labour at a premium, Inco's unions gained in strength, thus increasing the cost of labour and making the company vulnerable to strike action. Since then Inco has engaged in a strategy of mechanization and automation to reduce its reliance on labour in general and the Canadian union in particular. This approach was combined with a strategy of diversification and internationalization.[47] Labour has been an active agent in shaping the direction of Inco, not because it has been drawn into the circle of decision-making but because its militance and solidarity, reinforced during an eight-and-a-half-month strike in 1978–79, have made it a force of consequence. Inco's response – internationalization and capitalization – has been costly, especially with the squeeze of high energy costs required for its Indonesian and Guatemalan operations and high interest costs to pay for that expansion plus capitalization. The highest price, however, has been paid by the thousands of Inco workers who have been systematically laid off as a result of company policies and inept managerial decisions.

Table 3 also highlights the importance of forest-related firms to Canada's exports. In 1984 there were 260,000 forestry workers and the value of forest product shipments was $26.8 billion, of which $14.5 billion, or over half, was exported.[48] Two-thirds of Canada's pulp and paper output was exported to the United States, while Canadian lumber exports accounted for a third of the US market (valued at $3 billion in 1985).[49] The forest industry has been subject to particularly close examination within Canadian political economy. Patricia Marchak's *Green Gold* places it within the broader political economy of the forests: "B.C. imports approximately $60 million of the $62 million worth of pulp and paper machinery consumed in a given year," while "half of the wood harvesting and processing machinery purchased in B.C. is imported."[50] Ian Radforth's work on the labour process of forestry workers emphasizes the dynamic role of labour in influencing change within the industry: "Workers in this resource industry have done much to shape the pace and nature of technological change." Radforth notes, in particular, problems of attracting labour caused by the decline of agriculture; farm workers often served seasonally in the woods. He argues also that unionized workers forced wage rates higher; to remain competitive, firms sought mechanization to increase productivity.[51] This is an outstanding illustration from the new political economy of dynamic, relational understanding of the connection between capital and labour.

DIRECTIONS AND DEVELOPMENTS

There is yet another way to examine the effects of Canada's resource development on its social fabric. Most research has focused on the broad levels of capital drains and export dependence or on detailed case studies of specific industries and labour processes. Recently there has been an attempt to understand the implications of these various phenomena on Canada's total class formation. Using data produced within the International Class Structure Project, Don Black and John Myles have compared Canada, Sweden, and the United States: "Canadian class structure bears the imprint of a truncated development process but, in addition, has to a large degree incorporated a distinctly American set of practices for the organization of the capitalist production process." They detect clear effects of "uneven development" in terms of the size of the petite bourgeoisie and working classes in Canada and "conclude that dependent industrialization has resulted in the 'Americanization' of the Canadian class structure. Within those sectors of the economy traditionally dominated by US capital (and US labour unions), Canada has developed a class structure that is distinctly American." As would be expected, Canada's extractive sector is larger than that of either Sweden or the United States, and its transformative sector is smaller, but within these sectors production is organized through administrative and supervisory patterns resembling those practiced in the United States but unlike those in Sweden. In those sectors dominated by the United States there is much more surveillance and control of workers than in other Canadian sectors or in Sweden.

Canada's social structure is a product of its historical relations – with the United States in particular and the world in general. While there are other nations that rely strongly on trade, no other advanced industrial society has such a clear pattern of large resource exports and manufacturing imports. The cumulative effect on Canada's class structure has been telling; the implications for cyclical unemployment have been substantial. Canadian workers seem to be responding by moving away from international unions into autonomous unions that can more readily express their interests. The Canadian state, however, seems intent on intensifying trade with the United States. There are no signs that the content of that trade will improve the fortunes of Canadian workers, whose instincts have been to oppose such a direction. Canada's trade record would suggest that their instincts are correct.

NOTES

1 See Lucas, *Minetown, Milltown, Railtown*.

2 Innis, *The Fur Trade in Canada*, 384-5, emphasis added.

3 Innis, *Empire and Communications*, 5-6.

4 Watkins, "A Staple Theory of Economic Growth," 53.

5 Watkins, "The Staple Theory Revisited," 83; for an elaboration of his argument, see Watkins, "The Innis Tradition."

6 For an extensive outline of literature on resources and staples, see my section in Drache and Clement, eds., *The New Practical Guide to Canadian Political Economy*. A recent comprehensive collection of papers and bibliography can be found in Burrill and McKay, eds., *People, Resources and Power*.

7 Watkins, "From Underdevelopment to Development," 8.

8 Innis, "The Canadian Economy and the Depression," 138.

9 See Clement, *Class, Power and Property*, chap. 3.

10 See Panitch, "Dependency and Class," 8.

11 See Clement, *Hardrock Mining* and *The Struggle to Organize*.

12 Gordon Laxer, "Foreign Ownership," 335.

13 Ibid., 315.

14 Ibid., 320.

15 See Brown, *Strangers in Blood*; Van Kirk, *"Many Tender Ties"*; and Bourgeault, "The Indian, the Metis and the Fur Trade."

16 Mackenzie, "Women's Responses to Economic Restructuring," 84.

17 Bradbury, "Women's History," 25, 38-9.

18 See Marilyn Porter, "Peripheral Women."

19 See, for example, Antler, "Women's Work"; Connelly and MacDonald, "Women's Work"; Marilyn Porter, "Skipper of the Shore Crew"; Muszniski, "Class Formation and Class Consciousness"; Neis, "Doin' Time on the Protest Line"; and McCay, "Fish Guts, Hair Nets and Unemployment Stamps."

20 Connelly and MacDonald, "Women's Work," 54, 64.

21 See Luxton, "Two Hands for the Clock."

22 See Luxton, "From Ladies Auxiliaries to Wives' Committees."

23 See *OECD Economic Surveys 1984/85: Canada*, 5.

24 The OECD makes a special point of qualifying the interpretation of manufacturing export figures by notes "a) non-manufacturers' share in Canadian merchandise exports (43 per cent on average over the past five years) and b) bilateral automotive trade with the United States (within the framework of the 1965 Auto Pact) which accounts for one-third of all manufacturing exports"; ibid., 47 n 9.

25 See Clement, *Continental Corporate Power*.

26 Commission of the Yukon Territory, Brief, 12.
27 Clark, "The Canadian State and Staples," v. A revised version is Clark-Jones, *A Staple State*.
28 Clark-Jones, *A Staple State*, 468.
29 See Glen Williams, *Not For Export*.
30 See Clement, "Regionalism as Uneven Development."
31 See *OECD: Canada*, 27.
32 Desmarais, *Labour-Management Relations*, 1.
33 See *Financial Post*, Report on the Nation (winter 1985–6) 25.
34 See Clement, "Labour in Exposed Sectors."
35 See Clement, *Class, Power and Property*, chap. 10.
36 See ibid., chap. 8.
37 See *Globe and Mail* 9 April 1986. B1.
38 Task Force on Atlantic Fisheries, *Navigating Troubled Waters*, 97.
39 See *Financial Post* 29 Sept. 1984, 13.
40 See Patton, *Industrial Development and the Atlantic Fishery*.
41 See Energy, Mines and Resources Canada, *Mineral Policy: A Discussion Paper*, 1.
42 Ibid., 9.
43 Ibid., 113–14.
44 See *Globe and Mail* 20 Nov 1985, B6; 29 Nov 1985, 12.
45 See Clement, "Contemporary Developments at Inco and Their Impact on the Sudbury Region."
46 See *Globe and Mail* 10 March 1986, A3; *Toronto Star* 10 March 1986, A7.
47 See Clement, *Hardrock Mining*.
48 See *Globe and Mail*, Report on the Forestry Industry, 5 Dec 1985, B27.
49 See *Globe and Mail* 31 March 1986, B11.
50 Marchak, *Green Gold*, 351.
51 Radforth, "Logging Pulpwood in Northern Ontario," 271.
52 Black and Myles, "Dependent Industrialization and the Canadian Class Structure," 3, 23, 28.

CHAPTER THREE

What Went Wrong? Explaining Canadian Industrialization

Neil Bradford and Glen Williams

A centrepiece of the new Canadian political economy has been its far-ranging exploration of the origins and development of Canadian manufacturing. Although freely employing different research agendas and theoretical perspectives, most contributors to the new Canadian political economy have highlighted themes related to industrialism. This focus is scarcely surprising, given the centrality of industrial advancement, with its attendant explosion of innovation, technique, and trade, in the economic history of this century. And it is also not surprising given Canada's unique participation in this industrial expansion: combining impressively large absolute increases in productive capacity with a warped industrial structure characterized by intense technological dependence, abysmally small exports of finished manufactures, and atypically high foreign ownership spread through almost all key sectors. These distortions have given Canada virtually the poorest record among developed countries in industrial innovation and a cumulative trade deficit in highly manufactured end products significantly greater than $250 billion for the 1970s and 1980s.

While researchers have often coalesced around questions about what went wrong with Canadian manufacturing, both the 'old' and the 'new' political economies have explained in many ways the peculiar trajectory of industrialization. However, important methodological similarities distinguish these responses from mainstream Western political science and orthodox neo-classical economics. Canadian political scientists have typically organized their study of industrial policy around a rather confined examination of "the set of selective measures adopted by the state to alter industrial organization";[1] most Canadian economists have dogmatically stressed the role of comparative advantage based on factor endowment.

Political economy, in contrast, has projected a far broader scope of inquiry. Although individual practitioners have sometimes emphasized a single factor, Canadian political economy as a whole would suggest four interrelated preconditions for the successful study of Canadian industrialization. (1) Such work must incorporate a spatial dimension, relating Canadian manufacturing to manufacturing in more advanced centres and examining regional differences within Canada. (2) It must recognize that industrialization has largely been socially determined (rather than being the simple product of innate factors combining to produce a lack of comparative advantage) and is the result of a complex network of human choices made primarily by firms and the state. (3) It must proceed in a historical developmental fashion that builds explanation in any one period through analysing the implications of choices made by firms and the state in previous periods. (4) It must recognize that manufacturing and resource sectors are relationally linked: the relative weakness of manufacturing industries can in part be attributed to the relative strength of resource production.

In employing these general insights, most political economists have assumed that the limitations placed on the industrial development of "marginal" countries like Canada by the international system are not powerful enough to determine, in a straightforward fashion, the pattern of national development. To proceed from such an assumption would obviate the need to study the relationship between external forces and internal socio-political conflicts, which arise often over alternative strategies for promoting national and/or regional accumulation within the world economy. It would also obscure the mediation and direction of these social forces by state actors, whose policy decisions unfold within a complex matrix of constraints and opportunities, both domestic and international. However, if broad consensus exists around the need to analyse across time the development of linkages between the regional, national, and international political economies, important differences persist over how best to describe the manner in which these evolving relations have affected Canadian industrialization. As we will discover, many of these differences are rooted in the distinctive characteristics and research demands of the three principal organizing concepts that have been used by political economists to examine Canadian manufacturing: the staples trade, foreign ownership, and social relations.

For the early staples writers, specifically Harold Innis, the exchange between countries at the centre and at the margin of the international industrial economy provided the essential backdrop for a sweeping historical interpretation of Canadian economic, political, and cultural development. Situated in this global context, Innis's analysis began with detailed studies of the character of successive staple commodities, tracing their impact on the organization of industrial production. Innis highlighted both the obstacles to balanced economic development and the opportunities for rapid industrialization inherent in Canada's situation. Recent inheritors of Innis's staples framework, in pursuing his theme of obstacles and opportunities, have focused more on the evolving relationships of power – both political and economic – that condition the exploitation of natural resources under the aegis of multinational corporations . Their work argues that opportunities for development have emerged most clearly when Canadian elites have sought to capture a major share of the linked industrial benefits arising from the staples trade.

A second recent group of writers, focusing on foreign ownership, has stressed obstacles to industrial progress. It believes that the international configuration of class interests, as currently manifested in the power of the multinational corporations, has propelled Canada's political and economic elites to sustain a resource-based staples trade at the expense of domestic industrial capital formation. A third approach in the new political economy, centred in an examination of social relations, has conceptualized industrialization as a dialectical process involving exploitation and struggle between classes within the Canadian social formation. From this vantage point, this approach has pointed to the influence of subordinate classes on the course of industrial development.

INNIS, STAPLES, AND INDUSTRIALISM

According to Harold Innis, Canadian economic history revolved around the exigencies of natural resource export to markets in more economically advanced regions of the world. Armed with this insight, Innis drew attention to the peculiar elements shaping economic development in the "new countries" like Canada, where industrialism had arrived "at a comparatively late date."[2] Innis's writings sketched a staples-led pattern of industrialization characteristic of the new countries: cumulative concentration of productive resources in staples exploitation, implying "weakness in other lines of development;"[3] piling up of massive public debts to underwrite heavy fixed capital charges for building the extended transportation infrastructure necessary to reach distant markets; pronounced vulnerability to external market fluctuations leading to adjustment crises with their deleterious effect distributed unequally across regions; and, finally, the national government's active role in implementing policies for both supporting staples production and countering the "rigidities" and "disturbances" inhering in such a development strategy.[4]

As is well known, Innis did not provide a theoretical formulation of economic development in the marginal country that addressed systematically the causal relations among these evident problems.[5] Nevertheless, his writings on Canadian development stressed the importance of moving beyond conventional economic thinking. Established theory, Innis argued, was impoverished by its insensitivity to historical processes and institutional factors in different societies. The specificity of political-economic developments at the margins of Western civilization, initiated when other countries already had achieved substantial industrialism, could not be captured through models that attempted "to fit the phenomena of new countries to the economic theories of old countries."[6]

For the new country, industrialism was not so much the culmination of incremental developments, as it was a sudden wholesale arrival. "Industrialization of the new countries," Innis suggested, "given suitable political and social organizations, tends to become cumulative – the United States became industrialized more rapidly than Great Britain, and Canada more rapidly than the United States." Its effect on the new country was unknowable in advance: "We have been unable to interpret or predict the lines of Canada's development either because of its complexity or the rapidity, and magnitude of its changes."[7] The "sweep of industrialism" across the northern half of the continent was "cyclonic" – its intensity ebbing and flowing in different regions of the new country in accordance with the unpredictable rhythms of technological breakthroughs, emanating from the mature economies and applied holus-bolus to virgin natural resources. Under such conditions, said Innis, "the effects of capital investment differ materially from the gradual investment of labour and capital for which economic theory is accustomed to allow in a discussion of the dynamic state. Violent swings are set in motion according to the prediction of unpredictableness."[8]

In the new country, Innis argued, industrialization occurred rapidly and its subsequent course was unpredictable. Whether its economic "storms" provided the foundations for stable, long-term development was far from certain. Balanced development presupposed containment of destructive tendencies. In this regard, Innis focused on the Canadian state, in particular the federal government, as the key institution managing the forces unleashed by industrialism. Hence, he saw Confederation and the National Policy as rational business-state collaborations designed to consolidate the gains from the burgeoning European demand for foodstuffs.[9] These policies responded to the specific challenges facing Canada in its first experience with industrialism: to secure overseas wheat markets while integrating east-west trade flows and maintaining Canadian national integrity in the face of formidable continental economic pressures.[10] State intervention provided the institutional basis for integrated national expansion based on wheat export, iron and coal mining for rail construction, and protected manufacturing – buttressed by American branch plants – for the domestic market. The political-economic cornerstones of Canada's initial Britain-centred staples-led industrial strategy – what Innis referred to as "the old industrialism" – were thus in place by the last decades of the nineteenth century.[11]

In the early twentieth century, Innis observed, the centre of gravity for Canadian industrial development began to shift. While dependence on staples exploitation continued unabated, the particular mix of resource products and markets was altered. Explicitly oriented to booming American industrialism, Ontario's minerals, pulp and paper, and hydroelectric power emerged as the leading sectors. Canada's place in the second industrial revolution would not be marked by extensive participation in its strategic electrical, chemical, or motorized machinery sectors, except through establishment of branch plants "fostered by government policy in tariffs and extension of imperial preferences."[12] In the face of clearly established American leadership in these industries, "the new industrialism" meant for Canada the transition to new staples integrated into a continental production structure. Innis believed that the new staples industries would not herald a fundamental structural transformation of the economy. Rather, he argued, the sophisticated technical requirements of their production deepened Canada's established pattern of dependence on imports of capital and capital goods.[13]

Moreover, Innis stressed that the rigidities – government debts and regional disparities – inherited from expansion in earlier periods not only hampered the progress of the new industrialism in Canada but became increasingly debilitating with the onset of a global economic downturn. The market collapse of the 1930s exposed the special weaknesses and vulnerabilities of countries riding "the crest of modern industrialism": rapid growth without stability, and substantial industrialization without the capacity for self-sustaining development. "Industrialism," he concluded, provided Canada with "an abundance of goods but not the first luxury of security."[14]

Thus, the movement from the National Policy's "wheat-coal economy" to the new industrialism was severely complicated by the Depression. The transition also witnessed the decline within Canada of the federally directed east-west trade geared to European markets. In its place, the development of minerals, oil, and gas called forth a continental-provincial focus that posed new problems for national integration. Innis emphasized the degree to which the new staples industries accentuated the regional unevenness of capitalist development in Canada. While they enabled Ontario to make substantial advances toward "an efficient, balanced, and relatively elastic economy," this progress was made at some cost to resource-producing regions: "The emergence of Ontario to maturity has brought problems for the province as well as for the Dominion. The elasticity of the economy of Ontario has been based on a wealth of developed natural resources and has been obtained in part through inelastic developments which bear with undue weight on less favoured areas of the Dominion. The strength of Ontario may emphasize the weakness of the federation."[15]

By "elasticity" Innis meant the capacity, based on economic diversification, to make rapid institutional adjustments or adaptations in response to unforeseen external economic shocks. The peculiar rigidities of the Canadian economy accentuated the impact of these disturbances, as reliance on a few export commodities reduced overall resilience. At the same time, adjustment and stabilization were complicated greatly by the unequal effects of such shocks on different regions. Politics and the state system faced considerable constraints in the search for "elastic machinery by which the burdens imposed may be adjusted."[16] A constitutional structure that combined "feudalism," in the form of provincial jurisdiction over land and resources, with "modern capitalism," in federal control of domestic and foreign commerce, involved "a drain on economic energies and inability to direct them effectively": "The advance of technology, which created paper from spruce and balsam and converted the vast waste areas of the Precambrian formation into a region with paper plants, power sites, and mines producing chiefly for the American market, accentuated the feudalistic character of federalism . . . The Canadian federal structure is wrenched between the influence of British policies and their effect on wheat, and of American policies and their effect on minerals and newsprint."[17]

Innis's economic history set out a reality quite unlike the one depicted by practitioners of orthodox trade and growth theory.[18] Where they predicted cumulative progress sustained by diversification around the staples base, Innis admitted progress but saw it staggered by internal unevenness and external vulnerability. Where their neo-classical models of comparative advantage counselled reliance on the unfettered direction of the market, Innis, despite his reticence in proffering policy-related knowledge, believed strongly that the state had a central role to play in mediating Canada's economic relations with the international system and in restructuring domestic arrangements to ensure equity across regions and sectors.

Offering a panoramic view of the broad contours of Canadian economic development, Innis's work captured the dynamic linkages between geography, foreign demand for raw materials, borrowed technologies, and rapid yet unstable forms of industrialization confined primarily to resource-related sectors. While he devoted little attention to potential problems arising from foreign ownership, Innis showed how industrialization in Canada took root within, and never really escaped, the constraints arising from initial reliance on staples production for advanced economies. Pointing to the special role assumed by the state under such conditions, he illustrated the shallowness of theorizing divorced from history.

Nevertheless, because it lacks a systematic discussion of the social determinants of state and business policies, Innis's economic history leaves many unanswered questions about the process of industrialization in Canada. Which interest coalitions and class alignments concretely express the unequal power relations implied by his discussion of Canada's place in the global political economy? As we know, mobilized around particular ideological conceptions of the Canadian "national interest," such alliances have frequently played determining roles at specific historical conjunctures. For example, how do we account for the choice of an inward-focused industrial strategy like the late-nineteenth-century National Policy? How do we explain the persistent failure, described clearly by Innis, to recast this strategy when its considerable limitations became evident in the early twentieth century? Further, what explains the variations in policy approaches to staples industrialization in different provinces?

In sum, while laying out strong foundations, Innis failed to provide a complete map of the forces shaping Canadian industrialization because his materialism was insufficiently informed by consideration of social processes and political struggles. Speaking to Innis's silences, we will see that all three streams addressing industrialization in the new Canadian political economy emphasize in different ways the role played by human agency in developing manufacturing in Canada.

STAPLES REVISITED: LINKAGES AND DEVELOPMENT

Mel Watkins made the pivotal contribution to the new political economy's renovation of the staples thesis by transforming the rather diffuse writings of the earlier staples writers into more systematic propositions about economic development. In 1963, he distilled from Innis's work the rudiments of a theory of economic growth applicable specifically to the "atypical case of the new country" like Canada. New countries, Watkins argued, were distinguished from underdeveloped nations by their "favourable man/land ratio and an absence of inhibiting traditions."[19] On this foundation, economic development organized around the familiar staple-exporting, technology-importing axis could be expected, under certain conditions, to produce manufacturing diversification around the staples base. These conditions reflected not only the economic considerations of investment opportunities arising from the production of staple commodities but also political or sociological factors related to the quality of local entrepreneurship. Important in this respect was the degree to which profits or surplus generated from staples exploitation were reinvested in the local economy, providing industrial linkages through machinery inputs for staples exploitation (backward linkages) or further downstream processing of the staple (forward linkages).

Assuming that the new country had specialized in an export commodity with potentially strong linkage effects, Watkins suggested that internal socio-political structures became the key to economic transformation. Explanations for the trajectory of the new country's economy required investigation of local élite behaviour, because the key variable was local retention of benefits from staples exploitation. Where these benefits flow outward, the "staple trap" is the likely outcome. As Watkins explained: "The real difficulty . . . is that staple exporters – specifically those exercising political control – will develop an inhibiting 'export mentality' resulting in an over-concentration of resources in the export sector and a reluctance to promote domestic development."[20] Indeed, Watkins concluded, the source of inadequate performance by the Canadian economy was "an inhibiting export mentality the elimination of which lies within Canadian control."[21]

In this way, Watkins suggested the need to study the political bargaining, institutional structures, and ideological traditions shaping the new country's prospects for transcending the initial limitations and power imbalances accompanying the staples trade. He warned that "staple economies are often believed to be much more at the mercy of destiny than they actually are."[22] Thus onset and consolidation of the "staple trap" were not attributable primarily to externally imposed constraints on investment choices in the new country. This recasting of Innis's framework effectively established a research agenda for the new political economists continuing to probe relations between natural resources and industrialization. Indeed, we will see that the benchmark contributions to this approach are organized around the core assumption that forces in the marginal society may organize to renegotiate the relations of dominance initially structuring the staples trade within the international economy. In exploring the particular historical circumstances opening up such a possibility, these writers have traced the entrepreneurial strategies pursued by state and business élites in their quest to capture resource linkages.

H.V. Nelles has offered a rich historical analysis of the early-twentieth-century policies pursued by the Ontario government in addressing the leading sectors of Ontario's "new industrialism" – forest products, minerals, and hydroelectricity. What factors account for the relative success and failure of Ontario's commitment to the "manufacturing condition" which placed restraints on export of unprocessed lumber and minerals and fostered public ownership of hydroelectricity? From Nelles's perspective, industrialization on a staples base was a multidimensional process. Starting from the province's location within the continental production structure, its complex dynamics were discernible in the historically contingent, spatially specific interpenetration of economic structures, political institutions, and organized social forces. Nelles employed sectoral studies to illustrate the mix of factors facilitating and constraining the provincial state's resource-based industrial strategy and, in the end, concluded that the manufacturing condition must be considered a "qualified failure."[23]

In lumber and hydroelectricity, the success of local business spokespersons in mobilizing public support behind their "home manufacturing" and "cheap power" campaigns pushed the provincial state to legislate against the interests of American capital and its continental supporters in the Canadian financial community. However, the institutions of Canadian federalism greatly complicated the implementation of the manufacturing condition. Ottawa's free-trade commitments made it ill disposed to Ontario's "nationalist" interventions and receptive to American complaints. Moreover, as long as other provincial jurisdictions – in this case, neighbouring Quebec – permitted the export of raw logs and unprocessed pulpwood, Ontario's achievements would be limited.

In the mining sector, Nelles argued, structural constraints embedded in the industry's technical and market conditions proved more forbidding than with lumber or hydroelectricity. The concentration of expertise in large American firms in conjunction with dependence on American capital markets presented immediate barriers to extending the processing regulations to include mineral resources. These factors materialized in the form of threatened capital strikes, downward credit-rating adjustments, and prohibitive American tariffs on Ontario nickel. At the same time, American mining interests were well organized and well represented in the Canadian political process – again, particularly at the federal level.

Written in the context of the 1970s oil boom, John Richards and Larry Pratt's study of post–Second World War developments in Alberta and Saskatchewan (*Prairie Capitalism*) examined state-led strategies for economic diversification around the "New West's" leading staples – oil, gas, and potash. Like Nelles, Richards and Pratt assumed that strategic interventions by local élites could shape and modify the accumulation process and that structural relations conditioning staples development in regional economies were not immutable across time. Initial resource endowments could be altered if external dominance over staples accumulation were challenged by politically mobilized entrepreneurship.

Richards and Pratt argued that a "nascent regional bourgeoisie" that coalesced around its provincial government could direct the transformation away from staples dependence by learning to "bargain for linked industrial developments" with major foreign resource companies. Over time, the provincial élite's experience in dealing with resource development can allow it to overcome an "initial imbalance in power and knowledge."[24] If bureaucratic expertise and self-confidence are merged with the requisite political will, the state can capitalize on the region's comparative advantage in scarce natural resources. Whether following Saskatchewan's "social democratic" or Alberta's "*dirigiste* capitalist" path, strategic bargaining with external groups could provide for local retention of an increasing share of economic rents. Industrial development would then be predicated on reinvestment to build the kind of linkage effects described by Watkins in his staple theory of growth.

Prairie Capitalism remains the new political economy's most forceful elaboration of the position that state action can lead to a definitive break from the staple economy's structural deficiencies and dependent relationships. Indeed, this detailed study of Alberta and Saskatchewan institutions, élites, and policy capacities was cast, in part, as a critique of the reductionist and static view of political life that often characterized previous work on Canadian industrialization from both the staples and foreign-ownership perspectives.[25] Whereas Nelles highlighted the blockages, located in both the institutions of federalism and the power exercised by transnational corporations, to full implementation of Ontario's industrial strategy, Richards and Pratt played down these issues. Concluding that "the ideas of politicians and the actions of governments . . . mattered most of all" in stimulating regional entrepreneurship, they assumed that the provincial state had considerable autonomy from any particular societal interests and stressed its administrative capacity to formulate and implement strategic goals.[26]

Tracing economic development in nineteenth-century Quebec and Ontario, John McCallum's investigation of the wheat staple's legacy followed a different tack in pursuing the connection between natural resources and industrialization patterns. In contrast to the "politics of industrialization" focus common to both Nelles and Richards and Pratt, McCallum's primary concern was the broad economic conditions facilitating emergence of an "independent entrepreneurial class" in staple-producing regions. Assuming that natural endowments have provided the basis for a viable export product, two issues were crucial in determining whether the staple will become the "engine of industrial growth": alternative transport routes, ensuring that the producing region is not beholden to an outside monopoly; and sufficiently modest barriers to entry in staples-linked industries such that discrepancies in "initial endowments" between centre and margin do not pre-empt the latter's entrepreneurial initiative.[27]

With Ontario's wheat staple, McCallum argued that these conditions were met on terms very favourable to local producers. Conversely, Quebec and the prairies offered examples of where the absence of a "good agricultural staple product, or external control over the benefits from a potentially powerful staple, resulted in flawed industrial growth. For the prairies, the dynamic of wheat-led industrialization was arrested. In a period when the scale and technologies of production were undergoing massive changes, Ontario's established industrial advantages were reinforced by Canadian Pacific's rail monopoly over commodity transport. By a similar logic, efforts of Montreal merchants to appropriate the linkages from Ontario's wheat failed: "The increasing use of the American trade route [was] a means by which Ontario towns reduced their dependence on Montreal . . . The small-scale technology of the mid-nineteenth century had served to promote the local retention of staple-related linkages."[28] Deprived by nature of an agricultural staple, Quebec's low-income subsistence farming led to "enclave industrialization" concentrated in a few urban centres. The province entered the age of industrialism along a "route founded on cheap local labour, in combination with external markets, capital, transportation facilities and raw materials." Only in Ontario, then, did agriculture provide a sound basis for "an evolutionary pattern of industrial development based on the internal market, internal sources of capital, internally generated transportation facilities, and locally produced raw materials."[29]

FOREIGN OWNERSHIP

Instead of elaborating the limits placed on Canadian industrialism by staples development, writers focusing on foreign ownership have explained that Canada's industrial weakness can be traced to the exploitative power relations that accompany the foreign ownership of Canada's branch-plant manufacturing base. The opening salvos in this approach came at the end of the 1960s from both the report of the federal government's Task Force on Foreign Ownership, headed by Mel Watkins, and Kari Levitt's widely read *Silent Surrender*. Watkins and Levitt supplemented a common view that "the Canadian public interest would be served by new national policies which recognize the need for a stronger government presence to countervail the power of multi-national firms" with a comprehensive statistical overview of the towering extent but shallow performance of foreign direct investment in Canadian manufacturing.[30]

Levitt argued that a "new mercantilism" of large American-based multinational corporations had "recolonized" Canada. Lacking the capacity for either independent entrepreneurship or technological dynamism, US branch plants reduced their Canadian managers to passive overseers of foreign-controlled operations: "In key sectors of the Canadian economy, decisions concerning what is to be produced, where it is to be sold, from whom supplies are to be purchased and what funds are to be transferred in the form of interest, dividends, loans, stock-purchases, short-term balances, charges for management, research or advertising services, and so on, are made externally in accordance with considerations of global strategy of foreign corporations ... "In this manner the free market is being replaced by internal transfers within multinational corporations. Correspondingly, intergovernmental relationships resemble increasingly those of the old mercantilist systems."[31] Under such conditions, Canada's "rich, industrialized underdeveloped economy" maintained relatively high economic growth, per capita income, and industrialization yet remained unable to develop new technologies or compete in finished product exporting.

With her focus on how the national interest had been compromised by entrepreneurial failures, Levitt cleared the path for this genre's most ambitious attempt to explain the limitations of "hinterland" industrialization. In a sweeping critique of mainstream "colony to nation" historiography, R.T. Naylor argued forcefully that successful industrialism in Canada was undermined not by a general lack of entrepreneurship but by the overwhelming presence of a specific entrepreneurial class: powerful merchants and financiers. Instead of "creating profitable productive opportunities through various forms of innovative activity," commercial élites based in the staples trade actively opposed the consolidation of an indigenously controlled industrial capitalism in Canada."[32] And the commercial elite's privileged position within the colonial state apparatus, amply supported by imperial powers, ensured the pre-eminence of its strategic interests.

Two alternative routes to industrialization were open to Canada in the formative years of the nineteenth century, Naylor believed: "Manufacturing industry can grow up 'naturally' from a small scale, even artisanal mode of production where capital accumulation is a largely internal phenomenon based on the reinvestment of the firm's own profits. A second path implies direct development to large-scale oligopolistic enterprise where outside capital is invested to facilitate its expansion and where the state takes an active, direct role in its growth. The outside capital required could come from commercial capital accumulation, from the state, or from foreign investment."[33]

Naylor contended that Canada's commercial-financial class fraction was able to impose its own peculiar variant of the second route. Its alliance with British financial capital at first channelled scarce investment funds into transport infrastructure for staples export; later, its support for National Policy tariffs amounted to a policy of industrialization by invitation, where American direct investment was welcomed, leading to an extensive network of branch plants. These initiatives, Naylor observed, were the legacy of an archaic mercantilist ideology still dominant within the colonial state, favouring low-risk investment outlets and maximum inflow of foreign productive factors. Starved for financing by the banking community and overwhelmed by the state's support for American branch plant industries, nascent Canadian manufacturers were marginalized in an economy increasingly oriented to large-scale, staple-related enterprises. Their stultification extinguished the possibility of independent capitalist industrialization and produced "inefficient, non-innovative, and backward industrial structure with a penchant for dependence on foreign technology, foreign capital, and state assistance."[34]

In his studies of elite formations within the continental political economy, Wallace Clement has followed Naylor's interpretation of the relationship between class, dependence, and industrial retardation. Accepting Naylor's historical explanation for the persistent commercial bias in Canada's capitalist development, Clement attempted to advance it by unravelling the interlocking network of corporate élites held to be responsible for diverging industrial paths of the United States and Canada. He provided documentation to update, through the post-war period, Naylor's view that transnational élite linkages forged around the staples economy undermined Canadian manufacturing. A detailed portrait was drawn of a comfortable, if unequal, partnership between Canada's indigenous elite, concentrated in finance, transportation, and utilities, and an American-controlled comprador élite directing Canada's resource development and secondary manufacturing.[35]

Industrial stultification resulting from the distorted economic management of a dominant class misshapen by imperialism is also a theme developed by Daniel Drache. Canada, he submitted, has been saddled with an incomplete form of capitalism, "advanced resource capitalism," in which government intervention has been only partially able to "offset the worst effects of profit-taking, resource exploitation and industrial retardation brought about by American domination."[36] Canadian banks have been fattened by the resource trade while hopeful Canadian manufacturers have been starved of capital. Even apparently nationalist industrial initiatives like the nineteenth-century National Policy, Drache asserted, respond to an external dynamic: "It is clear that neither the state nor the capitalist class controlled or even set the pace of Canadian development. The motor forces of development clearly lay elsewhere. State and capital could react; they could influence; they could take initiatives; but they could not control in any fundamental way what happened. They were a subservient state and bourgeoisie, continually on the defensive reacting to events over which they had no real control."[37]

For Gordon Laxer, the Naylor thesis approached the question of Canada's "aborted" industrialization too narrowly. Using a "modified Gerschenkron approach," he attempted to demonstrate that Canadian manufacturing "held its own with other late follower countries at the end of the nineteenth century" and was poised with countries like Sweden and Japan to progress toward an independent, fully developed industrialism.[38] While agreeing that the early-twentieth-century rise of branch plant production sealed the unfortunate fate of Canadian manufacturing, Laxer explained that this was not the inevitable outcome of political and economic domination by a dependent commercial ruling class. "Instead of pointing a finger at Canadian capitalists for not protecting their own bailiwick," he said, "I have indicted the whole of the social formation."[39]

In other "late-follower" countries, the political power of the subordinate classes had produced conditions favourable to the development of a nationalistic industrial strategy often associated with the pursuit of military objectives. However, Laxer asserted, Canada's agrarian and working classes were relatively weak, sectionally divided, and generally incapable of mounting a serious challenge to "big capital." As well, military defence was left to the British and the Americans. Accordingly, "Canada did not develop a domestically-owned and innovative engineering industry under the protective care of an independent military policy."[40]

A more fundamental critique of Naylor's position can be found in the work of Glen Williams. Focusing on the failure of Canadian industry to become internationally competitive, he has taken direct issue with the assumption that foreign direct investment broke the back of either an existing (as in Levitt and Gordon Laxer) or potential (as in Naylor, Clement, and Drache) class of independent Canadian manufacturers. Instead, Williams has stressed the essential continuity in the various periods of industrial expansion that followed the National Policy. This continuity stems from the logic imposed on investment decisions of firms and the state by Canada's unique location within the international political economy.[41]

During the earliest period, this meant an import substitution industrial (ISI) strategy characterized by extreme technological dependence and orientation to the domestic market. Once ISI was established as the prevailing pattern, it became progressively more difficult for firms to risk capital on developing world-competitive, export-oriented manufacturing. US branch plants, whose growing dominance in Canadian manufacturing could be explained largely by their initial location in the growth industries of the twentieth century, simply reinforced and further institutionalized the earlier ISI model by becoming "Canadian regional" production centres within the continental economy.

Williams has also taken issue with the "dependent state" position typical of the foreign-ownership school, suggesting that the Canadian state system not only has the capacity to challenge branch plant production but might, under certain conditions, even use it.[42] However, in spite of sometimes detailed appreciation by our political and bureaucratic elites of the many deficiencies of the ISI model, both the power of foreign capital in the Canadian economy and the prevailing continentalist orthodoxy of officials have made the state loath to implement corrective policies. Williams's most recent work has recorded the serious challenges to the ISI régime's stability caused by the economic and trade dislocations of the last decade. As well, he has surveyed the various adaptive strategies employed by firms and the state in attempting to cope with the new international environment.[43]

Turning away from this approach's historical debates about the origins of Canadian industrial weakness and returning to the Watkins-Levitt call for "new national policies . . . to countervail the power of multinational firms" in Canada's manufacturing sector, many authors have argued for a state-directed industrial strategy. The Science Council of Canada, in general, and John Britton and James Gilmour, in particular, struggled to flesh out an often elusively imprecise slogan.[44] Because of the branch plant economy's failure to provide for "technological sovereignty," the Science Council, with others, like Abraham Rotstein, has argued that an industrial strategy must be a precondition for any move toward Canadian-US free trade.[45]

James Laxer has long been a proponent of an industrial strategy. He first began to warn in the early 1970s that a declining American empire would mean deindustrialization for Canada.[46] In the 1980s, suggesting to the left that Canada faces a greater crisis in production than in distribution,[47] he has contended that Canadian-US free trade will strip Canada of the ability to mount an industrial strategy at the time it needs one most. He finds considerable irony in this situation: "The East Asian economic miracle has decidedly not been based on the individualistic model of competitive economy favoured in the United States. Rather, it has been based on the synergy between public and private sectors which takes advantage both of long-term strategic planning and of competition. . . . We will be adopting the American model in spite of the fact that our own economic history in Canada gives us a model far closer to the one that has been emerging elsewhere in the industrialized world."[48]

SOCIAL RELATIONS

Employing various approaches within Marxist or neo-Marxist class analysis, writers interested in social relations have sought to understand industrial development in a broader social context than can be found in the simple bipolar relationship between capital, domestic or foreign, and the state. Although the capitalist class is given a central and ultimately determining role in the growth of manufacturing, weight is also placed on the particular contribution of the working class and other subordinate classes. As we shall see, these popular social forces are seen to be an important moderating influence on the direction of industrial expansion both through the elaboration of state policies and within the accumulation process itself.

Recording the place of labour and farmers in the origins of Canadian manufacturing, H.C. Pentland and Stanley Ryerson broke ground during the 1960s for those who subsequently followed in the new political economy. The prelude to Canada's industrial revolution, they agreed, was the 1850s. During this decade, the first explosion of railway building occurred. The railways were to become the key to consolidation of a Canadian domestic market and laid the groundwork for transformation of craft production through application of more advanced industrial techniques.

In Pentland's view, the 1850s provided for "a mature capitalistic labour market with, on the one hand, adequate supplies of skilled workers and an abundance of cheap unskilled labour, and, on the other hand, the sustained demand that would retain them in the market."[49] Through the free availability of skilled immigrant workers from Britain, Canadian factories enjoyed considerable savings in time and capital as they adapted to the modern technology and impersonal labour discipline of the new industrial capitalism. Ryerson stressed the manner in which the investment capital required for industrial transformation represented a social product historically accumulated from the labour of the subordinate classes: "Merchant's capital, accumulated in the fur-trade through profit extracted from the labor of Indian trappers and French-Canadian canoemen, merged with capital derived from land-company speculation, exploitation of settlers and the farming community; and thence to banking operations, railway speculation and profiteering, and the commandeering of the government apparatus and public exchequer."[50]

Introduced in Ryerson's and Pentland's work, the contribution of labour to the trajectory of Canadian industrialization has also been a theme within the new political economy. Greg Kealey has observed that as Canadian industrial capitalism progressed toward "maturity" in the last three decades of the nineteenth century, the working class struggled to keep pace as production shifted from an artisan to a machine base. Workers reacted both by looking for ways to slow the onslaught of new technologies and by recognizing that "their strength no longer lay in their skill but rather in their ability to organize all workers."[51] This organization involved both formation of trade unions and a search for labour influence within the political process. Through examining the decade after 1900, Paul Craven has emphasized that the craft-based unions that then dominated Canadian labour "were dragged extremely reluctantly, and with faces firmly turned toward the past," into the new industrialism. Neglecting the interests of workers in mass-production manufacturing and defending instead "the old aristocracy of craft," the newly organized Trades and Labour Congress (TLC) greatly restricted the potential influence of Canadian labour on the character of modern Canadian industry. With acceptance of the "employment hierarchy" at the heart of the craft model, the TLC was concerned with simple "fairness" rather that "equality." Craven believed that its "emphasis on making a fair bargain in the market place reaffirmed the legitimacy of the existing economic order, without raising complementary questions about distinctions between employer and worker."[52]

Leo Panitch has outlined a more structural relationship between industrialization, the accumulation process, and the character of Canadian labour. Canada's position in the international and continental political economies dictated that on a world comparative basis Canadian workers constituted a relatively "high wage proletariat." This meant that "industrial production in Canada had to expand on the basis of *relative* surplus value, the application of extensive fixed capital to the production process to expand labour productivity, and not on the basis of cheap labour with the extension of working hours and absolute immiseration of the direct producers" as it did in less favoured parts of the world capitalist economy. With a later start and more limited domestic markets, Canadian manufacturers were inevitably led to dependence on US technology and investment. "Thus the very struggles of the Canadian working class . . . over the shorter work week, factory discipline, the importation of cheap foreign labour, or resistance to wage cuts," Panitch argues, restricted the potential for the evolution of a Canadian industrialism not dominated by American branch plants.[53]

The new political economy has also investigated the manner in which the subordinate classes have helped to shape the essential elements of state industrial policies. Kealey has argued that working-class support for National Policy tariffs was key to the 1878 electoral success of the Conservatives. A populist wing of the Tory party eagerly pursued this "cross-class political alliance," and labour, in the context of unemployment and bad times, responded to the point where "the 1878 campaign in Toronto was fought almost entirely on the issue of protection and its effect on the working class."[54]

Craven and Tom Traves have offered a three-class model to account for the subsequent evolution of the first fifty years of National Policy industrialization. Unlike countries where industrialism polarized society into direct confrontation between workers and capitalists, National Policy economic development also produced a powerful agrarian petite bourgeoisie. Thus the complex politics that framed the industrial tariff produced "grounds to unite class interests as well as divide them." Workers and manufacturers found common cause as an "industrial interest," farmers and workers intersected as "producing classes," and industrialists and farmers joined together as "propertied classes." However, as industrial capital "gradually consolidated its power at the expense of the others, it found it decreasingly necessary to build such cross-class alliances. Instead, its priority became to forestall the possibility of an alliance against itself: hegemony, once established, must be maintained."[55]

Traves's own work on Canadian industry from the First World War to the Depression documents the difficulties of maintaining this hegemony in the face of organized resistance from the subordinate classes. Despite the desire of industrial capital to use the state to structure and regulate the market on its behalf, "there was never a simple translation of economic might into political power." Instead, politicians had to learn to "tread carefully between powerful corporate interests and outraged public opinion."[56] Nowhere is this more clear than in Traves's description of how popular forces were able to decisively influence the automotive production régime in Canada: "It is clear that after 1926 political and institutional imperatives affected the course of structural change in the Canadian industry at least as much as the changing nature of the market . . . Once automobile prices became the focus of class and sectional politics in Canada the industry was especially vulnerable to pressures to change the terms of the tariff schedule under which it operated. After 1926 these forces, together with changing market conditions and altered entrepreneurial capacities, decisively reshaped the environment within which auto producers made their investment decisions. Ultimately the auto industry adapted to changed circumstances, but adaptation was slow and hesitant."[57]

Confirmation of the potency of subordinate classes in pushing and pulling state industrial policies has also been recorded since 1945. Lying at the heart of Quebec's Quiet Revolution, according to William Coleman, was a project for industrial renovation bringing together the common interests of three classes in allowing "the francophone community to become a full participant in the advanced industrial economy of North America." While the francophone business class saw obvious opportunities in extending its sphere of operation, the nationalist middle class believed that a new francophone "capitalist order could be directed so as to be compatible with the established culture of the French-Canadian community." Organized labour, meanwhile, hoped that the strengthening of francophone enterprises would prove "a means of regularizing the business cycle and stabilizing employment." All three classes coalesced around the 1960 program of the Parti liberal calling for state intervention both to increase French-Canadian control of the Quebec economy and to extend industrial development through processing of Quebec's resources within the province.[58]

Wildly successful at first, this alliance ultimately broke apart over issues such as the degree of government intervention, layoffs and instability attending industrial restructuring, and competing views of cultural nationalism. Ironically, Coleman notes, the more successfully integrated into North American production " the francophone capitalist class becomes, the less interested in nationalism it is likely to be."[59] However, important sections of the organized working class channelled into the independence movement their disenchantment with the failure of the Quiet Revolution to increase job security.

Subordinate classes also play a meaningful role in Rianne Mahon's account of the restructuring of Canadian textile manufacturing in the wake of post-1960s tariff liberalization. The changing tariff régime, Mahon believes, was in the interest of the "hegemonic" resource-exporting or staples fraction of the Canadian capitalist class, and the burden of much of her analysis is to demonstrate how labour became marginalized in the formation of state policies to cope with industrial restructuring. Faced with potential deindustrialization in their industries as tariffs fell, textile and clothing unions attempted in the late 1950s and the late 1960s independently to lobby the state for a "corporatist planning" solution, involving unions, corporations, and the government. Because of the organizational fragmentation of the unions concerned as well as the generally weak representation, compared with western Europe, of Canadian labour within the federal state structure, they met with no success.

It was through a producer-initiated and -led alliance that labour was eventually able to gain some leverage in the policy process. In a period "marked by generalized labour militancy," and given the Quebec base of textile production, the Canadian Textile Institute was able to establish a connection between the plight of the manufacturers it represented and "the state's more fundamental concerns: labour unrest and Quebec separatism." And so "the coalition led by textile capital did manage to present its case for a 'new national policy for textiles' in a manner that forced the state to recognize that inaction might ultimately place in jeopardy the staple fraction's hegemonic position."[60] Nevertheless, subordinate classes did not play a direct role in negotiating the concessions that were made in 1971 to help textile capital modernize: "Clothing capital and labour in both industries were kept at a distance from the process . . . Other forces – consumers and importers – were even more marginal." Mahon warned that the outcomes for workers in other industries that face tariff-induced deindustrialization "are unlikely to be better than those provided under the textile policy," unless "labour is able to produce a decisive shift in the basic balance of power."[61]

Mahon's discussion of the competitive challenges posed by multilateral tariff liberalization for one of Canada's "traditional" manufacturing sectors usefully introduces broader questions about the place of subordinate classes in the ongoing restructuring and transformation of production in countries of the advanced industrial bloc. Basing their analyses on the French *regulation* school, François Houle, and John Holmes and Colin Leys, have traced the protracted period of recession during much of the last two decades to the erosion of the particular socioeconomic structures sustaining the Fordist régime of accumulation.[62] Constructed around the relationship between mechanized mass production and mass consumption, Fordism, by the end of the 1960s,began to suffer from chronic productivity and profitability crises accompanied by intensified international competition. In general terms, industrialists have been responding by reorganizing labour markets and processes, introducing new technologies, and relocating manufacturing to low-wage sites.

Panitch has observed that firms have been seeking "to organize production so that they can respond flexibly and quickly to an environment they don't and can't control monolithically." Part and parcel of the search for flexibility have been "a strategic attack on labour." This has included heightened reliance on part-time and short-term contract work, decentralized collective bargaining which seeks to institutionalize new forms of worker identification with management goals, and extension of job ghettos in the burgeoning service sector.[63]

For North America, these upheavals have brought not only decline relative to the global industrial economy but also a relative shift in output and employment from manufacturing to services. As Jorge Niosi and Phillipe Faucher have documented, these trends have made "more explicit" the structural weaknesses of Canada's branch plant economy. These authors warn of the "very expensive" social costs associated with industrial decline. Increasingly, "high productivity, high value added" jobs are exchanged for "low productivity, low value added" ones.[64]

Female workers have been particularly affected by restructuring. While most factory workers are men, female workers are concentrated in especially vulnerable industries like textiles and electrical products. Accordingly, Pat Armstrong has argued, although more men will likely lose their jobs to restructuring than women, the future is bleak for female workers in manufacturing, "since women are concentrated in the sectors characterized by low productivity, in those targeted by the government for technological transformation and in those facing the greatest competition from abroad."[65]

CONCLUSION

Through amassing an impressive inventory of empirical studies, the new political economy has developed the most robust analytical framework in contemporary Canadian social science for understanding the peculiar trajectory of Canada's industrialization. Reflecting this strength, this chapter has reviewed outstanding contributions in three research dimensions: the staples trade, foreign ownership, and social relations. It has argued that these research foci are generally linked through four underlying methodological assumptions which stress that outcomes are socially determined and historically developed across relationally linked economic sectors and territorial spaces. Nonetheless, contributors to this field have engaged frequently in fierce internal debates on, among other things, the nature of state-society relations and Canada's position in the international political economy. Other chapters record these debates. This chapter seeks to outline what we have learned about the substance of "what went wrong" in Canadian manufacturing.

The current debate over free trade underlines the enduring importance of the research dimensions and methodological assumptions that we have identified. Bowing before the commands of the international market, free trade promises to deepen Canada's historic reliance on export of staples to the United States. This will be particularly so insofar as it is cast as an alternative to a state-directed industrial strategy as a means of adjusting to restructuring in the international economy. Here Innis's exploration of the national government's fragile capacity to mediate the impact of "economic storms" in the world economy speaks directly to the current retreat from interventionism. Equally timely is the work of the later staples writers on the regional dimension of industrialism, encompassing analyses along both the federal-provincial and Canadian-US axes. Much more work needs to be done from this perspective.[66]

Similarly, as it centres on the effect of technological change and the labour process, research adopting a social relations approach must be carried forward to consider in greater depth the labour market upheavals and "adjustments" that have attended liberalized trade and the international redivision of production. Further, the strategic response from the corporate sector and organized labour to both these upheavals and the federal state's re-energized continentalist thrust must be examined through more studies of specific industries and sectors.[67] Finally, of course, there remains the broad problem of "Americanization," pivoting around the contemporary behaviour of multinational corporations and the effect of foreign ownership on Canada's manufacturing prospects. We still know too little about the new roles that branch plants will be expected to play in the ongoing rationalization of continental production.[68]

NOTES

1 Blais, "Industrial Policy," 4.
2 Innis, *Problems of Staple Production in Canada*, 100.
3 Innis, "Transportation in Canadian Economic History," 66.
4 Innis, "The Canadian Economy and the Depression."
5 Aitken, "Myth and Measurement."
6 Innis, "The Teaching of Economic History in Canada," 10.
7 Innis, *Problems of Staple Production*, 91, 82.
8 Innis, "A Defence of the Tariff," 150.
9 Innis and Easterbrook, "Fundamental and Historic Elements," 368.
10 Innis, "A Defence of the Tariff." See also his "Introduction to Canadian Economic Studies," 162-8, and "Transportation in Canadian Economic History," 71-2.
11 Innis, "The Penetrative Powers of the Price System," 258-64.
12 Innis, "Introduction to Canadian Economic Studies," 173; "Economic Trends in Canadian-American Relations," 235; and "Recent Developments in the Canadian Economy," 305.
13 Innis and Easterbrook, "Fundamental and Historic Elements," 369, and Innis, "The Canadian Mining Industry."
14 Innis, "The Canadian Economy and the Depression," 135.
15 Innis, "An Introduction to the Economic History of Ontario," 122.
16 Innis, "Government Ownership and the Canadian Scene," 96.
17 Innis, "The Wheat Economy," 277-9.
18 For a discussion of how the orthodox view has been manifested in Canadian analysis, see G. Williams, *Not for Export*, chap. 7.
19 Watkins, "A Staple Theory of Economic Growth," 53.
20 Ibid., 62-3.

21 Ibid., 73.

22 Ibid., 63.

23 Nelles, *The Politics of Development*, 309.

24 Richards and Pratt, *Prairie Capitalism*, 10–11.

25 Ibid., viii–ix, 307–19.

26 Ibid., 329.

27 McCallum, *Unequal Beginnings*, 120, 116–17.

28 Ibid., 119.

29 Ibid., 91–2.

30 Canada, Privy Council Office, Report of the Task Force on the Structure of Canadian Industry, 345–6. Also important in developing the early critique of the branch plant economy were Bourgault, *Innovation and the Structure of Canadian Industry*, and Canada, Information Canada, *Foreign Direct Investment in Canada*, (Gray Report).

31 Levitt, *Silent Surrender*, 118–19. For contemporary illustrations of the stifling effects of foreign ownership on industrial entrepreneurialism, see Saul, "The Secret Life of the Branch Plant Executive." For an excellent discussion of the difficulties of maintaining an independent Canadian economic policy in the face of US pressure, see Clarkson, *Canada and the Reagan Challenge*.

32 Naylor, "The Rise and Fall of the Third Commercial Empire of the St. Lawrence," 3.

33 Naylor, "Dominion of Debt," 52. See as well his *History of Canadian Business*, I, 38. Volume II focuses on industrial development. A collection of more recent essays can be found in his *Dominion of Debt*.

34 Naylor, "Dominion of Debt."

35 Clement, *The Canadian Corporate Elite* and *Continental Corporate Power*.

36 Drache, "Canadian Capitalism."

37 Drache, "The Crisis of Canadian Political Economy," 34.

38 G. Laxer, "Foreign Ownership," 330.

39 G. Laxer, "Class, Nationality and the Roots of the Branch Plant Economy," 46.

40 Ibid. See also his "The Political Economy of Aborted Developments."

41 G. Williams, *Not for Export*, chap. 2. For an explicit critique of Naylor's position, see his "The National Policy Tariffs, 333–8." On Glen Williams's view of Canada's location in the international political economy, see his chapter in this volume.

42 G. Williams, *Not for Export*, 169–72.

43 Ibid., chap. 9, and "Canadian Sovereignty and the Free Trade Debate."

44 Britton and Gilmour, *The Weakest Link*. Also see Canada, Science Council Industrial Policies Committee, *Hard Times, Hard Choices*.

45 Britton and Gilmour, *The Weakest Link*, 153, and Rotstein, *Rebuilding from Within*, chap. 2, 3.

46 J. Laxer, "Canadian Manufacturing and U.S. Trade Policy."

47 J. Laxer, *Rethinking the Economy*, 97–9.

48 J. Laxer, *Leap of Faith*, 80.

49 Pentland, *Labour and Capital*, 170.
50 Ryerson, *Unequal Union*, 270.
51 G.S. Kealey, *Toronto Workers*, 293.
52 Craven, *"An Impartial Umpire,"* 138-9, 189-90.
53 Panitch, "Dependency and Class," 19.
54 G.S. Kealey, *Toronto Workers*, 156.
55 Craven and Traves, "Class Politics," 15-16.
56 Traves, *The State and Enterprise*, 9.
57 Ibid., 120.
58 Coleman, *The Independence Movement*, 92-3.
59 Ibid., 128-9.
60 Mahon, *The Politics of Industrial Restructuring*, 76-7.
61 Ibid., 90, 150.
62 Houle, "Economic Strategy," and Holmes and Leys, "Introduction." See also Houle, "L'état canadien."
63 Panitch, "Capitalist Restructuring," 136-7. See also Panitch and Swartz, *From Consent to Coercion*.
64 Niosi and Faucher, "The Decline of North American Industry," 72-3, 76.
65 P. Armstrong, *Labour Pains*, 156. See also A. Porter and Cameron, "The Impact of Free Trade."
66 An outstanding account of recent developments in the BC political economy can be found in Marchak, "The Rise and Fall of the Peripheral State."
67 Some specific industry case study material has begun to emerge. See, for example, Muszynski, *The Deindustrialization of Metropolitan Toronto*; Grayson, *Plant Closures and De-Skilling*; and Holmes, "The Crisis of Fordism."
68 L.K. Mytelka looks insightfully at changing multinational behaviour from the perspective of the organization of technological change in "Knowledge-Intensive Production." A quite conventionally orthodox, but recent, treatment of some similar themes is provided by Conklin and St-Hilaire, *Canadian High-Tech*.

CHAPTER FOUR

Through Different Lenses: The Political Economy of Labour

Paul Phillips

Dioptic lens: a lens used to focus light on a single plane
Prismatic lens: a lens used to correct errors of vision

The Canadian tradition of political economy – the "fusion of economic and political theory into one single social theory"[1] – has been long and honourable. The "old" political economy reached its peak under Harold Innis and the Toronto school, complemented in the west by a coterie of hinterland political economists at the University of Saskatchewan. But political economy in Canada entered a "dark age" in the 1950s and 1960s with the triumph of economism, the divorce of economic theory from political and social theory. The economic crisis of the 1970s and 1980s and the failure of orthodox economics either to explain or to correct the resulting stagflation and unemployment crises brought renewed interest in political economy. The "new" political economy, however, differed significantly from the old. While the earlier political economy was hardly monolithic or homogeneous, given the differences between the metropolitan and hinterland perspectives, the differences were less in the type of "lens" used to focus on their subject than in the direction in which they chose to point them.

By contrast, the new political economy embodies a number of disparate and competing strains, most notably, the schism between the left-nationalist, dependist school and the more classical Marxist class analysts, though it would be a mistake to see this as the only basis of "dioptic" or "prismatic" division.[2] Far from being an indication of a crisis in Canadian political economy, however, vigorous competition among approaches indicates an intellectual vitality that generates perhaps equal amounts of light and heat.

The political economy approach to labour has used numerous lenses, each focusing on different aspects of the labour experience. At one extreme is labour as an abstract factor of production – a commodity used in the production of other commodities. At the other, labour is viewed as a class, both in the objective sense of its social relation to capital in production and as a vehicle of conscious social and economic change. It is viewed as an institution, in both the widest sense employed by social historians and institutional economists – "collective action in control of individual action"[3] – and the narrowest, the formal political and economic organizations of workers to achieve specific or general ends. At one time or another, all these approaches have been used in Canadian political economy. The purpose of this chapter is to review the contribution of the various approaches to our knowledge of Canadian labour and to attempt a synthesis that will enlarge our understanding of the political economy of labour in both contemporary and historical Canada.

THE STAPLES TRADITION

With respect to the treatment of labour in Canadian political economy, it is possible to identify a number of dioptic and prismatic lenses, approaches that illuminate quite different facets of the labour experience. Historically, the first is the staples approach identified with Innis and his Toronto and Saskatchewan colleagues. Innis, despite his innovative staples approach to patterns of Canadian economic development, remained in the liberal economics tradition by treating labour primarily as a factor of production, that is, in a conventional economics manner. He was not interested or concerned with class as an analytical tool and, in this sense at least, cannot be connected with the Marxist approach to labour and development.

Perhaps Innis's clearest treatment of labour occurs in "Labour in Canadian Economic History," primarily a discussion of labour migration to Canada and its regions, labour's contribution to the defence of Canada from American absorption, the impact of economic fluctuations and war on the welfare of workers and farmers, and the consequent early organization of craft unions and farm organizations. Innis's abstract factor-of-production approach can be illustrated best by this quotation from the conclusion to the article:

The importance of staple products . . . [implied] wide fluctuations in price and yield, distance from the market, dependence on the share system, the truck system, intensive self sufficiency, and marked fluctuation in the standards of living. The increase of industrial development . . . have involved increasing efficiency and extension of the monetary structure. These developments have been accompanied by increasing flexibility and increasing mobility. On the other hand the shift from commercial capitalism to industrial capitalism has been striking . . . and has led to a later stage of capitalism with the attendant rigidities of capital structure . . . The conflict between a price structure dominated by Great Britain and a price structure increasingly dominated by the [United States] has serious implications for the Canadian economy in the inequalities between groups and regions.[4]

This is clear confirmation of McNally's critique of the staples approach as "commodity fetishism," which, "rather than revealing the 'essential relations' of capitalist society, reproduces the reified images in which capitalism immediately presents itself." Further, the theory continues classical "market abstractionism" and "technical determinism," which conceives production as "the production of things by things . . . and not as a process in which social (class) relations are produced and reproduced in the process of producing things known as commodities."[5]

A further confirmation of this critique is Innis's failure to distinguish between farmers, fishers, and native trappers – all independent commodity producers in a commercial or exchange relationship – and wage workers in an industrial or production relationship. Innis was concerned primarily with the staples trades (cod fish and fur in particular but also timber and agriculture), where industrial capitalism and the formal subjugation of labour to capital were minor or fringe elements. Indeed, the staples approach fell into disuse (and orthodox disrespect), in large measure because it failed to explain the development of staples industries after the advent of industrial capitalism and the emergence of an alienated working class. Its re-emergence followed two developments – the application of Marxist class analysis and accumulation theory to the staples industries (the neo-Marxist approach) and the application of Marxist exchange and primitive accumulation theory to metropolis-hinterland relations (the left-nationalist or dependency approach). As I have tried to show elsewhere, the expropriation of surplus may be accomplished directly from labour, in the sphere of production, or indirectly, in the sphere of exchange; hence the two approaches may well be complementary rather than contradictory.[6]

Having made this fundamental criticism of Innis's treatment of labour, we should recognize his major insights about Canadian labour. Two points are paramount: the contribution of successive waves of staples expansion to segmenting and conditioning the labour experience and the influence of a continental labour market (before the First World War) on wages, on wage structures and the Canadian workers' standard of living, and on the shape of Canadian labour institutions. Daniel Drache has pursued the first point, in particular the differences between the experiences of exposed workers in the staples industries and protected workers in domestic manufacturing: "Using an Innisian perspective, it is possible to show how both the implementation of the labour market and the gradual development of the working class reflect the productive forces of each successive staple. The principal notion . . . is that each staple determines its own relationship, labour requirements and labour markets."[7]

Each expansion of staples development tended to be accompanied by a corresponding wave of immigration. Most waves were composed of various ethnic and racial groups, with different labour and industrial experiences. Schmidt has recognized the importance of this point for the development of Canadian labour:

The divisions within the working class created by language and ethnicity were one source of disunity, as was the ability to create wage competition between immigrants and the more established work force. More to the point however, immigration created a series of disjunctures within a common history of the development of the class struggle. Each wave of immigration corresponded to a distinct stage of accumulation, and immigrants were incorporated in a specific manner and through specific struggles – regionally and sectorally, depending on the period – and within the class hierarchy as skilled or unskilled, as independent commodity producers or wage labourers.[8]

The influence of a common labour market on Canadian wages and wage structures has been stressed by Leo Panitch,[9] though I would not agree that high wages were instrumental in the invasion of American branch plant capital into Canadian industry. Nevertheless, a North American labour market, as Babcock has demonstrated, certainly assisted the invasion of American "branch plant unionism."[10]

Not all the traditional staples scholars ignored class as a significant factor in the production and reproduction of the economic system. Donald Creighton, the Tory historian, in *The Empire of the St. Lawrence*, championed the commercial or merchant class.[11] However, "merchants" and "mercantile system" take up four or five column inches of his index; "land" almost two; "labour" and "worker" get nary a mention. Vernon Fowke, the western populist and leading economic historian of Canadian agriculture, quite consciously recognized farmers as a class of independent commodity producers by paying "special attention to the agricultural segment of the economy and to the relations between agriculture and commerce in particular" and to "the place of agriculture within the *price system*," the latter term "being synonymous with 'competitive system' " or the open market.[12] Here again we are returned to Innis's 'price system' – the sphere of circulation where labour is an abstract factor of production or, simply, a commodity of exchange.

THE INSTITUTIONALISTS

Historical Narrative

Contemporary with Innis was the labour economist Harold Logan, perhaps the founder of trade union history in Canada, who played a role not unlike that of the Webbs in Britain and Commons in the United States in describing and chronicling the emergence and evolution of unions. This approach to Canadian labour is subject to severe limitations. While unions are the most concrete subject matter for research and description, they have always represented a minority of paid workers, particularly among women and the service, trade, and financial sectors. In addition, such an approach tends to ignore the role and contribution of unpaid labour in the home.

Unionism also involved only part of the working-class experience, that "on the job." It largely excludes cultural, ethnic, religious, community, family, and, to a lesser extent, political experience. Trade union histories tend to reify labour organizations and laws, giving them human qualities and values independent of the individuals who comprise them.

There is a further difficulty when attempting union history within an orthodox economic (partial-equilibrium) framework, which can be summed up by the subtitle of a popular post-war collection of readings on wage determination – power or market forces. Conventional economic theory is singularly unsuccessful in incorporating institutions into the analysis of labour. As a result, Logan's pioneering work was largely descriptive, as is Desmond Morton and Terry Copp's recent "social democratic" history of Canadian labour, *Working People*. Institutional labour studies have tended to remain in the same general mould, culminating in Eugene Forsey's massive exercise in investigative reporting, *Trade Unions in Canada, 1812–1902*. Not all institutional studies have been quite so narrowly historically descriptive, though most lack a broadly theoretical, political-economy underpinning such as the Webbs developed in *Industrial Democracy* or Commons in *Institutional Economics*. As such, they represent necessary building blocks or inputs into more complex political-economic analyses of Canadian labour in historical perspective.[13]

Historical Analysis

The designation "historical analysis" is meant to convey a subtle, but important distinction among the institutionalist writers; the embedding of institutional histories in a theoretical framework. This subgroup was concerned with analysing the institutional experience in order to test or to demonstrate an argument or thesis about the nature of the Canadian political economy. Let's take some examples. Horowitz attempted to show how the unique political culture of Canada, reflecting its British roots, shaped the evolution of the political institutions of Canadian labour (the "red Tory thesis"). Robin explored the interaction of union and socialist movements in the early period of industrialization, while Abella attempted to explain the rise and course of the Congress of Industrial Organizations (CIO) in Canada in terms of the conflicting social democratic and communist ideologies and the role of the state. Bercuson identifies the western labour revolt (the One Big Union, or OBU) with the nature of economic development and the capitalist class in western Canada; McCormack takes his political analysis much further, identifying the ideological strata and noting fragmented working-class consciousness and its role in determining the structure and tactics of unions and other labour institutions. In my own early work on British Columbia and western Canadian labour, my main concern was to determine and illustrate the impact of patterns of economic growth and stagnation, and of inflation and unemployment, on the evolution and behaviour of organized labour in both its industrial and political forms. Perhaps the most significant contribution to this genre of studies has been the work of Stuart Jamieson. His specific focus has been on industrial conflict, with emphasis on the economic and technological determinants of conflict and on the role of the state in controlling overt conflict. However, he has also sketched out elements of a continental political economy with respect to Canadian unions and industrial relations.[14]

There is no consistent theoretical framework embodied in these institutional studies. The only study of this nature that adopts an explicitly Marxist lens is *The Trade Union Movement of Canada, 1827-1959*, by Charles Lipton.[15] Even Lipton, however, lacks a consistent theoretical framework, and his book becomes, more often than not, a mere partisan narrative of the struggles of organized labour against capital and the state. The other institutionalists generally focus through social democratic or reformist liberal, often nationalist-tinted, lenses.

These institutionalist approaches, while not in themselves indefensible, limit the analysis in two major ways. First, they restrict study to formal institutions. Second, they have tended to be partial, within the limits imposed by conventional economic, political, and social theory. On the first limitation, Palmer has noted:

This first generation of labor historians broke new ground decisively in their studies of the working-class experience, but they accomplished their tasks (and defined them) in the old ways. . . . Only rarely (although recently with more frequency) did they seem concerned with the international literature in the field, seldom with theory. Untouched by radical sentiment, much of this generation reflected a hard-nosed tough-minded approach to their subject. . . . Like Dickens' Gradgrind, they sought only "the facts." Their commitment, their engagement, was and is in the service of *professional* historical writing. . . .

For all of their strengths, however, these "realists" face certain problems. Briefly stated, they often appear as prisoners of their sources, incarcerated by the period which they study. Twentieth-century evidence is top-heavy with royal commissions, "official" union correspondence, prime ministers' papers, RCMP files, and justice department collections. Small wonder that such data yields histories of an essentially institutional/political character, and zeroes in on the labor movement and the working-class experience from a particular vantage point.[16]

The second limitation, in part an extension of the first, is the result of a failure of paradigm. Contrary to Palmer's assertion, lack of concern with theory was not the root of the problem; rather, the conventional theoretical paradigms in the social sciences provided few tools for the study of working-class experience as multi-dimensional, but many for abstract, ahistorical, and partial analysis. Unfortunately, in the post-war boom period, under the influence of Cold War academic censorship and the takeover of many of the social sciences by advocates of narrow quantification, the political-economy tradition of multi-disciplinary, historically informed analysis virtually disappeared in Canada – but not completely.

THE NEW POLITICAL ECONOMY

Pioneers

The Cold War and the hysterical anti-communism that accompanied it for the best part of two decades after the Second World War were very destructive of radical and Marxist-informed political economy in Canada, and perhaps even more so in the United States, where increasing numbers of Canadian social scientists were receiving their graduate training. Throughout this period, however, a few rather isolated scholars were making a significant contribution to the rebirth, beginning in the late 1960s, of a more radical Canadian political economy. Perhaps the two most important were Stanley Ryerson and Clare Pentland. Ryerson's Marxist reinterpretation of Confederation, *Unequal Union*, a synthesis of ideas and work dating back to the 1940s, was published in 1963. Clare Pentland wrote a series of articles that appeared between 1948 and 1959 on nineteenth-century labour and capital. They were a byproduct of his pathbreaking 1960 thesis (published 1981), which circulated widely in manuscript form among the younger generation of political economists.[17]

These two pioneers brought a Marxist approach, and thereby class analysis, to the study of Canadian labour, thus avoiding the institutionalists' narrow preoccupation with unions and electoral politics. This might well be expected in Ryerson's case as he was a leading intellectual for the Canadian Communist Party through much of this period. Pentland, however, was a very different case, refusing any Marxist label and insisting on his debt to Innis's staples tradition. Nevertheless, he greatly admired the work of a number of British Marxist scholars, particularly Eric Hobsbawm and Maurice Dobb, who undoubtedly informed his choice of subject, scope of inquiry, and theoretical approach.

Ryerson's central preoccupation in *Unequal Union* was the inequalities of Confederation, particularly the political and economic inequality between French and English Canada. (See Coleman's contribution to this collection.) He finds the cause not in an English plot or the failure of French capital but in the processes of the emergence of a capitalist industry and class and of a class of industrial wage-earners within a nation-building, capitalist state.[18]

Perhaps more important is the perspective Ryerson brought to the study of history, and hence to the study of labour:

History is made by people acting, collectively and as individuals, in three intersecting areas of social being: that of the "metabolism" of man and nature, with man gradually ... extending his mastery of natural forces, multiplying the productivity of labor, creating new technologies; that of class antagonism and conflict, rooted in social and economic contradictions, posing with mounting insistency the necessity of resolving the dilemma of social labor versus private appropriation; and ... the area of relations between national communities, the tensions and conflicts born of oppression of one people by another, and the urge to banish inequality, to break through to the "republic of man," the world community.[19]

Pentland's was the first in-depth study of the making of the Canadian working class and the transformation of relations between labour and capital from pre-industrial, staple-extractive to capitalist, industrial forms during the first industrial revolution:

To make the [labour] material suitable required a complex and unknowable educative process, conducted largely in the school of experience with the goad of harsh impersonal penalties for failures. Nor was the means to success capable of reduction to a precise dose of new discipline and new ambition that could be injected, once and for all, like a coin in a machine. Success was attained rather by an indistinct and never-completed process of interacting stimulation and response. Human transformation was bound to be partial, and mostly unplanned, because men were remaking themselves without much comprehension or consciousness of it, because deliberate changes sent out other ripples of subtle, unrecognized adjustments to preserve the tension and balance of existence, and because the inanimate machinery of production to which man had to fit himself could only itself be transformed bit by bit and year by year.[20]

Pentland has recently come under considerable criticism, particularly for his treatment of the Irish, but however flawed certain aspects of his study may be, it remains a landmark in the social history of Canadian labour.[21] Pentland followed up this major work with another, as yet unpublished, seminal work on Canadian labour.[22] It again reflects the broad scope of his inquiry, though with considerably more attention to the institutions of industrial relations and the role of the state in adjudicating class relations, and less attention to the process of the remaking of the working class. Pentland at various times employed many lenses and explored many different areas by combining a broad historical, political-economy approach with class analysis in the context of social and institutional history.

The Social and Class Historians

Pentland's and Ryerson's class-based "lenses" were not the only influences on the developing historical analysis of the political economy of Canadian labour. Another was the expansion of social history, in part made possible by the new computer technology (which allowed for meaningful quantification of the experience of the common people), in part an expression of primarily left-leaning younger scholars who were more concerned with the lives of the common people than with the parlour games of the high and mighty. One particular "filter" that offered new understanding of Canadian labour in a historical context was ethnicity. A second was gender. For the first time, women's work was being integrated into our understanding of the political and economic importance of the family as the basic unit of production and reproduction in a developing capitalist country. A third filter was the rural/urban experience, in particular the extent to which the urban unskilled poor bore the brunt of the social and economic change associated with industrialization. A fourth was region, which emphasized historical, geographic, social, economic, and cultural differences between Canada's economic areas.

These various filters undermined any concept of homogeneity or of a monolithic structure of working-class experience. It also paved the way for a significant departure in Canadian labour studies from the previously dominant institutional approach: studying working-class culture (or experience) in order to analyse Canadian labour in a historical context. This new approach is associated most closely with the writings of Kealey and Palmer and also reflected frequently in the pages of *Labour/Le travail*, the Canadian journal of labour history.[23]

To understand this lens, it is helpful to go back to two of this school's American mentors, historians Herbert Gutman and David Montgomery (though perhaps the most influential scholar in the field was the British historian E.P. Thompson).[24] Gutman, in referring to the genesis of one of his innovative articles, noted that he went to England to learn from the British historians and to Americanize their work:

What these British colleagues – Thompson, Hobsbawm, Rudé, Pollard, and several Harrisons, among others – had done was far more than simply study the whole worker. They had begun to reexamine the processes by which new subordinate classes are formed, how they develop. They were studying class conflict and social change in new ways ... It is an analysis of the ways in which who workers *had been* affected who they *became*. Our task was to Americanize ...[25]

Montgomery describes the relationship between his study, the evolution of the political-economic order, and the task of an "engaged" historian. His approach is to study the history of capitalism from the vantage point of working-class history, particularly shop-floor relations: "My study of both shop-floor struggles and the Reconstruction period has underscored for me the fact that the working class has always formulated alternatives to bourgeois society in this country, particularly on the job. What I find myself looking for is new forms of political struggle that come out of the everyday lives of working people . . . If, as radical historians, we are doing work that has some sort of meaning to politics and to the daily lives of working people, then it's got to be shared with them."[26]

In Palmer's own words, the practitioners of this approach have "learned of the importance of culture, of conflict as a way of life, and of the values of exploring class as a relationship with its own dynamics, internal and external, rather than as a static category acted upon, molded by, impersonal forces and hegemonic groups."[27]

Perhaps the most enduring contribution made by this group in Canada is to show just how different the work experience was in the nineteenth and early twentieth centuries from what it is today and, in the process, shedding considerable light on differences in regional and gender experiences. In particular, they have focused on the struggle of the skilled worker to maintain control over the work process, to resist the real subordination of labour embodied in the technological and work-organization changes associated with the emergence of factory production and large-scale capitalist production. At the same time, they have been accused of romanticizing the "idealized working man" of the past and exaggerating the importance of culture as a unifying theme of working-class experience. (One caustic wit has commented that if a worker farts, some of these historians immediately interpret this as a working-class movement.) Unfortunately, the important contribution that the class/culture historians have made to our understanding of this important period in the development of Canadian capitalism has sometimes been overshadowed by intemperate and counterproductive attacks on those who might view labour through such a different glass.[28] However, their emphasis on the organization of work and on the battle between workers and employers for control of that organization has contributed significantly to one of the most exciting approaches to both historical and contemporary political economy of labour, namely, the study of the labour process.

The Labour Process Analysts

In 1974 Harry Braverman published *Labor and Monopoly Capital*, his classic and influential study of the labour process and the determination of control of the workplace under monopoly capitalism.[29] It opened for study and debate an area largely ignored since Marx introduced the subject. How is work in a specific workplace organized? More important, why is it organized in this manner? Braverman's study encompasses control at both the point of production (sale or provision of service) and the point of employment and in the employment relationship. Critics commented that he concentrated on management and the technological control of work, largely ignoring workers' response and struggle, which in many cases significantly affected the final form of the labour process. Canadian political economists have, by and large, avoided this problem.

There have been two (not mutually exclusive) approaches to studies of labour process – historical and contemporary. At least initially, the historical studies were strongly influenced by the work of (indeed in many cases done by) social historians. The focus was on the attack by capital on the position of the autonomous skilled worker in the 1870-1914 period. Indeed, much of labour history for this period revolves around the struggle for control of the workplace and the real subordination of labour, first of the earliest deskilled trades – shoemaking and coopering being classic examples – and later of some of the iron- and steel-making and related metal-working trades. But the historical studies soon branched out and encompassed women's work, both in the home as well as in the paid labour market as clerical and service workers.

Much, but not all, of this work was done by historians. Contemporary studies have become dominated more and more by sociologists, as sociology has come virtually to eclipse an increasingly irrelevant economics as the premier discipline in the study of industrial relations and the politics and economics of labour. One need refer only to the studies of Pat and Hugh Armstrong, Clement, Connelly, Lowe, Marchak, Muszinski, Neis, and Reiter to illustrate this point. Economists have made a significant contribution to this field in Canada, often in the context of "women's work," such as MacDonald and McFarland on the Atlantic region.[30]

What is the gist of labour process analysis? Simply, employers attempt to maximize surplus value by organizing work, introducing technology, and structuring employment relations and labour markets in such a way as to purchase labour power (the capacity to work) at the lowest price and to exact the maximum labour (work effort) out of the employed workers. Workers resist such exploitation and adopt opposing strategies, from institutional and collective responses and political action to individual action – turnover, absenteeism, poor-quality work, systematic soldiering, and so on – but only when they perceive a wrong. To the extent that employers have been able to use racism, sexism, and other prejudices to disguise the wrong, capital has been able to use these divisions to structure work and the labour market to its own advantage. This last aspect of the political economy of Canadian labour, however, has not yet received much systematic treatment, particularly by economists.

Economists

Throughout this review of the various perspectives on labour, economists as a group have hardly stood out as major contributors in Canada. Innis, of course, cannot be ignored, but his treatment of labour was hardly satisfactory. Pentland and Jamieson (and perhaps myself in a rather more modest way) among economists have seen labour in a systemic sense, as both factor of production and conscious agent. However, conventional economics cannot adequately conceive of labour as both an economic and a political force. Rather, labour is treated as a passive and homogeneous element of production.

It is only with the revival of a more radical economics, where labour is treated as both an active agent and a heterogeneous element of production, that sense can be made out of the contemporary labour market. In this area, the most significant recent contribution has been Gonick's *The Great Economic Debate*, which situates labour firmly at the centre of the debate between competing paradigms over economic and social policy in the current economic crisis.[31] Workers' fates hang in the balance, awaiting the outcome of this debate.

Adoption of various lenses has allowed us to focus on selective aspects of the labour experience. What remains is to attempt to outline the main features of a synthesis, a new political economy of labour, which integrates the various perspectives outlined above with the major themes of the developing radical economics, to provide a composite lens with which to analyse labour.

A NEW POLITICAL ECONOMY OF LABOUR

The institutional treatment of labour within orthodox economics has led in the direction of ahistorical, mechanistic, partial-equilibrium (systems) analysis.[32] The new labour historians to some extent arrested this development by giving historical, class, and cultural contexts and placing the whole subject within a process – the making and remaking of work, worker, and working class. Marxist industrial relations approaches see industrial relations also as a process of constantly evolving class, employment, and interpersonal relations, evolving out of conflicts of class interests under the capitalist mode of production and distribution, with the state anything but a neutral arbiter.

In many ways the culmination, or coming together, of these diverse approaches is the study of power relations in the labour market and the workplace – the labour process. It is this study that must integrate institutional, social, economic, cultural, and ideological forces – all historically conditioned – within the constraints of available technology, to explain the processes of the determination of power at the workplace and of worker consciousness and the nature of class conflict, both historically and today. One American attempt at a global interpretation is by Gordon, Edwards, and Reich.[33] Their explanation is rooted in their concept of social structures of accumulation within the contours of long waves of economic accumulation. As of yet there are no such global attempts to explain the Canadian experience. Briefly, however, we will try to sketch out the main elements of such a political economy of labour.

The Labour Process

The very nature of the capitalist employment relation creates three planes on which conflict between labour and capital can and does exist. The first, and most obvious, is at the point of employment – the labour market. It is there that traditional labour economics has perhaps most notably failed to deal adequately with the inequality of power – despite Adam Smith's attention to the question over two hundred years ago. In reference to the power differential, Smith wrote: "It is not difficult to foresee which of the two parties must, upon all ordinary occasions, have the advantage . . . In all such disputes the masters can hold out much longer. A landlord, a farmer, a master manufacturer, or merchant, though they did not employ a single workman, could generally live a year or two upon the stock which they have already acquired. Many workmen could not subsist a week . . . without employment. In the long run the workman may be as necessary to his master as his master is to him, but the necessity is not so immediate."[34]

However, American institutional economists (following Commons) as early as the 1940s recognized the effect of labour market structure on the distribution of labour market power, but these insights tended to be lost in the neo-classical–Keynesian synthesis of the 1950s and 1960s. In any case, this tradition was never very well established in Canada. In the 1970s, the failure of the US war on poverty and the collapse of the neo-classical–Keynesian paradigm, in the mire of rampant inflation, rising unemployment, and a stagnant economy brought renewed interest in the structure of the labour market, most notably in the dual labour market theory or, more generally, segmented labour market theory.

The manner in which segmented labour market theory treats the structure and distribution of power allows incorporation of discrimination (by sex, race and ethnicity, and age), labour institutions, class consciousness, class fractions (of both working class and capital), the availability and choice of technology, the historical evolution of labour markets, the role of the state, the stability and structure of the economy, and the reserve army of unemployed and underemployed.

Dual labour market theory postulates segmentation between a "primary job market," composed of relatively good jobs – with reasonable wages and job security and management by rule – and a "secondary job market," composed of relatively poor jobs – with poor wages, employment insecurity, and arbitrary management – and limited mobility between the two. The typical worker in the primary job market is a prime-age man from the dominant ethnic or racial group, protected by a union and working for a large corporation or the public sector. A typical worker in the secondary job market is a woman, young or aged, from minority racial or ethnic groups, unprotected by unions, and working for small competitive employers or in the service or sales sectors.

Such a structured, segmented labour market is largely the product of the twentieth century. Its development presupposes a capitalist labour market and the progressive relegation of a majority of productive workers to it, a process that began in the early nineteenth century in Canada. The creation of a capitalist labour market represents, as Marx first recognized, only the formal subjugation of labour to capital. The real subordination occurs when a worker controls neither the product of his or her labour nor the process of work itself.

The two major (though not necessarily independent) methods of achieving the real subordination of labour are the introduction of technological change, which replaces the workers' skill control of the work process with machine control, and changes in the organization of work, through "job-division," which may be designated as the classic case of "scientific management." Braverman describes three basic principles. The first is "dissociation of the labor process from the skills of the workers" – adoption of production technology that is not dependent on the skills or knowledge of the workers. The second is "separation of conception from execution," such that all the mental and technical functions of planning the product and work design are centralized and monopolized by management, leaving for labour only the execution of specific tasks assigned by management. The third is "use of this monopoly over knowledge to control each step of the labor process and its mode of execution." Work becomes a series of deskilled, simple tasks, such that workers do not understand the overall production process in which they work.[35] In short, workers lose control of the work process to management.

The initial expectation, including that of Marx, was that the real subordination of labour would homogenize the working class in low-skilled, repetitious work, encouraging the development of class consciousness and contributing to the growth of class conflict. Indeed, employers in the late nineteenth and early twentieth centuries became acutely conscious of this "labour problem" and evolved strategies to counter this development.[36]

The rise in class consciousness, however, was arrested in part by the emergence of monopoly capital – large (vertically and/or horizontally integrated) oligopolistic firms that allowed both for redirection of competition in the form of product differentiation, advertising, and monopoly controls (such as patents) and for restructuring of the labour process on a third plane, employment relations. This process was accomplished in part by both individualizing and bureaucratizing labour-capital relations through artificial internal labour markets – job ladders – which reward loyalty and discipline while dividing workers into different interest groups (for example, tenured, senior workers and untenured, recently hired workers).

As well, the welfare of workers was linked with that of their employers, primarily through the "welfarism" of the "soulful" corporation. A private welfare system for primary labour market employees supplements the state-provided welfare state. The latter, rather moderate by international standards, has emerged in Canada since 1945 as part of the "post-war accord" between labour and capital. In exchange for the recognition and acceptance of unions and collective bargaining and the provision of a minimum level of the welfare state, labour implicitly agreed not to challenge the capitalist system and to recognize and accept capital's prerogative and authority to manage and control the labour process. Before we can integrate the various streams of labour political economy into this segmented approach, it is necessary to amplify on the role of the state.

Labour and the State

In the orthodox, "systems" approach to industrial relations, the three "actors" are workers and their organizations, employers and their organizations, and government and its organizations. The general impression conveyed is that government is a neutral third party that intervenes to facilitate compromise and reduce conflict harmful to the "public interest." The traditional view of the evolution of the state's role in Canadian industrial relations has tended to be Fabian, "the erroneous notion that the expansion of the state's management of a capitalist economy represented the gradual advance of socialism."[37] Indeed, much of the earlier work (including my own) focused on party politics and the emergence of labour, socialist, and social democratic parties and their pursuit of legislative reforms in support both of unions and collective bargaining and of the elements of the welfare state. Alternatively, some attention has been given to labour as a pressure group within an essentially pluralist political system.

While such studies have illuminated Canadian industrial relations, they lacked a secure theoretical foundation. The resurgence of interest in Marxist theories of the state made available a consistent, applicable approach. The political economy of the state is extensively discussed elsewhere in this volume, and therefore only a brief outline of its application to the political economy of labour will be attempted here.

In a capitalist economy the three fundamental roles of the state and its apparatus are: aiding accumulation, legitimating the capitalist system, and ensuring social control. If accumulation is occurring apace and the system is accepted as legitimate, social control is limited to routine policing for control of deviance. However, once the legitimacy of the system comes into question, most frequently as a result of a crisis of accumulation, social control may become a dominant role of the state. Policing becomes increasingly directed at controlling dissent rather than deviance.

Some of the more recent studies of the evolution of Canadian labour law and economic policy have explicitly recognized the primary role of the capitalist state in aiding accumulation and maintaining the social system. However, a secondary issue is raised. To what extent is the state autonomous from the interests of capital in its policies and actions and thereby, at least to some extent, responsive to upsurges in the political power of labour, exerted through direct action and/or the ballot box. Or is the state, directly or indirectly, the instrument of capital?

The evidence would indicate that answers to these questions depend on several factors: the harmony of interests of the various factions of capital (national, multinational; commercial, industrial, and financial; small, large; goods-producing, service-producing); the strength and unity of labour and sympathetic political parties; the harmony of interests of labour or capital with those of independent commodity producers; and the state of the economy (i.e. the position in the business cycle and the long wave of accumulation). In periods of economic crisis, capital tends to speak with a single voice while labour tends to be fragmented and demoralized by unemployment. Under such conditions governments tend to act as instruments of capital.[38] Under more prosperous conditions, however, the state appears to have considerably more autonomy.

A Synthesis: Labour, Economy, Class, and Culture

The value of the labour process–segmented labour market approach to the political economy of Canadian labour lies in its singular ability to encompass many facets of the labour experience. In combination with an understanding of the evolution of capital, it also allows us to interpret political-economic change and reccurring crises in the capitalist system and see how these changes and crises affect the evolution of labour and the working class as both an objective and a conscious force. In this way we can synthesize the insights on the political economy of Canadian labour gained by the different "lenses" discussed above.

Despite revisionist criticism, the staples approach remains the most useful explanation of the successive waves of economic development in Canada, which spanned the pre-industrial staples trades, through independent commodity production ("settlement staples"), to capitalist staples industries. By stressing the dependent instability of these staples, it reveals the uneven development and the unequal experience and culture of workers in the various periods and regions that characterize the different staples – one element in the fragmentation of Canadian labour that is a hallmark of its history.

What the staples approach largely ignored was the social (as contrasted to the technical) relations of production, particularly in the industrial, non-staples, economies of central Canada and of the Maritimes after the mid-nineteenth century. Again, however, uneven penetration by industrial capitalism, differential application of the labour process, and different balances of classes and class fractions (including ethnic, racial, and immigrant minorities) in the various regions and industries fragmented the social relations of production. There is no reason to expect the experience of the industrial worker in Ontario to be the same as the textile operative in semi-rural Quebec, the marine worker on the east coast, or the resource worker of northern Ontario or western Canada. Institutional histories provide stark, though incomplete, evidence of some of these differences.[39]

Though the state of the economy is perhaps the most important determinant of labour's potential political and economic power, realization of that potential depends on the cohesiveness of working-class consciousness. More simply, all other things being equal, the more fragmented labour is, whether by organization, race or ethnicity, gender, skill, region, or ideology, the weaker will be its political bargaining power and its ability to work for common goals. As we have already noted, this fact was recognized early in this century by employers, who structured the labour process and explicitly exploited and intensified racial and gender divisions for economic gain. Labour process analysis and segmented labour market theory can help us understand the political economy of the period and the labour culture and institutions that developed.

In its degree of fragmentation, Canadian labour is quite notable. First, the working class (waged workers) in Canada became a majority of the labour force only as late as the Second World War.[40] As a result, it was frequently forced into a "collaborative electoral strategy" with either employers, on issues such as protection, or agrarian interests, on issues such as monetary policy and social reform.[41] Second, the French-English division of the main industrial region of the country split organized labour into two distinct religious-linguistic groups, a split that remains, though no longer based on institutional religion. Third, the development of a capitalist labour market in Canada was marked by a series of ethnic migrations that undermined any sense of cultural or class homogeneity. Fourth, regional disparities in income, employment, and economic structure have promoted a regional consciousness that has proved a powerful competitor for class-consciousness.

Some researchers have argued against the regional concept of "western exceptionalism" associated by labour historians with the western economic revolt that culminated in the 1919 Winnipeg General Strike and the rise of the radical One Big Union in 1919–20. One argument is that similar radical views were also held in central and eastern Canada.[42] But the west *was* different, in its industrial and occupational structure, its income composition, and its capitalist class. It would be remarkable indeed if these material differences and the uneven development of capitalism in Canada were not reflected in differences in consciousness, at least in degree, though not necessarily in kind.

Further, skill has often divided Canadian labour, frequently contributing to craft, rather than class, consciousness. In the nineteenth century, the social division between skilled and unskilled contributed to a sizeable social and cultural gulf and supports the concept of an "aristocracy of labour." This split was augmented by ethnic and racial division, perhaps most notably between Catholic and Protestant Irish in nineteenth-century Ontario and white and oriental workers in British Columbia before the First World War.

The destruction of many skills in the second industrial revolution (incorporating Taylorism and scientific management) and the organization and general triumph of industrial unionism from the late 1930s on have lessened the older craft consciousness, though it still exists, as evidenced by the recent breakaway of the building craft unions to form the Canadian Federation of Labour. However, this shift has not lessened the skill division resulting from the growth of white-collar technical and professional unions, primarily in the public sector.

Perhaps the most important new divisions in the working class in the last two or three decades are between private and public sectors and between workers in the primary labour market (largely unionized) and those in the secondary labour market (most not organized). The first division has been encouraged by employers and the state, pitting public-sector workers, who are pictured as parasitical, overpaid, underworked, and overprivileged, against productive, hardworking, goods (surplus value)–producing private-sector workers. As a result, the fiscal crisis of the state can be blamed on the public-sector worker. At the same time, inflation has been blamed on the wage demands of the unions in the private sector, allowing governments to attack all unions, largely with impunity.

Combined with this caricature of unionized workers, public and private, is the misrepresentation of the secondary labour force (including women and minority groups) and the unemployed and welfare recipients as lazy, lacking in career commitment, and unreliable, hence a drain on public services and a cause of the high taxes assessed against more productive workers and employers. The resulting tax revolt by wage- and salary-earners has hurt the poor, women, and public-sector workers.

Perhaps the most important division among Canadian workers has been that based on gender. Women have endured a double burden of work, both in the home, as unpaid housework, and in the labour market, where they have disproportionately stocked the secondary labour market and the non-unionized clerical, financial, retail, and service sectors. Suffering wage and job discrimination, women in the paid labour force have an average income only three-fifths that of men. Though not barred from unions, they have been underrepresented in union ranks, particularly at the executive level and in the ranks of the elected members of labour political parties, and women's issues have only recently become a major item on organized labour's agenda.[43]

Finally, Canadian labour unity has historically been fragmented by so-called international unions, US-based, with branches in Canada. The internationals have dominated private-sector unionism in Canada from 1902, when the American Federation of Labor engineered a takeover of the Trades and Labour Congress of Canada. Only within the last decade or so have an increasing number of private-sector unions broken with their American headquarters to establish autonomous national unions. Probably the most significant recent breakaway was that of the Canadian Automobile Workers, who left the United Automobile Workers in 1985. The immediate issue was concessions to the major automobile companies, which the Canadians rejected. Behind that issue, however, was a more cultural and ideological division. In general, Canadian workers appear more conscious than do American workers of the common (or class) interest and seem more willing to struggle for it, as manifested in the constant or rising percentage of Canadian workers organized in unions, compared to a steady downward trend in the American labour movement.

The reasons for American dominance over Canadian labour institutions have been debated, as have been the material costs and benefits of that dependence. Whatever the benefits, the costs in terms of fragmented institutions and consciousness are undeniable and continue to harass organized labour in Canada. The current (1987) manifestation of national fragmentation is the attempt by the US-based United Food and Commercial Workers to prevent Canadian east coast fishers from breaking away to ally themselves with the Canadian Automobile Workers and form a purely Canadian union.

Given these divisions, a consistent and enduring consciousness and culture have not emerged among workers in Canada. In times of labour crisis, a passing culture/consciousness has emerged, only to succumb to the many divisions in the working class and the systematic use of these divisions by capital to divide and conquer.

CONCLUSION

In the current economic crisis, Canadian labour is undergoing a new remaking in response to changing technology, restructuring of the labour process

and of the labour market, and the combined assault of increasingly multinational and concentrated capital and a relatively non-autonomous state on
labour institutions and the social system. The eventual outcome, of course, is
not clear at this point. A great deal depends on the extent to which capital
exploits divisions among the working class and the consciousness that develops among labourers in the struggle. These factors will depend on the
leadership that emerges, both from formal labour institutions and other
organizations of the "ordinary" people and from among middle-class intellectuals. For, as Marx reminds us, "[People] make their own history, but they
do not make it just as they please; they do not make it under circumstances
chosen by themselves, but under circumstances directly encountered, given
and transmitted from the past."[44]

NOTES

I would like to thank the editors, Wallace Clement and Glen Williams, and Cy
Gonick for their useful comments on an earlier draft of this review. While many
of the standard works in Canadian labour studies are referred to, this is not primarily a bibliographical essay, and therefore no attempt is made at comprehensive coverage. Rather, sources mentioned are meant as a representative sample
of specific approaches or, in some cases, representative sides of controversies.
For a more complete bibliography see Drache and Clement, *The New Practical
Guide to Canadian Political Economy* in particular, chaps. 3 and 7.

1 Horvat, *The Political Economy of Socialism*, xiv.
2 For a sample of this debate see Drache, "The Crisis of Canadian Political Economy," and G. Williams, "Centre-Margin, Dependency, and the State."
3 Commons, *The Economics of Collective Action*, 22.
4 Innis, "Labour in Canadian Economic History," 198.
5 McNally, "Technological Determinism," 162–3. See also his "Staple Theory as
   Commodity Fetishism."
6 Phillips, "Staples, Surplus, and Exchange," 27–44.
7 Drache, "Formation and Fragmentation," 46.
8 Schmidt, "Canadian Political Economy," 87.
9 Panitch, "Dependency and Class," 17.
10 See Babcock, *Gompers in Canada*.
11 Creighton, *The Commercial Empire of the St. Lawrence*.
12 Fowke, *The National Policy and the Wheat Economy*, 289.
13 Logan, *Trade Unions in Canada*; Desmond Morton with Terry Copp, *Working
   People*; Forsey, *Trade Unions in Canada 1812–1902*. There will be no extensive
   bibliography of writers in these schools. For other references see Drache and
   Clement, *The New Practical Guide*, particularly chap. 3 and 7.
14 Horowitz, *Canadian Labour in Politics*; Robin, *Radical Politics and Canadian La-*

bour; Abella, *Nationalism, Communism and Canadian Labour*; Bercuson, *Fools and Wise Men*; McCormack, *Reformers, Rebels and Revolutionaries*; Phillips, *No Power Greater*; Jamieson, *Times of Trouble*; and Cox and Jamieson, "Canadian Labour in a Continental Perspective."

15 Lipton, *The Trade Union Movement.*

16 B. Palmer, "Working-Class Canada," 600.

17 Ryerson, *Unequal Union*; Pentland, *Labour and Capital*; Pentland, "The Development of a Capitalist Labour Market," and Pentland, "The Lachine Strike of 1843."

18 Ryerson, *Unequal Union*, 418 ff.

19 Ibid., 25.

20 Pentland, *Labour and Capital*, 176-7.

21 The major attack on Pentland was by Greer, in "Wage Labour." It was, however, confusing and confused. It criticized Pentland for relying on available secondary sources, for not being a classical Marxist (in a peripheral economy where classical Marxist analysis is at best problematic), and for not dealing in depth with independent commodity production and with pre-industrial society, not Pentland's central issues. However, Green made valid criticisms of Pentland's racial and ethnic stereotyping and useful references to more recent research related, however peripherally, to the emergence of industrial capitalism and a capitalist labour market.

22 Pentland, *Study.*

23 B. Palmer, *Working-Class Experience* and *A Culture in Conflict*; G.S. Kealey, *Toronto Workers*; B.D. Palmer and G.S. Kealey, *Dreaming of What Might Be.*

24 See B. Palmer, *The Making of E.P. Thompson.*

25 Gutman, "Interview," 194.

26 Montgomery, "Interview," 176-80.

27 Bryan Palmer, "Working-Class Canada," 601.

28 For an example, see Bryan Palmer, "Listening to History."

29 Braverman, *Labor and Monopoly Capitalism.*

30 For an excellent sample see Heron and Storey, *On the Job.*

31 Gonick, *The Great Economic Debate.*

32 For perhaps the best example see Dunlop, *Industrial Relations Systems.* "System" here cannot be equated with "systemic" and has quite a contrary meaning. For a critique of the systems approach see Hyman, *Industrial Relations.*

33 Gordon, Edwards, and Reich, *Segmented Work, Divided Workers.*

34 Adam Smith, quoted by Gonick, *The Great Economic Debate*, 48.

35 Braverman, *Labor and Monopoly Capitalism*, 112-20.

36 For a discussion of the Canadian case and the importance of Mackenzie King in the state's strategic response, see Craven, *"An Impartial Umpire."*

37 Panitch, "Yesterday's News," 15.

38 Panitch and Swartz, *From Consent to Coercion.*

39 Palmer, in his defence of *the* Canadian labour experience, "doth protest too

much" in his response to Drache's thesis of a fundamental fracture between the experience of the resource proletariat and that of the industrial worker. See Bryan Palmer, "Listening to History," and Drache, "Canada's Fragmented Working Class." On balance, at least on this issue, I side with Drache.

40 Leo Johnson, "The Development of Class," 141–85.
41 Schmidt, "Canadian Political Economy," 84.
42 See, for example, G.S. Kealey "1919."
43 For an extended discussion of these issues see Paul Phillips and Erin Phillips, *Women and Work*.
44 David McLellan, ed., *Karl Marx, Selected Writings*, 300 (from *The Eighteenth Brumaire of Louis Bonaparte*).

CHAPTER FIVE

The Political Economy of Gender

Isabella Bakker

To date, the new political economy has incorporated only a limited analysis of the interaction of class and gender inequalities. In order for political economy to move ahead, it must, at a minimum, recognize the fundamental importance of sex/gender systems in its broader goal of understanding "the dynamic relationship between people within a specific society by identifying how that society has unfolded historically and, in particular, how its economic system is organically linked to the social/cultural/ideological/political order."[1] Feminism can benefit from the developed analysis within political economy of how social relations are conditioned by economic structures and processes. As Luxton and Maroney pointed out in their recent consideration of feminist political economy: "What political economy offers feminism is powerful conceptual categories, a (usually sex-blind) macrostructural theory of economic, political, and social structures and a body of historical research."[2] Because both feminism and political economy understand power as a fundamental category situated within a historical and materialist context, the two approaches appear congruent.

Feminism, however, challenges political economists to systematically grapple with gender and sexuality. It offers political economists not merely a more complete analysis of politics and economics but also a political commitment. Nevertheless, feminism cannot be said to address equally well all aspects of social phenomena.[3] Indeed, the women's movement is currently readjusting because of its limited analysis of questions of race and ethnicity (see Abele and Stasiulis in this volume).

A strong argument can, accordingly, be made for greater commitment to rather than rejection of political economy. Elizabeth Wilson has pointed out that the increasing integration of women into the labour force and the greater commodification of reproduction and private life make Marxism more, not less, relevant for feminist analysis.[4] This being said, a feminist political economy is key to recognizing that all classes are characterized by gender and that gender is fundamental to conflicts between classes as well as within them.

The specificity of the Canadian economic and political context has shaped Canadian feminism in a fashion that differs from its American and British counterparts. This chapter will focus on factors that have contributed to the unique character of feminism in English-speaking Canada and Quebec and will argue that the women's movement has effectively established an indigenous theoretical and political project while still engaging in the international debates.

What follows is a limited treatment of the feminist literature: first, a brief look at the political economy tradition and the place of the various feminist perspectives within this tradition (much of the discussion relies on Luxton and Maroney's comprehensive treatment of the subject) and more detailed consideration of the economic, political, and cultural aspects of Canada that have helped to shape the intellectual and political movement that is feminism; an examination of the extent to which feminists have redefined and extended political discourse in this country; and, third, consideration of some of the contributions dealing with the social reproduction process and the reproduction of gender. The state and its institutional relations affect all these areas, and some of the implications of this influence will be drawn out in the text. The goal of the chapter then is to analyse the articulation of gender relations within the Canadian political economy.

WHAT IS THE POLITICAL ECONOMY OF GENDER?

As with any attempt to provide an overview of a vast and complex subject, it is important at the outset to define the boundaries of the discussion. What needs to be defined is the meaning of "the political economy of gender." Fortunately, several recent collections on feminism and political economy provide useful elaborations of this concept. Maroney and Luxton situate their discussion of feminist political economy within several distinct political economy traditions: liberal political economy, Marxism, and Canadian political economy.[5] This allows them to trace the different feminist revisions of the traditional political economy approaches.

Maroney and Luxton isolate seven key elements of a feminist political economy. (1) Gender differentiation is universal and of fundamental importance on a par with class divisions. (2) All classes are characterized by gender conflicts. (3) There is a co-determination with economic structures of sex/gender systems. (4) Biological reproduction is not a naturalistic phenomenon but socially organized. (5) Gender is central to culture. (6) Sexuality is shaped by gender, class, race, and economic structures. (7) Individual identity is shaped by gender, race, and economic divisions.[6]

In their collection, Hamilton and Barrett emphasize the diversity of feminist theoretical and political practices in English Canada and Quebec.[7] Pat Armstrong and Hugh Armstrong incorporate "material that takes a broadly defined political economy perspective or is explicitly critical of such an approach" in their introduction to the literature on women in *The New Practical Guide to Canadian Political Economy.*[8]

The early Canadian political economy did not concern itself with questions of gender. Instead, according to Maroney and Luxton's review, the focus was on Canadian economic development, especially extractive industries and dependency, state formation, the national question, regionalism, the composition and formation of the ruling and working classes, and the media and cultural production.[9] It was not until the more recent mobilization of women politically, with its resulting theoretical probing, that gender became a conditional element of what Mary O'Brien would call "malestream" political economy analysis.

Feminists critical of the early Canadian political economy have argued that introducing gender into accounts of early Canadian industries such as the fur trade transforms and deepens previous analyses. For example, Sylvia Van Kirk's *Many Tender Ties: Women in Fur Trade Society* examines gender divisions of labour within white and native societies and uncovers the central role of native women in the fur trade.[10] Bourgeault sees the subjugation of Indian women as a central factor in the establishment of the fur trade in northern Canada.[11]

Many socialist feminists remain critical of the current revival of political economy, as signalled in the pages of *Studies in Political Economy* (see issue no. 6). While recognizing that "women" exist as a social category and as a political force, it has not for the most part incorporated this understanding into the body of its work.[12] The new political economy tends to "add on women" instead of making genuine attempts at theorizing gender. Increasingly, feminists are cautioning that "political economy must realize that 'gender' is not just a fancy word for 'women' but a fundamental social structure."[13]

This resistance to gender as an organizing concept of political economy was (and still is) reflected in academic writings on the subject. Attempts have been made to appropriate feminist categories into political economy in different ways by fitting women into existing Marxist categories, constructing two separate and distinct systems with their own laws of motion (patriarchy and capitalism), or attempting to synthesize a political economy of gender with malestream political economy. This has led writers such as Mary O'Brien to reject a political economy framework altogether in favour of either radical feminist alternatives or a "mode of reproduction analysis." Feminists not concerned with political economy but situated within a liberal framework have avoided such problems by emphasizing equality of opportunity but limit their analysis by ignoring the fact that class society and the family itself are patriarchal institutions.[14]

In addition to theoretical controversies, cultural duality has also served to inhibit the full incorporation of gender into the new Canadian political economy. The English-Canadian political economy tradition had little resonance for Québécois feminists, given its focus on Quebec as a province rather than as a nation.[15] In Quebec, the rise of nationalism restricted the early development of the women's liberation movement and made the recognition of Quebec as a nation (as opposed to the Engelsian focus in English Canada on the abolition of private property and class) a necessary prerequisite for women's liberation (see Coleman in this volume). This contextual view of the feminist struggle is best illustrated by a slogan of the feminist movement in the 1960s: "Pas de libération des femmes sans Québec libre, pas de Québec libre sans libération des femmes."[16] Early influences in Quebec were based on an anti-colonialist version of Marxism and theories of underdevelopment, which were later eclipsed by developments in feminist theory in France, in turn informed especially by French structuralist analyses of the role of the state.[17] These different influences, in conjunction with divergent views on the national question and English-Canadian non-expertise in the French language, ensured a rather autonomous development of the English- and French-Canadian feminist communities.[18]

TOWARD AN INDIGENOUS FEMINISM

Gender and the Political Economy of Canadian Development

Hamilton and Barrett, in their consideration of feminism in Canada, write that, given the American and British influences, "the women's movement threatened to become a rather colonized affair."[19] However, Canada posed unique challenges to feminist analysis. Regional disparities, the national question, class and race differences, and jurisdictional conflicts between the federal government and the provinces all required a uniquely Canadian perspective.[20] This diversity in the development of the Canadian polity and economic structure has shaped feminism in both practice and theory. At the early stages, international concepts and categories were superimposed wholesale (with the exception of pioneering efforts by Margaret Benston, Peggy Morton, and Wally Seccombe on women's work in the home). Current efforts are beginning to reflect uniquely Canadian approaches to feminism and involve a reformulation of Canadian political economy categories.[21]

The dual nations of English Canada and Quebec have had a substantial impact on the women's movement and its theories. In many respects, dual nations led to dual movements and different theoretical emphases. Because of the varying historical, economic, and cultural roots, institutions such as the family took on a different importance in English Canada as opposed to Quebec.[22] In addition, the unresolved political status of Quebec lent much force to what can be considered a constant of Quebec history – nationalism.[23] The early 1960s were witness to the Quiet Revolution, a massive *deblocage* in Whitaker's terms, which signalled the secularization of Quebec society, liberation from Duplessis's backwardness and repression, and a challenge to the 'unequal union' of English and French Canada.[24] According to some observers, this new nationalism was, aside from its genuine cultural identification, expressed mainly as a nationalism of the new state middle class and others, whose self-interests were closely allied with the Quebec state. The Parti québécois itself evolved from a mildly social democratic party to one that, after taking power in 1976, was in tune with right-wing nationalist forces and unabashedly capitalist in its economic development policies.[25] Such a perspective goes a long way in explaining the contradictory position of the Parti québécois toward women and its restrictive policies on trade unions and women's issues in the later years of governing.

An example of the tension between feminists and more conservative values was crystallized in the concern with the declining birth rate in Quebec. In its 1981 campaign, the Parti québécois promised monetary incentives for having children, signalling a return to traditional assumptions about the family and the role of women in ensuring the survival of Quebec culture. This so-called revenge of the cradle (la revanche des berceaux) and the ideology of survival (idéologie de la survivance) have been a concern since the English defeat of the French on the Plains of Abraham in 1759. As Diane Lamoureux has pointed out, this ideology "accorded a double importance to the family as the institution responsible for the physiological and cultural reproduction of the nation."[26] It has forced Quebec feminists to grapple with fertility questions "from within a perspective which seeks to understand the political, ideological, and economic substructures of the high birthrates typified as 'la revanche des berceaux.' "[27]

With the Parti québécois's defeat in the sovereignty-association referendum, the political forces that had been united around the goal of constructing a national state were in disarray; further, it brought into sharp focus the necessity for feminism "to develop its theoretical foundations away from the scope of nationalism."[28] Because the women's movement was the first to refuse to accept the subordination of its struggles to the so-called primary national struggle, it may have been more successful than other social movements in achieving this task and consolidating its political position after the defeat of the Parti québécois.[29] Also, the Quebec women's movement (as opposed to its English-speaking counterpart) was more conscious early on of the need to define its goals as explicitly political.[30] Nevertheless, as alliances are rebuilt, feminists in Quebec must still confront the "apparent contradiction between feminist emphasis on women's autonomy and independence, and the anxiety about national 'survival.' "[31]

National survival in the context of complex relations of dependence, exploitation, and uneven regional development has also shaped the responses of the women's movement in English Canada, with economic history providing an important backdrop to women's political demands and struggles in the 1970s and 1980s.[32] In particular, the rise of "province-building" strategies and the growth of provincial states affected the organizing tactics of the women's movement: increasingly a focus was being placed on provincial or regional lines. This was reinforced by the successful challenge of the provinces, especially the newer resource-based provinces, to undermine the federal state's superior position in fiscal arrangements. These changes divided responsibility for development strategy and fiscal policy among two levels of government; because several key provinces had sufficient revenues, they could also proceed with their own strategies.[33] For the women's movement, this shift diffused claims toward the state and confused the jurisdictional questions around economic and political issues.

Canadian economic development and the Canadian political economy tradition have fostered a unique body of literature that has evaluated the effect of economic policies and periodic crises on women. These analyses have been generated by feminists working both within and outside the state. Patricia Connelly and Martha MacDonald have written a careful account of a regional economy in Nova Scotia encompassing both a rural and a fishing community and have examined the effect of increasing reliance on wage labour (the transition from independent commodity production to capitalist production) on women's commodified and non-commodified labour. Their work shows how in the context of underdevelopment "the allocation of women's work between the home and the labour force has occurred as a response to the family household changes in the needs of the economy."[34] More generally, their analysis points out how "the various regions of the country are linked by complex relations of dependence and exploitation that are mediated and organized politically through the provincial governments within Canada."[35] Marilyn Porter has also examined the political economy of the Atlantic periphery and re-evaluated it in the context of feminism.[36] These inequalities in economic and political relations are in turn mirrored in the women's movement and tend to accentuate the effect of geographical distance as Hamilton and Barrett have suggested.[37] Meg Luxton, updating her mid-1970s study of changes in women's double day of labour in a small Manitoba mining community, Flin Flon, links women's increased attachment to paid employment to "a crisis in the way labour is currently distributed and accomplished in the family household."[38]

These and other micro studies that use the tools and concepts of political economy[39] have been complemented by a host of analyses of the effect of economic restructuring and crisis on women's labour.[40] Pat Armstrong, in *Labour Pains: Women's Work in Crisis*, examines the effect of economic crisis on various sectors, occupations, groups of workers, and the household from the 1930s to the current period. She analyses in particular the effect of restructured domestic and wage labour, arguing that while the combination of segregation and uneven development may have protected women (who tend to be concentrated in the expanding service sector) from more recent economic downturns in the primary sectors, women start with a more precarious position in the labour market (less security, lower monetary returns) and have suffered more severe, though less visible consequences in the household. Armstrong has also shown how increases in part-time work and the privatization of state services will threaten women's jobs as well as their collective strength.[41]

Marjorie Cohen has presented a sectoral analysis of the economy and women's employment to argue eloquently against the free trade proposals put forward in the Report of the Royal Commission on the Economic Union and Development Prospects for Canada. Arguing that freer trade would reduce employment in female-dominated industries, Cohen points to a necessary rethinking of economists' perceptions of the labour force.[42] I have suggested elsewhere that, given uneven patterns of economic development, the effect of any macro policy linked to a specific economic strategy must be assessed separately for population groups in observably different conditions, such as women.[43] More generally, the exclusion of women from economic planning in the context of far-reaching economic and social changes has been a concern of several regionally based groups which have been particularly hard hit by recession and the turn to a more neo-conservative political environment. Women against the Budget and the Women's Research Centre in Vancouver have undertaken evaluations of the economy that include all aspects of women's work and that look at the effect of single-industry towns and mega-resource projects on women and families.[44] In Quebec, the committee on the status of women of the Confédération des syndicats nationaux (CSN), which represents province-wide unions, produced an anaylsis of the economic crisis in the 1980s and urged that the CSN maintain equal status for women as one of its priorities.[45]

The focus on economic issues (and the earlier concern with economic rights, which reflected the predominance of liberal feminists' concern with equality of opportunity) increasingly was complemented in the 1970s by a broader concern, expressed by socialist and radical feminists, with social and moral issues. Nevertheless, regional disparities still continue to shape very different approaches to these political questions. The struggle around the insertion of an equality clause in the Canadian Charter of Rights and Freedoms is such an example. As Chaviva Hosek points out, no consensus reigned, as "women were residents of different provinces, with various political party affiliations and different views on patriation, the amending formula, the division of powers and other issues."[46] Regional sentiments played a key role in women's approach to an entrenched Charter of Rights, with women in Quebec and the west arguing against it.[47] The former group felt that women's issues were understood better by their provincial government, and the latter was against giving the Supreme Court and central Canada any final say on human rights. Ontario women, in contrast, wanted an entrenched charter, perhaps because of their historically advantageous political and economic position within Confederation.

Due to the very size of Canada and its federal structure, the centrality of the Canadian state as the maintainer of economic and political hegemony has in turn influenced the political and policy focus of the women's movement. Repeated duelling with the state has also contributed to the education of feminists. Liberal feminists' initial conception of the state as emancipatory, as spelled out in the pages of the Royal Commission Report on the Status of Women, has been displaced by a more sophisticated analysis of the role of the state and its unequal structure of representation.[48] Structurally, pressure from the women's movement did help to create various departments and agencies within the federal government to deal with women's issues. Socialist feminists have come to realize the importance of continually confronting the state, given its historical role in shaping the capital-labour relationship through legislation and policies and its pervasive influence on the everyday lives of women, including the ideological facets (such as the construction of sexuality).[49] Recognizing the state's need for legitimation, socialist feminists have intervened in certain periods to secure positive reforms for women while recognizing that "the potential for successful challenges depends on the extent to which feminists inside the state have been able to maintain their relations with the women's movement."[50]

Women Redefining the Political

Part of the process of challenging and testing the limits of the state has involved women's effort to expand their political influence. Political action, according to Jane Jenson, can be limited by not only "the range of actors who are accorded the status of legitimate participant" but also "the range of issues considered to be within the realm of meaningful political debate . . . the policy alternatives considered feasible for implementation and . . . the alliance strategies available for achieving change."[51] Basic social arrangements such as the expanded post-war labour market for inexpensive and unskilled labour and the expanded welfare state have necessitated a change in the terms of political debate, not only in Canada but in most OECD

(Organization for Economic Co-operation and Development) countries. As Jenson notes, however, these social arrangements only facilitate rather than guarantee a change in the political agenda, which will come about only in the context of political struggle.[52] The feminist movement has been able, with various degrees of success, to insert a new collective identity into the political process, which includes not only new actors but new policy alternatives as well.

Feminists' intervention in the political process and their sparring with the state have led to the redefinition as "political" of certain issues previously considered on men's terms or relegated to the private or religious (for example, abortion and pornography) and therefore not part of the political agenda. However, feminists realize that the state itself has at times shaped the political definition of these issues in a way that disarms the feminist struggle. Defining abortion as a "medical" question, with doctors as the legitimate controllers, is but one example.[53] The struggle for reproductive freedom has been and remains at the forefront of feminists' attempts to widen the political agenda, and their success, although not complete in terms of their goal of a woman's own control over her reproductive capacities, is shown by this issue's continuing dominant place on the political agenda.[54]

Pressure has also been exerted on political parties and state actors by the feminist and union movements to expand their consideration of women's work and related policy menus. The example of legislation on equal pay for work of equal value for both the public and limited private sectors in Ontario (Bill 154) highlights the manner in which feminists can shape legislative debate on women's issues. It is not yet clear whether the expanded parameters will lead to significant, concrete changes. Results at the federal level, where equal value has had legal expression since 1978, discourage optimism about the extent to which inequality can be overcome through these avenues.[55]

Women as political subjects and actors have had an effect on the legislative arena. But the limited gains achieved through the formal political process are in large part due to the momentum of extra-parliamentary action. Grassroots reaction to the intransigence of federal politicans about inserting an equality clause into the charter is but one example of this process. Another striking, albeit largely symbolic example was the 1984 national leadership debate sponsored by NAC (National Action Committee on the Status of Women). It reflected the established parties' concerted effort to make a special appeal to women voters, an appeal that has not been made to other so-called subordinate groups, such as unionized workers and ethnic and visible minorities.[56] The 1984 campaign also saw twice as many women candidates in each of the three major parties, and the two largest parties reserved several priority ridings for women.[57] Thus in recent years the entrenched gender bias of Canadian political parties has become an openly discussed issue.

Part of the growth of the feminist movement in the 1960s and 1970s was caused by the unwillingness of parties to deal with women's issues.[58] This "conspiracy of silence" between the two major political parties is not exclusive to women's issues. As Brodie and Jenson observe, the extent to which the existence of class conflict has been avoided or reinterpreted by the Liberal and Conservative parties has effectively limited federal party politics to two major themes: bicultural politics and consensual politics.[59] Apart from the bourgeois parties' ideological and organizational dominance in defining politics in these non-class terms, they have also been successful in excluding sex and race from the social relations that should be considered political.[60]

Again, studies by Bashevkin, Vickers, and Brodie suggest that limited inroads have been made into the parties in the last two decades, but the parties often lag behind the general public in their support for women's rights. In a study of delegates to both the 1983 Progressive Conservative and the 1984 Liberal leadership conventions, Brodie asked delegates whether women should have more rights. Among Tory men and women, the affirmative response was 28 per cent and 46 per cent respectively; among Grit men 38 per cent and women 63 per cent. In overall public opinion polls, 80 per cent of men and 85 per cent of women thought that more should be done for women's rights in Canada.[61] Because political parties in liberal democracies help shape consciousness and define issues and politics, such studies indicate that women have made only partial gains. Research does show that social democratic parties have been more receptive to women's issues and concerns, and this is certainly the case with the New Democratic Party in Canada.[62] This would suggest that it is quite important for feminists to foster a socialist or, at a minimum, a social democratic tradition if they wish to have a broader range of gender issues included within the narrow limits of formal political struggle in liberal democracies.

These observations on the exclusionary nature of party politics need to be situated in the context of feminists' relatively ambivalent attitude to electoral politics. Elections in particular have been interpreted in several ways: some feminists view them as an instrument of social control and co-optation; others look to their educational and mobilizing role or see them as the means through which group interests are represented. Beyond this, a great deal of feminist political analysis simply "rejects a definition of politics that sustains the conventional focus on electoral processes or on institutions of government."[63] Feminist demands cannot be exclusively subsumed under the category of the political. They go beyond political equality or political rights and require that the socio-economic-cultural-racial roots of women's oppression be addressed. As Elizabeth Wilson notes: "The existence of the women's movement in the 1970s and 1980s has certainly confirmed that reforms in the civic and juridical field do not, on their own, achieve the equality that is sought."[64] Socialist feminism, then, remains a movement that goes beyond the electoral consensus on women's rights.

Social Reproduction and Feminist Political Economy

A more far-reaching analysis, which goes beyond reconceptualization of women's work and redefinition of the political, is offered by feminist considerations of the social reproduction process under capitalism. Such analyses are concerned with the construction and reproduction of labour power (as a commodity in capitalist society), taking into account the economic and extra-economic institutions and processes of reproduction. They place the interrelationship of three basic institutional realms – the state, the household, and the economy – in the context of productive and reproductive aspects of society. The three realms involve "the productive consumption of capital by labour within the economy; the formation and maintenance of working class households through individual consumption; and the social interventions of the modern state which constitute collective or social consumption."[65] These realms constitute the productive and reproductive moments of capitalist society, and recent work on social reproduction attempts to specify the interlinkages of these three realms and their role in the reproduction of the population. Feminist work on the social reproduction of gender and on the politics of sexuality and motherhood has provided additional insights that must be integrated into political economic analysis. Feminists have correctly noted that exclusive emphasis on institutional relationships, such as domestic labour and capitalism, loses sight of sex relations and offers a necessary, although limited focus on labour and capitalist reproduction.

The early literature on social reproduction stresses that capitalism conditions a specific mode of reproduction of labour power. Most strikingly, labour power is the only commodity that cannot be produced as a commodity proper; it is reproduced within the household both on a daily and on a generational basis. Many of the changes in domestic labour and the reproduction of labour power have in turn found their impetus in capitalist production. Dorothy Smith has shown how the market process increasingly provides for the daily needs of individuals and how this change has displaced labour and skill from the domestic production of subsistence to industry.[66] Recent work has challenged the notion that reproduction is a contingent process and argued for an expanded concept of modes of production that takes into account subsistence activity and biological reproduction. By conceptualizing reproduction and production as part of a singular material base, this view poses a radical challenge to historical materialism and its uses.[67] Finally, considerations of the social reproduction process since 1945 need to take into account key forms of state intervention, such as welfare policies that regulate capitalist consumption of labour power; interventions that set parameters to the labour market, such as minimum wages; and interventions directed to the point of reproduction, such as state regulation of procreation (abortion, contraception), marriage, and family property, as well as state provision of the social wage, which is designed to reproduce and maintain households through the provision of a substitute wage.[68] Dickinson and Russell's recent volume develops this extended analysis of the reproductive sector as a series of interconnected private and public institutions.

The writings on social reproduction represent to some extent the fruits of earlier debates between Marxism and feminism. These debates questioned the efficacy of Marxist analytical tools for providing a framework for understanding the sexual division of labour[69] and other aspects of women's oppression. "At issue," write Maroney and Luxton, "is the relative weight of class structures and sex/gender systems as fundamental determinants of different modes of production and social formations."[70] Domestic labour provided an initial entry into Marxist debates on the reproduction of labour power, as the private household remains the primary site of such reproduction.

Unfortunately, initial attempts to understand the specificity of women's oppression under capitalism and to link it to work in the home degenerated into functionalist arguments about capitalism's physical requirements as a system of production.[71] The debate became increasingly technical and conceptual and, at worst, relegated women to a reproductive sphere that conflated biology and social processes.[72] However, as the Armstrongs have noted in their extensive discussion of this literature, the best elements of the debate gave way to a historical materialist analysis that highlighted "the centrality of domestic labour and sex divisions to capitalism, to wage labour, and therefore to our theorization of how capitalism operates."[73] Such a view of the daily and generational reproduction of workers extended our understanding of women's oppression and allowed for the insight that "women are simultaneously subject to capitalism, male dominance and their bodies."[74] Situating patriarchy and capitalism within the same system should not, however, exclude the fact of class and, indeed, ethnic and racial differences among women.

This theoretical journey has allowed for a new approach that locates the sexual division of labour at the centre of capitalism. This approach is developed by Johanna Brenner, Maria Ramas, Michele Barrett, and Susan Himmelweit in the United Kingdom[75] and by Pat and Hugh Armstrong and Pat Connelly in Canada. At the heart of the new literature on the sexual division of labour is a debate about whether such a division is inherent to and necessary for capitalism. For Pat and Hugh Armstrong, "the sexual division of labour is essential to this mode of production, at the highest level of abstraction." They argue that because capitalism is premissed on free wage labour (and not biological differences per se) reproduction must take place outside the sphere of production of goods and services. Because women bear children, they are relegated to the home, which further intensifies the separation of home and work. Hence, the sexual division of labour and its implied segregation of women are a result of capitalism's need to create and reproduce the commodity free wage labour.[76] Connelly presents a contrasting viewpoint, citing Michele Barrett, who argues that "the relegation of women to the home and to low-paid, segregated wage labour was a long and uneven process which involved a struggle between women and the better-organized male craft unionists. The questions of who would be responsible for childcare and whose skills would be recognized as more valuable in the workplace were resolved in the interest of men according to a division of labour and an ideology of gender which pre-dated capitalism and which served to disadvantage women in their struggle."[77]

This debate has led to reconsideration of biological reproduction and its mediation by historical and social forces. What is socially assigned and what is biologically determined? To what extent is biology influenced by class society? New historical and materialist approaches to motherhood and questions of sexuality have also been introduced by socialist feminists. The development of a political economy of sexuality has been especially difficult, but authors such as Brustyn and Valverde[78] have laid the foundation by raising four key questions. First, is there a relationship between sexuality and class structures? Second, how is sexuality shaped by commodity relations? Third, what are the broader links between sexual liberation, socialism, and feminism? And fourth, "What accounts for foregrounding sexuality as a dimension of identity?"[79] Feminism's new tendency to embrace motherhood has come under scrutiny for returning to separate spheres and what Maroney calls a "new feminist essentialism."[80] Maroney believes that the new theories of motherhood reject a separate-spheres approach and, using O'Brien's transposition of the Marxist notion of alienation from production to biological reproduction, argues that the new motherhood is part of the radical transformative project to create a feminized world. Her work and other aforementioned contributions point to the growing diversity of inquiry that constitutes feminist political economy.

CONCLUSIONS

This chapter has been not so much a summary or review of the literature as an attempt to examine some of the new and unique research and theoretical directions in Canadian feminist political economy. The chapter out of necessity has not touched on all the available material. References to primary sources or recent collections that offer broader treatment of the political economy of gender should help the interested reader trace the various strands of this now complex and extensive field.

A concerted attempt was made here to argue that Canadian economic and political developments must be taken into account when trying to understand feminist theory and politics. However, the new political economy must recognize the importance of sex/gender systems as a necessary part of its theory of other social, economic, and political structures. Building on this "materialist" base, feminism and political economy begin to establish a new common ground that offers a powerful set of conceptual and practical tools. I have linked changing material conditions to developments in feminist political debate and practice. I have also suggested that as women's issues become more political, institutions such as the state are increasingly challenged; at the same time, new strains are being placed on the women's movement itself. There are many forces and tendencies in Canada's political economy that reinforce the diversity rather than the unity of feminism. In addition, certain tendencies within capitalism, such as women's increased labour force attachment and the erosion of the breadwinner/homemaker family, may be sharpening class and race differences among women.[81] Uneven regional development, the federal-provincial division of power, and the monopoly of the two major political parties on defining the parameters of the political process all contribute to conflicts between different strands of the women's movement. These conflicts reflect the growing importance of the women's movement. More than ever, feminists are involved in broader debates on, for example, free trade and economic conditions. In addition, key areas of feminist political action, such as reproductive rights and pornography, have a high degree of exposure on the Canadian political scene. The prominence of these debates is a reflection of the fact that Canadian feminism has, for the most part, successfully built on historical divisions rather than ignoring them.

The political economy of gender is becoming a central part of Canadian political struggle, and the recognition of women's vital productive and reproductive roles has underlined the centrality of gender in both theory and practice.

NOTES

I am indebted to Riel Miller, Lise Gotell, Sandra Burt, Glen Williams, and Wallace Clement for their insightful comments and assistance.

1 Drache and Clement, "Introduction."
2 Maroney and Luxton, "Feminism and Political Economy," 6.

3 See ibid.
4 Wilson with Weir, *Hidden Agendas*, 21.
5 See Maroney and Luxton, "Feminism and Political Economy," 5.
6 See ibid., 27–8.
7 Hamilton and Barrett, "Introduction," 5.
8 P. Armstrong and H. Armstrong, "Women," 37.
9 See Luxton and Maroney, "Feminism and Political Economy," 8–9.
10 See also K. Anderson, "A Gendered World," 121–38.
11 Bourgeault, "The Indian, the Metis and the Fur Trade."
12 See Luxton and Maroney, "Feminism and Political Economy," 5.
13 See ibid., 11.
14 See Jaggar and Rothenberg, eds., *Feminist Frameworks*.
15 See Maroney and Luxton, "Feminism and Political Economy," 8.
16 Lamoureux, "Nationalism and Feminism in Quebec," 53; translation: No women's liberation without a free Quebec; no Free Quebec without the liberation of women.
17 See Marks and deCourtivron, *New French Feminisms*.
18 See Maroney and Luxton, "Feminism and Political Economy," 7.
19 See Hamilton and Barrett, *Politics of Diversity*, 9.
20 See ibid., 10.
21 See P. Morton, "Women's Work Is Never Done"; Benston, "The Political Economy of Women's Liberation"; Seccombe, "The Housewife and Her Labour."
22 See Burt, "Women's Issues."
23 See Whitaker, "The Quebec Cauldron," 34.
24 See ibid., 39.
25 See Slater and Molnar, "The Decline of Quebec Nationalism," 12.
26 Lamoureux, "Nationalism and Feminism," 55.
27 Maroney and Luxton, "Feminism and Political Economy," 23.
28 Ibid., 63.
29 See Monique Simard, quoted in Slater and Molnar, "The Decline of Quebec Nationalism," 11.
30 See Burt, "Women's Issues," 148.
31 Hamilton and Barrett, *Politics of Diversity*, 27.
32 State intervention in economic development has not only reinforced this uneven development but has indeed fostered it since the days of the National Policy. See Jenson, "Economic Factors."
33 See ibid., 61.
34 Connelly and MacDonald, "Women's Work," 78.
35 Hamilton and Barrett, *Politics of Diversity*, 5.
36 Marilyn Porter, "Peripheral Women."
37 Hamilton and Barrett, *Politics of Diversity*, 6.
38 See ibid., 50.
39 See Mackenzie, "Women's Responses," and Gannage, "A World of Difference."

40 There was also concern with what constitutes "work." See Part Armstrong and Hugh Armstrong, "Beyond Numbers"; Bakker, "Paradoxes."

41 See P. Armstrong, *Labour Pains*, 17.

42 See M. Cohen, "The Macdonald Report," and *Free Trade and the Future of Women's Work*.

43 See Bakker, "Women and Economic Development in Canada."

44 See Women's Research Centre, *Women and the Economy Kit*.

45 See Burt, "Women's Issues," 147.

46 Hosek, "Women and the Constitutional Process," 283.

47 See ibid., 283-4.

48 See Findlay, "Facing the State."

49 See M. Barrett, *Women's Oppression Today*, and Adams, Biskin, and McPhail, *Feminists Organizing For Change*.

50 Findlay, "Facing the State," 48.

51 Jenson, "Struggling for Identity," 7.

52 See ibid., 8.

53 For a good discussion see McDaniel, "Implementation." Thanks to Sandra Burt for alerting me to this piece.

54 See Gavigan, "Women and Abortion."

55 Bakker, "Pay Equity."

56 See Brodie, *Women and Politics*, 125.

57 See ibid.

58 See Burt, "Women's Issues," 135.

59 See Brodie and Jenson, *Crisis, Challenge and Change*, 2.

60 According to Brodie and Jenson, "Political parties shape the interpretation of what aspects of social relations should be considered political, how politics should be conducted, what the boundaries of political discussion most properly may be and what kinds of conflicts can be resolved through the political process." ibid., 8.

61 Brodie, "The Gender Factor."

62 See Bakker, "Paradoxes."

63 Katzenstein, "Feminism."

64 See Wilson with Weir, *Hidden Agendas*, 114.

65 Dickinson and Russell, *Family, Economy and the State*, 5.

66 See Smith, "Women, Class and the Family."

67 P. Armstrong and H. Armstrong, "Beyond Sexless Class and Classless Sex"; Seccombe, "Reflections."

68 See Dickinson and Russell, *Family*, 10-11. Elsewhere I have quantified the historical trends in Canada of these three key elements for the reproduction of labour power – the direct wage, the social wage, and domestic labour. See Bakker, "Reproduction."

69 I do not distinguish between "sex" as biologically determined and "gender" as socially constructed because I believe that the two are interdependent. Barrett,

for example, takes a different approach and uses the term *gender divisions*, relating it to an analysis at the level of the social formation.

70 Maroney and Luxton, "Feminism and Political Economy," 12.

71 See Hamilton and Barrett, *Politics of Diversity*, 17.

72 See Maroney and Luxton, "Feminism and Political Economy," 21.

73 P. Armstrong and H. Armstrong, "Beyond Sexless Class," 27.

74 Ibid., 29.

75 See Himmelweit, "The Real Dualism"; Brenner and Rmas, "Rethinking Women's Oppression."

76 P. Armstrong and H. Armstrong, "Beyond Sexless Class."

77 Connelly, referring to Barrett's argument of the English case in Connelly, "On Marxism and Feminism," 244.

78 See Valverde, *Sex, Power and Pleasure* and Burstyn, *Women against Censorship*.

79 Maroney and Luxton, "Feminism and Political Economy," 25.

80 Maroney, "Embracing Motherhood."

81 See Wilson with Weir, *Hidden Agendas*, 93.

CHAPTER SIX

Canada in the International Political Economy

Glen Williams

Few tasks have proved as divisive to the new Canadian political economy as that of determining Canada's place within the hierarchy of the world economy. Extreme exponents of the various positions have uncompromisingly rebuked each other in scholarly journals. David McNally, for example, has ridiculed his rivals as bourgeois political economists – "fetish-worshiper[s] trapped in a mysterious, topsy-turvy world in which people are merely the means by which things construct their own social relations." Daniel Drache has suggested that his opponents have a debilitating "blindspot" that comes from their adherence to "a generalized, often ahistorical neo-Marxism" and are "surprisingly intellectually conservative . . . [with an] unhealthy reliance on universal models and . . . rather narrow views."[1]

Since the late 1960s, the new political economists have offered at least four descriptions of Canada's role within the international order: dependency, intermediary, advanced imperialist, and region within the centre. The dependency school, dominant in the 1960s and early 1970s, argued that Canada is an economic colony with a client state. Later, neo-Marxist class analysis held that only Canada's historical specificity separates it from other advanced Western societies and polities. Moderates temporized: Canada is an intermediary, sharing features of both the dominant and dominated tiers in the world capitalist economy, and, depending on the weight of their analysis, moderates have frequently suggested that Canada is progressing or regressing in one direction or the other.

In contrast to both the dependency and the class frameworks, which posit the nation-state as their basic unit of analysis, the fourth approach interprets Canada as a lesser political, economic, and cultural region within a succession of powerful empires. Accordingly, Canada is seen to mirror in its own particular fashion the political and socioeconomic formations characteristic of the centre. In one dimension the Canadian liberal democratic and federal state system serves as a locus of struggle for competing social classes and provincial elites. In a second, related dimension, the state system serves as a point of balance for the political instability that attends our standing both inside and outside empire. In this second dimension federal and provincial states can be seen to carry out their roles in focusing, mediating, protecting, and developing the regional position of the Canadian social formation within the continental political economy.

The ghost of Harold Innis can be discovered haunting all four positions. Perhaps surprisingly, the most important contributor to classical Canadian political economy has become the central figure in framing the heated modern debate on Canada's place in the international hierarchy. Although both praised and pilloried by the various protagonists for his opinions on this question, Innis's views have been widely misinterpreted. Accordingly, we will begin with a survey of his position.

INNIS AND CANADA'S PLACE

Innis held a clear, if somewhat imprecise by today's standards, conception of hierarchy within the international political economy and Canada's location within this hierarchy. His world view saw human history as a succession of "civilizations" marked by "empires" that arose within them and determined the character of their development. When civilizations collided, it could be with devastating consequences for the economy and social organization of the weaker.

Recent centuries had been dominated by "western civilization," composed of Europe and its overseas colonies of settlement. Western civilization's progress had been fuelled, at least to some extent, by the unbalanced relations it had developed with the rest of the world.[2] In the Americas, Innis observed how the European search for gold had harnessed the labour of "the aborigines" of Africa and North America. For the Africans, this had meant plantation slavery;[3] for the native North Americans, a near-genocidal catastrophe "for which no remedy was adequate."[4]

Within Western civilization, Innis's attention was drawn primarily to the "Anglo-Saxon world." This research focus shaped his view of the international political economy. British imperialism, in contrast to other European empires, had linked a high-wage, settler economy to the institutions necessary for the evolution of liberal democracy.[5] The Anglo-Saxon economies became characterized by an "emphasis on consumer's goods and the use of advertising as a device for persistently educating the consumer to a higher standard of living."[6] Mass economic participation reinforced mass political participation.[7]

Innis never tells us that Canada is anything but a full member in the North American branch of the Anglo-Saxon community within Western civilization. Indeed, as if in fear of how his work might later be misinterpreted, he declared that "fundamentally the civilization of North America is the civilization of Europe" and specifically located his intellectual project in opposition to "the stress placed by modern students on the dissimilar features of what has been regarded as two separate civilizations."[8]

This is not to suggest that Innis saw Canada as being at the "centre" of Western civilization. After a decade and a half of the new Canadian political economy, we are all by now very much aware that he saw Canada at the "margin" and that its economic history had been "dominated by the discrepancy between the centre and the margin of western civilization."[9] We should also be familiar with the many economic disadvantages that Innis believed associated with marginal status: most notably, that Canada's staple export specialization and relative industrial backwardness left its pace of economic development vulnerable, conditioned by the shifting demands of more advanced industrial centres for resource products.[10]

Innis's portrayal of weaknesses in the Canadian position, however, can be understood properly only within the context of his international schema, in which Canada stood prominently among those at the centre of the world political economy. Whatever the "handicaps" flowing from impossible geography, plentiful resources, and scanty population, Western civilization had developed, not underdeveloped, Canada. Even though "no country has swung backwards and forwards in response to such factors as improvements in the technique of transport, exhaustion of raw materials and the advance of industrialism with such violence as Canada," Innis noted, "the elasticity of Canada's political, economic, and social structure" cushioned the blows of cyclonic resource development and allowed it to adapt.[11] Always central to this process of adaptation was the Canadian state.[12] "Elasticity" also allowed the "new" or "frontier" countries of western civilization to progress on the base of the earlier industrialization of the older centres. "Industrialization of the new countries, given suitable political and social organizations," Innis wrote, "tends to become cumulative – the United States became industrialized more rapidly than Great Britain, and Canada more rapidly than the United States. The more recently the country has been industrialized, the more rapid tends to become its industrialization." However, the character of industrialization tended to reinforce the relative resource specialization of the new countries by increasing the efficiency with which they produced raw materials.[13] Innis portrayed the prospects of the underdeveloped tropical resource export political economies as bleak; their comparative inelasticity made them far more vulnerable in the world economy.[14]

Innis was not elaborating a theoretical model of economic exploitation or underdevelopment of the new countries like Canada. His, rather, was an inquiry into regional relationships within that same civilization. Unquestionably, because the new countries followed the pace and pattern of industrial development set in more advanced centres, the regional relationship was asymmetrical. But in economic development, as measured by productivity and living standards, and in political development, as measured by liberal democracy, the centre and margins of Western civilization were largely equivalent. The asymmetry was also balanced to some degree by the reciprocal way in which economies of the new countries and the centre caused "disturbances" for each other. Innis's views on the manner in which the changing demand by the centre for Canada's staples presented Canada with structural problems and a series of adjustment crises are well known, but it is still not sufficiently appreciated that his focus also encompassed the disruptive effects of staple production on the centre.

The peculiar geographic setting of Canada has made its economy a source of disturbance to the economies of other countries. The enormous importance of water navigation and the vastness of the Precambrian formation have necessitated concentration on large scale production of basic commodities and intense pressure on the markets of other countries. The markets of Europe were bombarded in turn with such staple products as fur, timber and wheat and of the United States with minerals and newsprints. Wheat production, supported by energetic governmental assistance, brought a revolution in British agriculture and led European countries to impose barriers or to undergo revolutions. Pulp and paper production supported by provincial governments facilitated the rapid growth of advertising in the United States, and contributed to the problems of industrialism and the destruction of a stable public opinion.[15]

One final element in Innis's view of Canada's position internationally is the nature of the continental relationship between Canada and the United States. Following the establishment of a European civilization in North America, the continental economy became separated into three distinct areas: a northern, Canadian territory, which developed as a region within the British economy; a diversified centre, which achieved industrialization; and a southern region, producing cotton for Europe. After the US Civil War, the southern region was integrated in a "subordinate" relationship with the centre, "just as," after the First World War, "the northern fur-producing area, at present producing the staples, wheat, pulp and paper, minerals, and lumber, tends to be brought under its influence."[16] Canada, then, while remaining within Western civilization, simply shifted from one Anglo-Saxon empire to another.

It is quite true that Innis became increasingly concerned with the deleterious effects of Canada's entry into the regional orbit of the American empire. It could scarcely have been otherwise, as Innis himself witnessed the chaotic manner in which the Depression exaggerated the strains of the transition from a British to a US focus for Canadian economic activities. In his schema, structural problems and adjustment crises always seemed more of a feature of life at the margins than at the centre. Nevertheless, there is little to suggest that he believed Canada any more likely to be radically "underdeveloped" by this new association than by the old.

What then are we to make of the oft-cited essays published at the end of Innis's career in which he railed against US imperialism in Canada? "American imperialism has replaced and exploited British imperialism," he wrote, and, "Canada has had no alternative but to serve as an instrument of British imperialism and then of American imperialism."[17] Innis had no precise definition of "imperialism." Suggesting nothing more than its general dictionary sense of aggressive cultural, political, economic, military, or diplomatic behaviour by one nation toward another, he used it from time to time in a variety of contexts. As Reg Whitaker has pointed out, it would be incorrect to read into his work "a consistently anti-imperialist bias. On the contrary, balanced empires sum up what is best in human aspiration."[18] Innis from time to time even referred to Canada's "mild imperialistic policy."[19]

American economic imperialism in Canada was certainly discussed by Innis, but it was not toward this aspect of imperialism that his anti-American passions were primarily directed. The "dangerous" conduct of US military and diplomatic affairs was most often his principal target. Innis had been deeply disturbed by the loss of life in the two world wars. "The basic post-war problem," he wrote, "is that of stopping the loss of blood or the problem of peace." Innis believed that the wars represented "the breakdown of western civilization" and blamed them partially on "instability" manufactured by the press.[20] Developed in the United States, the "new journalism," with its dependence on attracting advertising, had emphasized international instability as a means of increasing circulation.[21] Indeed, the mechanized transmission of information that characterized American society degraded Western civilization and threatened world peace.[22] Further, "surely the lowest ebb in any civilization was reached when it was possible to threaten the lives of thousands of people with atomic bombs, with scarcely a protest in the interest of common humanity."[23]

Innis linked this analysis of journalism and international instability to a critique of the manner in which the populist American political system led to the "military domination of foreign policy." In the "instability" that characterized US political life, he wrote, "foreign issues are too apt to be dominated by the immediate exigencies of party politics."[24] Canada was also implicated by Innis in the development of this "peril." In keeping with the reciprocal manner in which staple "disturbances" were manifested in both centre and margin, he observed: "Newsprint production in Canada is encouraged, with the result that advertising and in turn industry are stimulated in the United States, and it becomes more difficult for Canada to compete in industries other than those in which she has a distinct advantage. Increased supplies of newsprint accentuate an emphasis on sensational news. As it has been succinctly put, world peace would be bad for the pulp and paper industry."[25]

THE DEPENDENCY SCHOOL: APPROPRIATING INNIS

Although a faithful interpretation of Innis's views on any topic is never easy, those who helped establish the new political economy rendered his opinions on Canada's position in the international political economy in a decidedly one-dimensional fashion. It need not have happened this way. Mel Watkins, one of the leaders of the revival, had published in 1963 an account of staples theory that closely mirrors the manner in which Innis developed his own beliefs:

The staple theory is . . . not . . . a general theory of economic growth, nor even a general theory about the growth of export-oriented economies, but rather [is] applicable to the atypical case of the new country. The phenomenon of the new country, of the 'empty' land or region overrun by the white man in the past four centuries, is, of course, well known. The leading examples are the United States and the British dominions. These two countries [sic] had two distinctive characteristics as they began their economic growth: a favourable man/land ratio and an absence of inhibiting traditions . . . These conditions and consequences are not customarily identified with underdeveloped countries, and hence are not the typical building blocks of a theory of economic growth. Rather, the theory derived from them is limited, but consciously so in order to cast light on a special type of economic growth.[26]

Had Watkins maintained at the centre of his work this interpretation of the staples approach as a special theory of economic growth, it would have branded him a heretic in the new dependency school. Dependency theory had first been developed to account for the failure of economic growth and modernization in Latin America. Derived from Leninist theories of imperialism, its earliest models argued that the world capitalist economy was ordered by a rigid chain of international economic exploitation that accelerated development at its centre while locking its dependent periphery into underdevelopment.[27] Comparisons between Canada and semi-industrialized Latin America were rendered plausible by the considerable similarity in selected economic indicators, such as high levels of foreign investment, resource export specialization, and a technologically weak and internationally uncompetitive manufacturing sector. Later, more sophisticated dependency models placed social and political factors at the centre of their analysis and allowed for the possibility of "associated" economic development.[28] However, because of the unbridgeable divide between the principal features of Latin American and Canadian political and social formations, these refinements had little impact on the Canadian dependency school.

The early 1970s were littered with Innis citations as the dependency school sought to present its analysis as an updated edition of classical Canadian political economy. Drache submitted that Innis was a Canadian nationalist and "resolutely anti-American," believing continentalism "imperialistic." "It is perplexing in reading Harold Innis' writings in the 1930s and the 1940s on the political economy of Canada and on the theme of American imperialism in this country to realize that his work went apparently unnoticed by the Canadian left," Drache observed.[29] James Laxer argued that Innis and Creighton were an "essential" starting-point for socialist historians who wish to understand "Canada's continuing character as a resource-extractive country dependent on outside imperial powers."[30] Watkins suggested that "Innis' anti-imperialism argues powerfully for the necessity of a Canadian nationalism of the left."[31]

Parallels between Innis's scholarship and dependency theories were drawn. Kari Levitt wrote that "Innis was the chronological antecedent of the Latin American economists in developing a 'metropolis-periphery' approach to American staple economies."[32] Ian Parker contended that Innis analysed "more deeply than Marx had the forms of dependency which characterize colonial relations, from the standpoint of colonial margins."[33] John Hutcheson noted that "Innis showed us" that "Canada has been in the position of a 'peripheral' country, dependent on a series of imperial 'centre' countries."[34] Drache explained Innis's view that "Canada's staple-oriented economy would remain fundamentally dependent because centre-margin relations under capitalism are such that dependencies are prevented from developing into self-generating industrialized economies."[35]

Innis and the Latin American school were seen as legitimate because they were both outside the hegemony of US scholarship. Watkins observed:

I think that the way in which the Latin-American economists have developed this [metropolis-hinterland] schema for purposes of studying Latin America [has] probably generated more useful insights and more useful models than, certainly, those we have in Canada, with the exception of some of the things that Innis said. My argument here is that if we want to study the Canadian condition, we would be much better off reading what Latin Americans write, or reading what Europeans write, when faced with American penetration than anything we will ever learn by reading what American social scientists write about. There is virtually no literature produced by Americans on multi-national corporations that can be taken seriously.[36]

This theme also figures in the more recent work of Watkins. Claiming that orthodox "branch plant" economists in Canada "ignored and suppressed the essence of Innisian theory because it was necessary to do so to avoid facing its implications of inherent tendencies toward hinterland dependency," he argues that "there has been a revival of interest in Innis precisely *because* of his understanding of Canada's satellitic position, his distrust of orthodox economics and . . . his nationalism when it mattered. In the context of the revival of political economy *and* the right-wing bias of the dominant monetarist, or neo-conservative economics, Innis became, by default, the property of the left."[37]

And so, by invoking Innis, we were brought to a Third World dependency perspective on Canadian underdevelopment. Levitt built the prototype, concluding that it demonstrated our "regression to a condition of underdevelopment in spite of continuous income growth."[38] The contradiction at the heart of the "rich, industrialized, underdeveloped" formula, however, always left it exposed to attack: how to account for all the other, obvious socioeconomic indicators of Canada's high wage location within the international hierarchy. Some, like Cy Gonick, merely argued that Canada had "stopped developing."[39] Hutcheson warned that Canadian development was "threatened." "The succession of capitalist development by underdevelopment has been a common fate for many regions of capitalist countries, as the history of the Maritimes testifies," he pointed out. "In fact, as the example of Argentina may show, this is a fate which can be visited upon whole countries."[40] James Laxer attempted to make an empirical case for "de-industrialization" resulting from US domination of Canadian manufacturing.[41] Drache saw Canada being brought to the "point of collapse . . . on a not too distant horizon" and concluded that "Canada's status has regressed from that of a semi-centre economy to a semi-peripheral one."[42]

Canadian economic underdevelopment was directly linked by the new dependency political economy to "underdevelopment" of the Canadian bourgeoisie and the weakness of "their" state. Levitt opined that "Canada provides a dramatic illustration of the stultification of an indigenous entrepreneurial class" by foreign capital.[43] Watkins wrote that Canada was dependent "because a full-blown industrial capitalist class does not emerge." He reasoned that "the only obstacle to independent capitalism was foreign domination; the obverse of this, is that the failure to remove that obstacle, as in Canada[,] is sufficient to explain – indeed it defines – the persistence of dependency."[44] Drache asserted that "the Canadian bourgeoisie have never sat at the high table as an industrial bourgeoisie in their own right. A colonial bourgeoisie gains admittance to the club for its weakness, not its strength." "Their national programmes reflect a simple design," he clarified, "making Canadian resources cheap and accessible to British and American capitalists."[45] R.T. Naylor became the leading figure within the cult of the enfeebled Canadian capitalist class. In his highly influential 1972 account, dependency and underdevelopment in Canada were the unfortunate result of the playing out of a form of species hostility toward independent industrialists on the part of the dominant but colonized merchants and financiers who organized Canadian resource capitalism.[46]

A weak and dependent capitalist class was matched with an "underdeveloped" Canadian state that functioned in its hands, and in the hands of foreign capital, as an instrument of dependency. Gonick remarked: "The developing continentalization of Canada has led to the deterioration of Canada as a nation-state. The policies which guide the direction of Canada's cultural and economic future emanate more and more from Washington and from the board rooms of the multinational corporation in New York, Chicago, and Detroit. Consequently, it has been the task of Canadian governments to administer this country and its provinces as a region and as subregions of the great American metropolis."[47] James Laxer spoke of the "informal American imperial control of the Canadian state" and of "American capitalist control of the Canadian state both directly by American corporations and indirectly through the military and political sway of the US state over Canada."[48] Gary Teeple was puzzled by those who held that "Canada is a politically independent state" when it is remembered that "little control of industry lies in the hands of Canadian capitalists." "The appearance of autonomy is illusory," for "this nation has the trappings of independence but not the reality because politics under capitalism are ultimately subordinate to the amassing of capital by individuals and corporations, the most powerful of which in this country are American."[49] Naylor argued that the merchants' and financiers' control of the Canadian state enabled them to defeat their industrialist rivals at the price of collaborating with US branch plants in their own eventual subordination as American capital came to dominate Canadian economic life. This "ruling class of the hinterland" became "virtually irrelevant to the management of the northern periphery of the continental system." "A Canadian capitalist state cannot survive," he concluded, "because it has neither the material base nor the will to survive, the former contributing substantially to the latter."[50]

The political project that underlay the academic analysis of the dependency school was at once Canadian nationalist and socialist. "An antiimperialist struggle is the only way to break through the tight circle of Canadian history," Drache wrote. "Anti-imperialism, anti-capitalism and Canadian independence are an inseparable unity."[51] In its pursuit of this project, the dependency school claimed both lineage from, and the legitimacy of, Innis's staples approach. Some of the more significant points of divergence between the dependency school and Innis on Canada's international position can now be summarized. Where Innis was concerned with understanding the relationship between the centre and marginal regions of "western civilization," the dependency school inquired into relations between the centre and periphery of the world capitalist economy. Where Innis suggested that reciprocal "disturbances" attend centre-margin relations, the dependency school proposed exploitation. Where Innis set out a model of economic growth under structural constraints, the dependency school suggested aborted development or a tendency toward underdevelopment. Finally, where Innis attached great importance to the Canadian state as an adaptive mechanism during adjustment crises and to liberal democracy as an essential characteristic of the "anglo-saxon world," the dependency school reduced the state to an instrument subject to the control of external forces.

These points of divergence take on special significance in the light of a recent attempt to present Innis's work as a more formal theory of underdevelopment that can be considered "a natural bridge between neoclassical economic theory and Marxist theory of dependency." Drache has proposed that Innis be read as a "general theory" of peripheral capitalism, and, inspired by "Innis' insights," he has consolidated this theory into a ten-item "staple mode of development." Suggesting that Innis divided the international political economy into two regions, centre and periphery, Drache draws parallels between the work of Innis and the Third World economist Samir Amin:

There is a striking similarity between Innis' theory of rigidities and Amin's theory of extroversion. Even though one must tread cautiously and avoid superficial comparisons between developed dependency and stark underdevelopment, Innis and Amin share a common perspective in their respective efforts to discover the dialectic of incomplete development and the complex means by which centre economies have been able to impose through intensive specialization a division of labour on periphery formations ... In language which echoes Innis' reasoning, he explains how a country at the periphery has a narrow range of productive activities and expansion of the economy via export-led growth in primary resources means that indebtedness grows faster than income.[52]

When one notes that Innis placed Canada prominently at the centre of the world economy, that Amin himself has specifically classified Canada as a central formation, and that an application of Amin's "structural characteristics of underdevelopment" confirms Canada's centre status, the unintended irony in Drache's argument is breathtaking.[53] Drache's "general theory" cannot come from a strict reading of Innis himself. Rather, like others in the dependency school, Drache mistakenly seems to have read theories of dependency and underdevelopment into Innis, interpreting selected passages as if Innis had indeed been a scholar of dependent "peripheral capitalism."

SUCCESSORS TO THE DEPENDENCY SCHOOL

The intellectual hegemony of the dependency school within the new Canadian political economy fell into serious decline in the late 1970s. However, an important aspect of its discourse continued to define the neo-Marxist,

class approaches that succeeded it. Using a model derived from theories of
imperialism, the dependency school sought to represent Canada's position
as the resultant of a lost, aborted, or forgone conflict between national
capitals. This, as we have observed, set it far apart from Innis's conception of
Canada as a regional staples case within the empires of "western civilization." We will soon see that Innis's regional theme has re-emerged as one
perspective in the post-dependency era. However, the more orthodox, neo-
Marxist scholars who came to dominate the new political economy regularly
passed over the thorny questions surrounding Canada's unique location
within the international hierarchy. And, when class analysis did contest
directly the dependency position, it typically remained within the theoretical
framework of imperialism: arguing simply that Canada has an intermediate
or higher rank in the ongoing conflict of national capitals.

The dependency school and the more orthodox, neo-Marxist approaches
have also commonly shared an inability to adequately theorize the Canadian
state by putting together a full account of the unique specificity of its
internal and external dynamic. Put simply, the study of the political economy
of Canada, whether through employing "multinationals" or "classes" as the
primary units of analysis, has often suffered through the subjugation of its
political world through the overdevelopment of economic categories. Where
the dependency school has portrayed the Canadian state as an instrument of
foreign capital, the neo-Marxist school has too frequently highlighted the
instrumental use of federal and provincial state structures by various fractions of the Canadian capitalist class. Neither has been particularly adept at
coming to terms with the exceptional and problematic nature of Canadian
state sovereignty. Historically, this sovereignty has been politically defined
through elite and class struggle over various images of Canadian nationality
in civil society and expressed through the state system's historic role in
reproducing the Canadian accumulation process through bargaining the
regional relations of empire.[54]

A brief survey of the three distinct perspectives on Canada's position in
the international political economy that developed outside the dependency
school will serve to illustrate these general points. The categories created
here, like the "dependency school" above, are meant only as an analytic
shorthand to guide our discussion of the development of these ideas within
the new Canadian political economy and not as prisons for their occupants.

Canada as Intermediary

Those who have looked at Canada as an intermediary have suggested that
Canada's tendency to be "imperialized" is largely balanced by its participation in imperialism. This perspective uses primarily economic and social
variables in its analysis, attempting to account for indicators of both weak-

ness and strength in the structure of Canadian production, trade, and capital investment and in the composition of the Canadian bourgeoisie. Accordingly, it seeks to accommodate within itself the arguments and the evidence of both those who hold that Canada is a dependency and those who believe Canada to be a fully developed socioeconomic formation.

Tim Draimin and Jamie Swift first launched this perspective within the new Canadian political economy in 1975. Working from research on Canadian investment in Brazil, they argued that Canada, along with Israel, Iran, and South Africa should be considered "sub-imperial powers," neither wholly developed nor wholly underdeveloped. On the one side, Canada's relationship to world capitalism and to the United States has fragmented its internal economy. On the other, it acts as an economic "trouble-shooter for American imperialism": "Canada is very successfully able to utilize the conventional mechanisms of imperialism (aid, trade and investment) to drain resources from Latin America and the Caribbean for the ultimate benefit of the main imperialist centre, the United States."[55]

The most important intellectual figure within the new political economy adopting the intermediary perspective has been Wallace Clement. Because his approach has been thoroughly eclectic, his vision is far wider than others in this group. For example, he alone has attributed some significance to the political realm in classifying Canada's position in the world economy, although it is not a theme he systematically pursues. "Canada is not a puppet state," he noted, "because it is a liberal democracy, a society which maintains a distinction between public and private power."[56] Concentrating his research on capital flows and the composition of the Canadian and US economic élites, Clement concluded that Canada's position in the "world system of inequality is ambiguous." Located midway in the world economic system, it is both a receiver and a sender of multinationals. However, "taking a broad view of the world order, it is clear that Canada sits firmly among the advantaged."[57] As an alternative to the dependency perspective, he has proposed Galtung's "go-between nation theory" as a way of identifying "both Canada's specific location within the continental economy and its general world position": "Certain members of the Canadian economic elite . . . are integrated into the world order in two distinct ways: as go-betweens of foreign, predominantly United States, interests and through their own indigenously controlled corporations. Canada has a rather unique role as mediator of foreign-controlled capital, as holder of its own foreign investments, and as host to extensive foreign investment. Thus a framework differing somewhat from the one emerging from the dependency literature is needed for placing Canada in the world system."[58]

P. Ehrensaft and W. Armstrong have recommended that we place Canada in a group of five "dominated economies" which they call "dominion capitalist" countries: Argentina, Australia, Canada, New Zealand, and Uruguay.

These are located within the international political economy at the top of an intermediate "semi-industrial" category, between the "dominant capitalist societies" and the "periphery" of the world economy. Because of the structural weaknesses of their economies, these countries face an inherent tendency toward "declassification." A number of characteristics of dominion capitalism are set out – indicators that display "their fundamental character as an extension of the European social space" and their "truncated economic base."[59] Curiously, given the rather obvious parallel, state structure is not treated as one of the characteristics of dominion capitalism. Instead, state policy is treated as an extension of the economic policy of the bourgeoisie, mediated only partially by the social and political expressions of other classes.[60]

More recently, Jorge Niosi has argued that Canada should be seen as a "semi-industrial" country with an "intermediate" position in the international political economy. As a consequence of this intermediate position, the Canadian bourgeoisie is fragmented, with a comprador fraction linked to foreign capital and a national fraction controlling domestic capital and interested mainly in finance, commerce, resources, services, and transportation. The national bourgeoisie is dominant and has a "continental or rentier nationalism" development strategy, concentrating on competing with the many financial and non-financial industries in the North American market while buying back foreign subsidiaries in the resource sector.[61] In a less than complex account of the political relations between the state system and Canadian society, Niosi submitted that "continental nationalism" had developed as a "compromise" between "conservative elements" of the Canadian bourgeoisie and "the more nationalist wing of industry and the upper state bureaucracy who advocate a full-fledged industrial policy."[62]

Canada as Advanced Imperialist

Those of the "advanced imperialist" school argue that Canada is itself a minor imperialist nation presenting, in most respects, the normal profile of any full developed socioeconomic formation. Like the "intermediary" perspective, it uses primarily economic and social variables in its analysis but argues that any weaknesses in the structure of Canadian production, trade, and capital investment and in the composition of the Canadian bourgeoisie are far outweighed by growing strengths in all these areas. As a consequence, this perspective has dismissed as an epiphenomenal consideration the central line of general agreement between Innis and all the other approaches in the new political economy – namely, that Canada cannot be understood apart from its relationship with more advanced metropolitan markets. David McNally, for example, has categorized the staples approach as "commodity fetishism – the attribution of creative powers in the historical process to the staple commodity as a natural and technical object." He has contended that "it is high time that the fetishistic preoccupation with staples was abandoned in favour of a concentration on class formation and capitalist development in Canada. And it is high time that vulgar materialism was supplanted by historical materialism."[63]

This perspective first made its appearance in 1975. Rejecting completely the analysis of the dependency school, Steve Moore and Debi Wells classified Canada as a "secondary imperialist power," along with Britain, France, Japan, and West Germany, although they conceded it was "near the bottom of the barrel." Nor did they accept the thesis that Canada is a "sub-imperial" power like Israel or South Africa, for these countries lack an "independent economic basis." An analysis of a series of statistical indicators relating to the structure of the Canadian economy and Canadian investment led them to conclude "that Canadian monopoly capitalism is well developed and highly concentrated; that the Canadian bourgeoisie is holding its own in home market expansion; that foreign control of the Canadian economy is declining slowly on a relative percentage basis in recent years; that Canada's industrial growth statistics are comparable with other imperialist countries; that there is a substantial Canadian-controlled section of the bourgeoisie that has large numbers of branch plants abroad; that Canadian investment is rapidly increasing in the Third World; and that there has been a much more rapid increase in Canadian investment abroad than in foreign investment in Canada."[64] Moore and Wells argued that the "strategy" of the Canadian bourgeoisie in relation to the inter-imperialist struggle was to "increase its control of natural resources at home and abroad as an economic base for buying back Canadian subsidiaries of foreign firms and purchasing new multinationals abroad." This will set the stage for heightened "inter-imperialist rivalry between the U.S. and Canada" in the future.[65]

During the 1980s, William Carroll has developed similar themes. Hypothesizing that "to the extent that a fraction of Canadian capital manifests a capacity to control its own extended reproduction, we may entertain the possibility of a national bourgeoisie with some degree of autonomy from foreign dependence, and of an independent Canadian imperialism," he has examined statistical data sets on foreign ownership and interlocking directorships in post-1945 Canada.[66] His results indicated that indigenous Canadian capital has controlled not only the financial sector but a steadily growing portion of the industrial sector as well. In addition, he pointed to a "dramatic" increase in the value of Canadian-controlled investment abroad. On this basis, he reasoned that, "on balance, Canada seems to present the example of a middle-range imperialist power in an era of thoroughly internationalized monopoly capitalism."[67]

Phillip Resnick has been a convert to this perspective from the dependency school. Reviewing a statistical set similar to Carroll's, he has explained that while it might have been possible a decade ago to use a Latin American dependency model when describing Canada, because of its excessive degree of foreign ownership and "American client state" status, both Canadian capitalists and the Canadian state have now "come of age." This change has been the result of the many dislocations in the international economy in the 1970s and 1980s, the "maturing of Canadian corporate capitalism," and "the emergence of the Canadian state as the mid-wife of economic development."[68] Resnick has cautioned Canadian political economists to "break with an analysis that spoke in terms of dependency . . . The left must begin to see Canadian capitalism as a First World capitalism analogous to metropolitan capitalisms like the U.S., Western Europe, or Japan."[69]

Canada as Region within the Centre

In contrast to the dependency, intermediary, and advanced imperialist positions, which all focus on Canada's place in the inter-imperialist struggle of national capitals, this fourth perspective evokes Innis's views on the position of Canada in the world hierarchy by treating Canada as a lesser region within the centre of the international political economy. Placing stress on the decisive role played by cultural and political variables in determining the structure and content of Canada's socioeconomic formation, this approach reads the Canadian political economy through the prism of its links with more advanced regions.

As with the intermediary and advanced imperialist perspectives, this one emerged in the mid-1970s as a critique of the dependency school. In 1976, I suggested that the comparisons repeatedly indulged in by nationalist political economists between Canada and poor Third World resource exporters were misleading because they accounted for neither the basically autocentric (developed) nature of Canada's economic structure nor the long-term stability of its position near the top of the international hierarchy of wealth, as measured by living standards. This "rich" basis to Canada's social formation, I argued, was the direct result of Canada being developed historically as an extension of the centre: "Canada and the other white Dominions stood in sharp contrast to the colonies of conquest and impoverishment. The colonies of settlement were developed as overseas extensions, miniature replicas, of British society, complete with a large measure of local political autonomy. In terms of the standard of living, Britons who emigrated did so for the most part freely, induced by relatively high wages and opportunities to improve their material conditions."[70]

This thesis was elaborated by a presentation of Arghiri Emmanuel's contention that the relatively high wage levels in the white dominions of the nineteenth century accelerated their industrialization.[71] By his account, high wages created consumer demand through a rich internal market and forced industries to invest in labour-saving machinery to increase productivity in order to remain competitive with low-wage countries. Following a discussion of how, around 1900, the issue of "high wages" had received political expression through debates on tariff and immigration policies, this article concluded with the observation that Canadian political economists should begin to pay greater attention to the "political implications" of Canada's position at the centre of the world order.[72]

Five years later, Leo Panitch developed and extended in several essential new directions the "implications" of white settler colonization. "We can't understand the place of a society in terms of economic dependence alone," he suggested. "Socio-political distinctions, domestic political institutions must enter the picture as well."[73] Panitch made three original and valuable contributions to the debate. First, he drew attention to the central importance of the continental labour market in conditioning wages, industrialization, and class conflict in Canada.[74] Second, he observed that the institutions of liberal democracy have framed and determined Canada's position in relation to both the centre and the periphery of the world order. Finally, he suggested that it is not the "client" state, working on behalf of foreign capital, but rather the popular culture of our continent that "sustains American imperialism within Canadian society" – "not so much the "haute culture" of the intellectuals but the popular culture which is produced and reproduced in advertising, the mass media and the mass education system. Just as it is by virtue of a cultural hegemony in civil society that bourgeois domination is made compatible with liberal democracy in advanced capitalist societies, so Canadian dependency remains compatible with liberal democracy by virtue of the penetration of civil society itself by American culture."[75]

Gordon Laxer has recently suggested that "we must go beyond the givens of geography and external influence and look at the role of Canada's internal social formation" if we are to understand the incomplete character of Canadian economic development. "By volunteering to be a 'Dependency of the Empire' " during the formative period before the end of the First World War, Canada "discarded the first line of defence against foreign ownership and technological dependence."[76] The commercial capitalism that thrived on the imperial connection and dominated this formative period, Laxer adds, was not threatened by popular nationalist movements, as it had been in other countries, because of sectional divisions in Canadian society and the relative weakness of the agrarian classes.

My own inquiry into the arrested nature of Canadian industrial development contends that initial location within the British Empire accounted for its peculiar character (import substitution), while later organization as a regional extension of continental industrial production rendered its modern branch plant form.[77] In a parallel archival survey of Canadian production and trade in the new industrial staples of oil, nickel, and forest products, Melissa Clark-Jones has concluded that since 1960 the Canadian state has been "formalizing the relationships of a mode of production" which she calls "continental resource capitalism." This has involved "treatment of the Canadian political economy as a specialized (resource-producing) adjunct to the American political economy."[78] In this regard, a number of excellent studies in the new Canadian political economy document the active role played by provincial states in promoting the interests of local or sub-regional social formations within the fluid production régime of the continental economy.[79]

Indeed, when investment, production, and trade are considered, the Canadian economy may now be usefully conceptualized as a geographically large zone within the US economy. While itself regionally divided, this zone has until now maintained the capacity to reproduce its own unique social and political formations rooted in various popular and elite conceptions of a distinct Canadian nationality and culture.[80] As continental economic integration has grown, however, far-reaching constraints on the ability of the federal and provincial states to challenge US power in Canada with nationalist programs have resulted not only from the primacy of the continental relationship in economic policy-making but also from the continentalist definitions of the Canadian national interest found both generally within civil society and especially among state elites.

While the formal autonomy of the Canadian state, which makes possible nationalist initiatives, cannot be directly challenged, nationalist threats to the continentalist status quo can often be forestalled, muted, or repudiated after a concerted campaign of pressure by US multinationals and the US government. These campaigns need never step outside the normal decision rules of Canadian liberal democracy but can simply use all the many points of political access and leverage available within a multi-party, executive-dominated federal system. In making their representations, Canadian branches of multinationals are typically accorded the same legitimate "corporate citizen" status by state élites as domestically owned firms. This allows foreign firms to press with vigour their own (continentalist) version of the Canadian national interest. As the fate of the Trudeau government's nationalist initiatives on the Foreign Investment Review Act and the National Energy Program of the early 1980s vividly demonstrate, essential to the success or failure of American pressure is the degree to which factions within the executive class of the bureaucracy, the cabinet, and the leadership of the political parties resonate within their own decision forums the multinationals' arguments for a continentalist vision of the Canadian national interest.[81]

Essential, as well, is the manner in which the maintenance or cultivation of the global continental relationship can hold even nationalist Canadian policy-makers hostage on specific issues.

CONCLUSION

In reference to the debate on "Canada's position within the circuit of international capital" which we have just reviewed, Paul Phillips has recently argued that, "given the importance of understanding the nature of Canada's past economic development to the on-going free trade debate in the context of the contracting American economic empire and a stagnant Canadian and world economy, it is important that some kind of resolution take place – soon." Phillips has suggested that no resolution of the debate between the dependency and neo-Marxist approaches is possible "without incorporating perspectives from both schools."[82]

The "Canada within the centre" approach is neither as well known nor as explicitly developed in the literature as its competitors. It can nonetheless usefully serve, if not as a point of intersection or reconciliation, at least as an indigenously generated framework for the productive re-evaluation of the new Canadian political economy's first generation of analytic models, which were derived from the study of European and Latin American experience. It would do this by asking the partisans of the neo-Marxist and dependency positions to be more sensitive to the positive implications of employing a spatial focus that gives primacy to the regional relations of empire rather than assuming that Canada relates in the first instance to the international political economy through the struggle between national capitals. As with the dependency model, the "Canada within the centre" perspective demands consideration of the spatial dimensions of uneven development. However, these considerations are not at all incompatible with the deeper insights provided by the more sophisticated neo-Marxist literature addressing the internal dynamic of Canadian socioeconomic formation. Indeed, because of the central role given by this approach to political, cultural, and social institutions in reproducing Canada as a region within the centre, such sophistication is essential.

NOTES

1 McNally, "Technological Determinism," 165; Drache, "The Crisis of Canadian Political Economy," 26, 27, 43.

2 Innis, "On the Economic Significance of Cultural Factors," 102. See also "The Political Implications of Unused Capacity," 372-3.

3 Innis, *The Cod Fisheries*, 501.

4 Innis, *The Fur Trade in Canada*, 42, 83.
5 Innis, "Economic Significance," 88.
6 Innis, "Reflections on Russia," 259.
7 Innis, *Political Economy in the Modern State*, 122-3.
8 Innis, *The Fur Trade*, 383.
9 Ibid., 385.
10 G. Williams, *Not for Export*, 130-7.
11 Innis, *Problems of Staple Production in Canada*, 82, 88.
12 This is a theme repeated throughout Innis's work on Canada. For an introduction to his views, see "Government Ownership and the Canadian Scene" and "Decentralization and Democracy."
13 Innis, *Problems of Staple Production*, 90-2.
14 Innis observed: "The demand for salt cod in tropical and Catholic countries has been more directly exposed to the effect of fluctuations in economic activity incidental to regions producing tropical commodities. These tropical products, being luxuries, are subject to wide variations of demand from countries in the temperate zone. Such variations are due to many things – to cyclical business disturbances; to the influence of mechanization on tropical commodities as, for example, citrus fruits, bananas, sugar, and coffee; to the weakness of government machinery in countries whose peoples have low standards of living, as is made evident in bankruptcies, exchange rates, and revolutions ... Demand for luxury products fluctuates sharply, as it does for dried cod, whereas fluctuations in the cost of provisions and supplies such as flour, salt pork, and salt beef from temperate continental areas have been less pronounced." *The Cod Fisheries*, 493.
15 Innis, *Political Economy in the Modern State*, ix-x. Leo Panitch has also drawn attention to Innis's "appreciation of imperialism as a contradictory phenomenon" in his "Dependency and Class," 28.
16 Innis, *The Fur Trade*, 393.
17 Innis, "Great Britain, the United States and Canada," 395, 405.
18 Whitaker, " 'To Have Insight,' " 828.
19 For example, "Having exhausted our more available resources, we may continue to thrive by sharing in the exhaustion of the resources of less industrialized parts of the Empire and the world. Our mild, imperialistic policy will look for new territory. British imperialism was brought face to face with Canadian imperialism at the Imperial economic conference." Innis, *Problems of Staple Production*, 121. "The character of Canadian imperialism became evident in the growing insistence on nationalism shown in the defeat of the Reciprocity Treaty, in the peace treaty of Versailles, in the Statute of Westminster, and finally in the acquisition of Newfoundland. It would not be difficult to collect a series of slogans comparable to those of the United States illustrating our imperialistic ambitions." Innis, "Roman Law and the British Empire," 69-70. See also "Great Britain," 411.
20 Innis, "The Problems of Rehabilitation," 57.
21 Innis, "The Press, a Neglected Factor."

22 Innis, *Empire and Communications*, 169-70.

23 Innis, "Roman Law," 70.

24 Innis, "Great Britain," 408. Further discussion of the theme of militarism in US politics can be found in "Military Implications of the American Constitution" and "Roman Law."

25 Innis, "Great Britain," 396.

26 Watkins, "A Staple Theory," 53. Watkins, as a leading member of a dependency school obsessed with Canadian "underdevelopment," lost interest in developing Innis's position of the Canadian political economy as a special type of centre political economy in the world hierarchy. To his credit, however, this perspective did not disappear entirely from his analysis. After completing his work with the Dene in the mid-1970s, Watkins suggested a scenario in which "the aboriginal population, which we would have to assume was much larger, had not been easily pushed to the margins of society, geographically and socially. Rather than being a 'colony of settlement' Canada might have been a 'colony of conquest' analogous to those of Asia and Africa. Or it might have been a 'white settler colony' proper, like the Union of South Africa or Rhodesia. Or it might have been a mixed case such as abound in Central and South America. In any event, Canadian development would have been different and much more difficult. A precapitalist indigenous population that could not be ignored would be reduced to underdevelopment, and either slowly converted to the capitalist mode of production or contained by massive repression and discrimination. We would not have our very high *average* standard of living; though the European stock – if it had not yet been turfed out – might be doing very well. Methodologically, there would be no special case amenable to the literal staple theory." Watkins, "The Staple Theory Revisited," 90.

27 See, for example, Frank, *Capitalism and Underdevelopment*.

28 See, for example, Cardoso and Faletto, *Dependency and Development*.

29 Drache, "Harold Innis: A Canadian Nationalist," 7, and "The Canadian Bourgeoisie," 24.

30 J. Laxer, "The Political Economy of Canada," 28.

31 Watkins, "The Dismal State," 205-6.

32 Levitt, *Silent Surrender*, 46.

33 Parker, "Harold Innis," 561.

34 Hutcheson, *Dominance and Dependency*, 28.

35 Drache, "Rediscovering Canadian Political Economy," 14.

36 Watkins, "The Branch Plant Condition," 39.

37 Watkins, "The Innis Tradition," 21, 26.

38 Levitt, *Silent Surrender*, 48.

39 Gonick, "Foreign Ownership," 59.

40 Hutcheson, "The Capitalist State," 166-7. See also *Dominance and Dependency*, 26-8.

41 J. Laxer, "Manufacturing and U.S. Trade Policy."

42 Drache, "Canadian Capitalism," 10, and "Rediscovering Canadian Political Economy," 41.

43 Levitt, *Silent Surrender*, 58.

44 Watkins, "Economic Development in Canada," 75.

45 Drache, "The Canadian Bourgeoisie," 19–20.

46 Naylor, "Rise and Fall." Naylor subsequently shifted his thesis onto somewhat higher ground, suggesting that the imperatives of commercial capitalism, rather than the machinations of mercantile-financial capitalists per se, stultified Canadian industrial capitalism, not capitalists. "The strength of commercial capitalism in Canada was the result of the British colonial connection and together they served to lock the Canadian economy into the staple trap. The domination of the Montreal commercial community in the colonial economic and political structure was the outgrowth of the pattern of dependence, and the stultification of industrial entrepreneurship followed from their control of the state and state policy." *History of Canadian Business*, II, 283.

47 Gonick, "Foreign Ownership," 69.

48 J. Laxer, "Political Economy," 35.

49 Teeple, "Introduction," x.

50 Naylor, "Rise and Fall," 36.

51 Drache, "The Canadian Bourgeoisie," 22.

52 Drache, "Harold Innis and Canadian Capitalist Development," 49.

53 Amin, *Accumulation*, I, 297; G. Williams, "Canada," 29–30, and *Not for Export*, 3–4.

54 I gratefully acknowledge Leo Panitch's assistance in clarifying this view of Canadian sovereignty.

55 Draimin and Swift, "What's Canada Doing in Brazil?" 7.

56 Clement, *Continental Corporate Power*, 300. See also p. 14.

57 Ibid., 131, 289.

58 Ibid., 23–4.

59 Ehrensaft and W. Armstrong, "The Formation of Dominion Capitalism."

60 Ibid., p. 143. W. Armstrong has recently moved away from the "dominion capitalist" position and now stresses the "political, economic and cultural chemistry developed between each society of European settlement and the dominant power of the nineteenth century, Great Britain ... [which] locked the economic development of each society into the expansion of the century's industrial, financial and commercial giant." See his "Imperial Incubus."

61 Niosi, "The Canadian Bourgeoisie," 133, 141–2.

62 Niosi, "Continental Nationalism," 63.

63 McNally, "Staple Theory," 38, 57.

64 Moore and Wells, *Imperialism*, 92–3.

65 Ibid., 96–7.

66 Carroll, "The Canadian Corporate Elite," 90.

67 Carroll, "Dependency," 45. P. Stevenson comments critically on the underdevel-

oped notion of the state in both Carroll's and Niosi's work, in "Capital and the State in Canada."

68 Resnick, "The Maturing of Canadian Capitalism," 11-12.

69 Ibid., 22.

70 G. Williams, "Canada," 30.

71 Emmanuel, *Unequal Exchange*.

72 G. Williams, "Canada," 32.

73 Panitch, "Dependency and Class," 26. For a disappointingly rhetorical and misdirected critique of this article see Drache, "Crisis."

74 Panitch, "Dependency and Class," 19-20. The manner in which the continental labour market affected the Canadian political economy was also a theme of considerable interest to Innis. See, for example, *The Cod Fisheries*, 152, 425, and "Labour in Canadian Economic History," 196-9.

75 Panitch, "Dependency and Class," 26-7.

76 G. Laxer, "Foreign Ownership," 336, and "Class, Nationality and the Roots of the Branch Plant Economy," 46-7. See as well his "Political Economy of Aborted Development."

77 G. Williams, *Not for Export*, chap. 2, 6.

78 Clark-Jones, *A Staple State*, 11, 211.

79 See, for example, Coleman, *The Independence Movement*; Marchak, "Rise and Fall"; Nelles, *The Politics of Development*; and Richards and Pratt, *Prairie Capitalism*.

80 G. Williams, *Not for Export*, chap. 9. See as well his "Canadian Sovereignty and the Free Trade Debate."

81 For relevant discussions of this point see Clarkson, *Canada and the Reagan Challenge*; Doern and Toner, *The Politics of Energy*; and G. Williams, *Not for Export*, chap. 8. Prime Minister Mulroney recently indicated how pursuit of the continentalist vision guided the Conservative government's dismantling of FIRA and the NEP during its early years: "We did not do that because we were doing the Americans a favour," he argued; "we did that because we were building a stronger Canada." See House of Commons, *Debates*, September 23, 1987, p. 9232. So traumatized were some continentalists by these early 1980s manifestations of nationalism within the federal state that they have sought, through the 1987 Canadian-US free trade agreement, to place any future nationalist initiatives in foreign investment controls or energy policy permanently beyond the legislative capability of the Canadian state. Deputy Prime Minister Donald Mazankowski described the energy provisions to Calgary oilmen as "insurance against your own government." See *Globe and Mail*, 17 Oct 1987, A4.

82 Phillips, "Review," 206-7.

CHAPTER SEVEN

The Political Economy of Regionalism

Janine Brodie

Few political economists would disagree with the assertion that regionalism is a "profound and fundamental" feature of Canadian political life.[1] Canadian politics revolves around persistent and divisive conflicts about the spatial distribution of economic development, state activity, living standards, governmental services, and political power. And, unlike the experience of other advanced capitalist countries, spatially based conflict in Canada has not decreased as the pace of development accelerates. The centrality of regionalism to Canada's collective political experience has prompted many scholars, especially revisionist historians, to advocate a fundamental reorientation in thinking about Canada, one in which region would "rival, if not replace, the nation-state as the central construction in Canadian studies."[2]

The revisionists argue that the most popular interpretations of Canadian history, the so-called national schools, are centralist in bias and contain a vision of economic, social, and political development that is profoundly at odds with the Canadian experience. Recently, similar charges have been levelled against the current generation of Canadian political economists.[3] Both the "old" and "new" schools of Canadian political economy incorporate considerations of space and geography in their analysis. Unlike its predecessor, however, the new political economy, especially the class and dependency streams, has not been particularly self-conscious about questions of regional definition and integration, that is, explaining what a region is and how regions relate to one another and to the nation-state of which they are a part.[4] This essay examines selected contributions of the old and new political economies to the study of Canadian regionalism. It attempts to show that the early political economists, particularly Harold Innis and Vernon Fowke, provide a useful point of departure for a future political economy that is sensitive to the spatial dimension of Canadian development and politics. We begin with some terminological considerations.

THINKING ABOUT REGIONS

Canadians are very familiar with thinking about the country in terms of cross-provincial spatial partitions. Moreover, they are constantly bombarded with subtle messages suggesting that these spatial partitions have political relevance. Politicians bemoan the lack of regional representation in federal institutions, public opinion polls are reported according to regional variations, and governments devise policies for regional development. Indeed, references to region are so familiar and pervasive that Canadians have accepted these divisions as natural, without ever questioning why they have come to think in these terms or what meanings these spatial abstractions convey.

There are actually a variety of meanings and a great deal of confusion associated with the spatial dimension of Canadian politics. Matthews points out that much of the confusion arises from the fact that four analytically distinct terms – region, regional differences, regionalism, and regional disparities – are often used unconsciously and interchangeably.[5] The first term, *regions*, refers to some sort of spatial unit. It is, as Stevenson argues, "a territorial entity having some natural and organic unity or community of interest that is *independent* of political and administrative boundaries."[6] Constitutional arrangements such as federalism may set administrative boundaries on a map, but this does not mean that provinces are equivalent to regions. The term suggests a sameness within a geographic space that separates or differentiates it from some other geographic space. To designate a region, in other words, is to simultaneously assert differences.

Any high school atlas demonstrates the multiplicity of partitions that can be imposed on geographic space, with each line of demarcation signifying similarities within and differences without. Regions can be defined in terms of topography, climate, land use, and demography, to name a few common criteria of demarcation. And all of these criteria simultaneously signify regional differences. Yet most of these analytic distinctions are "quite irrelevant to the phenomena which Canadian scholars and writers are attempting to explain when they invoke the concept."[7] The spatial dimension of Canadian politics involves more than sterile analytical distinctions, drawing lines on a map and searching for empirical regularities in the location of things, attitudes, and events. Regions in Canada have concrete political and social dimensions that are deeply embedded in collective historical experience. They are much more than arbitrary intellectual constructs.

Regionalism and regional disparities, the other two terms in Matthews's spatial vocabulary, attempt to capture the social and political dimensions of the phenomenon. Regionalism is a socio-psychological factor that involves identification with and commitment to a territorial unit.[8] Moreover, Breton argues, regionalism is necessarily political, because economic, political, and cultural interests are defined and articulated in spatial terms. Regionalism means that politics and political conflict revolve around the distribution of resources across geographic space.[9]

The term *regional disparities* refers to differences in the distribution of resources and development across space. And, as Matthews correctly observes, the expression of differences (such as unemployment rates) as disparities is also an expressly political process. When a region is declared to be "in disparity when compared to other regions," it is "not merely a declaration that certain differences exist among regions but a judgement about the *meaning and implications of such differences.*"[10] It is a judgment that gives substance and form to political conflict, setting an agenda for remedial action to which governments in liberal democracies must respond.

The concepts of regionalism and regional disparties are at the heart of the spatial dimension of the Canadian political economy. Politics is judged to be about "place" instead of "people" prosperity, and, therewith, conflict revolves around the allocation of power and resources across geographic units rather than, for example, among social classes. It highlights relationships in geographic space in which some territorial units gain or lose in relation to other territorial units. It is thus a class of political expression and, often, mobilization that focuses on the spatial inequalities resulting from uneven capitalist development. Having established some terminological clarity, we now turn to the conceptual problems of regional definition and intergration. What is a region, and how does it relate to other regions?

REGIONAL DEFINITION AND INTEGRATION

There are primarily two analytic procedures for defining regional boundaries - the *formal* and *functional* methods.[11] Each procedure for definition, in turn, contains specific assumptions about integration, or how regions relate to one anther. Formal regions are designated by homogeneity or similarity in features. We have already seen that there are many ways to determine a formal region. In practice, however, students of Canadian history have relied uncritically on environmental and, more recently, institutional criteria for designating regions.

When environmental criteria are employed, Canadian regions typically are characterized by similarity in physical features and separated from other regions by prominent topographical features. The familiar configuration of Canadian territory into the Atlantic, central, prairie, Pacific, and Arctic regions is a product of this approach.[12] More recently, political scientists have equated regions with provinces and the formal boundaries of federalism. Elkins, Simeon, Smiley, Breton, and others have argued that to become mobilized, regional differences must have an institutional focus and that provincial political institutions now provide that focus.[13]

I argue in detail elsewhere that both formal approaches often promote misinterpretations about the nature of regionalism and regional interaction.[14] The environmental approach, for example, is often accompanied by a kind of cultural determinism which assumes, incorrectly I believe, that a common environment gives rise to common political, social, and cultural characteristics. It searches for the causes of regionalism in the inanimate and immutable features of the landscape.[15] Similarly, by reducing regional boundaries to the institutional boundaries of federalism, researchers run the attendant risk of explaining regional tensions solely in terms of institutional imperatives and rivalries. Regionalism loses its conceptual distinctiveness because it is forced into the "strait-jacket" of federalism.[16]

The other approach to regional definition has been variously termed functional, polarized, relational, or dualist. It differs from the formal procedure in a number of ways, but, most fundamentally, it does not propose concrete regional boundaries that isolate one region from another. Nor is it concerned primarily with discovering similarities and differences in geographic space. Instead, as the above terms imply, regions are seen as part of an interconnected whole in which one regional configuration is largely a function or an expression of another. Regions, in other words, are not arbitrary constructs but effects or consequences of historical relationships. Following this account, regions are shaped and reshaped by "flows of some kind" – political, social, and economic links that connect geographic space in relationships and interdependencies.[17]

Thinking about regions relationally may be unfamiliar to many of us, but it opens many new perspectives on the spatial dimension of Canadian politics not offered by the formal procedure. First, this perpective de-emphasizes geography and nature in the determination of regional boundaries. Regions are the product of historical experience, human organization, and social interaction. From a functional perspective, regions are in a very real sense political creations. Second, this perspective encourages us to think about regions not as being fixed but, instead, as fluid phenomena that change as their interrelationships change. Third, it enables us to study regionalism synchronically and diachronically, that is, at a given moment in time and across time. Finally, a functional approach can be readily adapted to the study of sub-regional relationships such as exists between northern and southern Ontario. It is, therefore, a much more demanding approach, which obliges us to identify the forces or links that alter relations among territorial entities and thereby reshape them.

The formal and functional approaches also provide quite different perspectives on regional integration. In brief, the formal approach is accompanied most often by what have been termed theories of regional self-balance.[18] In these theories, no links between regions are postulated, and, as a result, factors explaining the character of the region necessarily are sought within the region itself.[19] Theories of regional self-balance have attributed a region's underdevelopment to such factors as the forces of nature which provide an inadequate resource base or an inhospitable climate, insufficient entrepreneurial skills among local capitalists, lack of infrastructure, and an unskilled labour force. In contrast, the functional perspective demands a theory of regional imbalance because it identifies the character of a region as an effect of its interrelationships with other regions. Both the old and new political economies, as we shall see, rely heavily on a functional or relational interpretation of regional definition and integration. Innis's staples theory, the metropolitan-hinterland thesis, dependency theory, and some neo-Marxist applications all argue that regions are defined by their interrelationships with other regions. They differ, however, over the forces or links responsible for the creation of Canadian regionalism. It is to this debate that we now turn.

CREATION OF REGIONS: THE EARLY TRADITION

Innis's Staple Theory

We begin our survey of the early political economy with Harold Innis's staples theory. This may seem a questionable point of departure. Some have argued that staples theory is not a relational approach to regional definition and integration but, instead, an example of vulgar geographic and resource determinism.[20] This accusation is largely, though not entirely, unwarranted and appears to derive from two sources in particular. The first source is Innis himself. Innis's work is often frustratingly imprecise and makes sweeping assertions about the importance of geography, staples, and technology. Critics have taken some of these assertions as evidence that Innis was a determinist who allowed little room for political agency in the explanation of regionalism.[21] Admittedly, strong currents of determinism do run through his work, but they are not sufficiently deep to dismiss Innis's potential contribution to the study of Canadian regionalism.

Second, more often than not, the charge that Innis's work is little more than vulgar resource determinism results not from a close reading of Innis but rather from the liberal laundering of his staples theory. This "laundering" coincided with the growth in popularity of quantitative economics and reduced Innis's staples theory to little more than a neo-classical theory of international trade and comparative advantage.[22] Not surprisingly, this interpretation of staples theory has been embraced by such conservative think-tanks as the Economic Council of Canada. In a major study on regionalism in Canada, it concluded: "The varying economic fortunes of different areas of Canada are . . . explained, according to the staples approach, by varying availability and marketability of natural resources."[23] Similarly, Pomfret, an economic historian following in this tradition, argues: "Staples theory asserts that the pace and nature of an area's economic growth is determined by the characteristics of its staple product."[24] These interpretations of staples theory do provide examples of vulgar resource determinism but bear little resemblance to the complexity of Innis's argument.

Innis was not the first Canadian political economist to emphasize the centrality of staples production in Canadian history. Mackintosh, who argued that the exploitation of staples was a necessary transitional stage on the path to economic maturity, first alerted him to the idea of the staple.[25] Innis, however, doubted that staples trade would inevitably lead to industrialization. In fact, he disagreed strongly with the assumption that the course of economic development in a new country would eventually parallel that of Britain or Europe. For Innis, it was simply defective thinking to attempt "to fit the phenomena of new countries into the economic theories of old countries."[26]

A central thread underlying Innis's work is that Canadian political economy must be understood in relation to its unique historical antecedents.[27] The experience of North America was simply different from that of Europe. It came into contact with the old world only after capitalism had emerged as the dominant model of social organization. Innis, like Marx, was acutely aware that geography is continuously shaped and reshaped by explicitly historical and social forces such as the organization of production and new technologies.[28] For him, the key to understanding the pattern of Canadian development was to trace how the invasion of European culture and the price system left its imprint on a geography that previously corresponded to the non-capitalist forms of social organization of the aboriginal peoples.

According to Innis, the new white settler colonies of North America were, by definition, economically weak and were forced to engage in staples trade with a series of imperial centres, first France and later Britain and the United States, in order to obtain necessary material and technological goods. The form and location of economic activity within these colonies, however, were determined by the centre's demand for staple products. The exploitation of a series of staples – fish, fur, timber, wheat, and minerals – meant that different areas of the country developed at different times as the demands of the centre as well as technology and transportation made them accessible. New countries, in other words, developed in relation to old countries.[29] However, it was not the staple itself that stimulated growth but rather prices, markets, and the monopoly of markets, all of which are defined historically.

Innis argued that the succession of staples exploitation explained much more of Canadian history than simply the location of economic activity at any given period. Each staple was also characterized by specific patterns of settlement, linkages to other economic activities, interactions with the centre, culture, and institutional arrangements. "Concentration on the production of staples for export to more highly industrialized areas in Europe and later in the u.s.," he writes, "had broad implications for the Canadian economic, political and social structure. Each staple in turn left its stamp, and the shift to a new staple invariably produced periods of crises." Moreover, "the tendency has been cumulative."[30]

Innis provides us with a relational and diachronic analysis of the link between uneven development and political arrangements in Canada. Each staple was characterized by a complex web of forms located in geographic space that changed across time. Innis asked us to think about geographic space abstractly and relationally. It was as if Canadian history could be represented as a series of transparencies, each representing a different matrix of economic growth and political organization, laid on geographic space, one on top of the other, as the international political economy changed. Each staple led to different geographic configurations that were unstable across time. Boundaries – whether national or regional – were not "in the land" but rather tied to the pattern of staples exploitation.[31]

Some have argued that Innis's work is anti-regional because he concentrates on patterns of national development – the whole rather than the parts. But his work is also valuable in illuminating the historical relationships among imperial centres and Canadian regional centres, between imperial centres and Canadian hinterlands, and between Canadian regional centres and Canadian hinterlands. In *The Cod Fisheries*, for example, he describes how the nature of the fish staple made Nova Scotia, and in particular Halifax, a regional centre in the Maritime provinces. "Her position, sensitive alike to competition from New England and to the effects of Imperial commercial policy, gave Nova Scotia a great influence with the administration in Great Britain."[32] Innis also recognized that the diversity of the Ontario economy gave it "undue weight on the less favoured areas of the Dominion."[33]

Innis saw political forms as necessarily emanating from the demands of staple production. This is because he ascribed the state a major role in facilitating the extraction of the staple. Thus, the east-west unity of Canada originated in the fur trade and trading ties with Europe, while the political form, Confederation, was tied to the wheat staple. The regions joined together at Confederation had developed independently in relation to Britain but were drawn into a new constitutional arrangement largely to underwrite the transportation costs necessitated by expansion to the interior. Heavy expenditures involved the development of a strong centralized government in Canada. They also placed the federal state at the heart of political conflict over the distribution of resources across geographic space.

Innis's analysis of state policy and political conflict is not particularly sophisticated, but he did acknowledge that the role played by the federal state in the economy was "unique" and more interventionist than most countries because of Canada's dependence on staples exploitation. During the development of the wheat staple, in particular, "heavy expenditures on transport improvements, including railways and canals, . . . involved government grants, subsidies, and guarantees to an exceptional degree."[34] Moreover, the costs and benefits accruing from government intervention were not distributed equally among the regions. "Western Canada," he wrote in 1923, "has paid for the development of the Canadian nationality, and it would appear that it must continue to pay. The acquisitiveness of eastern Canada shows little sign of abatement."[35] National policies, in other words, were often little more than thinly disguised regional policies, which, in turn, gave content to regional conflict.[36] "In regions bearing the burden of fixed charges and dependent on staples which fluctuate widely in yield and price, political activity became more intense. Relief was obtained by political pressure." "A less kindly critic," he confesses, "might say that currents of hot air flowed upwards from regions with sharp fluctuations in income."[37] Innis attributed regional conflict to the vagaries of staples exploitation and provided a point of departure for later work on regional protest movements in western Canada. More important, however, he suggested that the contours of regional protest changed with the pattern of staples exploitation.

Innis was especially concerned with the institutional maladjustments and regional conflict engendered by the shift from one staple to another. He argued that Confederation became obsolete when the wheat economy, complete with its east-west linkages, had run its course and staple production shifted to a north-south linkage, supplying pulpwood, minerals, and energy to the American market[38] – a theme adopted by Garth Stevenson in his treatment of federal-provincial relations.[39] Innis wrote:

The dangers to Canada have been increased by disturbances to the Canadian constitutional structure which have followed the rise of new industries developed in special relation to the American market . . . A division has emerged between the attitude of provinces which have been particularly fortunate in the possession of natural resources in which the American market is interested and that of the provinces more largely dependent on European markets . . . The strains imposed on a constitution specifically designed for an economy built up in relation to Great Britain and Europe have been evident in the emergence of regionalism.[40]

Innis's observations seem especially prescient in the late 1980s as Canada undertakes constitutional reform that corresponds to the realities of continental economic integration. His analysis of regionalism suggests that the form and content of regional protest change as major development strategies change. Moreover, the process is cumulative, as new symbols, forms, and tensions are layered onto older ones. In other words, the story of the spatial dimension of Canadian politics is not, as many now argue, that while once regions protested, provinces now do.[41] Instead, Innis argued that, with shifts in international demand for staples, certain *groups* of producing provinces would be placed in a new relationship with the United States and with central Canada, that is with the imperial centre and regional centres. The wheat staple had produced a particular pattern of regional definition, integration, and conflict, while the new staples, destined for the American market, produced another. This shift created tensions between the old and new orders and inevitably led to institutional crisis and adjustment. The position of Canada in the international political economy changed and, with it, the pattern and form of regional politics.

Innis suggests a necessary connection between economic development strategies, institutional and policy formation, and regional conflict. His formulations, however, are rudimentary and reveal one of the major weaknesses of his work. Innis's history, as history, is largely dehumanized.[42] Although he gave passing recognition to the impact of politics and policy in sustaining uneven regional economic development, the forces of the imperial centre and the price system always took conceptual priority. Staples exploitation limited the options and opportunities for a more equitable and controlled distribution of economic development, invariably leading the country deeper and deeper into a "staples trap" of dependency and stagnation. In this respect, Berger, Richards, Pratt, and others have grounds to judge him a determinist. Yet, as Berger explains, "paradoxically, to understand the magnitude and character of deterministic elements was for him to establish the margin, invariably narrow, in which men were free to make their own history."[43] In sum, Innis's contribution to the study of Canadian regionalism was his emphasis on an indigenous interpretation of regional development and the links between spatial configurations within Canada and changes in the international economic order.

The Role of the State

The other significant contribution of the early political economy is an elaboration of the role of the state and state policy in the creation of regionalism. This emphasis is traced most clearly through the work of the "hinterlanders," especially Fowke, Macpherson, Morton, and Mallory.[44] It is impossible within the confines of this chapter to survey the richness of this research, once judged to be the most "productive, detailed and perceptive contributions of the Canadian school of political economy."[45] These contributions are both unique and central to the political economy of regionalism, but share a common weakness. In contrast to Innis, who emphasized both external and internal forces structuring the contours of regionalism in Canada, the hinterlanders had a decidedly national perspective. They examined internal economic asymmetries, particularly those associated with the wheat staple, and the political mechanisms that held them in place. And it is their emphasis on the political dimension of regionalism, not their centre-periphery model, that commends their work.

Most students of Canadian political economy are familiar with the metropolitan-hinterland thesis of uneven development. It posits that western Canada was created as an internal colony of central Canada and held in a subordinate and dependent relationship through the mercantilist policies of the federal government and, in particular, the National Policy.

Smiley has summarized the key elements of the argument in his perceptive essay on Canadian development strategies. (1) Metropolitian policies confined the hinterland to the production of a small number of staples (although the focus of this group is the wheat staple). (2) Metropolitan policies required that the hinterland buy the manufactured products of the heartland. (3) The hinterland and the heartland were linked physically by transportation facilities, established and operated to the benefit of the latter. (4) Capitalist development in the hinterland was carried out through institutions centred in the heartland. (5) In the international context, the interests of the hinterland were usually sacrificed to those of the heartland. (6) Many critical aspects of heartland-hinterland relations were carried out through the instumentalities of large business organizations protected by imperial authorities from foreign or hinterland competition. (7) There was a continuing pattern controlling the political authorities of the hinterland in the interests of the heartland.[46] The result was an undiversified, non-industrial, and fragile resource economy tied to the uncertainties of the "boom and bust" of international commodities markets. Regional uneven development, in other words, was "created" by the economic and political power of the centre.

The detailed historical and empirical studies associated with this tradition remain some of the most significant contributions of Canadian social science to understanding how dominance is exercised and maintained in liberal democracies, in contrast to what House has termed the "pseudo-theory and pseudo-explanation" of "the new orthodoxy" in Canadian political economy.[47] One of the strongest works in the tradition is *Democracy in Alberta*. In it, Macpherson ascribes the rise of a regional protest movement to the uniquely temporal and spatial convergence of the "relatively homogeneous class composition" of independent commodity producers in a "quasi-colonial" relationship with the rest of Canada.[48] It remains one of the most sophisticated analyses of the contradictory position of the petit bourgeois in capitalist democracies and of the effective limitations that the middle class imposes on progressive movements. Indeed, his work should be reread by the current generation of political economists who are convinced of the efficacy of the "new" provincial state elite. Similarly, Mallory's work, *Social Credit and the Federal Power in Canada*, should alert us to the continuing importance of governmental institutions, particularly the constitution and the Supreme Court, as both mirrors of and instruments in the maintenance of particular developmental strategies and the patterns of dominance that they entail.[49] Finally, W.L. Morton's interpretation of the rise and fall of the Progressive Party, with its uniquely hinterland perspective, demonstrates how regional grievances are shaped by democratic elections and, thereby, become embedded in our political history and culture.[50]

Unfortunately, too much success sometimes breeds failure, and, in at least one respect, this has been the legacy of the hinterland school for Canadian political economy. The hinterlanders provided a synchronic analysis – a historical elaboration of the political effects of the wheat staple – and they exposed the linkages that held this particular spatial relation in place. A centre-periphery model, however, has limited utility for explaining spatial patterns of uneven development, especially diachronically, or across time. First, it fails to explain the process of growth in the centre. Once a centre-periphery relation is established, it is assumed to be self-sustaining. The possibility that growth at the centre may be stopped or reversed by factors unrelated to the centre-periphery relationship is ignored. Second, the model assumes that the periphery has no autonomous capacity for change. The only source of economic change in the periphery is growth at the centre.[51] (These criticisms also are relevant to centre-periphery models applied on a global scale, such as Innis's staples theory or dependency models borrowed from South America and recently applied to Maritime underdevelopment.) Finally, the hinterlanders' neglect of the external forces acting on patterns of national economic development has encouraged overly rigid conceptualization of regional definition. The regional configuration outlined by the hinterlanders has been accepted as orthodoxy; it has become as rigid as "the old environmental/landforms structure of regions."[52] As a result, political economists who follow this orthodoxy have attempted to place quite different sets of relationships onto a regional configuration associated with the exploitation of the wheat staple – the functional region has become a formal one. As Westfall explains, however, "the old west . . . is considerably different from the new west and one cannot transpose the regional relations that characterize the former onto the latter."[53]

The limitations and conceptual problems associated with the hinterlanders' centre-periphery model should not detract from this school's important and necessary emphasis on the role of the state and policy in the creation of regionalism. Vernon Fowke deserves special attention here because he made the most significant contributions from this perspective. Like Innis, he had an explicitly relational approach to uneven development, but he moved the focus away from the concept of the staple to the more general process of capital formation and state economic development strategies. Fowke explicitly rejected geographic criteria for the determination or explanation of regional development patterns.[54] For him, "the frontier at any given point in time is whatever place and whatever economic activity gives rise to investment opportunities on a substantial scale." The "investment frontier may be geographically diffused but it nevertheless has concrete expression in the process of real capital formation."[55] Although Fowke's work concentrated on agriculture, he diverted our attention away from the explicitly conjunctural single-commodity and spatially rigid focus of the hinterlanders to the more general issue of the spatial implications of historical patterns of capital accumulation. Neither, however, did Fowke reduce the study of uneven development to the invariable laws of capitalism. Instead, he argued that the state played a major intervening role in the political economy of regions, but his state was not simply a reflection of the demands of staples exploitation, as Innis and others after him have argued.[56] For Fowke, the state was a necessarily political and somewhat vulnerable entity, responsible for developing a territory and designing policies to achieve this goal under conditions set internationally. These conditions were, by definition, outside its immediate sphere of influence.

Fowke argued that governmental policies could be ranked according to their impact on patterns of national economic development: "When the policies are grouped according to their collective purposes, gradations of importance can readily be distinguished. Some groups clearly relate to minor or temporary, others to fundamental and persistent governmental aims."[57] The thrust of Fowke's work was to show that the National Policy was an example of the latter group of policies, but for him this policy entailed much more than Macdonald's pronouncements of 1878. The term included "collectively the group of policies . . . [including Confederation itself] designed to transform the British North American colonies into a political and economic unit."[58] Moreover, he considered it a policy of desperation, dictated by the disappearance of the favoured alternatives of imperial and continental economic integration. Its aim was to monopolize for Canadian capital the profits derived from the development of the west.[59]

At the risk of reading too much into Fowke, I would suggest that there are three streams in his work that should be pursued in future work on the political economy of regionalism in Canada. The first is his recognition that the overall process of capital accumulation during a period, not simply the dominant staple, shapes and reshapes geography and social relations. While this theme has been developed recently by radical geographers, it has been largely neglected by the new political economy.

Fowke's second theme is his emphasis on major state developmental strategies in the creation of different regions and regionalism. He asked us to periodize Canadian economic history into a series of "national policies," by which he means overarching state developmental strategies formulated in response to internal political pressures and to the demands of the international political economy. He regarded the period 1825–1930 as the era of the first national policy. With its goals accomplished and with changes in the international order, "the federal government worked gropingly and against substantial difficulties toward the formulation of a new set of national policies."[60] He and Donald Smiley suggest that the second national policy was the Keynesian state, and I suggest elsewhere that the past decade represents a third era, when the federal government has been searching for a new national policy.[61]

Fowke's third theme, and that of the hinterland school generally, was the class and spatial biases in purportedly "national" and neutral government development strategies. Just as important, he suggested that the class origins and substantive content of regional protest movements are tied to the specific developmental strategy of the period. His work detailed how the National Policy directed agricultural profits away from the producers to the appropriating classes and thereby became the focus of western Canadian farmers' populist revolt against eastern capitalism.[62] In other words, his work emphasized the material and class foundations of regionalism and, at the same time, suggested that the specific form and content of regional protest would be structured by the general developmental strategy of the period. Readers will detect an echo of Innis here (i.e. policy, instead of staples, sets successive regional imprints on geographic space), but Fowke's emphasis on policy directs attention to the political creation of uneven development and makes the state a necessary focal point in the study of the political economy of regionalism.

We have travelled some distance from Innis and have taken some liberty in the interpretation of the old political economy and its contribution to the study of Canadian regionalism. Its work, however, provides important perspectives on the persistent regionalism of Canadian political life. All the authors discussed here share similar points of departure. (1) The spatial dimension of Canadian political economy is an explicitly relational phenomenon. (2) It has fluid boundaries, which shift across time. (3) It centres on questions of uneven spatial development.

We have encountered some disagreement over the autonomous impact of politics and the state in the creation of regionalism, but much of the work of the early school suggests that the state establishes, legitimizes, and enforces particular spatial patterns of development in response to both internal and external pressures. Thus, while the new regional historiography proposes to replace the nation-state with region as the central construction in Canadian studies, the work of the early political economy indicates that the two cannot be separated so easily. State development strategies imprint patterns of accumulation and conflict in space, and the process is cumulative. These patterns, one after the other, become embedded in Canadians' collective political experience, opening options for some futures and closing others. We now turn to the contributions of the new political economy to the study of Canadian regionalism.

CURRENT TRENDS

Unlike its predecessor, the new Canadian political economy has not devoted much attention to uneven spatial development within Canada or to regional politics. Recently, there has been renewed interest in the political economy of Canadian regionalism, especially among radical scholars working outside central Canada. They have examined the uneven spatial development of Canada, but their approach has been eclectic. We can, however, discern two distinct trends in the current literature. The first borrows from neo-Marxist dependency theory and is an extension of the centre-periphery tradition in Canadian scholarship. The second stream, echoing Innis, examines the impact of continental economic integration on resource production and the activities of resource-producing provinces. This "provincialist" literature has provided rich historical analysis of the attempts by various provincial governments to promote accumulation and diversification within their respective boundaries. Neither stream, however, has elaborated a coherent theoretical approach to the spatial dimension of Canadian politics.

Scholars seeking to explain the persistent problem of underdevelopment in Atlantic Canada have relied heavily on various dependency models borrowed from South America. It would be impossible to review all this work here, but useful summaries are available for those wishing to pursue this theme.[63] In one of these, Barrett identifies three distinct trends in Atlantic scholarship which have emerged over the past two decades from debates and research in the dependency tradition: the Frankian model of the "development of underdevelopment," the "new dependency" (or dependent capitalist development) approach and the "modes of production" perspective.[64]

Archibald was the first to apply a modern theory of dependency, specifically, Frank's "development of underdevelopment" thesis, systematically to Atlantic Canada. According to Archibald, Atlantic Canada was reduced to the status of a satellite economy by a series of metropoles, first by Britain and then by central Canada and the United States. These metropoles drained surplus from the region, controlled patterns of development, and blocked industrial diversification of its resource-based economy.[65] Archibald's work shares the weaknesses of a centre-periphery model as described above and has been criticized for historical inaccuracy, especially for ignoring the fact that the Maritimes were not underdeveloped as much as they were deindustrialized.[66]

The "dependent capitalist development" school argues that the "development of underdevelopment" thesis misinterprets the nature of development in the periphery because it concerns itself with exchange relations rather than relations of production. Veltmeyer has been the key proponent for the incorporation of class in dependency models of Atlantic Canada. He argues that regional underdevelopment can be understood in terms of the universal tendencies of capitalism, especially the declining rate of profit and capital's requirement for an industrial reserve army. Atlantic Canada, he suggests, has been reduced to an industrial reserve army for central Canada.[67] He does not explain, however, why capital in Canada, but not elsewhere, requires such a peculiar spatial distribution of the industrial reserve army. He also fails to recognize the significant force of unemployed within the industrial heartland.

The "modes of production" approach also incorporates Marxist class analysis but departs considerably from popular dependency models. Employing this perspective, Sacouman argues that the underdevelopment of the rural Maritimes over the last century has been based on the "structural articulation of two apparent modes of production," petty primary production and monopoly capitalism. He uses this model to trace how the petty primary producer unit (tied seasonally to farming, lumber, and fishing) and the relative surplus population have been increasingly exploited by the strictly capitalist mode of production.[68] While more credible, his analysis is limited in scope, addressing only the issue of rural underdevelopment.

In a somewhat different vein, Clement has examined the interrelationship among three factors: Canada's dependence on the United States and multinational enterprises, its "distorted" class structure, and its uneven development. He argues that this external dependence causes internal spatial asymmetries because the weight of capitalist activities is located at the centre. He seeks to demonstrate how Ontario, with its disproportionate share of capitalists, multinationals, and corporate activity, dominates and exploits the rest of Canada.[69]

Clement's initial attempt to incorporate class and region provides little more than a description of a few of the consequences of uneven development and not an explanation of its causes. He and others working within this genre often confuse structural dualism (vertical class inequalities) with spatial dualism (uneven development across space). This confusion is evident in discussions of the transfer of surplus, which has very different meanings in class and regional analysis: extraction of surplus within capitalist relations of production and movement of capital across space, respectively. Evidence that more capitalists are located in Ontario than elsewhere may indicate spatial dominance – but it could indicate instead that capital in other regions is simply concentrated. In other words, a relatively few capitalists may be extracting surplus from workers within a region (names like Irving, McCain, Sobey, and Jodrey come to mind), and the capital thereby derived may or may not remain in the region.

Clement's work on Canadian regionalism has shifted emphasis in recent years, but he maintains a dependency perspective, arguing that "a region can only be underdeveloped if it is tied to an external economy which is responsible for its underdevelopment."[70] But a general confusion about structural and spatial dualism remains when he argues that "true" development is achieved only when "all those on site who participate in development share equally in the surplus produced."[71] By this latter criterion, regions identified as exploitative through the dependency lens, such as Ontario, cannot be considered developed, nor for that matter can any capitalist economy. This logical inconsistency can result only from the conceptual fusion of uneven spatial development and class exploitation.

Dependency models can be seductive, particularly when, as Williams points out, they conform to one's political objectives.[72] There are a number of reasons, however, why we should hesitate to employ them in an analysis of regionalism. First, there are logical problems with the dependency perspective's crude application of the spatial transfer of surplus. Flows of surplus are extremely difficult to measure empirically, and dependency theory ignores questions about the use of the surplus transferred.[73] Contrary to the assumptions of the dependency model, the region that gains value is not necessarily the one in which value is capitalized.[74] In fact, surplus may be used for takeovers and mergers and thereby actually contribute to contraction at the centre.

Massey's objections to the use of dependency models to explain intranational uneven spatial development are equally instructive. The dependency perspective was developed as a response to modernization theory in order to explain the effect of imperialism on a global scale. Massey, however, argues that it is a fallacy to "simply transplant" these models "to a lower level of spatial disaggregation." The interrelationships among nation states within world imperialism cannot be equated with interregional relations within a nation. In so doing, we ignore social divisions of territory and socially different types of territorial division.[75] In particular, we eliminate the role of national politics and policies and the state in the creation of uneven spatial development.

Clow has criticized the dependency literature on Maritime underdevelopment precisely on this point. He points to the detailed empirical work of revisionist historians such as Acheson and Forbes to demonstate that politics, beginning with Confederation and the National Policy, profoundly influenced Maritime underdevelopment. "The options for Maritime development were narrowed and channelled by the political fact" of Confederation and the National Policy, which "crystallized around rival strategies of economic development."[76] By the 1920s, the Maritimes had been effectively "deindustrialized" and suffered from the related maladies of depopulation and the loss of political power.[77]

The work on Maritime deindustrialization suggests a quite different perspective on regional development than that provided by centre-periphery models and dependency theory, both of which tend to assume that once a core-periphery structure is established it is resistant to change. Instead, the experience of the Maritime provinces demonstrates that as capitalists and governments shift their developmental strategies to correspond to the changing international political economy and to internal political pressures, certain localities for accumulation are favoured over others. As suggested by Innis and Fowke, each phase of accumulation tends to have its own geography, distinct from the geography of earlier phases. As a result, "the existing pattern of regions at any time is the result of the overlaying of these various phases of accumulation."[78] Capital, population, and political power also shift, but the structure is not immutable. Thriving industrial centres are deindustrialized by shifts in developmental strategies, a point that is currently being argued by opponents of free trade with the United States.

Revisionist Maritime historiography has begun to chart the interaction between politics, policy, and regionalism, but it remains largely a liberal history, which discounts the role of social classes in human agency. The conceptual priority given to class analysis, more than anything else, distinguishes the new political economy from the old. And it is precisely the historical coincidence of space, class, and politics that informs some of the most notable contributions of the new political economy to the study of regionalism. Several studies have appeared in recent years that examine the efforts of various coalitions of provincial élites and business interests to implement provincially based developmental strategies.

Nelles was one of the first to examine the class bases of provincialism, although, as we have seen, this theme also runs through the work of Innis. In *The Politics of Development*, he describes how, at the turn of the century, Ontario business interests, responding to American demand for energy and raw materials and unfavourable federal policies, joined in a coalition with political actors to engage in province-building. They pursued a combination of policies designed to promote a "manufacturing condition" and, thereby, ensured limited industrial diversification within the province.[79]

As Nelles demonstrates, Ontario's elites were the first to use the provincial state to construct regional development policies in response to continental and national pressures. Attempts by provincial governments, especially in the resource-rich provinces, to foster capital accumulation and economic diversification have accelerated since 1945 and have stimulated a number of important studies in the "provincialist" stream of the new political economy. Echoing the concerns of Innis, for example, Stevenson has argued that provincial governments have established close relations with resource capital and that federal-provincial conflict in Canada is an expression of conflict between competing fractions of the bourgeoisie.[80] Similarly, Marchak has explored how the pull of the international market, especially the United States, has shaped class conflict in British Columbia and the policies of the provincial government in periods of growth and decline.[81] Richards and Pratt, examining prairie capitalism, grant the provincial governments of Saskatchewan and Alberta more autonomy from resource capital than others working in this genre. They argue that the relationship between the provincial state elite and foreign capital changes over time, from dependence to interdependence, as provincial officials move up what they term a "learning curve" of skills, information, and expertise.[82] Finally, Coleman has examined the independence movement in Quebec as a shifting coalition of class forces that has promoted the continued integration of Quebec into the continental economy and the growth of an indigenous capitalist class.[83]

We cannot hope to survey the richness of this research here, but it does highlight one aspect of the spatial dimension of Canadian politics that has become increasingly evident over the past three decades, namely, the conflict between provincial and federal economic development strategies. In many ways this work reflects Innis, in its concern with resource production, continental integration, and the resulting political forms. This is, nonetheless, only one dimension of spatial politics experienced in Canada over the past century. The nation-state, sub-central units of government, and electoral politics are all organized around territory. Any one of these may be a vehicle for territorial conflict when classes or fractions of the same class centred disproportionately in one space bear the costs of a particular development strategy or wish to use political mechanisms to pursue alternative strategies.

Those working within the provincialist tradition therefore should be particularly cautious not to interpret the specifically conjunctural elements of the last few decades as being immune from the forces of history. The recent experiences of provincial governments, in fact, provide students of the political economy of regionalism with a number of important lessons. First, provincial developmental strategies are created within the contexts of national developmental policy and the international political economy and thus are vunerable to change or failure when conditions at either of the other two levels shift. As Coleman argues in this volume, the federal government should not be discounted in the analysis of provincialism. Second, while an analysis of the class forces and political coalitions behind regional initiatives is essential, these coalitions are temporal. Local capital will behave just like foreign capital when the locations for accumulation shift in space. Finally, while recognizing the apparent movement to province-building in the past two decades, we should not imbue provincial governments with excessive powers or consider them in isolation. The growth of provincial bureaucracies and their expertise is real, but their powers to effect change independent of the economic and political forces around them is limited, especially in a laissez-faire environment. The ability to break out of past accumulation patterns and construct a new geography requires a broader political base than a tacit coalition between regional capital and bourgeois political parties dedicated to creating favourable investment climates. It also requires more radical state developmental strategies than partnership with the private sector.

CONCLUSION

Both the old and the new political economies have tended to be centre-focused in both their theoretical and their empirical orientations. Nevertheless, a great deal can be learned about the Canadian political economy by looking inward from the margins rather than looking outward from the centre. As we have seen, the conceptual problems inherent in a regionally focused political economy are numerous and challenging. I have attempted to show that the early political economy school offers many insights into how considerations about space become interwoven into a social fabric. This indigenous tradition of scholarship argues that the spatial dimension of the Canadian political economy centres on questions of uneven development, is explicitly relational, and has unstable boundaries that shift in conjunction with national economic development strategies, themselves created in response to internal political pressures and the international economic environment. The state, in other words, is a key actor in what we shall term "the political creation of regions." A few political economists, particularly in the Altantic provinces, have begun to explore the relationship between politics and uneven development. It remains the task of a new generation, many of whom are centre-focused and -educated, to become sensitive to this persistent and fundamental fact of Canadian political economy.

NOTES

1 Elkins and Simeon, eds., *Small Worlds*, viii.
2 Westfall, "On the Concept of Region," 3. This insightful essay is valuable reading for all interested in this topic.
3 See, for example, Clow, "Politics and Uneven Capitalist Development"; Sacouman, "The 'Peripheral' Maritimes."
4 See Westfall, "The Concept of Region," 6.
5 See Mathews, *The Creation of Regional Dependency*, chap. 1.
6 Garth Stevenson, "Canadian Regionalism," 17.
7 Ibid., 16.
8 See Matthews, *Regional Dependency*, 22.
9 See Breton, "Regionalism in Canada," 59.
10 Matthews, *Regional Dependency*, 19 (emphasis added).

11 See Westfall, "The Concept of Region," 7–10; Gore, *Regions in Question*, 9–10.
12 See Westfall, "The Concept of Region," 7–8.
13 Elkins and Simeon, eds., *Small Worlds*, xi–xii; Breton, "Regionalism"; Smiley, *The Federal Condition*, chap. 1.
14 See Brodie, *The Political Economy of Regionalism*.
15 See Westfall, "The Concept of Region," 8. Students can find many examples of cultural determinism in the lierature on Canadian regionalism. One of the most obvious is the Report of the Task Force on National Unity (Hull: Supply and Services, 1979), pp. 24–31.
16 See Lithwick, "Is Federalism Good for Regionalism?"
17 Gore, *Regions*, 10; see Westfall, "The Concept of Region," 8.
18 See Holland, *Capital vs the Regions*; Barrett, "Perspectives on Dependency," 273.
19 Courchene's work is an example of this genre. See "Avenues for Adjustment."
20 See, for example, G. Kealey et al, "Canada's Eastern Question," 37.
21 Most often cited as evidence of determinism is Innis, *The Fur Trade in Canada*, 392, beginning: "The present Dominion emerged not in spite of geography but because of it." Also see Innis, "The Economic Development of Canada," 670.
22 For a discussion see Clement and Drache, *A Practical Guide*, 28–30: also Neil, "The Passing of Canadian Economic History," 73.
23 Economic Council of Canada, *Living Together*, 23.
24 Pomfret, *The Economic Development of Canada*, 33.
25 See Carl Berger, *The Writing of Canadian History*, 92.
26 Innis, "The Teaching of Economic History," 10.
27 See ibid., 85.
28 See Drache, "Harold Innis and Canadian Capitalist Development," 39; Marx, *Grundrisse*, 740.
29 See Carl Berger, *Writing*, 91.
30 Innis, *Empire and Communications*, 5; Innis, *The Fur Trade*, 385.
31 Westfall, "The Ambivalent Verdict," 48.
32 Innis, *The Cod Fisheries*, 490. I would like to thank Glen Williams for helping me develop this point.
33 Innis, *Essays*, 122.
34 Innis, *The Fur Trade*, 388.
35 Innis, *A History of the Canadian Pacific Railway*, 290–4, as cited in Carl Berger, *Writing*, 88.
36 See Westfall, "Ambivalent Verdict," 48; see also Innis's condemnation of the Rowell-Sirois Report in Review.
37 Innis, *Essays*, 396.
38 See ibid., 370.
39 See Garth Stevenson, *Unfulfilled Union*.
40 Innis, *Essays*, 396.
41 This is essentially the argument of Gibbons in *Prairie Politics and Society*, chap. 1.

42 See Carl Berger, *Writing*, 98.
43 Ibid., 102.
44 My use of "hinterlanders" is more open than that of Drache and Clement, who include Macpherson and Morton in what they call the post-Innisian stream in *Practical Guide*, 20-3.
45 Ibid., 20.
46 See Smiley, "Canada and the Quest for a National Policy," 43.
47 House, "The Mouse That Roars," 182; see also Drache, "Crisis."
48 Macpherson, *Democracy in Alberta*.
49 See Mallory, *Social Credit and the Federal Power*.
50 See W.L. Morton, *The Progressive Party*.
51 See Gore, *Regions*, 191.
52 Westfall, "The Concept of Region," 9.
53 Ibid.
54 See Phillips, "The Hinterland Perspectives," 77.
55 As quote in ibid. from Fowke, *Canadian Agricultural Policy*.
56 Drache, for example, argues that the Canadian state is autonomous in neither a relative nor an absolute sense. See Drache, "Harold Innis and Canadian Capitalist Development," 56.
57 Fowke, "THe National Policy," 272.
58 Ibid., 274.
59 Ibid., 272; see Phillips, "Hinterland Perspective," 81.
60 Fowke, "National Policy," 278.
61 Smiley, "Canada and the Quest"; Brodie, *Political Economy*.
62 Drache and Clement, *Practical Guide*, 18.
63 See, for example, Clow, "Politics"; Brym and Sacouman, eds., *Underdevelopment*; and *Canadian Review of Sociology and Anthropology* (Aug. 1980).
64 L.G. Barrett, "Perspectives," 277.
65 See Archibald, "Atlantic Regional Underdevelopment."
66 For example, see Acheson, "The National Policy."
67 Veltmeyer, "Capitalist Underdevelopment."
68 See Sacouman, "Semi-proletarianization."
69 See Clement, "A Political Economy of Regionalism."
70 Clement, "Regionalism as Uneven Development."
71 Ibid.
72 See Glen Williams, "Centre-Margin Dependency."
73 See Gore, *Regions*, 198.
74 See Webber, "Agglomeration," 4.
75 Massey, "Regionalism."
76 Clow, "Politics," 124, 125.
77 For a description of Maritime deindustrialization see Acheson, "The National Policy"; Forbes, *The Maritime Rights Movement*; Alexander, *Atlantic Canada and Confederation*.

78 Webber, "Agglomeration," 5.
79 See Nelles, *The Politics of Development*.
80 Garth Stevenson, *Unfulfilled Union*.
81 See Marchak, "Rise and Fall."
82 Richards and Pratt, *Prairie Capitalism*.
83 Coleman, *The Independence Movement*.

CHAPTER EIGHT

The Political Economy of Quebec

William D. Coleman

Why does a book on the new Canadian political economy have a chapter treating Quebec and not one on any other province? Quebec exists in Canada not only as one province in ten but also as a regional homeland for a distinctive national community, the nationalité québécoise. Discrimination, subjugation, and harsh oppression of the members of this community have occurred regularly in the history of Canada. This repression has evolved in tandem with the rise to dominance of the capitalist mode of production and has continued through the subsequent phases of capitalist development. A full understanding of Canadian capitalism requires the analysis of the relationship between class conflict and the nationalist movement based in Quebec. This movement was sufficiently strong as recently as a decade ago to pose the most serious threat to the legitimacy of the Canadian state and the hegemony of the Canadian bourgeoisie since the labour unrest following the First World War. The movement forced the political mobilization of big capital in a way seldom seen in Canadian politics in an effort to win in the referendum on sovereignty-association in May 1980. The reinforcing ties between nation and class in Quebec pose central questions for analysis in radical political economy.

According to Patricia Marchak, political economy is "the study of power derived from or contingent on a system of property rights; the historical development of power relationships; and the cultural and social embodiments of them.[1] Of particular importance in capitalist society are property rights related to the ownership of the means and objects of labour. Yet these same rights institute a relationship between capitalists and workers legitimized by the ideological form of individual freedom. A given worker enters into a contract with an employer to sell labour power, not himself or herself. The reproduction of capitalist relations of production depends both on individual men and women selling their labour power and on their "voluntarily" reproducing the species. Since capitalists do not own workers and their families, they rely on ideological beliefs and state policies to encourage a supply of workers who are healthy, properly socialized, and willing to work for a wage. Women are doubly implicated in the power relationships of capitalism. On the one side, they are workers and subject to class domination. On the other side, they carry and nurture babies and are expected to socialize the young in relations of patriarchal domination. Political economy, when sensitive to the issues of patriarchy, recognizes that all classes are characterized by gender and that gender conflicts are fundamental to struggles between as well as within classes.

What is distinctive about the case of Quebec when put under this prism is the degree to which both class and gender relations and struggles are overdetermined by nationalism and national/ethnic conflict. The relationship between the dynamic of class conflict and the struggle for national self-determination has occupied political economy in Quebec since the early 1920s and continues to pose difficult theoretical and investigative problems. The questions are evident. What is the relation between class conflict and the struggle for national self-determination? Does the latter take precedence over the former, or not? What role can be played by the provincial government? Is it a facilitator of national development, an agent of capital against labour, or an increasingly bureaucratized oppressor of the disadvantaged? What is the relationship between the national struggle and the women's movement? Does the fight against patriarchy and the economic oppression of women require first a resolution of the national question? Or should the feminist cause be addressed autonomously from nationalist struggles? What are we to make of the supposed rise of a new francophone capitalist fraction, so much celebrated in the bourgeois media? Is this the missing link in the necessary class alliance required for realizing the national aspirations of the francophone Québécois? Has the revolution in Quebec's capitalist class been as dramatic as it is often portrayed by pundits and politicians alike?

Such questions cannot be resolved in this chapter. Nevertheless they do provide an indication of the theoretical and empirical issues that the new political economy has sought to address in the study of Quebec. The consideration of these complex interrelationships among class, gender, and nation provides the common thread to the review and analysis of the political economy of Quebec that follows in this chapter. First, we review political economy analysis in Quebec prior to 1960. Second, themes and debates in more contemporary political economy are analysed, including relations between class and nation; state and nation; gender and nation; and party, class, and language policy. Third, we preview issues for further research: the rise of the francophone bourgeoisie and the future of Quebec nationalism.

POLITICAL ECONOMY IN QUEBEC TO 1960

As in most other aspects of social life, Quebec both shared in certain currents of thinking in English Canada and developed its own distinctive political economy tradition as well. In 1907, the government of Quebec established the Ecole des hautes études commerciales (HEC) in Montreal.[2] The school was charged with educating individuals who, it was hoped, might take over the management of business in the province. This nationalist objective and the support of francophone business organizations such as the Chambre de Commerce du District de Montréal helped propel scholars based at the HEC to develop a pragmatic, liberal, yet nationalist analysis of political economy. Edouard Montpetit, who began the first course in economics at HEC in 1910, which was to continue for 35 years, was the modern-day founder of this school of thinking.[3] His successor as dean of the school, Esdras Minville, was particularly prolific as a writer. The thought that has emerged from Minville and his associates has been described as "rather inductive, empirical, clearly interventionist and nationalist."[4]

Distinctive to the HEC tradition of Montpetit, Minville, and such students as François-Albert Angers was a constant tension between an almost virulent liberalism about employer-employee relations and a conservative attachment to traditional French-Canadian rural values on the one side and the promotion of state intervention to further the economic development of *la nation* on the other. Scholars at the HEC also have prided themselves on their involvement in policy formation. Minville and Angers contributed regularly to the Semaines sociales, the annual seminars on Catholic social thought put on for elites by the Jesuit Ecole sociale populaire. They also served as advisers to the Chambre de Commerce in Montreal when it became a strong voice articulating the interests of small francophone capitalists in the late 1940s and the 1950s. Minville chaired a conference on education in 1958 that gave the initial push to the educational reform of the early 1960s and served on the Conseil d'orientation économique which guided the Lesage government at the height of the Quiet Revolution. Prominent graduates of the school have continued the tradition of social involvement into the present day. Roland Parenteau played a leading role in state planning in the 1960s. Jacques Parizeau advised Quebec governments on economic policy over the course of the same decade and then went on to have a definitive influence on the economic thinking of the Parti québécois, where he was joined by other graduates, such as Pierre Harvey.

Less unique to Quebec were the writings on political economy by Albert Faucher and Maurice Lamontagne. Based at Laval, Faucher, who had studied under Innis, and Lamontagne also were willing to countenance state intervention, but not for nationalistic reasons like the Montreal school. Rather, they inherited from Innis and Keynes scepticism about the self-regulatory abilities of markets and saw the need for state action to correct for such structural weaknesses.[5] Such predispositions pushed these scholars to orient themselves more toward the federal government than was the case for the nationalists from the HEC.[6]

Whereas the writers at the HEC and Laval had their greatest influence in practical politics, Stanley Ryerson had more influence on those in the new political economy.[7] Ryerson sought consistently to place the struggles of French Canadians in Quebec in the larger context of capitalist development. He argued that the rebellions of 1837–8 should be understood as "bourgeois democratic" struggles linked to the arrival of industrial capitalism. Similarly, he suggested that the inferior economic position of French Canadians was more than the product of francophobia on the part of anglophones – a natural outcome of the process establishing a national industrial bourgeoisie. He worked with others to write the forgotten history of the development of the Quebec working class in the late nineteenth century. This project in itself reminded scholars of the complexity of Quebec society and helped political economists move beyond rather simplistic, nationalistic renderings of political struggles in the province. In raising questions about the relationship between class and nation in a historical perspective, Ryerson has contributed greatly to more recent political economy analysis of Quebec.

THE NEW POLITICAL ECONOMY

Analysts of Quebec society who might be loosely gathered under the umbrella of new political economy share one basic position, despite numerous other differences: the national struggle of the Québécois must be understood in the broader context of the development of capitalism in Canada and thus as a part of class and gender conflict. The national question neither supersedes nor runs parallel but is autonomous from class and gender struggles. This objective moves analysis beyond the Quebec-centred approach of the HEC school and accepts Ryerson's suggestion that study take more systematic account of the national and international development of capital.

Nonetheless, the task is difficult for political economy, as the following key questions would suggest. (1) Does the national struggle for self-determination override class conflict, does it run parallel to but autonomous from it, or is national alienation and struggle one dimension of the larger pattern of class conflict in Canada? (2) Is the Quebec state an arm of the Canadian capitalist state or sufficiently autonomous to lead a nationalist and socialist challenge to that state? (3) In the confrontation of patriarchy in Quebec society, what weight should be given in practice by women to autonomous collective action and the struggle for national self-determination respectively? (4) Is the Parti québécois the instrument of a bourgeoisie québécoise or the liberation instrument for the working class and the petite bourgeoisie?

(5) Do global policies on language facilitate the integration of the Québécois into North American capitalism, or do they represent a step toward national liberation? These questions are all inter-related but can help us organize this discussion of the new political economy of Quebec.

Its basic proposition and related questions are the fruits of a decade and a half of study and debate. Within the universities, progressive intellectuals had begun with a rather different basic premiss: "Quebec is the site of a nationality question – the so-called national question – upon which all socio-political analysis must give priority to its articulation."[8] Daniel Salée writes that the tendency to give priority to the national question characterized the work of sociologists such as Marcel Rioux and Fernand Dumont who viewed Quebec history through the historical manifestations of nationalism and the cultural uniqueness of the Québécois. He adds that the so-called modernist writers who emphasized the importance of a new middle class during the Quiet Revolution simplify too much the social order and thus share in the nationalist priorities of the cultural school. Nationalist questions also tended to dominate Marxist writings until the mid-1970s.[9]

Outside the universities, the trade union movement began to develop its own class-based analyses of Quebec society. Marcel Pépin, who became the president of the Confederation of National Trade Unions (CNTU) in 1965, called for a new vision of society and suggested that the trade unions open their own front for challenging and criticizing existing social structures. This campaign culminated in the issuing of manifestos by each of the three major trade union organizations in 1970-1.[10] Each of these documents departed from radical academic analyses of Quebec society by emphasizing the class struggle and seeking to interpret the need for political sovereignty in that context. This line of thinking and analysis was adopted more and more by radical political economists following the victory of the Parti québécois (PQ) in 1976. The meaning of the PQ victory and the various constraints that the party felt in exercising political power raised a series of questions about the role of the state in capitalist society and the relationship between the national struggle and socialism. Consequently, "the national question seemed to be interiorized and posed less and less as the dominant explanatory factor of reality."[11]

Looking retrospectively over many of these developments in the analysis of Quebec society, Arnaud Sales poses the question that summarizes well the agenda for the new political economy in Quebec:

Faced with a powerful integrating process among economies at the centre, and between central and peripheral economies, faced with the concentration and centralization of capital and power, faced finally with the process of transnationalization which touches equally institutions as well as numerous more informal aspects of social life, is it still possible to speak of national economic sovereignty? How does one manage the tension between this integrating process on the economic plane and a movement of political liberation (the quest for sovereignty) aiming to assure cultural and linguistic security as well as control of the economic levers of the state and more generally a new organization of economic power?[12]

Posing such a question forces the analysis of Quebec into a more global context and has led to a resurgence in the use of the concept of regionalism. Quebec is viewed as a region within Canada rather than as one distinct nation counterposed to another, that of English Canada. By stressing the ties that bind Quebec's economy to that of the rest of North America in particular and that restrain the actions of the provincial government, a more global and balanced understanding of the exercise of political and economic power may be realized. Each of the sections that follows traces the implications of such a change in perspective for the five key questions noted above.

Class and Nation

Until recently, analysts of Quebec society have sought an identity between class and nation and tended to stress as a consequence the primacy of national questions over class struggles. The earliest and most transparent example involved the elaboration of the concept of an "ethnic class" by Dofny and Rioux. In their view, the position of francophone Québécois as an ethnic group created such a powerful cultural identity and shared experience resulting from domination that this ethnicity overrode class differences.[13] Another prominent example is the emphasis on the new middle class by authors such as Guindon, Taylor and McRoberts, and Posgate.[14] The national aspirations of the francophone Québécois are articulated by this class as it seeks to control and use the levers of the provincial government in Quebec, the Etat québécois. My own work complicates this theme somewhat by arguing that the Quiet Revolution was led by a coalition of classes, including the traditional petite bourgeoisie, the non-monopoly francophone bourgeoisie, and organized labour.[15] Still the emphasis was on a class or set of classes indigenous to Quebec's francophone society articulating national aspirations. Each approach looked at Quebec society as autonomous from the rest of Canada and the nationalist struggle as a phenomenon that could be understood through an analysis of class forces within the francophone community alone.

In retrospect, the stress on homogeneity of class interests associated with such studies and on the autonomy of the francophone community in Quebec may be the product of a particular conjuncture. The Quebec of the early 1960s, for reasons I have discussed elsewhere, witnessed a short period of convergence of political interests among several classes.[16] This convergence may have led those analysing Quebec society to overestimate the durability of this unity of class forces and the autonomous strength of the political community that resulted. The identity relation between class and nation gradually came into question with the development of working-class reflection on the national struggle. Increasingly studies emphasized the complexity of class forces, both within the francophone community and more broadly within Canada. Particularly instrumental in this process of reflection was the wide-ranging study by Bourque and Legaré published in 1979.[17] As this complexity became better understood, the long-standing basic assumption about the class-nation relation came into question, namely, the primacy of nation over class.

It is difficult to reconstruct fully the process through which the primacy of national questions came into doubt. Two strands of analysis appear important. First, there was the debate over the character of the expanding francophone bourgeoisie. The principal protagonists in this debate were Pierre Fournier and Jorge Niosi.[18] They agreed that a significant big and medium francophone bourgeoisie had emerged in the 1970s and 1980s but disagreed on its definition and autonomy from the Canadian bourgeoisie writ large. Niosi suggested that the new bourgeoisie was oriented to pan-Canadian markets and hence growth within the broad context of the Canadian economy. Such an orientation explained, in his view, the fiercely federalist position of members of this class. Fournier countered that the new class was rooted firmly in Quebec's regional economy. Its markets were provincial, its suppliers were drawn overwhelmingly from within the province, and its financial support system (réseau financier) was Quebec-based. This bourgeoisie québécoise competed directly with the big Canadian bourgeoisie and was given cohesion and defended by the provincial government, particularly when that government was led by the Parti québécois.

Resolving the debate has not been easy. Niosi has continued his research into the nature of the Canadian capitalist class, noting a significant network of linkages between French- and English-speaking capital. I have found that even smaller, regionally oriented francophone firms belong to and participate in pan-Canadian business associations.[19] Yet the small regional firms described by Fournier appear to be oriented highly to the Quebec region and were targeted for special treatment by the Parti québécois when it was in power. In addition, some disputes within the Canadian capitalist class suggest that established anglophone firms have at time resisted francophone incursion (Power v. Argus, Campeau v. Royal Trust, Caisse de dépôt v. CP Enterprises).

More important are the lessons to be drawn from the debate.[20] The Quebec bourgeoisie cannot be viewed as an entity totally independent from the Canadian capitalist class, and thus analysis of it must take account of the larger dynamics of the latter. Yet it is also a mistake to conceive of the Quebec bourgeoisie as completely integrated into the Canadian capitalist class, without any capacity to compete with it or to act autonomously. Both of these propositions represent simplifications that ultimately distort the reality of class politics in Canada.

Another discussion of importance focused on social class relates to the new middle class. Analysis of this class had emphasized its central catalysing role in the nationalist movement and the Quiet Revolution. More recently, Jean-Jacques Simard and Gilbert Renaud have noted that the integration of its members into the provincial state apparatus has placed them in a position of considerable political power.[21] The reforms of the health and social welfare systems, emphasizing rationality, science, and technology, have helped produce a technocratic elite and what Simard has termed a "cybernetic society." Renaud, drawing on the work of Alain Touraine, writes about a "programmed society." Both authors describe the penetration and domination of the daily lives of workers and the disadvantaged by a technocratic and unyielding new middle class. The gulf that has grown between this elite and the popular strata has compromised seriously the capacity of the new middle class to mobilize these others behind its nationalist objectives.

The debates over the relationship between class and nation have pushed political economists to avoid giving nation primacy over class and in some cases to drop the nation as a category altogether. Instead they have moved to conceptualize nationalist alienation in the broader context of class struggle in Canada and to concentrate more on the confrontations between the disadvantaged and a technocratic state. Such a perspective brings them face to face with questions about the nature of the Canadian state.

State and Nation

Analysing national alienation within the context of class conflict raises questions in turn about the relationship between nationalist struggles and the provincial government, usually referred to in nationalist discourse as the Etat québécois. This very terminology suggests two problems that have emerged in political economy in Quebec. First, heavily influenced by the nationalist question, political economy has overemphasized the autonomy of the government of Quebec while failing to take sufficient account of the federal character of the Canadian state. Such an emphasis, in turn, has encouraged a perhaps naïve perception of the Quebec government as a potential agent of liberation for the nation québécoise. Second, fixation on the development of the Quebec state has blinded many analysts to the consequences of the excessive bureaucratization that has come with the state's growth.

Boismenu has reflected at length on the problems created by overplaying the strength of the Quebec government.[22] There results a temptation to simplify class relations at both the provincial and federal levels of government. Regional fractions of the bourgeoisie are seen to use provincial governments for the promotion of their interests, while the big, national bourgeoisie identifies with the federal government. Accordingly, the study of provincial class relations may be inappropriately truncated: "the provincial level of the state is placed in relation to classes more influenced in their composition by provincial territorial boundaries (the non-monopoly bourgeoisie, the *petite* bourgeoisie, the agrarian class), thereby singularly underestimating the principal component of the power bloc – the component that oversees the power structure within the federated state – to wit, the big bourgeoisie."[23] Linked to this tendency is a further problem, what Sales has termed "l'oubli de l'Etat fédéral."[24] In focusing on social classes in the francophone community and on the provincial government, nationalist-inspired political economy has either ignored the federal government or systematically underestimated its importance in Quebec society. On the other side, with the exception of Brunelle and Legaré, it has failed to appreciate the nationalist challenge to the legitimacy of the Canadian state.[25]

Moving to address these problems is not an easy task theoretically and is complicated further by the political context in Quebec. An attempt to study Quebec as one component of Canadian society among several leaves scholars open to the charge of playing into the hands of the federal government and undermining the nationalist struggle. Perhaps the most promising avenue of research is the work on regionalism by Jalbert and Boismenu.[26] Jalbert observes that the Canadian social formation was constituted, like many other capitalist societies, out of a number of pre-existing, more or less disparate social units. The gradual development of the social formation involved the unification of the bourgeoisie from these former colonies. The further expansion of the capitalist mode of production has included the assimilation of non-capitalist production forms and the homogenization of the social relations previously identified with these forms.

Such a process of unification and homogenization did not proceed easily or unopposed. As in all cases of capitalist development, the process worked itself out unevenly in various regions of the country. The particular mix of non-capitalist forms of production and economic sectors in a given region led to the development of regional identities in opposition to the process and thus to various movements of regional resistance. The challenges to the dominance of the big bourgeoisie therefore materialized differently depending on the region, its modes of production, and its history. In the case of Quebec, nationality repeatedly served as an organizing vehicle for the particular constellation of class forces resisting unification and homogenization, whether it be the Action libérale nationale of the 1930s, the Parti libéral du Québec of the early 1960s, or the Parti québécois.

Such an analysis has several implications for the study of the federal régime in Canada. First, these authors bring the federal government more fully into the analysis. For example, Boismenu emphasizes the importance of the Keynesian policies of the federal government and their impact on Quebec in his study of the politics of the 1940s and 1950s. He identifies the resistance to these policies under Duplessis with a class alliance that included American-based resource firms, the heavily francophone middle-sized bourgeoisie, and the agrarian class.[27] In seeking to restrict the advance of Keynesian policies, including social welfare measures, this alliance encouraged the idea of greater power for provincial governments, which, in Quebec, preferred a more classically liberal policy. Hence, Boismenu saw the provincial government as one player among several in a broader struggle within the Canadian bourgeoisie over the extent to which Keynesian macroeconomic policy and the social welfare state should be adopted in Canada.

Such a conceptualization allows for the autonomous action of provincial governments while placing it in a wider social context. These governments can seek to influence the terms of unification and homogenization. Beginning in 1960, the government of Quebec sought systematically to ensure opportunities for the medium-sized bourgeoisie to expand and become full partners in the big bourgeoisie. To further such aims, it has used alternatively public corporations, such as Hydro Québec, targeted fiscal policy, and its own financing institutions, such as the Caisse de dépôt. However, one should not exaggerate the importance of these actions or forget that they represented an attempt to integrate francophone firms further into the national bourgeoisie.

Moreover, as part of the Canadian state, the Quebec government, like all provincial governments, assumes a particular role in managing the labour force and containing working-class opposition. It is not as if the big bourgeoisie has no influence in provincial capitals. The Conseil du Patronat du Québec, which represents most of the large corporations in the province, and the Quebec Division of the Canadian Manufacturers Association are prominent in provincial politics, particularly in labour relations policy. In fact, such comprehensive business associations play a stronger role in integrating the various fractions of the bourgeoisie in Quebec than they do in any other province.[28] The general conflict between labour and capital takes place in all fields of the Canadian state, with provincial governments fracturing class opposition to capital into ten different battlefields and repressing labour unrest.

Viewing the Quebec state as part of the Canadian state is also characteristic of the second critique of state theory in the post-nationalist era: the development of a state-programmed society. As was noted in the discussion of class, writers such as Simard and Renaud have described the extension of technocratic state apparatuses into virtually all aspects of social life. Renaud writes: "Since the Quiet Revolution, the state has not ceased to extend its hold over the lives of citizens. New organizations are born, old ones have been transformed and their powers extended in ways that begin to generate conflict opposing these apparatuses to the populations they seek to domesticate."[29] Behind these observations lies a developing critique of social policy as implemented by both levels of the state.[30] Political economists have drawn on these critiques of state theory and social policy in attempting to account for the rise of new social movements in Quebec.[31] The actions of the state in these policy areas have worked against the development of a communauté nationale.[32] Ironically, the tool of liberation that was to be the state has become the instigator of division and the cause of alienation and despondency.[33]

Gender and Nation

The relationship between gender and nation parallels somewhat that between class and nation. In the first instance, the neo-nationalist discourse of the 1960s provided women with a language to analyse their own oppression;[34] the feminist struggle fused with the nationalist movement. As the nationalist movement developed and its ideology became better articulated, contradictions between the national struggle and women's concerns emerged. Many women still found misogyny a key element of nationalist thought.[35] While the PQ went some distance to resolve these contradictions, it never fully succeeded. Feminist analysis in the 1980s has taken a similar path to class and state analysis: it has broken with nationalist thinking and sought to develop its own categories. (See Bakker in this volume.)

Traditional French-Canadian culture celebrated the family as the microcosm of the nation and stressed the national significance of the mother's role in bearing and rearing children. As late as 1940, Rodrigue Cardinal Villeneuve, archbishop of Quebec, had reiterated these principles in a last-ditch attempt to prevent women from obtaining the vote. He reminded politicians and the faithful of the church's position on the unity and hierarchy of the family with the father as head, lamented the possible exposure of women to the passions of politics, and suggested that the reforms demanded by women in social policy could be obtained by women working in their own organizations on the margins of the political arena.[36] Similarly, the writings by traditional nationalists such as Lionel Groulx contained side by side demands for radical changes in the power of the Quebec state and paeans of praise to la femme traditionnelle canadienne-française.

This cultural role in the old nationalism came under review in the new nationalism of the 1960s, hastened by the arrival of the first wave of the women's liberation movement. The issues raised by this first wave were more cultural and sociological than economic - "it placed sexuality, marriage and the family at the centre, asserted that the long-term transformation of gender relations required sexual autonomy for women, and held that the rootedness of women's oppression in all social institutions required revolutionary transformation."[37] These cultural concerns had a ready affinity with the project of the nationalist movement in the late 1960s, which attempted to define a new cultural identity that was secular, socialist, and nationalist. Upon opening up to criticism most of the guiding principles of traditional French-Canadian culture, such groups naturally attracted feminists, whose project and that of national liberation seemed to be one. Those less committed to the radical change espoused by the women's liberation movement tended to be drawn into the federalist camp. The attempt to temper the pace of reform, in their view, was part and parcel of the struggle against nationalism. Hence, by the early 1970s, there had emerged what Maroney has called the Liberal bloc and the progressive nationalist bloc in the women's movement in Quebec.[38]

The development of autonomous women's organizations, an objective of the women's movement of the 1960s elsewhere, was delayed in Quebec: the national struggle took precedence. However, the women involved in the nationalist movement gradually found themselves confronted with the usual practices of male power and privilege and the persistence of traditional views on women. As Lamoureux has noted, the PQ sought simultaneously to valorize the institution of motherhood and to support women's rights.[39] The feminist movement responded to this ambivalence by reconceptualizing its ideology and by changing its organizational strategy.

Step by step, women moved to establish autonomous organizations within the political parties as well as more radical independent feminist associations. These steps coincided with the arrival of the second wave of feminism, which concentrated more on economic issues such as equal pay for work of equal value and day care. The social base of this second wave differed from the first in drawing from women in the working class, particularly in the trade union movement. Each of the three major trade union organizations in the province had set up committees to study women's issues by the mid-1970s. By 1978, each central had also published reports that pushed beyond workplace equality to demand abortion rights, the socialization of housework, and changes in the oppressive institution of marriage.[40] The trade union base of this second wave, when combined with significant support within the progressive nationalist bloc of the PQ, yielded in the end important advances. The PQ produced in its first government the best legislative framework for working women in Canada, "with the most generous maternity and parental leave provisions and the strictest equal pay provisions."[41] As in the case of the class-nation relation, the trade unions in Quebec played a pivotal role in bringing sex issues out from under the cover of nationalist struggles.

Similar to feminist thought elsewhere in North America, feminists in Quebec have found themselves confronted with a host of questions from different philosophical positions. Answers to these questions are far fewer. The critique of the state-programmed society that has emerged among other political economists has been joined by many feminists. Many of the new social movements examined by Quebec scholars in the 1980s have concerned themselves with feminist issues. The organizations of the women's movement are finding some common ground with these other movements and have entered into ad hoc alliances with them on several issues in recent years.

Party, Class, and Language Policy

Paralleling the debates within the new political economy on the relative primacy of class and gender conflict or national alienation and on the degree of autonomy of the Etat québécois from the Canadian state is a further discussion of the relationship between party, specifically the Parti québécois, and class. On the one side, Bourque and Legaré and Fournier have argued that the PQ exists as the political vehicle of the bourgeoisie québécoise, that bourgeoisie whose accumulation base and language predisposes it to identify with the government of Quebec and to compete with the English-Canadian big bourgeoisie.[42] Fournier writes: "The Parti Québécois is, in fact, a bourgeois party . . . The essential goal of its program is the expansion of the Quebec bourgeoisie at the expense of the Canadian bourgeoisie . . . The aim of the PQ is, thus, to a large extent, 'to make the Quebec bourgeoisie a hegemonic fraction.' "[43]

Such an argument contradicts some of the analysis already presented in this chapter. We have seen that it is difficult to sustain empirically the existence of such a Quebec bourgeoisie. More important, the brief references to the PQ in this chapter thus far suggest an organization that does not look particularly bourgeois. Its program treated economic issues and development in a way that put it well to the left of the New Democratic Party in English Canada. The party made a sufficiently serious attempt to understand and to respond to gender issues to keep the loyalty of all but the most radical feminists into its second government. Its policies on language and culture met with the deep-seated satisfaction of both the new and traditional wings of the petite bourgeoisie. The party espoused a constitutional option that was anathema to the whole bourgeoisie – big, medium, small, French, English, urban, rural, or whatever. Sales draws what must be the obvious conclusion: "It is necessary to recognize . . . that the francophone Quebec bourgeoisie . . . has never adhered to the nationalist project of the Parti québécois, that it has in fact vigorously opposed it, as it has several of its other social and cultural measures. From this point of view, the Parti québécois has never to this day been the preferred political vector of the bourgeoisie, be it monopoly, non-monopoly, francophone or anglophone."[44]

It is essential in this case to distinguish the social base of a political party and the internal processes leading to the construction of a party program from the actual exercise of state power. In neither case does a political party normally serve the interest of just one class. As a political party, the PQ served as the organizing vehicle for a coalition of interests that drew from a wide social base, including the petite bourgeoisie, organized labour, intellectuals, and feminists. One of its most distinctive attributes was the prominent place of intellectuals in its executive structures. Nor was the party simply a receptacle for the demands of these various groups. It possessed an intensive organizational life of its own, shaping and mobilizing militants from this diverse social base into a political movement which, in turn, defined successfully the agenda for political debate in the province for over a decade.

This being said, political economists, whether new or old, should not be at all surprised to find that the PQ government catered to the interests of the bourgeoisie upon its election in 1976. As a governing party in a capitalist society with liberal democratic institutions which was committed to the elimination of neither capitalism nor liberal democracy, it rules within the constraints of the capitalist state. Those constraints included, of course, those associated with being a component of a broader federated state, a point discussed above. Thus the PQ as government sought to ensure the continuity and expansion of the accumulation process in Quebec. It was conscious of the need to maintain and develop the potential of the material and human resources in its territory and to ensure that capital had an ample supply of co-operative labour power. In the pursuit of these basic goals of any capitalist state, it favoured the interests of capital over labour, thereby appearing to undermine its own social base as a political party.

To leave off the analysis here would, of course, be too simple. Similarly, to argue, as is the wont of Fournier, Bourque, and Legaré, that the PQ favoured one fraction of the bourgeoisie, the non-monopoly francophone Quebec bourgeoisie, at the expense of other fractions flies in the face of the facts. There is little doubt that the PQ devised policies designed to strengthen small and medium-sized firms, most of which are francophone. It targeted for special support the co-operative sector, sought to marshal financial resources under the jurisdiction of the state (the Caisse de dépôt) in favour of co-operatives and smaller firms, and built up, wherever possible, publicly owned firms. The same government, however, pumped millions of dollars into textiles and clothing, aluminum and pulp and paper, all sectors controlled principally by non-francophones. It favoured General Motors over a francophone firm for a major government contract to manufacture buses. It did not alter the basic investment strategy of the Caisse de dépôt which involved purchasing equity in large English-Canadian corporations. Over 65 per cent of the equity holdings of the Caisse were concentrated in 25 corporations, only two of which, Brascade and Provigo, generated the major part of their earnings in Quebec.[45]

Resolving the analytical problem of the relative impact of the social base of a political party within the constraints of the capitalist state is not an easy task. Elsewhere, I have suggested the use of distance from the accumulation process as a conceptual guide.[46] The closer the policy at hand is to the central factors in capital accumulation, the less freedom a party will have to manoeuvre as a government and the more it will respond to the dominant fractions of the capitalist class. As policies become less central to capital accumulation, the more freedom a party will have to respond to the specific concerns of its social base. One would expect this freedom to vary over time. In times of prosperity, parties will be more free to consider issues less central to the accumulation process than they will be in times of recession. Thus the PQ will have had less freedom to act on its own program during its second government, which coincided with the recession of the early 1980s, than it did in its first.[47]

The implementation of language policy illustrates well these variable constraints. On the broad plane, the language policy of the PQ contained in the French Language Charter continued the approach favoured by the Parti libéral in its Official Language Act of 1974.[48] The policy sought to integrate better the English-Canadian and American fractions of the bourgeoisie into Quebec society and served thereby to legitimate capitalism at a time when it was being attacked vigorously by the labour movement. When the PQ brought forth its first version of the policy in the form of Bill 1 in the spring of 1977, it was strongly attacked by all wings of the bourgeois class in the province. In the face of this attack, the party retreated in a number of areas of the policy when it reissued the legislation under a new guise as Bill 101. Systematic analysis of this process of retreat shows that the party changed the bill to suit the wishes of the bourgeois class primarily in areas closest to the accumulation process: the francization of communication in individual firms, the regulation of head offices, and the institutionalization of French as the language of work. Areas further away, such as the language practices of anglophone public institutions, including hospitals, municipal councils, and school boards, were left unchanged and thereby conformed rather well with the demands of the party base. Since the promulgation of the Canadian Charter of Rights and Freedoms, even these measures have been brought closer to the wishes of the francophone and anglophone fractions of the bourgeois class through the entrenchment of bilingualism.

Nor should one assume that the social base of a party is a given. On the one side, the PQ found that as it acted within the constraints of the capitalist state it gradually alienated the more radical elements of the working class. On the other side, the party sought to broaden its base to include elements of the capitalist class through a series of economic summits organized at the level of the macro-economy and of individual sectors.[49] These summits, when combined with the various policies favouring medium and small capital, were expected to produce a broad coalition in favour of political sovereignty. As is now obvious, the party failed in this regard. Nonetheless, the analysis of this failure and more wide-ranging analysis of the Parti québécois in power have advanced theoretical thinking on political parties in Canadian political economy.

QUESTIONS FOR THE FUTURE

I have sought to conduct this survey of the political economy of Quebec at two levels. First, what has political economy taught us about national alienation, gender and class conflict in Quebec society? Second, what are the important theoretical issues that have been raised in the context of political economy writing on Quebec, and how have these issues been resolved? I shall first reflect on two more practical issues for further research – the further integration of Quebec into the North American economy, and the dissolution of a nationalist progressive bloc. I shall then turn to some theoretical issues.

Any review of the past three decades in Quebec reveals a wholesale change in state organization from a rather clientelistic system to one that is highly bureaucratized and rationalized in the Weberian sense. A parallel series of changes in state policy at the provincial level affecting economic development, education, social welfare, culture, and language have furthered significantly the integration of Quebec society into the mainstream of North American capitalism. What remains unclear at this point is what the ultimate consequences of these changes will be in Quebec society. As Sales asks: "Will we conserve this Québécois sensitivity which has known how to give a direction to social change in a way that forces back dependency and subordination?"[50]

The history of this process of integration suggests that conserving such sensitivity will be difficult. One of the most obvious changes in Quebec over the past three decades is the emergence of a rather more vibrant and expansive francophone bourgeoisie. It is much easier to identify now a number of major francophone firms that have become a force in Canadian capitalism. These firms are supported by a financial network that includes the Mouvement Desjardins, the National Bank of Canada, the Caisse de dépôt, and the Laurentian Group. This network represents the culmination of an intensive process of centralization and concentration of finance capital that began in the early 1960s. It provides a source of capital for expansion independent of the English-Canadian chartered banks, and its members have been leaders among francophone firms in expanding outside Quebec's boundaries.

However, we must not overestimate the strength of this fraction. The most recent comprehensive study by Raynauld and Vaillancourt reminds us that changes in class structures may not occur as quickly as the mass media might suggest. They show that francophone firms have made advances in all sectors of manufacturing (save leather goods) and in construction, resources, and services since 1961. Francophones have thus improved on a traditionally weak position.[51] But the same data show that francophones are responsible for 12.8 per cent of the value added in mining, 22.3 per cent in manufacturing, 31.9 per cent in forestry, 42.2 per cent in transportation and communications, 44.8 per cent in the financial sector, 51 per cent in retail and wholesale trade, and 76.2 per cent in construction.[52] In none of these major economic divisions, then, do francophones control an amount of economic activity equivalent to their proportion of Quebec's population (81 per cent). Within the major English-Canadian and American firms, francophones now hold the majority of managerial positions. However, in many firms, a kind of division of labour has developed where francophones manage regional activities while anglophones take care of matters on the national plane.[53] The economic terrain, then, is still heavily tilled by English Canadians and Americans.

There is reason to be concerned that this francophone class will not show the sensitivity to subordination and dependence hoped for by Sales. Within the francophone community, it has been somewhat isolated from other social classes. Its natural instincts thus far on most issues have been to look to construct alliances with other fractions of the bourgeoisie rather than with other francophones. These alliances have been formed in both business associations and political parties. Perhaps these inclinations will change if the class finds itself blocked in expanding in English Canada. To date, however, there has been little evidence of such resistance.

The Quebec state itself over the past three decades has anchored a certain resistance to subordination and dependence but seems increasingly less inclined to continue in this role. Part of this reluctance comes from its own fiscal crisis. The government's willingness to intervene to shore up the economy and to act on unemployment declined precipitously with the onset of recession in the early 1980s. In 1982 and 1983, it passed legislation that cut back heavily the salaries and benefits of public-sector employees, restricted the collective bargaining process, and arbitrarily determined conditions of work for most public employees. In its new economic plan published in 1979, *Bâtir le Québec*, and its updates in 1982 and 1985, the PQ government stated explicitly its intention to rely on the private sector to resolve the province's difficulties.

The constitutional solution of 1981 gave no new powers to the government of Quebec. Rather, the new Charter of Rights, in combination with Quebec's own charter, opened the way in the courts for the "Canadianization" of Bill 101. Despite the vagaries of the "distinct society" clause in the Meech Lake agreement of 1987, the Canadianization trend was continued. What is more, Meech Lake transfers from democratically elected MNAs and

MPs to conservative justices all the important decisions relating to protection of language and culture and the interplay between English-Canadian and Québécois concerns.

If the process of integration is the first important development to be noted, the dissolution of a nationalist progressive bloc is a second. This bloc, composed of members of the traditional and new wings of the petite bourgeoisie, organized labour, and feminists, has come apart in the 1980s. The combination of the defeat in the referendum, the repressive labour legislation of the second PQ government and the triumph in the November 1981 constitutional accord of the bourgeois view of a bilingual, capitalist Canada with equality of opportunity (but not condition) for all has wreaked havoc on this bloc. Labour has lost its militancy and dynamism and finds itself isolated within the francophone community. To a lesser extent, the same can be said of the feminist movement. Quebec has become a French-speaking society with many cultural communities. This racial and ethnic heterogeneity has never been addressed well by nationalists and is of potentially great importance as the courts are pressed to decide upon what is "distinct" about Quebec society.

The expansiveness of the francophone bourgeoisie, the continued preeminence of the English-Canadian and American fractions, and the centralization and rigor mortis inherent in the constitutional settlement of 1981 may force labour and feminists in Quebec as well as the new social movements to reconsider their political strategy. Both have long traditions of autonomy from their English-Canadian counterparts. Both may no longer be able to act effectively without constructing some links with workers and feminists elsewhere in Canada who too are feeling the effects of provincial cutbacks and the transfer of important decisions on social and labour policy from legislatures to the courts. The retreat from parliamentary democracy very much in evidence on all fronts in Canada represents a serious threat to workers, feminists, and other disadvantaged groups, who have few tools at the best of times for redressing exploitation in a capitalist state.

While our conclusions on the practical, political plane are somewhat pessimistic, the same is not true on the theoretical plane. In working through the problems associated with giving the nationality question pre-eminence over class and gender conflict, important advances have been made by political economy writers in Quebec. The attempt to understand the complex relationships among these factors has led to a critique of our understanding of the Canadian state. Working out the full implications of the federal character of this state and attempting to understand Quebec nationalism in the larger perspective of regionalism in Canada show considerable promise. The comprehensive character of work on Quebec, covering the federal constitution, class conflict, regionalism, and economic structures, is most attractive and of great potential relevance to scholars examining other parts of Canada. To date, with the possible exception of Boismenu's study of Duplessisme and Jalbert's examination of third parties, there has not been sufficient empirical investigation aimed at further elaboration and refinement of what remains still rather abstract theoretical work. When this comes, as it will, the theory of radical political economy will be enriched.

NOTES

The author would like to thank Daniel Salée for his careful reading of an earlier version of this chapter and for his helpful suggestions. Unless indicated otherwise, all quotations in this chapter from French-language articles are translated by the author.

1 Marchak, "Canadian Political Economy," 673.
2 See Falardeau, *The Rise of Social Sciences*, 29.
3 Falardeau notes, however, that Montpetit followed two other social thinkers of the nineteenth century: Etienne Parent and Errol Bouchette. See ibid., 32-4.
4 Paquet, " 'Le fruit dont l'ombre est la saveur,' " 378.
5 See ibid., 379.
6 Paquet notes, however, that the Laval personnel were involved in the large planning exercise in eastern Quebec in the 1960s, BAEQ. Still this program was initiated with considerable federal funding. See ibid., 380.
7 The following discussion owes much to the excellent articles on Ryerson by Gregory Kealey: "Ryerson: Canadian Revolutionary Intellectual" and "Ryerson: Marxist Historian."
8 Salée, "L'analyse socio-politique," 15.
9 Salée cites, as examples the late 1960s journal *Parti pris* as well as Bourque and Laurin-Frenette, "Les classes et l'idéologie nationaliste" and "La structure nationale québécoise."
10 See CNTU, *Ne comptons plus*; QFL, *L'état*; and CEQ *Phase Un*.
11 Salée, "L'analyse socio-politique," 30.
12 Sales, "La construction sociale," 341-2.
13 See Rioux and Dofny, "Les classes sociales," 290-300; and Rioux, "Conscience ethnique."
14 See Guindon, "Social Unrest"; Taylor, "Nationalism"; and McRoberts and Posgate, *Quebec*.
15 See Coleman, *The Independence Movement*. For a critique of my work along these lines, see Bourque, "A propos du mouvement indépendantiste."
16 See Coleman, *The Independence Movement*, 94-9.
17 See Bourque and Legaré, *Le Québec*.
18 The key articles have been translated into English. See Pierre Fournier, "The New Parameters," and Niosi, "The New French Canadian Bourgeoisie."
19 See Coleman, *Business and Politics*, chap. 12.

20 See Sales, "La construction," 348-9.
21 See Simard, *La longue marche*, and Renaud, *A l'ombre du rationalisme*.
22 See Boismenu, "L'état fédératif."
23 Ibid., 52-3.
24 See Sales, "La construction," 351.
25 See Brunelle, *L'état solide*, and Legaré, "Towards a Marxian Theory."
26 See Jalbert, "Régionalisme," and "La question régionale"; Boismenu, *Le Duplessisme*.
27 See Boismenu, *Le Duplessisme*, 114 ff.
28 See Coleman, *Business and Politics*, chap. 5.
29 Renaud, *A l'ombre*, 60.
30 See Pelletier, *De la sécurité sociale*, and related essays in Pierre Fournier, ed. *Capitalisme*.
31 Of particular note here are Godbout, *La participation*, Hamel and Léonard, *Les organisations populaires*.
32 See Salée, "Pour une autopsie," 118-19.
33 For a reading of the despondency of Quebec intellectuals in the post-referendum era, see the articles in *Possibles*, 10: 2 (1986).
34 See Lamoureux, "Nationalism and Feminism" and *Fragments et collages*.
35 See Lamoureux, "Nationalism and Feminism," 55-62.
36 See Francine Fournier, "Les femmes," 347.
37 Maroney, "Feminism at Work," 53.
38 See Maroney, "Contemporary Quebec Feminism," chap. 4.
39 See Lamoureux, "Nationalism and Feminism," 62.
40 See Maroney, "Feminism at Work," 56. The reports were: CNTU, "La lutte des femmes: combat de tous les travailleurs" and "La lutte des femmes: pour le droit au travail social"; CEQ, "Condition féminine"; and QFL, "Femmes et syndiqués." For further discussion of the trade union treatment of feminist demands, see Mona-Josée Gagnon, "Les femmes" and "Les comités syndicaux."
41 Maroney, "Contemporary Quebec Feminism," 442.
42 Bourque and Legaré, *Le Québec*; Bourque, "Class, Nation and the Parti Québécois"; Pierre Fournier, "The New Parameters" and "Le Parti québécois."
43 Pierre Fournier, "New Parameters," 88.
44 Sales, "La construction," 355.
45 See Brooks and Tanguay, "Quebec's Caisse de dépôts."
46 See Coleman, "A Comparative Study."
47 This point is demonstrated well in Alain Gagnon, "A Tranquil Quebec."
48 See Coleman, "From Bill 22 to Bill 101" and *The Independence Movement*, chap. 7.
49 For a discussion, see Tanguay, "Concerted Action."
50 Sales, "La construction," 359.
51 See Raynauld and Vaillancourt, *L'appartenance des entreprises*.
52 See ibid., passim.
53 See Sales and Bélanger, *Décideurs et gestionnaires*.

CHAPTER NINE

A Contested Concept:
The Relative Autonomy of the State

Gregory Albo and Jane Jenson

The relationship between "the state and society" in Canada has been closely observed. Many commentators have suggested that much of Canada's uniqueness resides with the leading role that the state has taken in promoting economic development. Writing in 1929, Frank Underhill went so far as to describe "statism" as a cultural trait: "If we are to look for anything distinctively Canadian then, it must be found in the way in which we have handled social and economic questions which arise in the process of exploiting the resources on our half of the continent . . . One of the hopeful things about Canada is that we have not yet come to this complete despair about our politics, and that enterprises like Ontario Hydro and the National Railways show that we are still capable of using our political machinery for constructive purposes."[1] More recently, Leo Panitch argued that "the Canadian state was never a laissez-faire state and . . . Canadian economists and historians have well recorded this function."[2]

Several distinguishing features are generally invoked to account for the close integration of state and society.[3] The state has been crucial for regulation of trade and production in a dependent economy of production concentrated in export-sensitive sectors. Moreover, since Canadian geography creates great distances between production sites and markets, the state has provided commercial infrastructure and facilitated the financing of large overhead costs. Partly in consequence, there have been close ties between the state and the capitalist class. The state has underwritten the major institutions of capitalism: the capital market, through loans, subsidies, and depreciation allowances; and the market for labour power, through land, immigration, mobility, and education policies. The combined effects of federalism and uneven development have encouraged regional blocs of capital to cluster around the provincial states, thus creating competition in development strategies between the federal and provincial governments. The effect is further complicated by the existence of two nations within a single state.

Finally, although in the post-war period the overall size of the state sector has been restrained compared to European states (reflecting the under-developed welfare state in Canada), new interventions into social and economic policy have occurred.

NEW PERSPECTIVES ON THE STATE

Modern political economy has, in a sense, "caught up" with this long-standing Canadian analytical tradition. The interpenetration of state and economic structures across the advanced capitalist countries, as a result of the extension of welfare and Keynesian policies, has made analysis of the dynamics of the state and state policy a key area of debate for political economists. Any sophisticated understanding of advanced capitalism requires an investigation of the state as well as the class structures comprising civil society.

But to accomplish this, political economists have had to retrieve the concept of "the state", which had previously been associated with the legal-formal study of constitutions, and to combat pluralism's hegemony in so much of post-war social science.[4] In the pluralist account of politics, the task of government was simply to reflect an evolving consensus among social groups in its authoritative allocation of policy outputs. Rejecting pluralism and its notion of a neutral state, political economists returned to some of the classical concerns of analyses of liberal democracy. Two questions in particular dominated.[5] How was the continuing gap between the formal political equality of democratic institutions and the massive social inequalities of capitalist society to be understood and resolved? How do the institutions and power structures that comprise the apparatuses of the state – ranging from the government to the judiciary, Parliament, police, bureaucracy, and educational institutions – shape the structures of civil society, and how are they shaped by it? In response to these questions, the concept of the relative autonomy of the state emerged as a core theoretical premise.

The Marxist tradition contributes this concept. Early Marxist writings often described the state as a by-product of the class divisions of capitalist society. The ruling classes controlled the state and used it as an instrument to realize their common political and economic interests. The concept of the "relative autonomy of the state" was developed later to overcome this tendency to reduce the state to an instrument of domination, by granting it some independence from direct class control and economic determinants. Two major books in particular are often associated with this newer conception of politics and the state.

The State in Capitalist Society, by Ralph Miliband, has become the classic statement of what has been termed "instrumentalism." Miliband claimed that in capitalist society it was necessary to distinguish between the ruling class of civil society and the governing class which held positions in the institutions of the state.[6] In this way he mapped a real gap between the state and society, but one that was almost inevitably closed through the direct social and economic links of state personnel to the capitalist class. In his account, moreover, the possibility of democratic control of the state was limited further by the economic constraints of private ownership and ideological processes that produced popular consent to the class-based rule of capital. In this way the institutions of the state met the instrumental needs of capital, even when the state was relatively autonomous from the capitalist class.

The second book, which can be read as a clear statement of structuralist understandings of the state, is *Political Power and Social Classes*, by Nicos Poulantzas. Poulantzas was less concerned to establish direct links between the state and capital, arguing instead for objective structural relations that linked the state to class struggle. For Poulantzas, the relative autonomy of the state in the capitalist mode of production was due to a spatial separation of the juridico-political level from the economic level. In addition, in concrete historical conjunctures, the state had an autonomy from the power bloc (the political expression of the capitalist class) that meant that it "by its very structure, gives to the economic interests of certain dominated classes guarantees which may even be contrary to the short-term economic interests of the dominant classes, but which are compatible with their political interests and hegemonic domination."[7] The state, then, was not an isolated set of institutions, but a site of class struggles and political compromises, which, in turn, shaped the structure of the economy. In this way Poulantzas granted a critical role to politics but also made visible the structural constraints of reform within capitalist society. The concept of relative autonomy thus became a forceful explanation of both the gains made by social democratic reformers as they expanded social policy and the equally evident failure of such reformers to overturn the political and economic inequalities produced by capitalist social relations.

The concept of relative autonomy was, however, widely disputed. A first set of questions was raised: If the state is autonomous, from what is it autonomous – classes, the economy, the international system, organized interests? How important are concrete linkages between the state and capital? The second set of questions asked how the state actually operated. How do political compromises within the state occur? Does the state sometimes have more or less autonomy, and how do the pressures from civil society register in state policy? These issues are crucial to knowing how states vary across space, over time, and in institutional form.

In attempting to delimit the specific causal patterns of how states in fact intervene, concern with the concept's functionalism dominated discussion. In many theories of the state that used the concept of relative autonomy, there was an a priori assumption that the state's existence and actions were necessary to the continued functioning of the capitalist system. This assumption of an inherent functionality to the results of state interventions, no matter the precise nature of the relationship between state and capital or the class compromises within the state, was criticized extensively for explaining state policy only in terms of its results. Critics claimed that state theorists needed to specify the causal mechanisms that could lead to either positive or negative outcomes from specific state actions.[8]

The most prevalent line of criticism was that the concept of relative autonomy made state policy a reflection of societal structures and thus denied the state any responsibility for its own actions. For these critics, following Max Weber, the state has a "real autonomy" as an organizational structure with its own logic, internal dynamics, and processes.[9] States are autonomous actors in capitalist societies, having capacities to implement policy preferences and shape the structure of society according to their own interests. In stressing the salience of state structures and capacities, this statist approach looked to the policy legacies, institutions, and managers of the state to explain historical processes and national variations.

Neo-institutionalist criticisms of Marxism's concept of relative autonomy have, however, created their own set of theoretical problems. In advancing a state-centric perspective, they ignore any systematic connection between state interventions and the relations of production and, therefore, overstate the ability of the state to direct accumulation. Moreover, instead of being power struggles between social forces within civil society, "politics," for them, is dominated by the processes of bureaucratic conflict within the state. Only in returning to these larger social processes can one explain the differential forms and historical transformations of the institutions of the state, however.

The following pages trace the way political economy in Canada has grappled with the relationship between state, economy, and class. Its analytic trajectories have followed paths similar to those observed elsewhere, moving from varied types of instrumentalism toward both structuralist and neo-institutionalist analyses.[10] Yet throughout this evolution the central role of the state in Canadian history has remained an organizing theme.

STAPLES AND THE STATE

In developing the staples thesis, political economists opposed the prevailing constitutionalist bias of Canadian history. In suggesting that "history is emphatically not 'past politics,' "[11] W.A. Mackintosh's seminal 1922 essay argued that economic, technological, and geographical factors explained the historical trajectory. For the staples theorists, basic commodities (fish, fur, timber, minerals), and the associated commercial trade relations and technical conditions of production, provided the central dynamic of Canadian history.

Despite the state's considerable role, staples theorists did not isolate the state as a field of study.[12] This is not to say they ignored the state, but in the staples thesis, state actions followed from their functional role in facilitating the staples trade. The nature of the state – and the particular functions it performed in specific spatial and temporal locations – were *derived* from the needs of the staple commodity. The functions of the state included provision of transportation infrastructure for the export of staples; underwriting monetary obligations through the provision of credit guarantees and liquidity; and, as export demand altered, aiding adjustment from declining to rising staple sectors.[13] The special kinds of market structures and institutions imposed by staples directed the state's economic role.

Donald Creighton's *The Commercial Empire of the St. Lawrence* best illustrates the classic staples interpretation of Canadian political history. Despite recognizing conflict among elites, the text stressed the unmediated identification of the commercial state with the mercantile elite. For Creighton, then, western trade

largely determined the style of Canadian politics. Transcontinentalism, the westward drive of corporations encouraged and followed by the supercorporation of the state, is the major theme in Canadian political life; and it was stated, in its first simplicity, by the fur trade. The trade enforced commitments and determined policies. The state was based upon it: it was anterior to the state ... From the first, the government was committed to the programme of western exploitation by the river system. The St. Lawrence was an expensive monopoly; and its imperious demands could be met – and even then inadequately – only by the corporate effort of the northern society.[14]

If the staples thesis defined the state in terms of its functions, there was no uniform assessment of what these functions were. Just as Mackintosh and Harold Innis diverged in their conception of staples accumulation, so they assessed the modern role of the state differently. Mackintosh's notions of market equilibration suggested only a management role, a view that made him well suited to write the modest 1945 White Paper on Employment and Income, which laid the policy basis for the post-war state in Canada by oddly combining the staples thesis with Keynesian policies.[15] Intervening via sound techniques of economic management to smooth market processes, the state was to act as a rational balance-wheel easing the economy along a stable growth path.

In contrast, Innis was hesitant about endorsing the new economics. He remained sceptical of the narrow Keynesian view that adjusting nominal aggregate measures by fiscal and monetary policy could resolve real imbalances of industrial and spatial structures. For Innis, Keynesianism was too specific, too blunt, and too optimistic about the intelligence of the state.[16]

Innis's scattered comments on the state were simultaneously confounding and complex. While recognizing that the institutions of liberal democracy shaped political choices, his work gave little attention to the relation between the state and social classes. Instead, his analytic focus was on the pattern of exchange relations between centre and margin in the historical long run. For Innis, the state acted at the edges of staples extraction; its elasticity of adjustment was measured in relation to the central dynamic of external demand interacting with domestic technology and geography. The state was limited by the character of the staple, structurally bounded by the rigidities of overhead costs and external demand vulnerability on the liquidity side. Moreover, by adding to these institutional rigidities, the state played a contradictory role, since it was also an agency of adjustment to the altering price system. Innis expressed only studied ambiguity as to whether the state was a political agent or an institutional rigidity. As a result, his analysis clarified only that exchange relations within empire were primary. For Innis, the colonies, facing a problem in the staples trade, "began to concentrate on machinery designed to meet internal problems, ranging through Confederation to protection and construction of transcontinental railways. The political machinery was closely adapted to meet the severe economic demands of dependence on staples with their sharp changes in prices and income. Governmental devices stabilized in part and accentuated in part the fluctuations . . . The disturbances incidental to dependence on staples, including the essential importance of governmental support, created difficulties within Canada and without."[17]

Innis's critical pessimism about the role of the Canadian state remained unique. The principal legacy of the staples thesis came from other writers who embraced a more favourable view of the positive state. The functional promotion of a staples-led economy still explained state actions for them, but attention turned to the institutional and policy structures of the state. One direction, in the work of J.A. Corry and Alexander Brady, was explicitly statist, stressing the institutional and legal structures shaping "economic life." Corry's studies for the 1939 Rowell-Sirois Commission traced the interventionist history of the state, noting the juridical difficulties imposed by a disunified state structure.[18] Brady contended, after noting that capitalism had failed to maintain its self-adjusting character, that additional centralized economic planning was needed for "expert and dispassionate guidance to the Canadian democracy."[19]

The theme of reform from the top achieved its most forceful expression, however, in the social democratic tradition, notably in the collaborative *Social Planning for Canada*. After carefully analysing the staples economy and the class structure, the book outlined an alternative program of reforms to redistribute income and power. Social democracy would be built gradually by slowly expanding the state's functions with piecemeal reforms, pushed forward by pragmatic parliamentarians educated to support new policies. The state stayed above the fray of class conflict, being a neutral instrument capable of remedying the worst distributive defects of capitalism.[20]

Vernon Fowke and Hugh Aitken provided arguments even more influential for subsequent analysis of the state and helped shape mainstream understandings. Both posited the unifying role of the state at Confederation in securing the economic territory of Canada and the expanded role of the state for the modern period. In these two historical periods the state's role still followed from the requisites of staples exports, but Fowke and Aitken now conceived of it as part of a nation-building strategy.

Following many themes first presented by Innis, Fowke argued that the National Policy – a series of tariff, railway, and land settlement policies to promote economic development – followed the collapse of earlier strategies of imperial or continental economic integration. The state had to transform the "British North American Territories of the mid-nineteenth century into a political and economic unit"[21] and in doing so made itself the most prominent instrument for the creation of a national economy. The British North America Act was, for Fowke, as much an economic planning document as a political constitution: "the federal government was created an agent within the framework of the first national policy and continued to act as an agent until, with the attainment of the objectives of the national policy, it had exhausted its usefulness to its original principals, the commercial, financial, and manufacturing interests of the central provinces."[22] These state actions united the various fractions of capital around development and exploitation of the wheat staple of the western hinterlands as an investment frontier. They established, in Fowke's estimation, imbalanced internal exchange relations between regions, with the areas of concentrated wheat production facing a competitive market structure subordinate to the monopolistic interests of central Canada which backed the national policy.

Aitken's similar interpretation of the national policy was wrapped in the theme of "defensive expansionism." Here the state was paramount in inducing economic growth and defending Canada's economic space so as to contain the "imperialist" American economy. In promoting either the old staples or the new staples of hydroelectricity, pulp and paper, or oil and natural gas, the functions of the state were consistent:

The role of the state in Canadian development has been that of facilitating the production and export of these staple products. This has involved two major functions: planning and to some extent financing the improvement of the internal transport system; and maintaining pressure on other governments to secure more favourable terms for the marketing of Canadian exports . . . Each phase of expansion in Canada has been a tactical move designed to forestall, counteract, or restrain the northward extension of American economic and political influence. Primary responsibility for maintaining and strengthening this policy of defensive expansionism has fallen on the state.[23]

Aitken's essays were a fitting conclusion to the classical staples era. Defensive expansionism provided an integrated and linear account of Canadian political and economic history, describing it as a succession of staples for the purposes of nation-building. The interests of business and government elites were coterminous in this project. The state served a functional role by acting in the interest of the dominant elites to build a "new nation" within the shifting conditions of imperial relations. These themes would return in the 1960s, supplemented by a critique of pluralism and a growing query about the limits of the state's ability to construct an independent place for Canada in the modern world.

DEPENDENCY, CLASS, AND THE STATE

The staples theory collapsed with the fracturing of political economy at the end of the Second World War. The new economics focused more narrowly on formalistic explanations of incremental and equilibrating growth, isolated from the issues of class and power.[24] Remarkably, political science too turned away from these latter concerns. Study of the formal institutions of government declined, and the concept of the state disappeared altogether in a pluralist account of political processes in which the government was a neutral forum that adjudicated and reconciled the interests of competing groups. Departing from his earlier statist views, Corry captured the new consensus: "Genuine freedom bears its fruit in diversity of aim and interest. Individuals and groups will try to do what they find good, and the pursuit brings them into collision and struggle. Liberal democratic government exists to compromise these clashes without civil war and not to infuse us all with a sense of national purpose."[25]

One line of dissent to the separation of studies of politics and the economy continued in the Marxist tradition, however. Although only a small body of work, the writings of C.B. Macpherson, H.C. Pentland, and Stanley Ryerson carefully delineated the role that social classes played in mediating economic and state structures. While some of the themes of the staples thesis continued – notably that Canada's industrial structure was skewed toward resource production – the three authors emphasized the specifically capitalist form of accumulation based on free waged labour and the spread of industrial capital. The state, in this view, was not neutral or simply responding to the functional needs of the staples economy. Rather, it supported the interests of the ruling capitalist class. By making this connection between class and state structures, the Marxists could begin to explore areas the staples thesis had ignored.

Macpherson's study of what he called Alberta's quasi-colonial economy demonstrated the way that instabilities in the class structure dominated by the petite bourgeoisie led to oscillations in the politics of agrarian protest.[26] Pentland's studies traced over time the processes that structured the capitalist labour market in Canada, including the role of the state in shaping the institutional structure of the labour market via industrial relations law, employment policy, and immigration.[27] The classical Marxist treatment of the state dominated Ryerson's work, in which he depicted the class structure of the Canadian state as the "unequal union" of Confederation, which reflected the growing strength of industrial capitalists, who required "a state of their own, under their control, capable of providing a favourable framework for the home market and for securing advantageous terms for borrowing abroad."[28] Yet the Canadian state was still too weak to break from the imperial dominance of Britain. Moreover, since the new state structure failed to address the internal national question, the Quebec nation was incorporated on unequal political and economic terms into Canada. By identifying Canada as "two nations in a single state," Ryerson delineated the complex interaction of nation and class that traversed the Canadian state structure. Although a divergence between class struggles and national struggles was evident, a popular unity could be found across these divisions to oppose the capitalist social bloc that dominated the state.[29]

When the new political economy appeared in the late 1960s it also questioned the theoretical partition of economics and politics into separate spheres. Both neo-classical economics and the pluralism of political science failed to deliver convincing accounts of the systematic class and regional inequalities of Canadian society which shaped politics in the late 1950s and the 1960s, despite the redistributive efforts of the welfare state. Moreover, both paradigms were silent on the foreign domination of the economy. The new political economy built on the insights of the staples thesis but adapted it to a more critical understanding of the political and economic bases of Canadian society. The staples thesis's explanation of persistent resource dependence, truncated manufacturing and technology sectors, and reliance on foreign capital was coupled with Latin American dependency theory's emphasis on a pattern of exchange relations between centre and margin which locked the subordinate region into a process of underdevelopment. From this pairing, the core problematic of the new Canadian political economy emerged: the apparent paradox of a rich dependency with levels of socioeconomic development comparable to other advanced capitalist countries but imbedded in an industrial structure similar to peripheral societies. Kari Levitt set out this guiding thesis in terms of the new mercantilism of the multinational corporation and the fragmentation of institutions and processes of modern society. This fragmentation had evolved to the point that "present-day Canada may be described as the world's richest underdeveloped country."[30]

In taking up the staples thesis, the dependency school did more than simply radicalize the thesis by drawing out implications that the earlier liberalism of Innis and the rest had ignored. The new political economy subtly transformed the staples theory from an account of Canada's industrial development to an interpretation of how Canada had failed to develop industrially and, indeed, showed that the regression to dependency was a cumulative process.[31] By making the place of staples in the world system the logical starting point of analysis, the new political economy dissented from Marxism's stress on domestic relations between classes. Yet it also displaced the classical staples thesis – that interaction between technique, the character of the staple, and external exchange determined social structures. Instead, the extent and form of metropolitan penetration of peripheral economies became the primary causal factor, with dependency varying with the degree of integration into the international economy.

Given the importance of the world system, it was the "nature of capital," or more precisely the nature of the Canadian capitalist class, that maintained dependency. Lacking industrial entrepreneurship, dominated by commercial-financial elites, servile to American imperialism, contented as managers of branch plants, Canadian capitalists overdeveloped the resource and service sectors and failed in the difficult task of developing manufacturing. Indeed, antagonism of the commercial-financial fractions of Canadian capital to industrial capital blocked the internal development of Canadian manufacturing.[32] Moreover, commercial exchange solidified "an alliance between the leading elements of Canadian and U.S. capital that reinforces mutually the power and advantage of each."[33] Trade in staples had moved Canadian capital to adopt continentalism and to press continually for free trade.

What role could the peripheral Canadian state play between the faultlines of a stunted domestic social structure and the world system? Here too the new political economy overturned the classic staples thesis. The new political economy asked both who controlled the Canadian state and whether state managers would counter dependency. The response to these questions constituted a basic discontinuity in Canadian political economy. Whereas the earlier school had described the functional role of the state, it had also emphasized the capacity of the state to form the Canadian economy via the National Policy. The dependency school, in contrast, pointed to the weakness of the Canadian state resulting from its subservience to financial and foreign capital. Mel Watkins summarized the new stance: "The state itself is almost a by-product of the exigencies of staple production . . . Confederation and the National Policy [reflect] a state and a state-policy created by the merchant class in its own image. If anything of analytic substance remains to be said on this matter, it may be that more attention should be devoted to the process by which the Canadian state successively suppressed re-emerging domestic capital within the staple sector itself, and within the manufacturing sector, in the interest of foreign capital."[34]

As this statement makes clear, the state had to play an instrumental role vis-à-vis the dominant capitalist elites of the periphery. In this sense, the state had virtually no autonomy from particular capitalists, whether national or foreign. And since the structure of the capitalist elites was determined by the contribution and place of the staples trade in the world system, the degree of autonomy of the state was ordained by the amount of sovereignty the national economy had from foreign penetration. In this way, analysts did not ask about the relative autonomy of the state from national social classes but rather about the extent to which the dependent state could gain autonomy not only from foreign capital but from the structure of the world system itself.

In the essays of Levitt and Watkins, the nature of multinational capital inhibited the decisional autonomy of the nation state. For Levitt, foreign penetration blocked the normal evolution of an indigenous entrepreneurial class in Canada. Multinationals controlled the economic surplus internally and prevented domestic entrepreneurs from developing a national technological capacity. Where public-sector assumption of the entrepreneurial role might be an alternative, the conservative rentier-staples status of Canadian business stifled it. The dilemma, Levitt asserted, was that dependency structured weak political institutions: "Sovereignity is not compatible with branch-plant status; the greater the degree of foreign ownership and control of Canadian industry, the narrower the freedom of choice in economic as well as political matters."[35] The steady transfer of the locus of decision-making to the American metropole threatened to balkanize Canada.

Nevertheless, a window of opportunity remained for a nationalist project. The nation state might be diverted from its continentalist drift, the weak peripheral state replaced by a strong state capable of deepening domestic development and renegotiating autonomy vis-à-vis the metropole economy. In setting an agenda for the 1970s, Watkins affirmed the need for a new national (industrial) policy that would consolidate the capitalist class. In expounding the need for Canadian entrepreneurship, fostered by state interventions, he remained within the statist tradition: "The most important political dimension of a new National Policy would be the simple need to assume the burden of the old National Policy of 'defensive expansionism' vis-à-vis the United States."[36]

Most of the new political economy was far less sanguine, however, about the possibility of transforming the Canadian state from an instrument of American capital and Canadian financial capital to an agent for domestic

industrial capital. The constraint came not from the lack of potential entrepreneurial capacity in the state, or from the links between agents at the head
of capital and agents in the state – even though evident. The problem was
that the character of capital formed by staples dependency spawned a state
complicit in maintaining dependency. The most formidable expression of
this view was Tom Naylor's description of mercantile-financial suppression
of industrial capital. In a watershed essay for the new political economy,
Naylor suggested that the socioeconomic structure of the periphery was the
result of "internal changes in the metropole."[37] This tied the ruling merchant elites of the periphery to the metropole through a common interest in
expanding commercial trade and opposing peripheral industrial capitalism.
Tariff walls erected by the Canadian state were crucial to this logic of
accumulation, because they encouraged American branch plants to move to
Canada and thus discouraged nascent industrial entrepreneurs. With the
relationship between the periphery and centre the key determining structure, the state had only an instrumental role to play, acting at the behest of
the commercial-financial elite to mediate the relationship to the imperialist
centre. Naylor anticipated that no strong state could break with the long
nightmare of Canadian dependency. For him, in contrast to Levitt: "The
contradiction of continuity in change resolves itself in disintegration. A
Canadian capitalist state cannot survive because it has neither the material
base nor the will to survive, the former contributing substantially to the
latter."[38]

It was only a short distance from Naylor's position to a declaration that the
peripheral Canadian state was an instrument of foreign capital itself. John
Hutcheson took up the theme that the steady "sell-outs" to American capital
– from Defence Sharing Agreements to the Autopact – had demonstrated
that the "Canadian state was now in the control of the dominant section of
the ruling class in Canada – the u.s. corporations."[39] After studying the
integration of post-war Canadian and American resource policies, Melissa
Clark-Jones argued that the lesson to be learned was that the multinational
corporations and the internationalization of capital had so severely limited
the sovereignty of the Canadian state that it openly fostered foreign access
to public resources in the imperial interest.[40]

In these works, the concept of relative autonomy of the state was, in
effect, being cast as the sovereignty of the peripheral social formation from
the economy and elites of the centre. The failure of industrial capital to
develop as an autonomous force meant that the Canadian state lacked an
autonomous capacity. To the extent that resource dependence continued to
predominate, an autonomous capacity of the Canadian state would be ob-
structed, thereby perpetuating the vicious circle of dependency.

Political economists concerned with the structure of power detailed more
carefully the connections among the elites composing the peripheral ruling

class. By demonstrating the links among the occupants of elite positions of power within a dependent capitalist society, they both mapped Canada's stunted economic structure and rebutted pluralism's claim that all social groups had similar access to public and private power.[41]

Wallace Clement's two studies closely examined the types of corporate elite linkages that locked Canada into its dependent position. In *The Canadian Corporate Elite* Clement argued that through the multinational corporation American economic elites penetrated the Canadian power structure and produced a distorted elite formation. Canada's power structure was unevenly fragmented into an indigenous elite dominant in circulation and finance, a comprador elite of Canadian managers of branch plants in manufacturing and resources, and a parasitic elite that headed multinationals. The interlocking elite structure hindered smaller Canadian entrepreneurs from expanding. Moreover, the indigenous commercial elite and foreign industrial elite reinforced one another and dominated the state. "Indeed, it appears the alliance between business and government is not an alliance of equals but one dominated by the interests of corporate capitalism."[42]

The insight that these instrumental ties between the state and the corporate world might be understood best in a continental context served as the basis for *Continental Corporate Power*. Here Clement demonstrated forcefully that the unequal alliance between Canadian and American capital formed a continental elite, albeit with a section of Canadian capital being a dynamic component within the continental context. Within the world system, however, Canada had only an intermediary role, being a "supplementary structure of the United States."[43] This formulation established tensions between the Canadian state and the continental economy. On the one hand, the autonomy of the state was relative to Canada's place in the world system. Because the Canadian state did not control the decisions of corporations and allowed high levels of foreign investment there was "erosion of the autonomy of the state itself." On the other hand, the Canadian state operated in a liberal democracy and thus could "make decisions about the very existence of private power." Yet this potential autonomy was not realized because state elites depended on corporate elites for revenues, and both considered "corporate capitalism as the way to attain this goal."[44] Because of this dilemma, the continental capitalist elite ruled the Canadian periphery as part of a continental economy.

Clement's two studies represent a high point for the new political economy. Nevertheless, these elite-theoretical studies remained caught in the instrumentalist logic of focusing on the decision-making capacity of elites and on the direct ties between the state and capital. Other authors within the dependency school remained similarly tied to instrumentalism. For them, the world system was a constraint on the economic sovereignty of the periphery and, hence, on the autonomy of the Canadian state. In contrast to the earlier staples thesis, the new political economy did explore the relationship between the state and capitalist elites and the limits of private accumulation. Yet the conception of power remained monolithic and positional: powerful elites cut the path of Canadian dependency. Indeed, Daniel Drache, speaking for the school as a whole, was determined to turn the instrumentalist impasse of the new political economy into an axiomatic feature of a Canadian staples society: "In economic matters, the Canadian state is autonomous neither in a relative nor an absolute sense; rather as the creation of the imperial state, it functions as the instrument of foreign capital, and by direct intervention in the economy underwrites the strategies of accumulation and legitimation . . . The resource/financial/transportation bourgeoisie are the 'dynamic' and dominant ruling class formation in this mode of development."[45]

CLASS RELATIONS AND STATE POWER

The dependency school located its analysis of the state almost exclusively by reference to the capitalist class's place in external exchange relationships. As a result, the complexity of both inter-class and intra-class relations were ignored: the specificity of Canada is the result of the economic and class relations characteristic of the centre of the world system. Recognizing the limits of an analysis that dismissed internal social forces, many political economists advanced a class-theoretic analysis that focused on domestic social relations within the bourgeoisie and among the dominant and subordinate classes.[46]

The interest in the state by class theorists, particularly Marxists, was part of the international trend in political economy to rehabilitate the concept of the state. But Canadian writers responded also to their own national situation, which in the late 1960s brought radicalism, mobilized into nationalist movements in Quebec and English-Canada.[47] Therefore, new analyses of the class nature of the Canadian state and its role in the reproduction of unequal power relations appeared in a political context heavily influenced by nationalist projects. In English Canada, in particular, the nationalist movement settled on a strategy of cross-class alliances, defining the future of the subordinate classes as dependent upon an improvement in the conditions of indigenous Canadian capitalism. Faced with this political project, Marxists immediately had to assess the viability of a strategy that promoted state-led Canadianization of capitalism. Clearly dissenting from the dependency theorists, who accepted as the immediate task the nationalist project of breaking Canada out of the American orbit, class theorists asserted that the struggle against capitalism was the fundamental objective. Not surprisingly, then, the relations between the state and capital and relations among classes were of important theoretical and strategic concern for class theorists. The social and political limits of a nationalist project centred on an alliance of Canadian capital and subordinate classes against the interests of foreign capital had to be assessed.

With this political agenda, class-theoretical perspectives used the concept of the relative autonomy of the state as a framework for assessing both the limits of political strategy in the struggles with capital to democratize economic relations and the limits to anti-capitalist social reforms in a period of deepening economic crisis. This definition of the concept shifted attention from the structure of the international economy to domestic social relations. The first goal was to map the class structure of Canadian society and to demonstrate the patterns of class conflict that shaped political struggles. This concern produced a relational analysis, in which the unequal relations of class power provided the key dynamic to Canadian society.

Relational analyses looked at the ways structures of conflict between classes shaped state policy. They argued that capital was not an organic whole but was composed of various fractions and that the struggles of subordinate classes influenced state policy. There were, however, several interpretations of what these notions meant for the relative autonomy of the state, ranging from instrumentalism to structuralism. But they all located the explanation of state policies in the contradiction between the formal equality of the political sphere and the class divisions of the economic realm.

As a result, two foci organized class-theoretic analyses. The first was a demonstration of the means by which the class power of capital translated into state power, with the struggle between class actors being decisive. Differing conceptions of this process informed the varied interpretations of the relative autonomy of the state. The second focus has been reform of the Canadian welfare state in response to the needs of capital or the demands of labour.

A first version of class-theoretic studies was instrumentalist, differing from dependency only in its insistence on the internal class sources of state intervention. The most consistently instrumentalist study was Alvin Finkel's *Business and Social Reform in the Thirties*, which helped to dispel the notion that business systematically opposed state reforms during the Depression. Nonetheless, this revisionist insight was diminished by an insistence that the state had no autonomy from the capitalist class and that all its actions were the direct result of business lobbying and preference: while working-class militancy in the 1930s may have frightened the bourgeoisie into action, clear-thinking capitalists, acting through a captive state, designed the social programs that became the welfare state.[48]

More nuanced instrumentalist versions recognized the relative autonomy of the state and historical studies of business-government relations placed such links within a more sophisticated theory of state-society relations. Tom Traves, for example, in *The State and Enterprise*, delineated the state agen-

cies that arose to maintain the stability of production relations as industrialization proceeded in the first three decades of the twentieth century. Capitalists turned to the state because "in Canada, as in other developing capitalist
societies, the unlimited pursuit of private capital accumulation necessitated
the development of a political structure that would protect growing property
only by growing more powerful itself."[49]

While Traves never posited a straightforward translation of economic
power into political power, from his perspective the state acted as an instrument of class power to perpetuate the long-run stability of the capitalist
system.[50] A similar analysis by Paul Craven examined the role of the Department of Labour in stabilizing class relations in the same period. Faced
with widespread industrial conflict, the federal state moved to limit juridi-
cally and structure conflict in Canadian industrial relations, through com-
pulsory conciliation and statutory prerogatives designating essential
industries. In doing so, the state was meeting its responsibility for accumulation and legitimation of the system as a whole.[51]

Leo Panitch's introduction to *The Canadian State* has helped set the
agenda for studies of the state in Canada. Panitch combined, in a nuanced
instrumentalist analysis, the theoretical perspectives of Ralph Miliband and
James O'Connor. Panitch first clarified the distinction between a state that
acts simply at the behest of the capitalist class – as a simple instrument –
and a state that acts at a distance on behalf of that class to maintain the
capitalist system. Such distance provided, Panitch suggested, the state with
relative autonomy from particular capitalists, enabling it to intervene on
behalf of the long-run interests of the capitalist system; some decisions
generated objections from capitalists and their organizations.[52]

If the relative autonomy of the state was a general characteristic of
capitalist societies, the degree of autonomy depended upon specific conditions. The particularity of the Canadian state was unusually close links to
the capitalist class and deep interpenetration of state and society. Relying on
studies done by elite theorists, Panitch suggested that the "degree of co-
optation from business to government and of exit from cabinet to business
makes the very concept of an autonomous political elite in Canada a highly
tenuous one."[53] With this historical overview, Panitch demonstrated how
Miliband's approach helped direct empirical analysis and establish the parameters of autonomy.

Behind the empirical openness of the approach, however, were fundamental assumptions about structural relationships that rendered explanations of state actions functionalist. Panitch insisted that any adequate
theorization would specify the state's functions in the capitalist mode of
production.[54] He assumed that requisite functions of accumulation, legitimation, and coercion were always performed in order to maintain capitalist
social relations and thereby embedded functionalism within the theory.[55]

Empirical analysis then explicated performance of the various functions. So, for example, Panitch found that the Canadian state, acting on behalf of the capitalist class, put more resources into accumulation and coercion while neglecting welfare spending for purposes of legitimation.[56] By the mid-1970s, a potential legitimation crisis occurred, as accumulation faltered and unemployment climbed. Without the political support that a well-oiled welfare state might bring, the Canadian state was casting about for ways of resolving the developing economic crisis, attempting to institute a form of corporatism that would bind the trade unions to the state, capping wage pressures, and redistributing income to capital for industrial restructuring.[57]

The presumption in this early article was that the state must perform specific functions and would do so, whether it was relatively autonomous or completely entwined with the capitalist class.[58] The analytical task became, then, to label state actions as implementing primarily accumulation, legitimation, or coercion functions of the state. In later work, however, Panitch relied less on a three-function argument. His analysis provided a sustained critique of the new political economy's failure to pay sufficient attention to the social relations within Canada that have sustained the country's dependent status, and the argument took on a more structuralist cast.[59] Rejecting a focus on the ties between capitalists and the state, Panitch looked instead at relations between classes, arguing that the state became one of the terrains on which class struggle was played out. "If this has meant that our development has been based on the shifting sands of foreign investment, it has as much to do with the strength of the subordinate classes as with strategies imposed on the state by the bourgeoisie."[60] Panitch also took the dependency approach to task for its failure to recognize the importance of liberal democratic state forms for the balance of forces in Canadian society. The ability of the working class to mobilize in representative institutions has helped it gain collective power within the structures of contradictory class relations.

This shift from nuanced instrumentalism to a more structuralist analysis did not, however, eliminate the functionalism within the argument. Instead of performing three requisite functions, the state primarily facilitated accumulation: "To speak of the state as a capitalist state does not mean that certain or all capitalists rule directly at the political level. It means rather that the state's role primarily entails maintaining the social conditions for economic growth and the reproduction of classes in a way consistent with the dynamics of the capitalist economy. This means promoting capital accumulation, but within the framework of containing and mediating relations among the various fractions of capital and between the subordinate and dominant classes."[61] Thus the state continued to be directed in its actions by the functional necessity of preserving capitalist social relations.

Also following Poulantzas, Carl Cuneo's analysis of the development of unemployment insurance emphasized the organizational expression of working-class politics as well as divisions within the capitalist class. Thus, in the design of unemployment insurance programs in the 1930s, the Canadian state was relatively autonomous from the capitalist class because a "series of class contradictions and internal splits among class factions gave Bennett a 'relative autonomy' to intervene with his contributory plan."[62] In other words, state autonomy resulted from the structure of class conflicts and the advantages of autonomy as a mechanism of conflict-resolution.

With this understanding of relative autonomy, Cuneo was, of course, dismissive of Finkel's description of the development of social policy. Where Finkel could see only the influence of capitalists, Cuneo saw the effects of class struggle in the compromise legislation worked out first by Bennett (and declared unconstitutional) and subsequently by Mackenzie King. But this compromise, designed to avoid an escalation of conflict, had a cost. It fragmented working-class unity, by favouring the most moderate elements, and forced all capitalists to accept limits on their actions which only the most enlightened among them recognized as necessary to re-establish stability.

Despite the important role of class actors and the independent mediating role of the state, Cuneo still adopted functionalist categories to explicate the state's formation of the compromise. Thus the proposed insurance program "took the form of coercive tactics aimed at the most militant and unemployed sections of the working class, and legitimating (or conciliatory) tactics in dealing with the stably employed workers and business."[63] Cuneo concluded that it was, ultimately, the opposition of capitalists to a noncontributory unemployment insurance scheme, plus a split within the labour movement between the more radical demands of the Communist Party and the demands of the mainstream union organizations, that allowed the state to identify a path of mediation. Since Bennett and King remained relatively autonomous from direct influence by the capitalist class, they could perform the necessary mediating role among the class actors, and existing social relations were reproduced via a mixture of coercion and legitimation.[64]

Thus, for Cuneo, the state remained primarily a mediating institution, balancing the needs of capital and the demands of labour, yet ultimately favouring capital and the stability of the system. While the struggle between classes set the political agenda, as in Panitch's article in *The Canadian State*, its legitimation function compelled the state to locate a mediating point. The state, as an institution performing various functions, remained only relatively autonomous from the pressures of class conflict.

The role of the state in reproducing social relations was also important in Rianne Mahon's version of structuralist analysis. Mahon argued that the capitalist state reproduced the existing unequal structure of power by organizing an equilibrium, albeit unstable, of political compromise among the social classes.[65] The state helped construct a political hegemony within a social formation so that consent was forthcoming for the hegemonic project of the leading fractions of the capitalist class. The hegemonic bloc in Canada had been an alliance of staples and financial capital, though consent was obtained from both industrial capital and the working class through the incorporation of subordinate demands within the hegemonic project. Therefore, for Mahon, the state was not simply a set of institutions that existed in capitalist society to mediate among classes; nor could state interventions be categorized as contributing to the functions of accumulation, legitimation, or coercion. Rather, state interventions were a set of compromises, reflecting the unequal representation of social forces within the state itself.[66]

According to Mahon's structuralist logic, the welfare state existed as the product of the post-war construction of an unstable equilibrium of compromise. It met the requirements of the dominant and subordinate class, addressing simultaneously the capitalist system's needs for accumulation and the maintenance of social cohesion. The welfare state was more than the sum of social programs to maintain social order; it was the very condition, in a particular historical conjuncture, for both the disorganization of subordinate classes into their identities as individual "citizens" and the organization of the capitalist class into the ruling hegemonic bloc.

In determining how the state would respond to specific political issues, Mahon analysed the way unequal structures of power were inscribed within the state. Representation was constituted in such a way that the working class, represented by the Department of Labour, had a position in the structures of the state inferior to that of the dominant fractions of the power bloc, represented by the most powerful branches of the state, such as Finance. Mahon's *The Politics of Industrial Restructuring* argued, for example, that capitalist hegemony was reconstituted over time by state adjustment policies for the textile industry to prevent its deindustrialization. This compromise "cost" the state and the leading fractions of capital in the staples alliance, but it also thwarted a possible political threat to the continentalist strategy.[67]

Mahon's analysis met many of the criticisms made of earlier class-theoretic approaches. By being explicitly historical, it gave empirical content to the often abstract categories of structuralism. But it moved much beyond this. In recognizing the competitive structure of capital between various fractions, it also demonstrated how this structure was reproduced in the internal workings of the state, resulting in conflict among branches.[68] And, in contrast to instrumentalism, the unequal structure of representation reproduced class relations regardless of specific linkages between the state and capital elites. For example, the welfare state was not the result of direction by elites or of the functional needs of legitimation. Rather, it depended on post-war conditions, which made necessary an equilibrium of compromises incorporating some of the political demands of labour within the hegemonic project of the staples alliance.[69] In other words, the welfare state was simultaneously part of accumulation and part of legitimation; the two were inseparable, and it was no longer necessary to label any policy as primarily one or the other.[70]

Despite the advance of making the state a site of struggle between classes and the fractions of capital, Mahon's work retained a strongly functionalist explanation of the outcomes of specific state interventions. Studies based on Poulantzian structuralism were functionalist because all state policies by definition contributed to the overall reproduction of class relations as a result of the state's necessary and primary role as guarantor of the capitalist system. In other words, the particular structures linking the state and classes, including representation inside the state, could only help capitalism as a whole. All compromises were necessary compromises, following from the overall structure of class relations. Thus even when Mahon identified differing class bases in any state interventions – and granted the working class a central role – the accommodations remained functional to the continued hegemonic domination of the leading sections of the power bloc.

While functionalism was a general failing of class-theoretical approaches, two other widespread critiques have come from divergent directions. They were, paradoxically, either that class theorists were not statist enough or that they were too statist. The first criticism was that class-theoretical approaches, by deriving state policy always from the needs of classes, ultimately collapsed state actions into the relations of civil society. Whether the state was staffed by agents of the capitalist class, mediated the conflict between classes, or reproduced class relations by unequal representation within the state, the autonomy of the state was sacrificed to direction from the conflicts of civil society. In the last instance, it was argued, the state was only relatively autonomous: specific state interventions were always "read off" the balance of class forces.[71] Thus, while rejecting pluralism for its simplistic assumption that the state neutrally represented all social groups, class-theoretical explanations maintained a similarly society-centric stance in their conception of power. Therefore, for these critics, the state was not independent enough. They felt that greater explanatory space should be available for autonomous choices made by states and state managers.

It was a paradox, then, that the second criticism argued that class-theoretical analysis focused too exclusively on the existing form and policies of the state, paying too little attention to the ways in which new patterns of class relations might emerge and alter the behaviour of the state. While accounting for state interventions in terms of the contests and composition of civil society, actual studies looked at the ways state policy helped to reproduce capitalist social relations. Critics argued that this interpretation understated the capacity and role of the political and economic organizations representing the working class and of new social movements to mobilize opposition and affect the direction of state policy.[72]

All these criticisms were, in the end, directed against the legacies of functionalism in class-theoretical approaches. Whether claiming that the state was strong or that civil society was dense with organized interests, the critics rejected the notion that the state inevitably behaved in ways necessary for the maintenance of capitalist class relations. The lack of open-ended outcomes was troubling to some, who saw even in Mahon's hegemonic structure of representation, for example, the formulation of a research problem that could be explored only within the analytic grid laid over state and society. Inside the grid, only reproduction of the hegemonic domination of the power bloc, albeit in ways that alter historically, was possible. The lack of detailed consideration of the space for change within these class-theoretical analyses, it has been argued, represents the a priori definition of the role of the state as the reflection and reproduction of capitalist social relations. Breaking with this definition has been, therefore, the point of departure for treating the state as an actor in its own right or for deepening the analysis of civil society to account for the complexity of power relations, whose multiple forms of domination cross the categories of class and alter the inscription of social struggles within the state.

AUTONOMOUS STATE OR CIVIL SOCIETY?

The limits to the class-analytical approach provoked two divergent responses. One stressed the capacity of states to undertake autonomous actions, making choices in accordance with their own institutional needs. Hence the primary attention that class analysts gave to the relations of state and civil society disappeared. Instead, there was greater stress on the interests of the state itself and on conflicts within its internal bureaucratic and political institutions. This line of analysis can be called neo-institutionalism. The other response attempted to rethink how human agency shapes state actions, primarily by stressing the importance of struggles over ideology and meaning systems in determining the structures of power relations within civil society. In these studies, the relationship between state and civil society was still central, but the mapping of civil society into multiple forms of domination, based on social relations such as gender and race, reduced the focus on the role of class in the formation of social identities.

Neo-institutionalism within political economy should be distinguished from institutionalism within political science. For political economy, institutions and organizations have explanatory importance, but they are bounded – at least in general – by the processes of capital accumulation. The traditional political science use of institutionalism tended to examine institutions per se, in isolation from social processes. Neo-institutionalism analyses, in contrast, continued to stress that a country's social and economic conditions and international setting acted as constraints on the state. Yet they also argued that wide areas for autonomous activity were available to the state and state managers. Robert Brym, for example, has proposed a state-centric understanding of what he calls, in an odd usage, "relative autonomy." He found the space for autonomous action in "the mundane fact that state officials want to keep their jobs" (and therefore would not act to jeopardize them) and that state institutions reflected the crystallization of earlier struggles for political power.[73] These two reasons suggest that no a priori relationship existed between the state and civil society and, in particular, that the autonomy of the state was not the result of the state mediating current conflicts between classes. If the power of subordinate classes had been mobilized in the past, it would appear crystallized in the institutional structures of both state and society.[74] But Brym's neo-institutionalism disclaimed any particular link between state and civil society.

Glen Williams's *Not for Export* asserted the autonomy of the state even more. The history of state industrial policy, which helped fashion a dependent economy in Canada through a series of policy failures, was founded on the ways "political and economic elites chose to emphasize the development of resource extraction and staples trade over manufacturing."[75] This analysis not only marked a return to the category of "elite," designating state personnel as well as major business figures. It also revived many of the notions of the state from the classical staples thesis, though with a striking emphasis on the real autonomy of the state in making strategic policy choices. In Williams's view, the state mediated among differing interests in the Canadian economy and, though constrained by the accumulation process and liberal democracy, had wide scope for autonomous action based on elite choices.[76] The results of these decisions had an impact within the state's branches by either increasing capacity to make choices about industrial policy or further constraining freedom of strategic choice. But whatever the outcome, the choices made were a matter for empirical investigation and could not be "read off" the needs of class conflict.

David Wolfe's analysis of the post-war welfare state offered a similar example. Rather than forming part of a response intended to stabilize labour-capital relations, Keynesianism in Canada, according to Wolfe, had primarily an ideological role for political actors: "The postwar Liberal government was interested in the principles of Keynesian economics to the extent that they could be used to justify its policy of rapid economic expansion."[77] Economic policy resulted from choices made by key policy-makers, who then presented their selection in rationalizing language.

Richards and Pratt's study of prairie development also granted autonomy to state managers to make fundamental choices about the direction of accumulation. *Prairie Capitalism* is predicated on the notion that two different types of elites emerged in Alberta and Saskatchewan. These provincial "entrepreneurs" had real autonomy from the bourgeoisie of the resource sector, and, during the 1970s, each group was "capable of effective entrepreneurship within its respective resource sector," because of its ability to mobilize large economic rents from potash or oil resources.[78] In each case the established political and institutional structure was crucial to explaining the path chosen. Saskatchewan's elite was bureaucratic, drawing its support from the "remains of the traditional 'left populist' farm-labour constituency." The Albertan regional bourgeoisie was stronger, but, along with elites in the provincial state, it had a stake in maintaining a viable provincial economy. A break from a dependent development tradition could occur "when provincial governments have determined to exploit the region's comparative advantage in mineral staples, and have mobilized the requisite domestic entrepreneurial skills to capture the potential benefits from oil, gas and potash development."[79] This meant a public-sector strategy in Saskatchewan and private-sector diversification in Alberta. In each case, the political mobilization of elites in the provincial state, following their own strategic trajectory, altered the province's development path.[80]

Within neo-institutionalist analyses, the state was, of course, influenced by civil society; group conflicts set a series of constraints on strategic choices. The most obvious constraint on state choice – alongside Canada's international location – was elections. Laux and Molot, for example, claimed that the dual need to cut back the scope of Canada's state enterprises and to rationalize holdings, instead of undertaking more thorough-going privatization, appeared in the 1980s in large part because a state fiscal crisis made reduction of spending electorally unviable.[81] Similarly, Williams fell back on "electoral fortunes" to explain specific decisions put forward at several crucial moments.[82]

The attention given to representation in discussions of the state reflected, in fact, a sense even among structuralists of the need for more actor-centred theorizing and concern with human agency. Thus, in the most sophisticated class-theoretical works, too, there was growing recognition that modes of organizational representation of societal actors needed consideration. In *The Canadian State*, Panitch argued that liberal democracy created its specific political sphere, but that text was virtually silent on the role of parties and trade unions. But Panitch's later analysis of corporatism in Canada, while playing down parties, did examine other forms of representation in the postwar period, when new relations among capital, labour, and the state took shape.[83] Mahon's analysis emphasized the structure of representation of social forces within the various branches of the state, but she ignored other forms of representation, arguing that there was a shift away from Parliament and parties as sites of representation and toward bureaucracy, the executive, and corporatism.[84] For her, this change marked an actual shift in the structure of the state in the present period, but the instability in state structures and recomposition of the class structure continued to raise critical questions about the ways the working class and other movements organize within civil society and enter political struggle. In other words, the institutions of representation were important variables in determining the forms of state intervention.

The Gramscian concept of hegemony provided a most promising avenue for investigating representation. Mahon's concluding emphasis on the effects of the revival of popular movements, the breakdown of the post-war consensus, and the growth of neo-conservatism, as well as strategic shifts in the strategy of the trade union movement, provided evidence of the utility of the concept of hegemony for thinking about changing modes of representation.[85] Gramsci suggested the importance of the ideological and cultural dimensions of politics and the way in which social classes were mobilized. While a political party was fundamental to building a political alternative, construction of a counter-hegemonic political project also encompassed the need to advance democratic institutions throughout civil society. Thus trade unions in the workplace and social movements of peace, women, and ecology were an essential part of an alternative project for the future. Moreover, the importance of such struggles to the determination of the outcomes of these organizational efforts granted more openness to the political process than did the more functionalist accounts, which focused on the reproduction of class domination.

Brodie and Jenson's examination of the history of the party system demonstrated the importance of ideological struggle in forming classes as political actors.[86] Despite the existence of the social relations of capitalism since the late nineteenth century in most of Canada, there has never been a successful nation-wide organization of the working class into its own partisan formation. Asking why the working class has had such difficulty organizing into a political force, Brodie and Jenson argued that Canadian history has seen a series of crises in which the hegemony of the dominant class to organize politics has been challenged. But at each of these moments of possible change, although for different reasons, the capitalist class has managed to reassert its dominance within the state and the party system. A crucial weapon in its arsenal has been control over the ideological processes by which meaning systems develop. The language of politics in Canada, and thus the political identities with which Canadians approach politics, have been organized in ethnic terms – the ongoing crisis of Canadian unity. Class identities have never become the organizing mechanism, and thus working-class parties have been weaker in Canada than in other advanced capitalist societies. The lesson, in a sense, is straightforward: the political organization of workers is dependent upon class formation, which, in turn, requires building active political and cultural relations expressing a common class solidarity.

Socialist feminists have also stressed the importance of ideology, and the identities which follow from it, in the construction of gender relations in capitalism. Refusing to reduce the situation of women in capitalism to the effects of class relations, they have conceptualized the way the gender division of labour articulates to the overall social division of labour. At first the road to explanation was thought to lie in the labour that women did in the household, because it also structured the place of women in the labour market. But once this explanation was found wanting, attention turned to the role of ideology in giving meaning to the act that most clearly differentiated women and men – childbirth.

Pat and Hugh Armstrong argued that the unequal gender relations structured within capitalism were the result of the split between "the public" and "the private." In this split, women were confined to the realm of the private, because only they bear children.[88] Thus biological difference was constituted in capitalism along the dividing line between public (the economy, the state) and private (the family). State actions reproduced this division as they maintained existing structures of class and gender domination.

Jane Ursel, examining nineteenth-century factory legislation and the welfare state, emphasized the state's role in maintaining the gender division of labour for the benefit of capital accumulation. Fearing that the working class would not reproduce itself if women and children had to labour in the unsanitary and super-exploitive sweatshops of early industrialization, the state instituted restrictions on their labour, thus encouraging women's confinement to the home.[89] But socialist feminists have also exposed the ways women themselves – and not only bourgeois women – participated with the state in the maintenance of the traditional division of labour. Early reform movements promoted and participated in the implementation of social policy founded on a maternal feminism that presumed the existence of separate realms of competence and interest between women and men.[90]

If this is a pessimistic reading of the early reform experience and women's position in capitalist society, socialist feminists have nevertheless taken it as an inducement to understand the extent to which resistance to both gender and class domination can be mobilized in politics.[91] Since patriarchal relations are socially constructed, they can be dislodged through collective action. Yet mobilization requires conscious and organized struggle, based on an understanding of the ways relations of gender and class domination constantly arise, alter, and reproduce in ideology and practice.

The insight of socialist feminism is to re-emphasize the importance of the ways relations of domination are constituted in civil society and to direct questions about the state's role in structuring a gendered division of labour. Increasingly socialist feminists argue that while the state may currently reproduce patriarchal relations, the state is not compelled to do so. Moreover, they deny that the state is solely an instrument of male power. These refusals remind all students of the state that political space exists to challenge unequal structures, no matter the length of their existence and the power of those who benefit from them. It is a political lesson well worth remembering.

NEW QUESTIONS, NEW DIRECTIONS

Canadian political economy has travelled some distance from the notions of the state embedded in the classical staples tradition. The importance that neo-institutionalists have attached to the strategic capacity of the state and feminists' insights about the complexity of relations and the plurality of identities within civil society all mark this distance. Yet, if these two ways of theorizing the state broaden the conception of power and the relations of force, they do not challenge the premiss that the contradiction between social classes lies at the heart of capitalist social relations.

Class-theoretical discussions begin from this premiss, maintaining that the state's role in the reproduction of the relations of production provides the first step to understanding capitalist society. The agenda for further theorization about the state and civil society, then, is to acknowledge the insights of neo-institutionalism about the latitude of state autonomy and of feminists about the pluralism of power. Yet critical incorporation of such insights requires that we retain the fundamental propositions of class analysis about the contradictory social relations of capitalist democracies, in which the formal equality of liberal democracy coexists with class inequalities in civil society.

In pursuit of this agenda several issues are likely to emerge as crucial in advancing an understanding of the Canadian state. These issues are forced onto the agenda not simply by intellectual debate, however. Everyday politics has, and will continue to have, a major role in highlighting problems. From the politics of social movements, especially feminism, comes the issue of alliances for change. Feminist analysis insists that multiple identities do form in civil societies. Will these acting subjects mobilize along with or separately from workers? In addition, feminism reasserts the importance of the large theoretical question of the relative autonomy of the state from civil society, in part because it places less stress on the state itself and more on the social relations of civil society. Analyses influenced by feminism's insights tend to arrive "at the state" through considerations of representation and interest formation, rather than taking the state as a starting point. This shift in perspective accounts, in part, for the decline of interest in the state *tout court* within Marxism.

At the same time, the ongoing and rapid restructuring of global capitalism re-poses important questions about Canada's place in the international configuration and inspires state-focused analyses. Canada may be seen as either a distinct social formation, with unique economic and state structures, or as part of a single, integrated economy in which separate state institutions exist simply as a historical legacy. The last decade of policy efforts – whether to identify an "industrial strategy" or to formalize "free trade" – exemplify the political resonance of this question. The very existence of these pressing issues, on both the political and academic agendas, demonstrates that the traditional dichotomy of "internal" and "external" causes in patterns of Canadian development must be transcended. In a similar way, notions of state capacity – whether the Canadian state is weak or strong vis-à-vis the world system and domestic capital – continue to be useful for clarifying probable outcomes of economic strategies and for formulating political practice. In an international conjuncture with deep linkages between the advanced capitalist countries and in which national policy régimes appear to be diverging, it is all the more important to focus on any comparative institutional differences between the state in Canada and that in other advanced capitalist societies.

It is not surprising, then, to find discussions of the state contributing to the uncertainties and variety of Canadian political economy in the 1980s. Indeed, the new items on the agenda – representation and interest-formation, the relationship between state and civil society in a social formation of multiple identities, the precise institutional structures and strategic capacities of the state, the role of the Canadian state within the North American bloc – promise theoretical variety rather than agreement. Gone are the days when a single thesis – staples, dependency, instrumentalism – could organize all discussion.

Such variety is positive, to the extent that our understandings of Canadian capitalism deepen. However, theoretical diversity must not become an invitation to retreat into "academic" discourse, cut off from the political debates and controversy that form Canadian politics. Just as earlier debates about "theory of the state" arose from and responded to the politics of nationalist and socialist projects, so future scholarship on "the political" depends on continuing, committed opposition to the unequal social relations of the present.

NOTES

1 Underhill, "O Canada," 80.
2 Panitch, "The Role and Nature of the Canadian State," 14.
3 See Panitch, "Role and Nature," and Innis, "Government Ownership."
4 Pluralism's equation of politics to the competition between fragmented, roughly equal, interest groups in a stable political system was best illustrated in Dahl, *A Preface to Democratic Theory*. The systematic linkages between the state and

particular class interests, suggesting profound flaws in the pluralist conception, was demonstrated in Mills, *The Power Elite.*

5 See Hall, "The State in Question."
6 See Miliband, *The State in Capitalist Society,* 51.
7 Poulantzas, *Political Power and Social Classes,* 190–1.
8 This issue has been raised in numerous critiques of Marxist theories of the state; for example Skocpol, "Political Response." For a spirited defence of the utility and epistemological validity of functional explanation see G.A. Cohen, *Karl Marx's Theory of History.*
9 See Skocpol, "Bringing the State Back In."
10 The institutionalists who were so prominent in post-war Canadian political science were not working within a political economy tradition, as the political economists – represented perhaps best by the Mackintosh quotation given in the next section – well understood.
11 Mackintosh, "Economic Factors in Canadian History," 2. Also see C. Berger, *The Writing of Canadian History,* chap. 2.
12 One popular text at the time theoretically examined the state: MacIver, *The Modern State,* especially 316 ff.
13 The best empirical accounts of the staples role of the Canadian state are in: Mackintosh, *Economic Background,* and Easterbrook and Aitken, *Canadian Economic History.*
14 Creighton, *The Empire of the St. Lawrence,* 16–17. Although Creighton discusses in most of this book a pre-capitalist state, his views apply to the capitalist state as well. See Bernier and Salée, "Social Relations," 102–4.
15 See Wolfe, "Rise and Demise," and Owram, *The Government Generation,* 261.
16 See Innis, *Problems of Staple Production in Canada* and "The Role of Intelligence."
17 Innis, *Essays,* 381–2. Also see Easterbrook, "Innis and Economics," 294.
18 See Corry, *Difficulties of Divided Jurisdiction* and *Growth of Government Activities.*
19 Brady, "The State and Economic Life in Canada," 440. Also see Brady, "The Constitution and Economic Policy."
20 See League for Social Reconstruction, *Social Planning for Canada*; Brady and Scott, eds., *Canada after the War*; and Moscovitch, "Leonard Marsh."
21 Fowke, *The National Policy,* 8. Also see Phillip's insightful essay on Fowke: "The Hinterland Perspective."
22 Fowke, "The National Policy," 276.
23 Aitken, "Defensive Expansionism," 220–1. Also see Aitken, "Government and Business."
24 The best example in neo-classical economics remains H.G. Johnson, *The Canadian Quandary.* For the institutional approach in political science see Dawson, *Democratic Government in Canada.*
25 Corry, *The Changing Conditions of Politics,* 25.
26 See Macpherson, *Democracy in Alberta.*

27 See Pentland, *Labour and Capital.*
28 Ryerson, *Unequal Union*, 310.
29 Ibid., 422-3.
30 Levitt, *Silent Surrender*, 24-5. Also see Panitch, "Dependency and Class."
31 See Drache, "Staple-ization," 16.
32 See Naylor, *History of Canadian Business*, 3-4.
33 Clement, *Continental Corporate Power*, 6.
34 Watkins, "The Staple Theory Revisited," 89.
35 Levitt, *Silent Surrender*, 9.
36 Watkins, "A New National Policy," 163, 174.
37 Naylor, "Rise and Fall," 2.
38 Ibid., 36. Also see Naylor, *History*, II, 282-3.
39 Hutcheson, "The Capitalist State," 174. This was a theme throughout this Waffle text: R. Laxer, ed., *(Canada) Ltd.*
40 See Clark, "The Canadian State and Staples," 473.
41 John Porter argued that the linkages among Canadian élites were so strong that "there develops a confraternity of power in which the various institutional leaders share attitudes and values." This power structure, for Porter, did not constitute a ruling class, but the overlap of political and corporate worlds made Canada less than a "thoroughgoing democracy." See *The Vertical Mosaic*, 522.
42 Clement, *The Canadian Corporate Elite*, 117, 350.
43 Clement, *Continental Corporate Power*, 129.
44 Ibid., 299-301. The dependence of the state elite on corporate capitalism was also observed by Olsen, *The State Elite.*
45 Drache, "Harold Innis and Canadian Capitalist Development," 54.
46 This chapter will explore only class-theoretical analyses developed for capitalist societies. Other concepts are necessary for the examination of pre-capitalist formations. For example, Perry Anderson's concept of the absolutist state has been employed to explore state and society in Lower Canada in Bernier and Salée, "Social Relations and the Exercise of State Power."
47 Brym makes exactly the opposite point: there was "no logical connection between left nationalism *per se* and the left nationalists' early view regarding the state in capitalist societies." We disagree with this view. See Brym, "The Canadian Capitalist Class," 5.
48 Finkel, "Origins of the Welfare State," 345. Also see Finkel, *Business and Social Reform.*
49 These agencies were the Canadian Reconstruction Association, the Tariff Board, and the Board of Commerce. See Traves, *The State and Enterprise.* Paul Craven's examination of the early industrial relations system stresses the state's responsibility for accumulation and legitimation as well as for the cohesion of the system as a whole. See Craven, *"An Impartial Umpire,"* 159-61.
50 Stevenson, in discussing federalism and federal-provincial relations, makes use of an instrumentalist analysis as well when he claims that each level of govern-

ment "speaks for" different fractions of the bourgeoisie. See "Federalism and the Political Economy," 76-8, 90-1. Also see Swartz's study of state health care as a method of social control: "The Politics of Reform."

51 See Craven, *"An Impartial Umpire."*

52 See Panitch, "Role and Nature," 4. For Panitch, the capitalist state acts for capital even when it takes actions that capitalists may oppose. For Finkel, the state acts at the immediate behest of capital.

53 Ibid., 12.

54 Ibid., 5.

55 The major criticisms against functionalism are that it imputes needs to societies as if they were living bodies; it assumes a teleology without demonstrating the existence of goal-oriented planning mechanisms; and it involves circular reasoning, since any policy adopted is, by definition, functional, unless the system collapses. See Brym, "The Canadian Capitalist Class," 13-14. Brym's last two criticisms of functionalism – that it sets too strict limits on the possibility of reform and that it leaves no space for resistance via class struggle – are not about functionalism per se; they reflect disputes about the limits of agency. The difficulty lies in adequately specifying causality.

56 See Panitch, "Role and Nature," 18-19.

57 Ibid., 21-2. The state tried this corporatist initiative, however, without having the requisite conditions of centralized producer groups, a strong labour movement, and uniform labour jurisdictions.

58 "Noting that the legitimization function is relatively underdeveloped in Canada does not imply its total absence – it is a requisite of every state." Ibid., 19.

59 See Panitch, "Dependency and Class." Also see Panitch, "Elites, Classes and Power."

60 Panitch, "Dependency and Class," 25.

61 Ibid., 26-7.

62 Cuneo, "State Mediation," 47. Cuneo has the unfortunate instrumentalist habit of personifying the state. This makes unclear the extent to which his analysis has instrumentalist elements and, therefore, depends on the specific actions of state managers favouring capital. A similar "slippage" into instrumentalism is evident in his reply to Pal; see "Comment."

63 See Cuneo, "State Mediation," 44 ff.

64 Ibid., 47.

65 See Mahon, "Canadian Textile Policy," 170, 193 ff, and *The Politics of Industrial Restructuring*, 39.

66 Mahon, "Canadian Textile Policy," 170, 193ff. See also *The Politics of Industrial Restructuring*, 39.

67 See Mahon, *The Politics of Industrial Restructuring*, chap. 8.

68 Pal took Cuneo's structuralism to task for neglecting that aspect of the issue. Pal, "Relative Autonomy Revisited," 71-93, 99-101.

69 See Mahon, *The Politics of Industrial Restructuring*, 15. A similar argument, ex-

amining cultural policy, is made by Magder, "A 'Featureless' Film Policy."

70 David Wolfe pointed out that any policy may, in a contradictory fashion, incorporate both accumulation and legitimation functions. In discussing post-war Keynesianism, Wolfe suggested: "Full employment policy is an essential aspect of the accumulation function of the state because it ensures the high and stable level of demand which is the necessary incentive for sustained investment by private firms. At the same time, full employment policy is an essential aspect of the legitimation function of the state because it removes the most destructive consequences of the market economy." See Wolfe, "The State and Economic Policy," 254.

71 One way to avoid deriving the state from relations in civil society is by using the concept of "wage-labour relationship" to incorporate structural factors that shape relations between classes in specific periods. See Houle, "Economic Strategy."

72 Panitch, however, pointed out that parties and trade unions are not part of the state and that "class conflict does obtain political and industrial expression through the voluntary organisations of the working class." See "Role and Nature," 7. But in this text he does not analyse these organizations, nor does *The Canadian State* have any chapters on parties or unions. A notable "structuralist" argument has been that state institutions – including political parties in office – become encapsulations of class struggle themselves. See Bourque, "Class, Nation and the Parti Québécois."

73 Brym, "Canadian Capitalist Class," 14–15.

74 Brym claims (in "Variations") the absence of strong class parties in the 1980s is due to the institutional effects of the electoral system and other checks and balances on the generation of new parties. These limits are, in turn, the residues of past conflicts. He never explores, however, the reasons that earlier class conflicts did not empower the subordinate classes.

75 G. Williams, *Not for Export*, 36.

76 Ibid., 5–6. Given the importance he attributes to state choices, Williams pays a great deal of attention – appropriately so – to the development by intellectuals of frameworks for choice.

77 Wolfe, "Economic Growth," 15. In a later, more functionalist article, Wolfe describes the welfare state as a compromise between capital and labour which sets off contradictory tensions between accumulation and social consumption; see Wolfe, "Mercantilism, Liberalism and Keynesianism," 1–2.

78 Richards and Pratt, *Prairie Capitalism*, 10–11 and passim.

79 Ibid., 328.

80 Of course, the institutions of federalism have absorbed a good deal of the interest in the Canadian state. Garth Stevenson's work has helped set out an agenda of analysis. It ranges over a number of theoretical perspectives, from the quite instrumentalist analysis ("Federalism") in Panitch, *The Canadian State*, to articles that stress areas of independent action for state elites and the existence of a

structured relationship of dominance between the Canadian and American econ-omies, which limits the sovereignty of Canadian state managers. See G. Steven-son, "The Political Economy Tradition."

81 Laux and Molot, *State Capitalism*, chap. 8.
82 G. Williams, *Not for Export*, 130, 171, for example.
83 See Panitch, "Corporatism in Canada" and "The Tripartite Experience."
84 See Mahon, *The Politics of Industrial Restructuring*, 39–40. Coleman's overview of the literature of pluralism, clientalism, and corporatism provides a useful in-troduction to the issues of differing modes of representation within the state. See Coleman, "The Capitalist Class."
85 See Mahon, *The Politics of Industrial Restructuring*, 130 ff.
86 See Brodie and Jenson, *Crisis, Challenge and Change* and "The Party System."
87 This initial effort produced the "domestic labour debate": Fox, ed., *Hidden in the Household*. Also see the discussions in Hamilton and Barrett, eds., *The Politics of Diversity*.
88 See P. Armstrong et al., *Feminist Marxism*.
89 See Ursel, "The State and the Maintenance of Patriarchy." For another example of the consideration of capitalist states' interest in babies see Jenson, "Gender and Reproduction."
90 See Andrew, "Women and the Welfare State," and L. Kealey, ed., *A Not Unrea-sonable Claim*.
91 Of course, some have been quite pessimistic, seeing only the social control as-pects of state actions and women's involvement in them. For an instrumentalist view see Burstyn, "Masculine Dominance." For a different perspective see Smith, "Women, Class and Family."

CHAPTER TEN

Toward a Political Economy of Law

Amy Bartholomew and Susan Boyd

Despite the revival of the Canadian political economy tradition and the burgeoning critical legal studies movement, with its "radical" view of law,[1] a political economy of law remains relatively unelaborated and untheorized in Canada. Given law's centrality in contemporary capitalist societies, this is particularly surprising. Also inexplicably, few have observed that law received some consideration in the classical, liberal Canadian political economy. For example, Harold Innis's "Roman Law and the British Empire"[2] contained some provocative comments on the nature of law and made some connections between law, lawyers, and the political economy. Nevertheless, his attempt to relate imperialism to differences between written and unwritten law was fragmented and inconclusive. In contrast, J.R. Mallory's work on judicial review in *Social Credit and the Federal Power in Canada*[3] continues to provide an important framework within which political economists may understand courts. Finally, C.B. Macpherson's Marxist-inspired work provides a classic analysis of the form that law and rights assume under the capitalist mode of production, as well as an understanding of the importance of civil liberties and rights in contemporary capitalist societies. Unfortunately, the insights of these classical political economists have neither led the new generation of Canadian political economists to theorize law nor significantly affected the current debates in law in Canada.

Attempts have been made from outside the predominantly liberal view of law in Canada to expose the "tilted" political nature of capitalist legal systems and the inadequacies of traditional means of inquiry into the nature and roles of law. Some have criticized the view that posits law as an internally logical, natural set of rules possessing inherent validity and divorced from politics.[4] These critiques have been important for illustrating, if not adequately theorizing, the theme that law is politics. Other approaches have stressed the gap between the theory and practice of law, revealing the failure of law in capitalist democracies to live up to its extravagant claims.[5] While these are important developments, a further crucial step may be taken by analysing the nature of the interrelationships between the particular capitalist relations of production and attributes of civil society in Canada, on the one hand, and its law and legal institutions, on the other.

Despite the appearance since 1980 of several important publications dealing with law in a political economy vein,[6] the development of this approach to law is still embryonic in Canada. This chapter raises some points of inquiry toward an elaborated Marxian political economy of Canadian law. We insist that a political economy of law must attempt to theorize and capture both the limitations that law and legal institutions present for progressive movements and class struggles within capitalist societies *and* the potentialities of law and rights for class struggles and progressive forces within and beyond capitalism. Moreover, such an undertaking must be built on adequately theorized conceptions of capitalism, class relations, social relations and struggles involving gender and race, capitalist states, and ideology, all of which must be made concrete and particular to the Canadian social formation.

One central question that a developed political economy of law must ask is how economic and social forces influence or "determine" the development and trajectory of law-making, the content of law, and specific legal forms, institutions, and procedures. Equally important is the particular way in which law and legal institutions mediate and reconstitute, or "overdetermine," relations of power within civil society and the relations of production. Law, however, simultaneously is shaped by and shapes the political economy. Thus the relationship between "determination" and "overdetermination" is complex, and in empirical studies of laws and legal systems these aspects cannot be satisfactorily severed, except for heuristic reasons.

Our focus is primarily on law[7] as the coinage of the state – as discourse and practice – rather than other important aspects of legal systems such as enforcement,[8] powers of arrest, the police, and prisons. These latter issues have received attention by criminologists in Canada, although an adequately nuanced political economy approach to them also remains to be developed.[9] Nor do we elaborate on such issues as legal procedure, rules of evidence, levels and types of courts, or the possible role of the legal profession as the "conceptive ideologists" of capitalism.[10] These are not unimportant issues. On the contrary, a developed political economy of law must delve much more deeply into such issues and, in so doing, may benefit from the study of theoretical advances undertaken in Britain and Europe.[11] Guided by the existing Canadian literature, this chapter therefore merely scratches the surface of the full potential for a political economy of law and the legal system.

NECESSARY THEORETICAL PREMISSES

The relative underdevelopment of political economy approaches to law in

Canada is perplexing, since theorizations of law and the legal system face many of the same problems as do studies of capitalist states in general. Admittedly, states operate in illegal and extralegal as well as legal ways, and obviously there are important forms of "social control" - ranging from the family to social workers - that take place other than directly through legal institutions.[12] However, legal intervention by the state is crucial for articulating rights, duties, and obligations as well as sanctioning "discipline" and is a potent means by which power is structured within production relations and civil society (such as property rights, labour law, and family law) as well as within the state itself, through constitutional and administrative law. Moreover, just as other types of state intervention are not necessarily reproductive of capitalist relations, intervention through law may enhance contradictions within material and social relations.

Some "critical" work in Canada is weakened by insufficient conceptualization of class relations within capitalism, leading it to view both law and the state instrumentally[13] - as the unmediated will of a cohesive capitalist class. Many such approaches misunderstand capitalism - seeing it too much in terms of the cohesion and intentions of capitalists and "their state" rather than the dynamics of capitalism and the accumulation of its composite market dynamics. Some Canadian scholars view state agencies, particularly regulatory tribunals, as mere instrumentalities that may be "captured" by capitalists.[14] Other work is marred by an overly monolithic view of the state which treats it as a rather simple "agency of control," leading these scholars to exaggerated and debilitating anti-statist[15] and anti-judicial prescriptions.[16] Still other scholars fail to distinguish adequately among types of capitalist states by collapsing liberal democratic with authoritarian states.[17] Finally, there is a genuine lack of literature in the political economy tradition that examines the complex interaction between gender, race relations, and the law without falling into simplistic "social control" models.[18]

Any serious political economy of law must begin with an understanding that capitalist states are located within the dynamics of capital accumulation, capital restructuring, and the balance of class forces. While the balance of power within capitalist society may be and normally is unequal, typically favouring the capitalist class, that class is not omnipotent. Because class power is relational, subordinate classes are neither "inert political clay"[19] nor a "vanquished 'mass';"[20] rather they may, and often do, challenge and moderate the power of capital. Moreover, the capitalist class itself is not monolithic but is rent by divisions that may constitute distinct "fractions" with particular economic and political interests, a significant factor in the Canadian political economy.

Capitalist and other forms of domination are challenged from both outside and within the state and law by subordinate classes and other social forces. Not only the state in general but law and legal institutions constitute arenas of struggle.[21] Such a relational understanding of capitalist states and legal institutions indicates that the creation and interpretation of law, as well as legal practices such as law enforcement, depend rather more on the balance of class forces and the organization and mobilization of those forces than on the dictates of the bourgeoisie. This suggests that class struggle, as well as the workings of the economy, at least partially define and limit the potentialities of law for progressive social change.

It is not only class struggles that a political economy analysis needs to see in this way, however. Of equal importance are theorizations of gender, race, and other forms of domination as they develop within capitalism. Yet it may not suffice to simply add gender or race uncritically into Marxian analyses. Feminist and anti-racist struggles are not reducible to class struggles,[22] although there may be important connections, for example, between the respective difficulties of articulating claims for racial, gender and class "equality" using legal discourse. Theoretical frameworks for the analysis of law and state may well have to be reconsidered and amended, therefore, to successfully integrate issues such as gender and race.

Insofar as law may have a particularly important ideological place in liberal democratic capitalist societies, a developed political economy of law must also be premissed on an understanding of ideology as something more complex than a coherent world view or false consciousness. An appreciation of the variety and complexity of ideologies, and the interplay between them, would permit careful analysis of the role of law in structuring belief systems.[23] Legal discourse itself exhibits a particularly powerful ability to determine the legitimacy or illegitimacy of ideas and activities, so that conflicts over the meaning and form of legal discourse are significant. The outcomes of these conflicts may determine how "rights" and "the rule of law" – to take two important examples – affirm some activities, struggles, modes of organization, and life-styles, while condemning others.[24] Hence, an understanding of the ideological force of law itself, the power of legal discourse, and its corresponding ability to reinforce ideologies external to it may aid in exploring the complex and often contradictory "behaviour" of law.

Finally, the specificity of the Canadian political economy, the Canadian state, and Canadian law must be considered. The country's social formation, including its resource-based economy, its particular class relations, and its historical and current relationships with first the British and then the American empires may be among the most important particularities to be addressed. The state's federal form of government as well as the cultural and ethnic diversity of its civil society must also inform investigations of Canadian law and caution against indiscriminate adoption of theories enunciated for less complicated state formations or more uniform "peoples."[25] Moreover, although Canada's legal system has been shaped to a considerable extent by the reception of English common law, and French civil law in Quebec, local conditions may have modified the characteristics that otherwise might be shared with the "parent" legal system. A unique aspect of the common and civil law systems in Canada, underexplored to date, is their uneasy coexistence with the laws of the indigenous native and Inuit inhabitants of Canada.[26] The effects on law of such diverse factors as cultural, environmental, geographical, and spatial forces also merit serious consideration.[27]

In summary, we must begin to explore law as historically contingent in all its complexity. Analysis must be predicated on adequate theorizations of at least the following, related concepts: (1) the material and social relations constitutive of the capitalist mode of production; (2) the conflict and struggles between and among social classes; (3) gender, race, and other modes of domination and struggle; (4) the relationship of capitalist states to material and social relations; and (5) the role of ideology in (re)constituting legitimacy. Use of all these concepts must attend to the specificity of the Canadian political economy, civil society, and state.

DETERMINATION

A developed political economy of law must explore and explain how complex and often contradictory material and social forces may "determine" the emergence, change, and direction of the form and content of laws and legal systems. A timely illustration of the link between material and social relations and law is the current restructuring of Canadian labour relations law in response to capital crisis and economic restructuring. A massive overhaul of labour legislation by both provincial and federal governments has undermined many of labour's long-held rights to bargain collectively and to strike. Unfortunately, as we will see, Canadian political economy literature has generally eschewed theoretical consideration of complex questions such as how law and rights may represent the "relative social power and political coherence of different classes"[28] and the cogency of the very claim that there is a determining relationship between political economy and law. Instead, it has focused on how particular structures and conflicts have influenced concrete areas of law as well as judicial and administrative decisions. Before we turn to this literature, however, we will briefly outline two theoretical considerations that have influenced its development – property rights and the relative autonomy of law.

Macpherson: The Rise of Capitalism and the Form of Law

C.B. Macpherson's work represents the most ambitious attempt in Canada to theorize capitalist legal forms and rights. Macpherson's work is notable for its insistence that the transformation from pre-capitalist modes of production based on formal legal inequality to the capitalist mode of production demanded a system of private property rights, formal juridical freedom, and formal legal equality, including freedom of contract.[29] The newly dominant conception of property as absolute private property "can be seen to be the product of the new relations of the emergent capitalist society."[30] Macpherson, therefore, followed Marx to argue that capitalism required, and the concept of absolute private property entailed, specific and particularly limited notions of freedom and equality: the freedom to alienate labour as well as land, and formal equality in exchange relationships.

This type of analysis has recently encountered criticism in the "new legal history" literature[31] and elsewhere[32] for difficulties in claiming a relationship of determination between material conditions and legal constructs. The criticism draws on E.P. Thompson's suggestion that a relationship of determination cannot be maintained insofar as the capitalist mode of production required legally defined conceptions of private property rights in order to develop.[33] While Thompson's "imbricationist" position has not been explored in any depth in the Canadian literature,[34] the theoretical questions it raises are deserving of the most sustained analysis by the new Canadian political economy.

The new legal history literature also suggests that there are problems of periodization in analyses like Macpherson's by indicating that "possessive individualism," its legal underpinnings, and private property may be found prior to the transformation to capitalism or by pointing to qualifications on the juridical categories of free and equal individuals and private property – such as trusts, mortgages, and restrictions on the right of women to alienate property – which persist after the transformation in specific capitalist conjunctures. These renewed historical and empirical investigations may moderate the forcefulness of overgeneralized accounts such as Macpherson's. Indeed, political economists and historians might investigate the veracity of such generalized accounts for Canada by studying, especially, eighteenth- and nineteenth-century Quebec, with its seigneurial land tenure system.[35] It would, however, underestimate the complexity of the social formation to expect all aspects of it, such as property rights, to accord precisely with the predominant mode of production.

One important question raised by these analyses is whether the conceptual problem encountered in analysing the transformation of pre-capitalist into capitalist systems – " 'the problem of legality' in historical materialism"[36] – requires reconceptualization of the relationship between political economy and law. If so, it may have ramifications not only for studies of processes of transformation but also for how to think about the relationship between the political economy and law within capitalism. Despite important exceptions to the principles of private property and formal juridical equality within capitalist social formations, however, as Eric Tucker argues, these principles do appear to retain their primacy as girders of capitalist economic relations.[37]

Relative Autonomy and Uneven Development of Law

As one moves from examining core conceptions of private property rights, freedom, and equality accompanying capitalist relations to analysing particular laws, legal practices, and institutions within concrete capitalist conjunctures, it is necessary to conceptualize how law may be simultaneously "connected with" and "relatively independent of the economic movements of society."[38] The development of a richer examination of law has relied on the concept of the relative autonomy of law. The importance of using a concept like relative autonomy is highlighted by the need to be able to explain laws and legal practices that do not support the immediate interests of the bourgeoisie. Analyses premissed on the notion of relative autonomy have helped to explain, for example, the material basis for the persistent belief of trade unions and other progressive movements, not to mention individual citizens, that some laws confer benefits and some real measure of protection. While this concept is treated somewhat differently by its supporters,[39] is criticized in some legal literature for not sufficiently indicating its limits,[40] and is currently the object of more wide-ranging and scathing critiques,[41] it *has* provided a useful corrective in a Canadian literature sometimes too quick to adopt instrumentalist positions. However, as Leslie Pal has argued, Canadian political economy literature, while strong on an understanding of conflicts and pressures on the state, has not adequately addressed how relative autonomy may operate within the state.[42] This is a serious failing for analyses that theoretically treat the state as a terrain of struggle as well as understanding it as located within a context of societal struggles. The new political economy must come to terms with current debates regarding relative autonomy's purported shortcomings if it is to either reinvigorate it as a useful concept or seriously explore alternate modes of explanation.

Moreover, different forms and areas of law and legal institutions may be unevenly developed, even contradictory,[43] and may have their own patterns of determination. For example, increasingly repressive labour law exists alongside expanding protection of at least some civil liberties under the Charter of Rights. Hence each area of law will require specific analysis, as will various legal institutions and practices. The processes and nature of law-making in Parliament, the formalism of the courts, the role of administrative tribunals within the capitalist state, and the way each of these institutions may reflect and reproduce the "unequal structure of representation" within the state[44] all require further theorization and examination in the Canadian literature.

Origins of Legislation

The greatest portion of the Canadian political economy literature on law has focused on the origins and content of legislation. Much of this has come from a self-professed "structuralist" perspective which views law as a product of changes in the relations of production and the shifting balance of class forces. Also emphasized is a consideration of the broad historical context, especially the changing compositions of capital and labour.[45]

Many who write in this genre argue that earlier investigations into the emergence of early welfare state legislation did not adequately consider changing relations of production and class struggle. Russell Smandych's work on the introduction of Canadian anti-combines legislation around the turn of the century, for instance, analyses confrontations between labour and capital as well as fractions within the capitalist class.[46] In tracing the introduction of the Opium Act, 1908, to the rise of industrial capitalism in British Columbia, Elizabeth Comack rebuts explanations of that legislation based solely on racial conflict and efforts to control opium use by Chinese immigrants. When viewed within the broad historical context, the legislation is better understood, she argues, as part of a wider response to class conflict between the ascending capitalist class and increasingly organized and militant Canadian workers. In expanding numbers, these workers were drawn to socialist unions and parties which, unlike the older craft unions, were "intent on defining labour issues in class, rather than ethnic or racial, terms." Introduced at least partly to counter the increasingly class-conscious definition by unions and parties of organized labour's woes, the drug legislation helped to redefine those woes ideologically as racial rather than class-based by fermenting existing racist sentiment. This legislation drove "another wedge" into the working class as the non-socialist, conservative unions' racially oriented stance received a "symbolic concession," while the socialist movement's position was ideologically challenged.[47]

The marginalization of socialist organizations is similarly identified in Carl Cuneo's work on the Employment and Social Insurance Act, 1935.[48] An indication of the tapestry of possible state responses to crisis, conflict, and struggle can be found in his analysis of the Canadian state's mediation of class struggle and the reproduction of class relations in the midst of the Depression. Cuneo demonstrates that the state intervened with brutal, legally sanctioned coercion – including violent police repression, the use of labour camps, and deportation – as well as with "conciliation" in the form of an unemployment insurance scheme that was enormously at odds with the demands of the most militant workers' organizations, but not with those of more conservative workers' organizations. While the most radical working-class organizations pressed for a broad-based scheme not based on working-class contributions and with a significant element of workers' control, conservative workers' organizations had supported contributory schemes. At the same time, almost the entire Canadian bourgeoisie opposed unemployment insurance. Cuneo's treatment of this constellation of forces and struggles rejects instrumentalist analyses which suggest that the bourgeoisie's support was necessary to the introduction of unemployment insurance.[49] It also demonstrates the value of an analysis that insists that the state – partly through law and legal institutions such as the police – mediates struggles and responds to crises, contradictions, and tensions as a capitalist state.

Approaches such as Cuneo's have been criticized by Patricia Marchak for failing to present "compelling reasons to conclude that the state was doing anything but responding to claims from plural interest groups: why assume an interpretation about the long-term structural interests of capital if in fact labour unions . . . are the major source of pressure for legislation affecting workers?"[50] Cuneo's location of the emergence of the legislation in its broader context of legalized, sustained, overt repression against the most radical organizations and workers, however, raises doubts about Marchak's critique. Moreover, the resultant legislation constituted an extremely limited victory for the working class and was a *limiting* intervention, insofar as it circumscribed and marginalized future radical collective abilities of the working class by enhancing a split between radical and non-radical factions of labour. Most important, the form and practice of unemployment insurance that ultimately emerged specifically reproduce the social relations of capitalism. A pluralist approach cannot adequately account for these repressive responses and for the final form of the legislation.

Although the recent literature on the genesis of legislation contributes to the more copious political economy literature on the rise of the welfare state,[51] not all legal developments can be located directly within a class struggle paradigm. Other literature in the Canadian political economy tradition discusses, with perhaps a more sensitive posture toward other factors, the nature and origins of Confederation and the Constitution Act, 1867.[52] Garth Stevenson's work, for example, identifies geographic and defence, as well as economic, motives for Confederation.[53]

Literature on the Charter of Rights similarly stresses that its introduction may be partly a response to structural tendencies of capitalism insofar as a "legitimation crisis" can be said to have occurred in Canada,[54] but the Charter does not appear to have been a direct response to class struggles. Other political factors, including American hegemony,[55] a desire to check centrifugal federalism,[56] and Liberal party politics[57] have been suggested as significant contributors to the origins of the Charter. While an analysis that locates the Charter sufficiently within the context of capital restructuring remains to be undertaken, these contributions to the literature are important reminders that not all legal initiatives are the result of overt and collectively conscious classes in struggle. However, once the initiative to entrench the Charter was under way, participation in the hearings of the Special Joint Committee of the Senate and the House of Commons influenced the nature of rights ultimately entrenched. The contrast between the mobilization of women's groups and the refusal of organized labour to participate is reflected in the more advantageous wording obtained by the former.

Other recent research has explored ways the legal system responds, often through regulating gender relations, to the centrality of the reproduction (procreation, socialization, and daily maintenance) of human life and labour power to capitalism. These analyses do not ignore the role of class but concentrate on the interaction of capitalist and patriarchal relations. Leaving aside the debate about the precise relationship of human reproduction to the mode and relations of production, a certain balance between production and reproduction is integral to capitalism. Laws on marriage, infanticide, abortion, inheritance, and so on have played a role in seeking that balance.[58] Several authors have noted that the criminalization of birth control, punitive abortion law, and protective legislation prohibiting women from working in industry for certain periods surrounding the birth of a child all support reproduction of the labour force.[59] Jane Ursel, for example, explains labour legislation around the turn of the twentieth century as motivated partially by fear that indiscriminate consumption of the labour power of women and children might sacrifice future labour needs.[60] Thus legal systems have augmented in historically specific ways social relations that promote the availability of labour power through legislation directed toward shaping the reproductive practices of women.[61]

Judicial and Quasi-Judicial Decision-Making

The emergence of legislation tells part of the story of the link between the political economy and law. Less well developed in both Canadian and international literature[62] is the relationship between the forces and balances of power in civil society, on the one hand, and court and administrative board decisions and the development of legal doctrine, on the other. These issues are important because legislation is "interpreted" and moulded through judicial and administrative processes, sometimes in ways at odds with the original balance of forces that gave rise to the particular law in the first place.[63]

In the context of federal-provincial disputes, Mallory, like Garth Stevenson after him, argued that judicial decisions regarding the constitutional division of powers did not ultimately determine the federal balance. Judicial review instead represented a "sensitive indicator" of shifts in the "balance of power within the Canadian federal system." Further, Mallory argued, the Canadian constitution "is in a process of continuous evolution as the balance of forces which are brought to bear on it alter." These forces included "novel political and economic doctrines" as well as changes in economic relations.[64] As F.R. Scott also noted, many cases that went to the Judicial Committee of the Privy Council (JCPC) were not motivated by federal-provincial disputes but rather were challenges brought by those sectors of capital that were attempting to resist the rise of the "collectivist," or welfare state.[65] In addition, Mallory argued that the courts, in particular the JCPC, were "on the side of" those opposing the rise of collectivist state activity *rather than one or the other site of state power.* He concluded, "Thus, only on the surface has this struggle been a conflict between two conceptions of federalism."[66]

Mallory's analysis illuminated how rights struggles may be exploited in litigation by powerful forces attempting to resist the effects of legislation and is important for having posited both ideational and economic factors as significant. His approach went significantly beyond studies subsequently undertaken by constitutional lawyers – with the possible exception of his contemporary, F.R. Scott. Moreover, his analysis provides the new Canadian political economy with more insight than some contemporary approaches in the critical legal studies vein[67] and was more sensitive to the location of litigation within the societal balance of forces than some present-day Marxist analyses.[68]

Contemporary examinations of courts in Canada have not dealt adequately with either the importance of conceptualizing courts as part of the capitalist state or the relationship between social forces and struggles in civil society and courts. Glasbeek and Mandel's important piece on the Charter of Rights, for example, suggests how litigation may mediate disputes by individualizing and abstracting them from their historical and class settings. Nevertheless, their analysis of the relationship between struggles and social movements and the courts is oddly lacking. On the one hand, they treat courts as part of the capitalist state. On the other hand, when discussing court decisions, they disengage constitutional litigation from its material and social bases within changing relations of production, class struggles, and social movements. They characterize, for example, the US Supreme Court as having "almost single-handedly" decriminalized abortion.[69] This misleading underemphasis of the critical political struggle that preceded and surrounded the litigation in *Roe* v. *Wade* obscures the location of that court decision within women's struggles for abortion rights. At least in constitutional litigation, court challenges are often connected with more direct political struggles and social movements. Further, court decisions may not be simply responses to the litigation at hand, as Mallory's earlier work is important for underscoring, but may be more general reactions to capital restructuring and the balance of class forces within which litigation is embedded.[70]

Glasbeek and Mandel's failure to adequately conceptualize courts as located within broader societal conflict may help explain their conclusion that progressive groups should not engage in struggle in the courts.[71] An elaborated theory of the state, however, suggests that in addition to being embedded within the balance of class forces and overt political struggle, courts may be arenas of class, gender and other struggles, even though that struggle may be mediated in particularly legalistic ways. Such an understanding suggests the need to re-examine Glasbeek and Mandel's abstentionist position and raises the question whether refusing to participate in constitutional litigation may permit other interests, such as capital and the reactionary right, to define the issues unilaterally.[72] Hence, Peter Russell is correct to argue that Marxists have not yet developed a "positive and coherent theory of adjudication."[73] Theorizing adjudication as a terrain of struggle, as well as locating it within the economic and political context, may provide a fruitful direction for future analyses of court decisions and legal doctrines,[74] as well as administrative tribunals. Too often work on tribunals conceives of the relationship between capital and particular boards as one of "capture,"[75] an instrumentalist conception that obscures much about the complex ways bias may be reproduced within these agencies.[76]

Social Movements and the Law

Since the emergence of legislation and of court and administrative board decisions is also shaped by conflicts other than class struggles, it is necessary to inquire into how social movements influence the development of law. Shelley Gavigan has observed, for example, that while the capitalist mode of production created the precondition of formal legal equality, legal rights for women such as suffrage, equal pay, and equal division of family property resulted from persistent feminist struggle.[77] Even the particular form of discourse predominating in debates over law reform can influence the path of legal development. As Jane Jenson has pointed out, neither women nor the left had the political resources to express their voices during the early Canadian abortion law debates of the mid-1960s. As a result, the medicalized and liberalized debates dominated by doctors, lawyers, and churches led abortion law reform away from emphasizing access to abortion as a basic right for women.

According to Jenson, this situation could now change if a united feminist movement on abortion pointed out the real costs for women of restrictive abortion laws and challenged the casting of the debate within the discourses of medicalization and human rights which do not accommodate discussion of women's difference from men. She argues that other successful feminist campaigns concerning rights for women in the Charter and in matrimonial law succeeded because struggles over these issues in civil society threatened the existing balance of political forces.[78] Laureen Snider has argued similarly that by carefully examining the history of law reform efforts, the potential of particular reform strategies can be assessed. Not all law reforms are "traps." Particularly promising reforms may be those that increase working-class capacities[79] and/or social, political, and economic equality and that have a strong working-class base, establish alliances with other classes, are visible, create rights, and can be institutionalized.[80]

Important issues remain only partially treated by the determination literature. Underdeveloped is the influence of Canada's "rich dependency," first on Britain and then on the United States, and its particular constellation of class relations, including its high-wage[81] – but purportedly politically weak[82] – working class, on the development of Canadian law and the legal system. Other important matters include the role of American hegemony in such Canadian legal developments as the increasing privatization of social control, including prisons,[83] and the differences between the political economies of the various provinces, territories, and regions. It has too often been assumed that inquiry into central Canada is representative of the history of law in all parts of Canada.[84]

OVERDETERMINATION

A political economy approach to law must also attempt to grasp the ways in which law as practice, discourse, and institutions may be implicated in the reconstitution, mediation, or processes of "overdetermination" of the relations of production, thereby helping to shape social relations and struggles in the relations of production, in civil society, and within the state itself. In this regard, Canadian political economy has been concerned primarily with exploring the coercive aspects of particular areas of law such as labour law and how legal actions and institutions have helped reproduce and reconstitute capitalist relations of power. While this focus is crucial, the new political economy must now address strategic questions such as how rights, law, and legal institutions affect class capacities and the mobilization abilities of progressive movements. Law must be treated as a terrain "in which both reproductive and non-reproductive struggles are possible."[85]

Reconstituting Capitalist Relations

The Canadian state's historical involvement in reconstituting capitalist relations of production by fostering accumulation strategies has received much attention in the Canadian political economy literature.[86] Surprisingly, however, there have been few attempts to analyse the particular roles of law and legal institutions in those processes. Political economists such as Macpherson, Ellen Meiksins Wood, and Richard Devlin have elaborated on the "facilitative" role of law, in which it organizes capitalist relations of production and exchange. Macpherson and Wood, among others, highlight the place of law in defining private property rights and "freedom of contract." Devlin has posited the importance of contract law in organizing the exchange of commodities and potentially providing capital with an element of certainty for profit-making.[87] Criminal law as well is important in reproducing capitalist relations by protecting private property from trespass, theft, and the like[88] and by criminalizing various forms of dissent and resistance. Other laws positively sanction and strengthen various rights that employers already possess because of their superior economic power, for example by prohibiting collective bargaining over "management prerogatives."[89]

In this latter respect, Rosemary Warskett argues, in a discussion of union organization among bank workers, that the post-war juridification of labour relations in Canada has had "far reaching" and largely negative consequences for both the practice and ideology of the Canadian labour movement, demobilizing and demotivating trade unions.[90] While she recognizes the importance of protective labour legislation, reliance upon it has also brought into play substantial dilemmas, problems, and contradictions. Labour relations law has co-opted labour, obscured the real effects of law by appearing to be neutral, and imposed equality on unequal entities. Most crucially, perhaps, it has "naturalized" the historic struggles by labour for its rights by making it appear as if the state bestowed these rights on labour, rather than labour extracting them. Many Canadian commentators have emphasized that these highly juridified relations have imposed on trade unions a particular form of struggle in which unions have been encouraged to "police themselves."[91]

Other political economists have analysed the Constitution Act, 1867, and the involvement of Canadian courts in early cases involving interference with particular capitalists' private property rights. Work on the former provides an example of how legal forms may reinforce specific patterns of accumulation through constitutional mandate.[92] Barry Wright has studied how Canada's dependence on British markets and capital, the Canadian state's early promotion of accumulation, and Canada's reception of British common law conditioned the Canadian courts' responses to state intervention in the economy in the nineteenth century. His analysis indicates that in contrast to British and American courts at approximately the same time, and despite their usual deference to general English common law, the courts of Upper Canada were occasionally willing to interfere with particular private property rights in order to "promote the exploitation of natural resources"[93] through public economic activity.

Particular laws may also facilitate accumulation and capitalist relations of production by reproducing the "supply" of labour power and disciplining labour. Thus, while they may represent partial victories for subordinate classes and progressive movements, welfare state and family laws may also reinforce, for example, unequal gender relations. Welfare and family law arguably facilitate a balance between productive and reproductive capacities of the population, a balance conducive to a healthy and plentiful labour force.[94] Similarly, Cuneo's work demonstrates how the provisions of the first unemployment insurance legislation specifically reproduced aspects of class relations within capitalism by promoting a supply of " 'floating' reserve labour" as well as continued managerial control of capital, the capitalist labour market, the labour contract, and the status quo – which is to say the unequal strength – of trade unions.[95] Finally, Mandel has argued that both sentencing and parole, as implemented through the discretion of courts and administrative boards, may less protect society from crime than discipline "criminals" to accept their roles in capitalist relations of production and release those who have internalized this "discipline."[96]

The Organization of Violence, Coercion, and Consent

Law and legal institutions may also assist in reinforcing capitalist relations through the organization and legitimation of violence and coercion, while also contributing to the organization of consent. Drawing on Weber's insight, Devlin and others have noted that within capitalism, law has been both premissed on the "state's monopoly over the legitimate use of force" and has played a crucial role in codifying and justifying both that monopoly and the actual use of force.[97] Legally sponsored violence has been much in evidence in Canadian history, especially, but by no means exclusively, in labour relations and in the deployment of criminal law and the police. To recognize, however, that law is premissed on violence patently does not render "the liberal democratic state . . . an authoritarian state," as Devlin insists.[98] This sort of analysis obscures significant differences between liberal democratic and authoritarian capitalist states.

While state-sponsored coercion is not the only means of coercion in capitalist society – the relations of production are themselves coercive[99] – law does play a crucial role in organizing, legitimating, and administering state coercion in addition to the bold use of state-sponsored violence. As Mandel's work demonstrates, prison, sentencing, and parole – and, we would add, police and security agencies as well – are imbued with legitimacy through their legalized forms.[100] And, at least in labour relations, legal coercion has increased in Canada since the mid-1970s. Yet, as Panitch and Swartz indicate, assaults on labour rights do not necessarily quiet workers' resistance. Rather, in some periods and some conjunctures it has resulted in furthering contradictions and provoked renewed resistance. Hence, legal actions are clearly "not without their contradictions."[101]

Labour relations also demonstrate how the flexibility of law may facilitate state coercion. Panitch and Swartz illustrate, for example, how trade union actions that are legal under the general framework of collective bargaining statutes have been "increasingly declared unlawful for particular groups of workers or for all workers for a particular period of time" by virtue of particularistic and ad hoc legislation.[102] This legislation, combined with court injunctions, has, for example, rendered otherwise legal strikes immediately illegal. This flexibility of law, implemented through legislation, courts, and administrative boards, may facilitate the state's coercive responses to changing social conditions. That the form and appearance of rights, such as collective bargaining rights, may be retained while their substance becomes altered and undermined is also indicated by this work. The ability to retain the appearance of rights has obscured – although not completely – the real consequences of the changes imposed.

Thus in contrast to some liberal analyses which treat law as inflexible and certain, it is clear that the very flexibility of law is an important attribute that permits it to be wielded in chameleon-like fashion. Moreover, in contrast to some analyses of law emanating from the critical legal studies movement that treat the flexibility and discretion embodied within law and legal institutions – or the "indeterminacy" of law – as indicating the inadequacy, brittleness, and flawed nature of "liberal legalism,"[103] analyses like Panitch and Swartz's indicate its potential functionality.[104] As Ralph Miliband has noted, legal rules and rights are "all peculiarly elastic notions." The way discretion is used by courts, administrative boards, and police, for example, "must to a great extent depend upon the political climate in which they operate."[105]

Legal forms are crucially implicated in coercion, and the state does wield violence through legal institutions, but obviously the liberal democratic state does not rule by terror alone. Wright's work on the Upper Canadian treason proceedings of 1814 and 1838 augments that of Douglas Hay on the intimate relationship between terror and consent in eighteenth-century England.[106] Wright indicates that in Upper Canada, the hegemony of the "ruling elite" depended on the "ongoing historical mixing of expedient regulation of deterrence, terror and mercy with elite political views articulated and applied"[107] through the legal system. Thus, while the foundation of consent within capitalism lies pre-eminently in its ability to satisfy the material needs of its citizens, law, legal forms, and legal institutions may also help reproduce and reinforce that material basis of consent.[108]

Two important elements in the ability of law to organize consent are the elements of justice captured by the "rule of law" and the law's responsiveness to at least some class and other struggles. The ideological force of law is premissed precisely on the kernel of truth embedded within its claims – the real commitment displayed to justice and the rule of law. If justice "was not a nonsense" in eighteenth-century Britain, as Hay's analysis indicates it was not, neither is it a nonsense in twentieth-century Canada, in that law does not always manifestly oppress particular groups nor consistently benefit others. In addition, rule through law may circumscribe the power of capital. As Corrigan and Sayer have argued: "To the extent that capital rules in and through law . . . the specific forms and procedures of law circumscribe its freedom and constrain its modes of action."[109]

While "legality" is not a sufficient condition for consent, particular attributes of law may be especially adept at ideologically clothing class and other power "in the seemly robes of democratic consent in ways that are experienced intangibly"[110] as well as more directly. The "formalism," "majesty," "ritual," and "technicality" embedded in some legal institutions – notably in the courts – may contribute to the ideological force of legal results, especially of litigation. The persistence of formalism in the judicial proceedings of our century may call up an analysis similar to Hay's regarding eighteenth-century British criminal law administration: "The punctilious attention to forms, the dispassionate and legalistic exchanges between counsel and the judge, argued that those administering and using the laws submitted to its rules. The law thereby became something more than the creature of a ruling class – it became a power with its own claims."[111] The majesty and ritual found in contemporary court proceedings, at least in the higher courts, seem to represent more than a mere hangover of misguided "respect" for the legal system in their ability to focus attention and to provide the public moment around which both "terror" and mercy revolve. Litigation, as we have argued, is embedded within broader social movements and struggles. The process of litigation, the "handing down of a decision" by the courts, particularly where the court is acknowledging rights, may, however, obscure that material basis of the struggle.[112] The legal reasoning process, the use of stare decisis and precedent by courts, may also permit particularly conservative treatment of social and political issues which uses the past to justify existing processes, as Wright has argued.[113]

The ideological force of law in shaping belief systems and fostering consent must also be viewed in the context of a complex set of state and societal institutions and interactions. The dialectical relationship between legal and social relations, and the ideologies that they both produce and reproduce, is illustrated by the literature on family law. Contemporary Canadian family law rarely reveals direct capitalist or patriarchal interests. Instead, it may assist in reproducing consent to familial structures in a more indirect fashion. These structures may in turn institutionalize gender relations compatible with capitalism, including, in some social formations, the reinforcement of female economic dependence and devaluation of domestic labour and child care.[114] The important question is often not how law directly oppresses groups such as women, but how law assists in reconstituting social arrangements consistent with existing patriarchal and capitalist relations and how it interacts with other agencies and societal institutions that bolster consent.[115]

The law and legal arenas have considerable symbolic importance. In particular, the coding or selective mechanisms embedded within legal discourse – the encouraging of some forms of activity and discouraging of others by law's mechanisms – are significant. But law's effects on struggles go far beyond the symbolic. The quintessential form of law within capitalism, the modes by which it tends to individuate and abstract struggles from their social and material bases,[116] and the manifestation of formal juridical equality affect the shape of class antagonisms, conflicts, and struggles. Moreover, the technicality, and bureaucratism – or legalism – of law may undercut mobilization, as the literature on labour relations law reviewed above suggests. Finally, as Glasbeek and Mandel have warned, the technicalities and formalities typical of legal arenas may encourage the expenditure of resources and energies in "legalistic practice," potentially exhausting political resources.[117]

Juridical Freedom and Formal Legal Equality

Perhaps the most fundamental and problematic basis for the ideological aspect of law in organizing consent, legitimating oppressive social and material relations, and fragmenting collective endeavours emanates from the construction of "free" and "equal" subjects through juridical categories. Central premisses of law in liberal democratic capitalism are that individuals are "free" in the economic realm, insofar as they may strike their own bargains and dispose of their labour and property "freely,"[118] and free from the juridical inequality and dependence present in pre-capitalist modes of production. The ideological importance of these premisses is found in the way they may obscure and justify unequal and oppressive class, gender, and other relations. As many commentators note, "economic freedom" within capitalism is a particularly cramped notion of freedom. Moreover, as both Leo Panitch and Ellen Meiksins Wood have emphasized, because classes are constituted by the relations of production rather than directly by the state and law, the coercion that obtains within capitalist systems tends to be obscured.[119]

Formal juridical freedom and equality may thus obscure the fact that capitalist relations of production are neither free nor equal. By treating unequally situated individuals and groups as if they were equal at least some of the time, formal juridical equality also perpetuates unequal relations between classes, sexes, and races more directly. Rights are mediated by social, historical, political, and economic contexts which may be "invisible" to the law, a point illustrated by reference to struggles for formal equality rights. For instance, although obtaining the right to own property in the name of formal juridical equality with men was a significant victory for married women, other material and ideological constraints limited access by women to waged labour and the ability to acquire property in their own right. Similarly, capital and labour bargain collectively under conditions of structural inequality that include capital's greater material resources, greater "organizational and ideological resources," and "greater access to the state." Yet, in crucial respects, capital and labour are treated in collective bargaining law as if they meet on an equal footing.[120] Those who are "more equal" in reality are thereby favoured by the "neutrality" of law implicit in the concept of formal juridical equality, thus reinforcing the "net transfer" of power from those who do not own and control the means of production to those who do.[121]

Further, the discretion present in the law, operating against the backdrop of the presumed universal, neutral application of the law to "free and equal" individuals, simultaneously permits disparate and unequal treatment.[122] As Mandel points out, research into the invocation of criminal sanctions by courts demonstrates that "criminal law is applied in anything but an equal manner."[123] In labour law, the discretionary imposition of penalties by courts may be, and often is, particularly harsh when dealing with labour, as in the jailing of Jean-Claude Parrot in the last decade for refusing to order his workers back to work[124] and the recent jailing of Newfoundland labour leaders. The symbolic effects of such harsh example-setting should not be underestimated.

The juridical concepts of free and equal individuals are extended in capitalist democracies to the "interpellation" of people as free and equal citizens. Individual citizenship rights tend to both disarticulate classes and to rearticulate individual citizenship interests as the "national interest." In one fell swoop, classes are thereby fractured at the political level insofar as liberal democracies typically represent citizens, rather than classes, in the state. And political parties tend – at least in Canadian liberal democracy – to represent and articulate the "national interest," while the "national interest" represents pre-eminently the interests of capital. Hence, while subordinate classes may be disorganized by the categories of "free and equal," the capitalist class is brought together and represented broadly as if its interests truly expressed the common good. Thus, despite the fact that the franchise constituted a genuine victory for subordinate classes, oppressed races, and women, the exclusiveness of this mode of representation – the absence of class representation mechanisms, workplace democracy, and the like – may curtail genuine participatory possibilities.[125]

Predicated on the core concepts of "free" and "equal" individuals, and contingent on historical resistances and struggles, is the constitution of state subjects as bearing other, predominantly individual-based civil liberties and rights in liberal democracies. The presumed atomizing consequences of these configurations are often commented on in the literature. However, the law does not only atomize. Vera Chouinard has provided an important corrective in the Canadian literature by arguing that historical and concrete class antagonisms and struggles may prey on systemic contradictions in particular conjunctures, thus creating possibilities for struggles to resist the logic of atomization. Chouinard indicates that concrete struggles may achieve both legal restrictions on the "degree and manner" of subjection to the logic of production and legal recognition as collectivities. She further argues that precisely to the extent that struggles achieve collectivized class-specific rights and recognition, class capacities may thereby be enhanced.[126]

It seems clear that political struggles often revolve around rights claims in liberal democracies partly because of the cultural and historical commitment to at least some rights in such societies. But the pre-eminence of formal juridical equality may facilitate the appropriation of rights discourse by any political group, progressive or otherwise. Jenson has argued, for example, that instead of the abortion issue being seen as a debate between women and men as groups divided by sex, women's "right" to choose abortion has been pitted against pro-life arguments for foetal rights, thereby obscuring the gendered nature of the issue: "In such a discourse, women disappear as a group and reappear as individuals with needs which can only be assessed against those of all other persons, including foetuses."[127] These sorts of struggles are implicitly, if not explicitly, premised on formal juridical equality – positing equality of "access" to the enormously important claim to "right."

The concepts of atomization, freedom, formal legal equality, individual civil liberties, and political and citizenship rights may currently constitute the most complex and pressing " 'problem of legality' in historical materialism." The concepts of "free" and "equal" legal subjects do appear to fracture the subordinate classes, and the "centrality of a private, isolated, autonomous, egoistic legal subject possessed above all of a freewill" *may* "enforce . . . and legitimate . . . oppressive class relations."[128] At the same time, insofar as the ideological role of law requires some kernel of truth to its claims, individual civil liberties may help protect us against at least the most direct and obvious state coercion and intrusions – a not unimportant point in the era of Thatcher, Reagan, and Vander Zalm. Moreover, citizenship and political rights, as limited as they are in Canada, are valuable and were bestowed on us by neither a beneficent nor a cunning state, but rather were won through struggle. And the importance to disadvantaged groups of legal instruments acquired through struggles for formal legal equality should not be underestimated.

Much work in political economy of law in Canada does not adequately address these important and complex contradictions and problems. Indeed, an unmitigated hostility is displayed toward individual rights, most especially in the work emanating from legally trained scholars.[129] Glasbeek and Mandel, for example, undervalue individual constitutional rights, while some work in administrative law also denigrates the importance of individual claims against the state.[130] These approaches fail to seriously investigate the admittedly problematic but potentially emancipatory status of the individual legal subject endowed with free will and deserving of respect. An unexplored assumption that notions of "autonomy" and "community" are necessarily antithetical also abounds in both the work of Glasbeek and Mandel and in the critical legal studies–inspired work of Hutchinson and Monahan. Hutchinson and Monahan claim, in fact, that "rights-based theories have corrosive implications for communal aspirations."[131]

The complexity of formal legal equality, the importance of civil and political rights against and within the capitalist state, and notions of individualism and citizenship must be explored much more seriously in a developed political economy of law.[132] This task does not require us to concede significant ground to liberal approaches to law. It means simply refusing to throw the baby out with the bathwater. Ian Taylor has aptly criticized those who imply that we can simply take notice of the bourgeois form of law and then go home:

The danger . . . is that they frequently present law and legal institutions as an impenetrable and secure element in the apparatus of class domination, and that thereby they discourage the use of legal interventions as a useful move in political struggles. To say this is not, of course, to deny that one of the achievements of bourgeois law *is* to displace the *class* struggles that are constantly occurring in capitalist societies over commodities into disputes between *individual legal subjects* . . . legal discourse is a mystification of the true character of social relations in a propertied, unequal society, but it is none the less an important (imperfect) instrument in the defence of the liberties of the classes and the sexes.[133]

We would add that the new political economy of law could do worse than to recall the work of some of the "old" political economists, including that of Macpherson and F.R. Scott in their defence of "liberties."[134] Finally, work such as Chouinard's, which begins to theorize how the construction of legal subjects and rights can be challenged, how class-specific, collective rights may be secured in particular capitalist conjunctures, and how collective constructions may enhance the potential for transformative politics, constitutes an important challenge for the new Canadian political economy. While the questions surrounding appropriate forms of socialist legality have not even been broached in the Canadian literature, commentators have begun to consider the nature of collective and "activist" rights and progressive rights strategies.[135] Even this work, however, is all too sparse and limited in Canada.

CONCLUSION

We have stressed the complexity of the development and effects of law. Literature on periods of "crisis" of the state in Canada, for instance, illustrates how law both responds to and helps shape crisis,[136] indicating that law is a "complex, double-edged and deeply fissured condensation [of] social relations."[137] As may be all too evident in this chapter, it is arbitrary to separate, perhaps even for heuristic purposes, the "determining" forces on law from the "overdetermining" effects law has on social and economic relations. In reality, as the law responds to capitalist relations and to its attendant antagonisms, struggles, and social forces, it may influence in contradictory fashions the nature and direction of these relations.

Law, legal institutions, and rights represent both spaces and tensions, contradictions and possibilities, limitations and potential. We must, therefore, be cognizant of the ways in which law and legal institutions may contribute to the reconstitution and reproduction of existing relations of power. We must simultaneously begin to explore seriously what it means to say that law is embedded within struggle and is an arena of struggle itself; how and to what extent the discourse of rights and the forms of law may contribute to or detract from our struggles; how law, legal institutions, and rights may be used in strategic ways while minimizing the potentially demobilizing and integrative effects of participating within legal forms and legal arenas. If the new Canadian political economy meets these challenges, we will be that much better equipped to assess which strategies advance transformative and socialist politics.

NOTES

We would like to thank Wallace Clement, Shelley Gavigan, Alan Hunt, Leo Panitch, Wes Pue, Neil Sargent, Glen Williams, and Barry Wright for their helpful comments on drafts of this chapter. An earlier version was presented at the June 1987 meetings of the Canadian Law and Society Association, Hamilton, Ontario.

1 For overviews see Hunt, "The Theory of Critical Legal Studies"; Hutchinson and Monahan, "Law, Politics and the Critical Legal Scholars"; and J. Stuart Russell, "The Critical Legal Studies Challenge."
2 See Innis, *Changing Concepts of Time*, 47–76.
3 See Mallory, *Social Credit and the Federal Power*.
4 See Hutchinson and Monahan, "Law, Politics, and Critical Legal Scholars."
5 See, for example, Ericson, *The Constitution of Legal Inequality*.
6 See Neil Boyd, ed., *The Social Dimensions of Law*; Brickey and Comack, eds., *The Social Basis of Law*; Panitch and Swartz, *From Consent to Coercion*; Socialist Studies, *Critical Perspectives on the Constitution* II; Taylor, *Crime, Capitalism and Community*; White, *Law, Capitalism and the Right to Work*. Also see Brickey and Comack, "The Role of Law," and Ratner and McMullan, eds., *State Control*, both of which appeared after this chapter was written.

7 Hirst defines law as "a set of primary rules which function as guides to action and a set of rules of recognition whereby actors can verify the validity of rules .... [which may be differentiated from other rules] not by any formal properties but by the claim advanced by the agencies issuing them [legislatures, courts] to be the dominant and obligatory source of binding rules in a given territory." Hirst, "Socialist Legality," 125-6. While this definition excludes the "legal pluralist" view, it will be adopted for present purposes. See also Sugarman, "Law, Economy and the State," and Fitzpatrick, "Law and Societies."

8 See Snider, "Towards a Political Economy."

9 See Ratner, "Inside the Liberal Boot"; McMullan, "The 'Law and Order' Problem"; and Ratner and McMullan, "Social Control."

10 Cain, "Beyond Formal Justice," 348. For an early, critical review of the Canadian legal profession, see Scott, "The Future of the Legal Profession."

11 See, for example, Tom Campbell, *The Left and Rights*; Hall, Crichter, Jefferson, Clarke, and Roberts, *Policing the Crisis*; Hunt, "The Radical Critique of Law" and "The Ideology of Law"; Jessop, "On Recent Marxist Theories of Law"; Poulantzas, *State, Power, Socialism*; Smart, "Feminism and Law"; and Thompson, *Whigs and Hunters*.

12 Feminist literature often makes this point. See for example, Gavigan, "Women, Law and Patriarchal Relations."

13 See for example, Finkel, "Origins of the Welfare State." See also the early work of Snider, "Traditional and Corporate Theft" and "Revising the Combines Investigation Act"; Goff and Reasons, *Corporate Crime in Canada*. For critiques of instrumentalist approaches to corporate crime, see Snider, "Towards a Political Economy of Reform," and Sargent, "Law, Ideology and Corporate Crime."

14 See for example, Ison, "The Sovereignty of the Judiciary," and Pue, "The Law Reform Commission of Canada."

15 Much criminological literature in Canada adopts this approach. See for example, Ericson, *The Constitution of Legal Inequality* and *Reproducing Order*; Turk, "Law, Conflict, and Order." For a critical review see Ratner, "Inside the Liberal Boot." From a Foucaultian perspective see Hutchinson, "Part of an Essay."

16 Glasbeek and Mandel, "The Legalisation of Politics"; Mandel, "The Rule of Law"; Ison, "The Sovereignty of the Judiciary"; and Martin, "The Judges and the Charter." In a non-political economy, but "critical" vein, see Hutchinson and Monahan, "The Rule of Law."

17 See Devlin, "Tales of Centaurs."

18 For a discussion of this problem, see Chunn and Gavigan, "Social Control."

19 Panitch, "Elites, Classes and Power," 236.

20 Mahon, *The Politics of Industrial Restructuring*, 10.

21 For a concise review of state theories, see Stasiulis, "Capitalism."

22 Nor can feminist theory " 'catch up by walking in the footsteps of marxist legal theorists' ": Smart, "Feminism and Law," 111. See also Maroney and Luxton, "Feminism and Political Economy," and Bakker in this volume.

23 See Hunt, "The Ideology of Law"; J.B. Wright, *The Ideological Dimensions of Law in Upper Canada*; and Gavigan, "Law, Gender and Ideology."

24 See Chouinard, "Class Formation"; Corrigan and Sayer, *The Great Arch*; White, *Law, Capitalism and the Right to Work*.

25 See Snider and West, "A Critical Perspective" and "Canada and the United States."

26 See Morse, "Introduction," xi–xv; Sanders, "The Indian Lobby."

27 See Pue, "Review of Louis A. Knafla."

28 Sumner, "The Rule of Law," 68. See also Warskett, "Bank Worker Unionization."

29 See Macpherson, "Human Rights as Property Rights" and "Capitalism and the Changing Concept of Property," 105.

30 Macpherson, *Democratic Theory*, 124. See also Wood, *The Retreat from Class*, chap. 10.

31 Sugarman, "Law, Economy and the State in England."

32 For a review of the literature see Abercrombie, Hill, and Turner, *Sovereign Individuals*.

33 See Thompson, *Whigs and Hunters* and *The Poverty of Theory*. Also see Kaye, *The British Marxist Historians*.

34 But see Devlin, "Tales of Centaurs"; Tucker, "The Law of Employers' Liability"; and Wood, "Separation."

35 See Bernier and Salée, "Social Relations."

36 G.A. Cohen, *Karl Marx's Theory of History*, 217.

37 See Tucker, "The Law of Employers' Liability," especially 269–70.

38 Hall et al., *Policing the Crisis*, 200.

39 Tucker, "The Law of Employers' Liability"; Devlin, "Tales of Centaurs"; and Albo and Jenson in this volume.

40 See Hunt, "The Theory of Critical Legal Studies."

41 See especially Laclau and Mouffe, *Hegemony*. But see Geras's apt metaphor in "Post-Marxism?" And see Laclau and Mouffe, "Post-Marxism."

42 See Pal, "Relative Autonomy Revisited" and "Reply"; and Cuneo, "Comment."

43 See Smart, "Feminism and Law." Also see Perry Anderson, *Arguments*, 200.

44 Mahon, *The Politics of Industrial Restructuring*, "Canadian Public Policy," and "Regulatory Agencies."

45 See Snider, "Legal Aid," 178, for a good summary of these concerns, and Smandych, "Origins," for a cogent criticism of Bliss's work for failure to do so.

46 See Smandych, "Origins."

47 Comack, " 'We Will Get Some Good,' " 74, 75, 86.

48 See Cuneo, "State Mediation," 38, and "State, Class and Reserve Labour."

49 See Finkel, "Origins."

50 Marchak, "Canadian Political Economy," 693. Also see Brym, "Anglo-Canadian Sociology," especially 70–4.

51 See Panitch, "Role and Nature"; Swartz, "The Politics of Reform"; Finkel, "Ori-

gins"; Moscovitch and Drover, eds., *The Welfare State in Canada*; Moscovitch and Albert, eds., *The Benevolent State*; Myles, "The Aged"; Struthers, *No Fault of Their Own*; Tucker, "Determination"; and Walters, "Occupational Health."

52 See, for example, Ryerson, *Unequal Union*, and Naylor, "Rise and Fall." For a review see Stasiulus, "Capitalism."

53 Garth Stevenson, "Federalism," and *Unfulfilled Union*. See also Brodie and Jenson, *Crisis, Challenge and Change*. See Mallory, *Social Credit*, for a liberal, Innis-inspired explanation.

54 See Glasbeek and Mandel, "The Legalisation of Politics"; Mandel, "The Rule of Law." See Taylor, "Theorizing," for reservations concerning the applicability to Canada of Gramsci's theory of hegemonic crisis and Habermas's theory of legitimation crisis.

55 See Ratner, "Introduction."

56 See Peter Russell, "The Political Purposes."

57 See Whitaker, "Democracy."

58 See Ursel, "The State," 153, 154.

59 See ibid., 180; Jenson, "Gender and Reproduction," 16.

60 Ursel, "The State," 161.

61 For a discussion of child custody law and the socialization aspect of reproduction, see Arnup, "Lesbian Mothers."

62 See, however, Miliband, "Activism"; Kairys, "Freedom of Speech"; and Sparer, "Fundamental Human Rights." For a review of Canadian literature on courts and the constitution see Peter Russell, "Overcoming Legal Formalism."

63 See Devlin, "Tales of Centaurs."

64 Mallory, *Social Credit*, 4, 6, 7, 37. Also see Stevenson, *Unfulfilled Union*, 66.

65 Scott, "The P.C."

66 Mallory, *Social Credit*, 53, 55, also 182. Also see Scott, "The P.C.," 101.

67 See Monahan, "At Doctrine's Twilight."

68 Glasbeek and Mandel, "The Legalisation of Politics"; Mandel, "The Rule of Law." See also Martin, "The Judges and the Charter."

69 Glasbeek and Mandel, "The Legalisation of Politics," 103, 108.

70 See Mallory, *Social Credit*. Also see Kairys, "Freedom of Speech," and Sparer, "Fundamental Human Rights."

71 See especially Glasbeek, "Workers of the World." See also Devlin, "Tales of Centaurs."

72 Contrast with Petter, "The Politics of the Charter." See Hall, *Drifting*, 17.

73 Peter Russell, "Overcoming Legal Formalism," 24.

74 The recent Sunday closing decisions might usefully be assessed in terms of mediating struggles between fractions of capital and simultaneously between capital and the working class, as well as between organized and unorganized sectors of the working class. See *R. v. Big M Drug Mart* (1985), 18 *Canadian Criminal Cases* (3d) 385 (Supreme Court of Canada) and *Edwards Books and Art v. The Queen*, [1986] 2 *Supreme Court Reports* 713.

75 See Pue, "The Law Reform Commission," recommending more resources to tribunals in order to be able to resist "capture."

76 See Mahon, "Regulatory Agencies," "Canadian Public Policy," and *The Politics of Industrial Restructuring.*

77 See Gavigan, "Women and Abortion," 267; Gavigan, "Marxist Theories of Law," 10.

78 See Jenson, "A False Victory," 39.

79 See Chouinard, "Class Formation."

80 Snider, "Legal Aid," 176-7, 191. See also Snider, "Legal Reform"; Havemann, who argues that progressive groups should take procedural rights in the Young Offenders Act seriously: "Child Saving"; and Warskett, "Bank Worker Unionization."

81 See Panitch, "Dependency and Class," and Schmidt, "Canadian Political Economy."

82 See Schmidt, "Canadian Political Economy," and Taylor, *Crime, Capitalism and Community.* But see the important, conjuncturally specific working-class histories of Gregory Kealey (*Toronto Workers*) and Bryan D. Palmer (*Working-Class Experience*).

83 See Ratner, "Introduction," 2-3. See other contributions to *Crime and Social Justice* 26 (1986), especially Mandel, "Legalization of Prison Discipline."

84 Wright, "Towards a New Canadian Legal History," 366; Pue, "Review of Louis Knafla."

85 Chouinard, "Class Formation," 3.

86 See Panitch, "Role and Nature"; and Stasiulus, "Capitalism." The classic literature includes Fowke, *The National Policy,* and Nelles, *The Politics of Development.*

87 See Devlin, "Tales of Centaurs," 55; Tucker, "The Law of Employers' Liability," 272; Wood, *Retreat from Class*; and Macpherson, "Capitalism and the Changing Concept of Property." But see Macaulay, "Non-contractual Relationships," for a different view.

88 Glasbeek, "Corporate Deviance."

89 Tucker, "The Law of Employers' Liability," 271.

90 See Warskett, "Bank Worker Unionization."

91 Panitch and Swartz, *From Consent to Coercion,* 22; also see Jean-Claude Parrot, "An Interview"; Bryan Palmer, "Listening to History," 76; and Chouinard, "Class Formation," on the co-operative housing movement.

92 See Mallory, *Social Credit*; Scott, *Essays on the Constitution*; Stevenson, *Unfulfilled Union*; and Clark, "Continental Capital Accumulation," especially 220-3.

93 Barry Wright, "Towards a New Canadian Legal History," 372.

94 See Ursel, "The State."

95 See Cuneo, "State Mediation," 61, 53, 54-9.

96 See Mandel, "Democracy, Class and the National Parole Board," 179, and "Democracy, Class and Canadian Sentencing Law."

97 See Devlin, "Tales of Centaurs." Devlin is incorrect in saying that Poulantzas did

not note this; see Poulantzas, *State, Power, Socialism*, and Genovese, "Hegemonic Function."

98 Devlin, "Tales of Centaurs," 24.

99 See Whitaker, "Neo-Conservatism," 24.

100 See Mandel, "Democracy, Class and the National Parole Board" and "Democracy, Class and Canadian Sentencing Law."

101 Panitch and Swartz, *From Consent to Coercion*, 28.

102 Ibid.

103 See Hutchinson and Monahan, "Law, Politics and the Critical Legal Scholars."

104 See Hunt, "Theory," 35-6, for a similar discussion of the "function of incoherence."

105 Miliband, "Activism," 33. This point is also forcefully made by Hall et al. in *Policing the Crisis*.

106 See Hay, "Property."

107 See J.B. Wright, *Ideological Dimensions*, 67. See also Craven, "Law and Ideology."

108 See Przeworski, *Capitalism*, chap. 4.

109 Corrigan and Sayer, "How the Law Rules," 36.

110 O'Brien and McIntyre, "Patriarchal Hegemony," 74.

111 Hay, "Property," 112.

112 See Hall, *Drifting*.

113 See Barry Wright, "Towards," 360.

114 See Susan B. Boyd, "Child Custody"; Smart, *The Ties That Bind*.

115 See Smart, *The Ties That Bind*, 21. For the implications of the "intersection of medical practice and law, compounded by the overarching ideological significance of the family," see Gavigan, "Women, Law and Patriarchal Relations," 117. For ways in which legal education may reproduce in a majority of students "prescribed patterns of thought, conduct, and socio-political allegiances essential to both capitalist and patriarchal hegemony," see O'Brien and McIntyre, "Patriarchal Hegemony," 78.

116 See Glasbeek and Mandel, "The Legalisation of Politics."

117 Ibid. Also see Warskett, "Bank Worker Unionization."

118 See Macpherson, "Capitalism and the Changing Concept of Property"; Wood, *The Retreat from Class*; White, *Law, Capitalism and the Right to Work*.

119 See Wood, *The Retreat from Class*; Panitch, "Elites, Classes and Power."

120 See Panitch and Swartz, *From Consent to Coercion*, 20; see also Warskett, "Bank Worker Unionization." Family law too is now based on market assumptions, masking the gendered nature and disparate impact of the division of domestic responsibilities: Klein, "Individualism."

121 See Macpherson, *The Real World of Democracy*, 42-50.

122 On discretion, see Hay, "Property," and J.B. Wright, *Ideological Dimensions*. Also see Mandel, "Democracy, Class, and Canadian Sentencing Law"; Tucker, "The Law of Employers' Liability"; Warskett, "Bank Worker Unionization"; and

Craven, "The Law of Master and Servant."

123 See Mandel, "Democracy, Class and Canadian Sentencing Law."

124 See Glasbeek and Mandel, "Crime and Punishment."

125 See Boyle, "Home Rule for Women."

126 Chouinard, "Class Formation," 12.

127 Jenson, "A False Victory," 36; see also Smart, "Feminism and Law," 120-1.

128 Mandel, "The Rule of Law," 279.

129 See, for example, Glasbeek and Mandel, "The Legalisation of Politics"; Mandel, "The Rule of Law"; Ison, "Sovereignty"; Pue, "The Law Reform Commission"; Arthurs, "Rethinking Administrative Law"; Hutchinson and Monahan, "The Rule of Law"; and Hutchinson, "Part of an Essay."

130 See Glasbeek and Mandel, "The Legalisation of Politics."

131 Hutchinson and Monahan, "The Rule of Law," 114; also see 121.

132 See, for example, Panitch, "Liberal Democracy"; Wood, "Liberal Democracy" and *The Retreat from Class*. Also see Hunt, "The Politics of Law and Justice."

133 Taylor, *Law and Order*, 180, first emphasis added.

134 See, for example, Macpherson, *Democratic Theory* and *The Rise and Fall of Economic Justice*; Scott, *Essays on the Constitution*, especially "Freedom of Speech in Canada," 60-75.

135 See Miliband, "Activism"; White, *Law*, and Charles Campbell, "The Canadian Left."

136 See Panitch and Swartz, *From Consent to Coercion*. See also Comack, " 'We Will Get Some Good' "; Havemann, "Child Saving"; Hastings and Saunders, "Social Control"; Hastings and Saunders, "Ideology"; Taylor, *Crime, Capitalism and Community*; and MacCormick, "Deregulating the Economy."

137 Devlin, "Tales of Centaurs," 25.

CHAPTER ELEVEN

Canada as a "White Settler Colony": What about Natives and Immigrants?

Frances Abele and Daiva Stasiulis

This chapter selectively – and, we hope, provocatively – explores the treatment of race and ethnicity in English-Canadian political economy. Our focus is on two separate categories of changing social relations, involving Native peoples and immigrant groups (and their descendants).

"Native peoples" refers to the indigenous or aboriginal societies encountered by Europeans when they discovered what is now Canada. Analogous to the term *European*, "Native peoples" refers to a collectivity at a very general level. Included are all the various indigenous societies – the Dene, Nishga, Cree, Innu, Inuit, among many others – who inhabit North America.[1]

Native peoples currently comprise only a small minority of the Canadian population. The majority of Canadians are descendants of immigrants from virtually every part of the world. From an early stage in the development of the Canadian economy, ruling groups resorted to European, and to a lesser extent non-European (especially Asian), immigration as a source of labour for staples production, manufacturing, and (especially for women) domestic service.

Readers may question the wisdom of discussing Native peoples and non-Native "ethnic groups" in the same chapter. Native peoples have struggled against sustained attempts by the state to reduce their status to that of "just another disadvantaged ethnic group" and against the persistent inability of Canadians generally to appreciate their unique position.

We begin with the recognition that there are crucial differences in the circumstances and political concerns of Native people and oppressed immigrant groups. Native people were in Canada first, for many thousands of years before any other inhabitants. For each Native society, there is a very long history before European contact and then a particular history of contact with Europeans who were themselves enmeshed in evolving relations of production in Europe. All these histories comprise the history of Canada, but our attention is on only the most recent past. We shall argue that an understanding of the history of Native-European contact is essential to any analysis of Canadian state formation and economic development. Consolidation of state power over Native lands remained a central preoccupation of the federal government well into the twentieth century. Today, the presence of vast numbers of non-Natives has removed the need for a military or overtly coercive Native policy, but the battle over sovereignty continues, particularly in British Columbia, Labrador, and the territorial north.

Native peoples have a unique political and constitutional position arising from their history. In addition, for both legal and broader historical reasons, most contemporary Native societies find themselves, as societies, in a structurally different relationship to capitalist relations of production than do any other collectivities in Canada. From the point of view of Native people, everyone else in the country is an immigrant, all recently arrived (and uninvited) aliens. None of the transplanted ethnic groups is in a situation directly analogous to that of Native peoples.

Not all immigrants, however, are equal. Throughout the history of this country, many different peoples have come, often in flight from poverty or persecution at home, only to find themselves structurally and personally exploited here. From the days of first arrival, trade, and settlement by Europeans, there have been people in Canada of origins other than Native, French, or British. "Race" and ethnicity have always had an important sociological reality in Canada, forming features of legal-juridical, political, and social structures and conditioning the processes of class formation, mobilization, and conflict. The dominant British authorities, victors of the Conquest of French Canada[2] and heirs to the territory from which aboriginal societies had been displaced, followed two major imperatives in determining the national, ethnic, and racial composition of immigration: the desire to populate Canada with white, British people and the drive to meet the shifting demands of the labour market.[3] In several instances, these two imperatives clashed. In consequence, migrant and settler groups who departed from the British norms of racial, cultural, and political acceptability, but who were brought in to perform arduous and cheap labour rejected by British workers, were subjected to virulent forms of racism and nativism, often condoned and encouraged by government policies and state actions. Today, the material circumstances of immigrant groups and their descendants are varied. Within any given ethnic group are found both wealthy capitalists and wage workers, although some groups are collectively more privileged than others.

We choose to consider Native peoples and immigrant groups together for three related reasons. First, our interest is in assessing the adequacy with which the political economy tradition has advanced understanding of the roots of racism in Canada. We find that political economy, like mainstream history and social science, has often comprehended incompletely or inadequately two uncomfortable facts about Canada: the lands and resources were taken and continue to be taken from Native societies, at great cost to the members of those societies; and these lands and resources were integrated into a system of capitalist development that exploited and continues to exploit some immigrant groups more than others. Too much of the political economy tradition is colour-blind and amnesiac, failing to recognize the complexity of oppressive relations and the historical relations of struggle within which both Native peoples and immigrant groups are implicated.

Race and ethnicity are frequently treated as "add-ons" to political economy writings, as if these phenomena were peripheral to the way that Canadian society has unfolded historically and to the connections that have developed between the economic system and ideological, cultural, and political orders. Our argument is that engaging with a specific history of Native peoples and immigrant groups in a manner that recognizes the centrality and significance of race, ethnicity, and culture can say much about the nature of the Canadian social formation and its incorporation into the international political economy. In particular, such a materialist analysis will show that the categories of "race" and "ethnicity" are themselves socially constructed and historically variable.[4]

Our second reason for discussing Native peoples and ethnic minority groups in the same chapter follows from this observation. The assumption that human beings are defined by their "race" or "ethnicity" is reflected in the social science ghettos within which "Native studies" and "ethnic studies" have been placed. Yet the experiences of individuals and collectivities are better comprehended in an analysis of the matrix of social relations in which they are embedded. In Canada, as in all societies, relations of oppression are constructed through complex intersections among class, gender, racial, and ethnic forms of subordination. All Canadians are implicated in these intersecting relations of oppression. Just as sexism is not only women's problem, racism is not only a problem for Natives and "visible minorities." Racism affects the way that rights are imbedded in institutional contexts as well as the character of and restrictions in individual interactions for every member of Canadian society.

Our third reason pertains to the specific character of struggles engaged in by both Native peoples and ethnic minority groups. The politics, language, and self-organization among Native peoples and oppressed ethnic minorities is informed by notions of "nation" and "community," respectively, which bear a complex relation to class struggle. By respecting the specificity of oppression of different groups of peoples in the complex web of social relations, one can begin to understand similarities as well as differences in experience and strategies for resistance. In fact, only an analysis that respects specificity can show us how alliances might be built with and among Native and ethnic community struggles.

In this chapter, we hope to contribute to this long-range political project. An important theme in our analysis is a critique of applications to Canada of the description "white settler colony." This concept was used first by Canada's early colonial elites to describe their goals.[5] Later, it was employed by political economists to help explain Canada's peculiar pattern of development, which produced a relatively high-wage, "developed" economy heavily reliant on staples export and deeply dependent on foreign capital. As a descriptive category, "white settler colony" is useful for drawing attention to certain characteristics Canada shares with some other former colonies. However, it leads analysts away from directly confronting questions of race and ethnicity. In some applications of the concept, these factors are ignored altogether; in others, race and ethnicity are treated as unproblematic descriptions for attitudes that interfered with the smooth operation of the laws and relations of capitalist economic development and Canadian working-class and state formation. We try to turn this stance around, by arguing that it is necessary to begin with recognition of the gendered, racial, and ethnic complexity of class relations in all phases of Canadian economic and political development.

Our strategy in this paper is to introduce, briefly, some important applications of the "white settler colony" thesis. Then we review a number of analyses, first, of the circumstances of Native peoples and, second, of the role of immigrant groups and their descendants. Throughout we endeavour to consider the implications of these accounts for the political economy tradition. In this we rely on a literature generated by the energy of Native resistance and struggle and by the recent work of minority community activists and of feminist scholars to develop a politics that represents the interests of immigrant and minority women in Canada. The discussion deals, necessarily, with only a selection of each literature and omits much interesting and useful work. We cannot begin to do justice either to the histories of the original peoples of North America or to the experiences of the multitude of immigrant groups who have settled there.

"WHITE SETTLER COLONY"

The notion that Canada developed as a white settler colony or "white dominion" is a recurrent theme in the new political economy.[6] In accounts of the "peculiar" nature of Canada as simultaneously supportive of high wages and standard of living and retaining a dependent, resource-based economy, various political economists have referred to its "beginnings" as a white settler colony. Significantly, the key formative period for Canadian development is defined as the period from the 1860s to the First World War, or the "age of classical monopoly capitalism."[7]

In this model of development, Canada is classed together with Australia and New Zealand (and sometimes Argentina and Uruguay) as enjoying a privileged cultural, social, and political linkage to (British) imperialism, in direct contrast to colonies of military occupation, conquest, and impoverishment in Asia, Africa, and the Caribbean.[8] Unlike the latter regions, Canada and the other white dominions had small, sparse indigenous populations, who were "eliminated, assimilated or pushed into distant corners of the hinterland,"[9] and a temperate climate that did not favour the importation of either African slaves or indentured workers from India. These demographic and climatic conditions combined with the availability of cheap transoceanic transportation to encourage colonial ruling groups to construct a labour market by promoting large-scale European migration.

Several conditions coalesced to allow Canadian workers to capture wage rates and material standards that were among the highest in the world. These included the availability of large land reserves which in turn produced labour shortages, the advanced social organization of production, rich domestic markets for the development of import substitution industries, and the communication via immigrants' networks of gains achieved by mass struggles in Europe. Just as important, British and other European migrants shared with ruling groups a vision of Canada as a society which, in terms of living standards, political traditions, and cultural and moral values, would be created in the image of Britain. This is most directly argued by Glen Williams, who contends that "Canada and the other white Dominions . . . were developed as overseas extensions, miniature replicas, of British society, complete with a large measure of local political autonomy."[10]

Williams and, in a later article, P. Ehrensaft and W. Armstrong interpret the struggles of European workers to keep capitalists from importing Asian labourers as a key aspect of working-class strategy to maintain high wage levels by keeping out migrants "who came from regions where the socially defined standard of subsistence was far below what Europeans would accept."[11] These accounts recognize that a profound racism permeated the dynamics of both European-Native interaction and working-class formation in Canada, but they incorporate racism as a phenomenon of exceptional "ugly chapters" of Canadian history, rather than as a constituent and explanatory feature of Canadian historical development.

This tendency has had two effects. First, because racism and ethnic difference are recognized as characteristics of white settler colonies, but are not given central analytical attention, these factors tend to disappear in other work that draws on the white settler colony thesis. This leads to a second problem, perhaps more significant, because it has serious repercussions for solidarity and political mobilization. Where racism and ethnic differences are noted but not analysed, as in the white settler colony thesis, the dynamics of Native and ethnic minority resistance to exploitation become either invisible or very difficult to understand for those not directly involved.

In looking at analyses of the circumstances of Natives and immigrants, we return to these points. We focus on the potential distortions and dangers inherent in the white settler colony thesis that arise from its selective gaze on racially and ethnically dominant groups in selected phases of Canadian history. In the process, we are admittedly ignoring its strengths in accounting for the particular nature of Canadian economic development.[12] Although we argue that the notion of Canada as a white settler colony is racist in its implications, we do not mean to suggest that any of the authors we discuss have racist intentions. Rather, we are trying to show how the distortions and silences on race and ethnicity in the Canadian political economy tradition necessitate rethinking and reformulation. Our hope is that such work of reconstruction will broaden our understanding of the social forces that were and continue to be formative in Canadian development.

NATIVE PEOPLES

A central difficulty in writing about the political economy of Native peoples in Canada arises from the diversity of their pre-contact histories and the extraordinary complexity of their various and evolving relations with the state and with capitalism. Generalizations tend to conceal more than they expose. It is not surprising, then, that there exist very few synthetic works that offer a general analysis of "Native political economy" for any historical period.

In the political economy tradition, however, two authors have attempted a comprehensive overview: Harold Innis and Stanley Ryerson. Since their work was published, there have been hundreds, possibly thousands, of more narrowly focused studies of various aspects of Native peoples' history and current life circumstances. Native peoples' political struggles for self-determination have generated an enormous literature, most produced since the mid-1960s. Some analyses and histories have been written by Native people themselves, and some by non-Natives galvanized by Native political activity. Not all this literature of struggle may be accurately labelled "political economy," but for the political economist it provides an essential interpretive and factual base. Other work, not directly stimulated by Native political activism, has still been influenced; many scholars are now careful to avoid racist language and to recognize the role played by Native peoples in the events they are studying.

In this chapter, we cannot adequately reflect the richness of all of this scholarship.[13] We have space only to treat some of the major strands in some of the literature. Innis and Ryerson are discussed because of their general importance to political economists seeking to understand early state formation and capitalist development. Themes from the literature of Native struggle are then examined. Finally, we interrogate the political economy tradition as a whole concerning its analyses of the political economy of Native peoples. Here there is both satisfying progress and urgent need for improvement.

The Fur Trade

Innis's *The Fur Trade in Canada* offers an interpretation of early Canadian economic history that takes for granted that the analysis must be framed as "the history of contact between two civilizations, the European and the North American."[14] Although Innis declares his interest to be primarily the evolution of the transplanted European society, he includes careful descriptions of relations of production in the various indigenous societies that were drawn into the fur trade.

Innis's argument about the history of contact between European and North American civilizations may be briefly summarized as follows.[15] Early European colonists found themselves extraordinarily vulnerable. Their survival depended on both European commodities, such as clothing and metal implements, and indigenous food and technology. These circumstances required that a trade be established in which North American products could be exchanged for European goods. According to Innis, the indigenous societies welcomed the establishment of trade relations: "The limited cultural background of the North American hunting peoples provided an insatiable demand for the products of the more elaborate cultural development of Europeans. The supply of European goods, the products of a more advanced and specialized technology, enabled the Indians to gain a livelihood more easily."[16]

Ultimately the assimilation of European commodities and the change in productive activity forced by commercial fur gathering "disturbed the balance which had grown up previous to the coming of the European."[17] In combination, this change, new diseases, and warfare destroyed the indigenous societies. As the beaver were depleted and successive indigenous societies destroyed, the Europeans were drawn west and north – eventually to the Pacific coast and to the mouth of the Mackenzie River on the Arctic coast.

In reconstructing this history, Innis draws many lessons about the importance of geography, transportation, technology, and business organization. With respect to Native people, his conclusions are both startlingly oblivious of Native political activity and singularly pessimistic:

Canada has had no serious problems with her native peoples since the fur trade depended primarily on these races. In the United States no point of contact of such magnitude was at hand and troubles with the Indians were a result. The existence of small and isolated sections of French half-breeds throughout Canada is another interesting survival of this contact. The half-breed never assumed such importance in the United States.

"The lords of the lakes and forest have passed away" but their work will endure in the boundaries of the Dominion of Canada and in Canadian institutional life. The place of the beaver in Canadian life has been fittingly noted in the coat of arms. We have given the maple a prominence which was due to the birch. We have not yet realized that the Indian and his culture were fundamental to the growth of Canadian institutions. We are only beginning to realize the central position of the Canadian Shield.[18]

Innis published these lines just thirty-four years after Métis leader Louis Riel was hung (as a consequence of a "serious problem" in Manitoba) and Indian economic relations (as expressed, for example, in the potlatch) were being actively suppressed by agents of the state. "Pass laws" were still in force, requiring Indians who wanted to work for wages off the reserve to secure written permission from the local Indian agent. These and other state initiatives provide indirect evidence that "the lords of the lakes and forest" had not quite passed away and that their passage required further assistance.

Innis's concluding reflections are particularly startling in a work that has as its central theme the portrayal of Native peoples as members of highly organized societies and as self-conscious defenders of their own interests. When Innis turns his attention to his own period, Native people become invisible, and their ultimate significance is relegated to the symbolic.

For political economists, the great strength of Innis's work lies in his careful discussion of indigenous societies' relations of production histori-cally and in the way he relates Native-European interaction to the forces shaping formation of the Canadian state and economy. His weakness is that, despite the clarity with which he saw indigenous peoples of the past, he follows most of his contemporaries in ignoring their presence in his own time. Innis's obituary for indigenous peoples was premature; he mistook social distress and change for social and cultural collapse.

Both Innis's weaknesses and his strengths are replicated many times in later scholarly work. His preoccupation with understanding the interaction of Natives and colonizers during the fur trade has been carried forward in the work of other scholars. The line begins with E.E. Rich, who published his major study of the Hudson's Bay Company in 1953, and Abraham Rotstein, whose re-examination of the fur trade challenges Innis's interpre-tation.[19] Since 1970, many area-specific studies have been published. Most of this work proceeds from the premiss that what must be understood is the complex process of interaction between two radically different forms of civilization; the painstaking research of many scholars has shown just how variable this process was.[20]

Breakthroughs have been made. Sylvia Van Kirk's historical analysis of the role of women in the later fur trade demonstrates that social transformations cannot be understood unless women's roles are taken into account.[21] Van Kirk concludes: "widespread intermarriage between European traders and Indian women and the development of extensive kinship networks [were] fundamental to the growth of fur-trade society."[22] Fur trade society was thus multi-ethnic and highly stratified. Although there was certainly prejudice and racial tension, ethnicity was not a reliable predictor of economic position: at some conjunctures a few Métis women occupied superior class positions, and some Indian women played leadership and complex intermediary roles.

Bruce Trigger and Arthur Ray, in a number of exhaustive studies focused on different parts of the country, have shown how indigenous societies' social relations were transformed but rarely obliterated by contact with emissaries of European societies.[23] Building on this work and on previously unexamined historical records, Paul Thistle has shown that the Cree in northern Manitoba successfully resisted fur traders' efforts to control the terms of trade and to intensify Native labour, until disease undermined Native strength.[24]

The new fur trade scholars and historians like Trigger follow Innis in acknowledging the importance of the effect of the fur trade on both Native and European social relations. Their work reveals a long history of mutually transformative social interaction and in fact a most protracted "conquest." They show that during the long struggle, racial or ethnic lines were far from perfectly correlated with relations of domination and relations of economic domination were much less one-sided than perceived by Innis, writing fifty years earlier.

Few of the fur trade scholars share Innis's interest in studying fur trade relations for what they reveal about the dynamics of Canadian economic and state formation. The failure to connect insights about the significance of transformations in Native social relations to the bread-and-butter concerns of political economy is mirrored by many political economists' lack of interest in the salience of Native-European relations to their own research. The political economists' omission is perhaps less justified, for scholars in their tradition have laid a basis from which connections could be made.

The first of these was Stanley Ryerson, in his two-volume "reinterpretation of this country's history" published in the 1960s.[25] Ryerson's history of Canada was a formidable synthetic achievement, a Marxist counterpart to Innis's similarly broad interpretive project. Others have afforded this work sustained critical attention; here we focus only on Ryerson's analysis of Native social relations as these were transformed by European contact. Although he wrote well before the recent flowering of detailed "Native studies," Ryerson provides a complete and balanced account of Canada's beginnings, with the Native experience "read in."

Ryerson begins with a discussion of the Native social formations "that flourished for centuries before the Europeans invaded North America."[26] In analysing the period since Europeans arrived, he systematically relates developments in the colony to changes in European modes of production. At every stage, relations between labourers and their exploiters are documented, including Native labour in all phases. There is a careful exploration of "Negro" and Indian slavery. Like Innis, Ryerson sees a pattern of gradual destruction and displacement of Native societies, through European duplicity, warfare, and the introduction of devastating new diseases. Unlike Innis, however, Ryerson documents Native military and diplomatic resistance to European dominance. Ryerson recognizes the strength of Native societies even after they were enmeshed in commercial relationships with Europeans, and he sees a long, and continuing, history of political struggle. This quality imparts a dynamism and optimism absent from Innis's gloomy concluding assessment.

Weaknesses in Ryerson's account have become much more apparent in light of later scholarship. Ryerson's theoretical framework is, of course, Marxist – but it is the Marxism of the 1950s, before scholars discovered "the young Marx" and before the later challenges to mechanistic applications of European capitalism to non-European transformations. Ryerson applies the traditional categories, describing the social relations in most pre-contact Native societies as characteristic of "primitive communism." He follows Marx in assuming that movement through the European sequence of modes of production indicated "progress." He finds, for example, the agrarian society of the Iroquois more "advanced" than that of neighbouring hunter-gatherer peoples. Native spiritual beliefs are analysed as "mere ideology": "The world outlook of the Stone Age peoples was a reflection of the material conditions of their existence . . . The struggle for subsistence and survival had engendered skills: but about the nature of human consciousness and its relation to the material world there was ignorance and confusion."[27] Ryerson does not limit application of this principle to Native societies. He is equally scathing about the way bourgeois ideology and the religious project of the Roman Catholic church obfuscated the historical and material basis of social relations.[28]

Later work by Marxist anthropologists is less judgmental and less functionalist in discussing Native spiritual ideas, while continuing to relate these ideas to the material circumstances of the peoples who hold them.[29] Ryerson's unequivocal dismissal of "totemism" and mythology is related to his acceptance of the stages hypothesis; in the most orthodox version of this theory, progress through the stages from primitive communism to feudalism to capitalism is understood to produce or permit greater, essentially scientific, knowledge about the human condition. Each mode of production includes a particular ideological universe; with capitalism, it became possible to penetrate ideological mystification and to see human affairs "scientifically." The implication is that people in all previous modes of production were "confused," or at least less comprehending, than socialists under capitalism.

A detailed response to this position is beyond the scope of this paper. We claim, however, that there is no particular virtue in seeking a replication of European stages in the evolution of social formations everywhere, and there is no reason to see only ignorance and confusion in Native cosmological and spiritual views. The point is surely to analyse the evolution of social relations in concrete instances for what this will tell us about domination and struggle; clearly, capitalist social relations developed in unique circumstances in England and extended from there into many areas of the world through different but comparable processes. In addition, given the current environmental and nuclear disasters now threatening humanity, it is not prudent to dismiss the interpretations of human experience produced by cultures that managed to survive, with considerable stability and without massive environmental destruction, for thousands of years.

No Canadian socialist has replicated the broad interpretive achievements of Innis and Ryerson.[30] However, a number of political economists have followed their example in trying to develop a materialist understanding of Native social relations and of the relations between Native and non-Native societies. Their work, discussed later in this chapter, complements another essential body of literature. As part of the process through which Native peoples in Canada have organized for political struggle at the local, provincial, and national levels during the last thirty years, many Native people have written chronicles of their own experiences of class, gender, and racial oppression, and some have produced political and economic analyses of the situation of Native peoples in Canada. Without attempting a comprehensive review of Native peoples' literature of struggle, it is possible to sample some common themes relevant to political economists.[31]

The Literature of Struggle

Native peoples' analyses of their own history supply two important elements for any analysis of Native political economy. The first is an exploration of the experience of race, gender and class oppression. The second is a consideration of relations between the social and philosophical characteristics of non-capitalist Native societies and personal and political struggles. In many accounts, both of these elements are present, although in different proportions and drawing different strategic conclusions.

Métis authors Maria Campbell and Howard Adams have written powerful personal accounts of the experience of living as a Native person in post-war Canada.[32] Campbell's story has become a touchstone for a generation of Métis people seeking to come to terms with their lives and an important source of insight for non-Native people. Campbell's is an angry book, but also hopeful and inspiring, because it chronicles her journey through oppression (both structural and internalized) to a position of greater insight and empowerment. In her story, the Native political movement is catalytic, but she identifies her reconnection with Native spiritual paths, through her grandmother, as the most important sustaining force.

George Manuel, Wilfred Peltier, and Harold Cardinal have all published complementary studies.[33] The "voice" in their work varies with the age, geographical situation, and biography of each author. But they all in different ways affirm the importance of maintaining a connection to their "native-ness," to traditional ways of being in the world that have continuity with the long pre-contact history. All recognize the difficulty of living this continuity in Canada as it is now structured for Native people. Many cherished traditional values are incongruent with both the racial oppression that they confront personally and daily and the confrontational, bureaucratized politics of the Native movement.

Howard Adams's *Prison of Grass* is a rare exception in the Native literature of struggle. Adams has written an angry, painful, confessional personal history in the tradition of Frantz Fanon and Eldridge Cleaver.[34] He explores the dimensions of his own internalized oppression and the way this was expressed in his relations with women. His resolution of the political question lies not in reconnection with his Native heritage but rather in revolutionary political activity.

Political economists have much to learn from these works. Native writers are concerned not with arcane refinements of theories of oppression, but rather with understanding their own "lived experience." While engaged in this process, all of them have traced the inter-related axes of class and racial oppression and, in the cases of Campbell and Adams, gender oppression as well. After reading these analyses, no one could possibly conclude that the Native societies have "passed away." Rather, Native peoples' literature of struggle emphasizes the salience of Native ways of being, even while it recognizes the distorting and damaging effect of capitalist social relations on Native collectivities. Contemporary political economy therefore must confront "the national question" in trying to understand Native societies and their relations with Canadian political and economic institutions.

The New Political Economy

Political economists have responded to the analytical and strategic challenges presented by the Native movement in a variety of ways. Some have taken the point and followed the example of Stanley Ryerson in building into their studies a recognition of Native specificity.[35] Others have followed Innis's example in prematurely banishing Native people from the present, affording them only historical importance. Still others have read Native people out of Canadian history and society entirely, ignoring the examples of both Innis and Ryerson.

Where this last occurs, it represents a serious analytical flaw. In a special issue of *Studies in Political Economy* on the political economy tradition, Leo Panitch and David McNally rely on the conclusions of the white settler colony analysis to describe Canada's beginnings, and both develop their arguments as if there were no workers in Canada until the Europeans arrived. Thus Panitch writes: "Unlike other dependent societies which were characterized by the attachment of mercantilism to a pre-capitalist mode of production (wherein direct producers were unfree, not directly engaged in market exchange, and sustained themselves by producing their own means of subsistence), Canada was a society where exchange value predominated in social relationships."[36] Although McNally cites Innis (including *The Fur Trade*) extensively, he writes as if – until what Ehrensaft and Armstrong call "the key formative period . . . from the 1860s onward" – there were no people in Canada at all.[37]

Similarly, Daniel Drache's influential work on the formation of the Canadian working class almost pointedly ignores the role of Native labour. For example, in a discussion of the complexities of labour market formation 1820–1920 (which emphasizes Canada's white settler, colonial status and cites Innis on the fur trade), Native people disappear from consideration after 1810.[38]

There was, of course, a long period in Canadian history "characterized by the attachment of mercantilism to a pre-capitalist mode of production," in the heyday of the fur trade. Until the Second World War, in large parts of the country, there were still Native people "not directly engaged in market exchange [who] sustained themselves by producing their own means of subsistence." Although the importance of Native labour power had declined by the 1860s, its significance accounts for state behaviour and even the very boundaries of Canada in the decades immediately preceding the formative period. Further, the fact that Native people still controlled or contested control of large areas of putatively Dominion territory (on the prairies until the 1880s and in the north until much later) shaped the national lands policy (not to mention policy toward Native people) well into the twentieth century.

Ehrensaft and Armstrong do take into account the presence of Native societies when Europeans arrived, arguing that because North America was sparsely populated, and because the climate did not favour large-scale plantation agriculture; "Europeans sought the land rather than the labour of indigenous peoples. Military conquest and land seizure were associated with a profound racism towards native peoples."[39] The accuracy of these state-ments, again, depends on which part of the country and which historical period they are discussing. Native labour was crucial in the long period before white settlement, and the development of systems for gaining access to and controlling native labour preoccupied the great trading companies and their imperial sponsors. It was only with massive European settlement (and the ravages of European diseases) that access to land became more important than access to Native labour. For the country overall, the moment at which this shift occurred varied. In the Maritimes, settlers arrived in relatively large numbers in the eighteenth century, and they consolidated their position gradually. In southern Ontario, white settlement occurred dur-ing the early nineteenth century; on the prairies, natives were not outnum-bered until nearly a hundred years later; on the coast and in different parts of the north, the timing was different again.

In light of this, one must ask why the period 1860-1914 is more "forma-tive" for Canada than any other. True, this period is conventionally consid-ered to mark the global transition from mercantile to monopoly capitalism. The effects of this global transformation were felt in Canada: industrial capital and an industrial proletariat began to form. The effects of the global transformation were felt unevenly, however, and very differently in different regions. Outside south-central Canada, there were different pressing im-peratives for both capital and the state 1860-1914. These were undoubtedly affected by global shifts in world capitalism, but an argument must be made to defend the proposition that these extraterritorial influences were of pre-ponderant "domestic" importance.

The decades *before* the emergence of monopoly capitalism in Britain and the United States may be seen as "formative" for Canada in several ways. First, as Innis argues, the fur trade established the pattern of non-Native geographical distribution and activity in most of Canada, and also the pat-tern of Native - non-Native interaction. Second, both pre- and post-Confed-eration state structures and practices were, arguably, shaped by the need to control the territory encompassed by fur trade activity - including the abo-riginal population (most coercively during the Métis rebellions, but also consistently through the treaty process, the reserve system, and Dominion lands policy). Finally, of course, the staples-led development strategy for Canada was formed during the mercantile period - that is, before the emer-gence of an industrial proletariat.

Elsewhere, we shall have more to say about the inadequacy of the white settler colony formulation. Use of this concept excludes from the analysis a central drama in Canadian development, from first European contact until the Riel Rebellion was defeated and final treaties were signed on the prai-ries. During this long period, Native societies presented a commercial op-portunity and a military challenge for the merchants and the colonial elite

who controlled the state apparatus. Today, in many parts of British Columbia and the provincial and territorial norths, the relationship between capitalist and non-capitalist relations of production is still a major – and open –
question.

A number of contemporary political economists have recognized this and
found in these areas a fruitful avenue of study. Ron Bourgeault has reinterpreted fur trade history along Marxist lines:

To understand the historical, political and economic existence of the native (including mixed-blood) people in North America, it is necessary to analyze them within
the context of the political economy of mercantilism. It is within this system that the
contradictions of race, class and nationalism have their antecedents and that the
foundations were laid for the formation of Canada as a nation-state . . . Class, racial
and sexist divisions came to be imposed upon the indigenous Indian population
through colonial relations based upon . . . [mercantilist] exploitation.[40]

Although his empirical research concerns the fur trade era, Bourgeault
presents this historical treatment as the basis of a strategic analysis of
contemporary prospects for alliances between Native and non-Native men
and women, to which, on his account, the class struggle is central.

Other political economists have taken these strategic questions into account in their research. Peter Usher and Michael Asch (and, in wonderfully
evocative books, Hugh Brody)[41] have effectively eliminated any ground for
conceiving of Native societies as either dead or doomed. In extensive field
research at various locations over nearly two decades, Usher has documented the continuing importance of Native land-based productive activity
for northern Native survival. In the process he has developed an analysis of
the modes of production in those parts of Canada still occupied mainly by
Native people: "The two modes of production in the North today are the
domestic and the capitalist. The capitalist mode has been superimposed on
the pre-existing domestic mode, but the latter survives in modified form.
The two coexist not as isolated, unconnected enclaves, but rather as interrelated parts of a larger social formation, that of industrial capitalism on the
frontier."[42] Usher argues that in northern Canada, as elsewhere in the world,
industrial capitalism is dominant but has neither overwhelmed nor eradi-
cated the domestic mode in which the distinctiveness of Native societies is
rooted.

In a complementary analysis, Michael Asch has interpreted evolving production relations of the Slavey (Dene) as responses to successive waves of
European emissaries and clearly demonstrated the resilience of these production relations and the adaptability of Native societies.[43] The work of both
Asch and Usher lays an analytical and historical basis for understanding the

strength of northern Native political activism, and it bridges the concerns of Canadian political economy and parallel preoccupations of other Marxist anthropologists such as Eleanor Leacock.[44] Although Leacock's work on the Naskapi-Montagnais is rarely as explicitly related to Native political struggles as the others, it is central to the revision of overly deterministic or mechanistic Marxist interpretations of Native social relations, particularly with respect to the situation of women.

Mel Watkins's research on the situation of the Dene in the Northwest Territories traces the ways in which capitalist non-renewable resource development is "underdeveloping" the northern economy. Native resistance to this is expressed in a struggle over control of the land; thus Watkins sees Native nationalism as a bulwark against penetration into Native lands of international capital.[45] Bourgeault is sceptical about the progressive potential of Native nationalism, fearing it will become a kind of Trojan horse that will lead the Native movement into co-optation and new forms of neo-colonial exploitation.[46]

Although both Bourgeault and Watkins address "the national question," neither has analysed closely the role of the state in these struggles. Two political economists, Murray Dobbin and John Loxley, have produced such analyses.[47] Each offers a case study account of a social democratic provincial government (in northern Saskatchewan and northern Manitoba) failing to develop or implement policies and programs to improve the living conditions of northern Native people. Both, in different ways, analyse Native peoples' economic relations with international capitalism as these are mediated by federal and particularly provincial states. Only Dobbin, however, systematically examines changes in the role of Native women.

A recent book by Dara Culhane Speck illustrates the analytical richness available when Native peoples' experience is interpreted in awareness of the complex interaction of class, race, and gender oppression.[48] Speck tells the story of the death from misdiagnosed appendicitis of Renee Bernice Smith, an eleven-year-old Kwakwaka'waka (Kwakiutl) in the BC coastal town of Alert Bay. The political and social struggles that followed are described in a gripping narrative, informed by analysis of the history of Native-white contact and of the political economy of a resource working-class town.

In assessing the treatment of Native issues in the political economy tradition, a number of observations can be advanced. Considerable analytical progress has been made by Innis, Ryerson, the fur trade scholars, Native authors, and some contemporary political economists allied with the Native movement. Central to their contribution is the recognition that Canadian history must be comprehended dualistically, in terms of both Native and non-Native experiences. They confirm the importance of the fur trade era for understanding Canadian development, not simply because the fur trade

established persistent patterns of Native/non-Native interaction (and created
in the process a new nation of people, the Métis), but also because the
structures of the Canadian state, the staples-oriented drift of the economy,
and the very geographical extent of the country were all established during
the period.

The mainstream political economy tradition has absorbed the force of
these analyses only incompletely. Where political economists rely on the
ideological construct "white settler colony," they deny centuries of human
experience and the aggression against Native societies by European economic and political interests. They also limit our capacity to understand
Canadian development.

Much work remains to be done. We require more case studies, more
debates, and much more theoretical work, in order to see Canadian history
for what it is and to study here revolutionary transformations in relations of
production. This work must find a firm basis in the lived experience of the
Native societies of Canada.

IMMIGRANT GROUPS

Immigration and ethnic minorities were peripheral concerns in English-
Canadian social sciences and historiography until the late 1960s.[49] During
the 1970s, the study of groups other than the British, French, and Native
peoples flourished, buoyed by support given through the federal government's multiculturalism policy. Much of the earlier research was of a cele-
bratory nature and projected a vision of immigrants as standard-bearers of
formal and ossified national cultures, rather than as participants in and
shapers of popular culture and Canadian institutional life. More recently, a
younger generation of scholars has begun to examine subjects traditionally
neglected, including the political economy of immigration, racism, the role
of ethnic minorities in labour struggles and radical politics, and the experiences of immigrant and ethnic-minority women.

Immigration, race, and ethnicity receive the most frequent consideration
in Canadian political economy, as they affect two central themes within that
tradition. The first is the formation of social classes, especially the making of
the Canadian working class. The second is the capacity of subordinate
classes to resist the policies and practices of the Canadian state and capital
in economic development and labour management.

In the ensuing discussion, Pentland is examined in some detail because of
his acknowledgment of the central role played by immigration in Canadian
capitalist development. Contemporary Canadian political economy has
adopted Pentland's contentious and problematic assumptions on the character of immigration, a line of inquiry we will briefly explore. Next, we
examine the relationship between race and class in the making of a racially

divided working class in western Canada. Finally, we consider some of the contributions to political economy of an emergent literature produced by the anti-racist and feminist movements.

Pentland on Immigration and Ethnicity

In scrutinizing how political economy in English Canada has theorized the role played by immigration, race, and ethnicity in capitalist class formation and subordinate class resistance, a logical starting point is the work of H. Clare Pentland. Because he placed the "man with the axe and shovel,"[50] rather than the man in the top hat, at the centre of his analysis of Canadian development, Pentland is frequently considered Canada's pioneering labour historian.[51] In his ambitious study, *Labour and Capital in Canada, 1650–1860*, Pentland traces the transition from pre-capitalist to capitalist (free-wage) forms of labour organization. Building on his earlier research on Irish canal and railway workers in mid-nineteenth-century Upper Canada,[52] *Labour and Capital* explores two centuries of Canadian history peopled by Indian raftsmen, French-Canadian voyageurs, Irish canal labourers, American millers, and English artisans.

Pentland's acknowledgment that immigration was a central process in the constitution of the incipient Canadian industrial (and resource) working class makes his work of particular significance to researchers interrogating the role of immigration and immigrant groups in Canadian economic and social development. In addition, Pentland insisted that ethnic diversity and conflict were especially germane in the shaping of the Canadian labour market, contrasting Canada's "ethnically complicated society" with the United States, where the "dominant group has been able to impose a high degree of cultural and ideological conformity upon minorities."[53]

Pentland focused on the role of labour institutions and mechanisms in establishing critical parameters for capitalist development. Directing his gaze at south-central Ontario, he argued that prior to 1850, the reserve of labour was too small and its character inappropriate for large-scale industrialization. To compensate for labour shortages, diverse forms of unfree and paternalistic labour systems prevailed, incorporating various groups of Canadian-born and immigrant producers. Unfree labour systems, including slavery and indentured and convict labour, as well as what Pentland refers to variously as "personal" or "feudal labour" in New France, organized production particularly of goods in the staples trades.

It was not until the second half of the nineteenth century that an inadequately supplied labour market gave way to a capitalist labour market marked by permanent reserves and requisite changes in the nature and organization of the labour force. Pentland contends that the migration of Irish Catholics from the late 1820s to the 1840s, initially drawn to labouring jobs in the construction of the massive canal systems, marked a watershed for Canadian capitalist development. For Pentland, the abundance and character of their free-wage labour effectively "solved" the major problem of labour scarcity for capital in Canada. This group of plentiful and highly mobile workers provided a reserve army of labour, and from their ranks emerged Canada's incipient industrial proletariat.

Unlike the majority of his contemporaries, Pentland made the character of ethnic groups, and the mostly conflictual relations among them (especially dividing French, English, and Irish), central to the development of the Canadian labour market. But his attention to immigration and ethnicity was vitiated by his eclectic and essentially idealist treatment of these phenomena.

First, Pentland's understanding of ethnicity is firmly culturalist, rather than materialist. A set package of cultural values, goals, outlooks, and capabilities accounts for the relative success or failure of each group in the Canadian labour market.[54] Racism and ethnocentrism pervade his depiction of both Indians and French Canadians as "cheerful and docile employees" of fur trading companies. These two groups could not become part of modern industrial development because of "some child like qualities that encouraged their organization into paternalistic labour systems."[55] Pentland's discomfort is evident in his afterthought: "Ethnic peculiarities were a subsidiary aspect of the matter and must not be pressed too far."[56]

The admiration Pentland exhibits for the physical strength and industriousness of Irish Catholic canal and railway labourers, and their willingness to undertake mean work shunned by more established British workers, coexists with his depiction of the Irish as intemperate, primitive, and prone to violence. Pentland fails to see these cultural values and predispositions as responses to oppressive conditions established by employers or state authorities, including government and corporate restrictions on owning land, starvation wages, and military suppression of combinations and strikes. As Ruth Bleasdale documents, these structural conditions and restrictions make comprehensible the wretched and violent lives of the southern Irish who flocked to canal construction sites in nineteenth-century Upper Canada.[57]

Further, Pentland's treatment of Irish Catholics as intemperate, disputatious, and violent takes as factual and unproblematic this depiction of Irish migrants by officials in England and Scotland.[58] However, the documentation of the violent treatment of Irish migrant labourers to Scotland during the first half of the nineteenth century, and their ideological portrayal as forming separate physical stock, prone to violence, drunkenness, and theft, and responsible for the moral corruption of the Scots working class, show that the Catholic Irish were the object of fierce racist stereotyping.[59] The fact that during the early nineteenth century the English and Scots conceived of the Irish as constituting a separate "race" highlights the elasticity and historical specificity of "racial" signifiers and indicates the elaborate ideological work done to secure and maintain various forms of "racialization" that have characterized different periods of capitalist development.[60]

Pentland similarly furnishes cultural stereotypes, but of positive valuation, to account for the entrepreneurial success of American settlers in Upper Canada ("mobile, adaptable and mechanically ingenious"). Approbation is also accorded to English immigrant craftworkers, who "contributed very greatly to make Canada's labour market a modern one by providing a regular and dependable supply of skilled labour and by insisting as a counterpart upon a suitable level of wages and conditions."[61]

The constructive, nation-building role of English skilled workers and (white) American settlers is a recurring theme in both the old and the new political economies: Canada began as a white settler colony or an extension of British society. As argued earlier, this theme renders invisible or distorts the role of both native peoples and successive waves of non-British and non-European migrants. It also plays down divisions within the early British migration that helped shape the Canadian labour market and the course of economic development.

Pentland's pronounced gender bias is prevalent in subsequent work on immigrant workers. Women are simply written out of the historical account of Canadian development, which is centred on men's work in the fur and timber trades, canal and railway construction, and the iron industry.[62]

The New Political Economy

The ethnocentrism and gender bias evident in Pentland's account of the effect of immigration and immigrant groups on the shaping of the Canadian labour market recur frequently in political economy writings. The authors are not themselves ethnocentric or sexist, but the white settler colony construct does not facilitate analysis of the influence of racial, ethnic, and gender differences. Two examples from the literature illustrate the consequences of reliance on it.

Panitch's use of the white settler colony thesis led him away from considering the importance of relations between Native and non-Native for Canadian state and economy formation; equal difficulties arise from application of the model to the non-Native labour force.[63] Citing Innis, Panitch avers that the attachment of migrants in a "white [British] settler colony" to the cultural standards of the homeland accounts for the predominance of production for exchange, thus marking Canada off from "other [presumably non-white] societies which were characterized by the attachment of mercantilism to a pre-capitalist mode of production."[64] Further, "Canada's roots as a white settler colony carrying with it the level of civilization achieved by Western Europe" helped Canadian workers in the early 1870s maintain high wage rates and thus, relative to European workers, constitute a "high wage proletariat."[65]

This analysis omits the historical role of Canadian immigration and immigrant groups. It ignores or treats as incidental the fact that ethnicity and race gave rise to significant conflicts, contradictions, and hierarchies in the structuring of the Canadian working class. The high wages won by English and Scottish urban-based craftworkers in Upper Canada provide a sharp contrast to the widespread destitution and misery experienced by famine Irish, eastern, central, and southern European, and Asian immigrant and migrant workers, brought in primarily to provide back-breaking and cheap labour.

With the exception of Ehrensaft and Armstrong, who refer to the ethnic segmentation in the capitalist labour market prior to the First World War, and its contradictory effects on the mobilization of the working class,[66] most white-settler accounts focus on the role of white, especially British workers. The selective gaze on ethnically privileged workers is present even within accounts that reject other aspects of the thesis. Descendants of the 15,000 Chinese who built the railways that linked together the vast area of Canada might be surprised to learn from Gordon Laxer that "workers wanted to keep out . . . cheap oriental labour, and in this regard they were largely successful."[67]

These analyses lack a focus on the class relations that promoted increasingly diverse immigration to suit the labour demands of employers. Trade unions, representing established British workers, agitated continuously against an open immigration policy which allowed employers to both lower wages and, by importing strike-breakers, weaken the union movement's ability to challenge employers collectively. While the labour movement occasionally obtained concessions from the state, such as the Alien Labour Act, 1897,[68] the chief enduring class beneficiary of immigration policy has been capital.[69]

Some political economists follow Pentland and recognize the profound influence of immigration policy and immigrants. Thus, Brodie and Jensen argue that both the hostility of English-speaking workers to non-English immigrants and the possibility that immigration could undercut working-class gains by constantly augmenting the number of unorganized and unskilled workers helped fracture the Canadian labour movement and discouraged "labour from playing the role of midwife to a viable socialist movement as it had in much of western Europe."[70] Paul Craven treats the polarized positions of manufacturers and unions on immigration as dooming the National Policy strategy of uniting the "industrial classes" (manufacturers and industrial workers). He also discusses extensively organized labour's militancy (and the reaction of capital and the state) with reference to early-twentieth-century immigration.[71]

Clearly, political economy does not ignore the development and effects of immigration policy. But the field as a whole has inadequately absorbed the impact of these factors. More work is needed on the state's exclusionary mechanisms and on the practice of employers and British skilled workers that served to maintain a hierarchy among groups of workers differentiated by race and ethnicity. Even while Britain and the United States continued to provide the bulk of immigrants during the early twentieth century, an ethnic/racial pecking order among workers had taken shape in legal-juridical and political status, desirability and skill levels of jobs, wage scales, segregation within the workplace, and opportunities for collective action. In the white settler colony, the "white (and Asian) slave trade" transported "human cattle" to the "slaughter yards of North American industry."[72]

The view that Canada was populated mostly as a settler society and thus, as Panitch contends, "constituted [from the beginning] in terms of free wage labour or tendentially free wage labour" also invites recasting.[73] The white settler colony thesis ignores the many waves of migrants to nineteenth- and twentieth-century Canada who were by their inferior "entrance status" neither settlers nor free wage labour. Even in late-nineteenth-century Ontario, many of the central, eastern, and southern European workers provided for labour-intensive resource industries and the transportation companies were brought over in a manner resembling the restrictions of seasonal-guest-worker schemes of labour migration. These sojourners lacked political rights, could not contract freely with employers of their choosing, and had few possibilities for collective action. They were often also ruthlessly exploited by ethnic intermediaries in a *padrone* system which, at the extreme, was analogous in its coercion to indentured bondage.[74]

Class and Race in the Canadian West

Relatively unfree labour systems and the distinction between settler and non-settler political status among ethnically divided workers were even more critical in the formation of the working class in western Canada. Unskilled Chinese labourers in British Columbia were frequently indentured to contracting companies for their passage to Canada, subjected by the federal government to increasing head taxes, and systematically denied settler status and the rights of citizenship. As Gillian Creese argues, this marginal political status (rather than any cultural predisposition) reduced the possibility of successful labour organization and militancy for the Chinese.[75]

Creese's study of ethnic cleavages in Vancouver's working class 1900–1939 pinpoints a further shortcoming of the white settler colony thesis – namely its reluctance to cede any explanatory significance to the ideology of race, especially in progressive movements such as labour. Yet the practices of Vancouver's white labour movement justified the exclusion of Asians not simply in terms of the fear of the cheapness, undercutting, and strike-breaking potential of Asian labour, but also in terms of racist assumptions about the social and cultural inferiority of Asians.[76] Thus the thesis is more usefully treated as an enduring, hegemonic ideology with origins in the intentions of British colonizers and with popular purchase among all segments of white, British society. It cannot be treated simply as a descriptive/analytic concept.

In his broad consideration of the formation and fragmentation of the Canadian working class, 1820–1920, Daniel Drache correctly identifies the British white settler colony as an ideology, but he errs in locating its working-class support only in one regional section of the working class, centred in south-central Canada and composed of members of skilled craft unions.[77] In searching for an essential unity among workers in English Canada, Drache finds the best approximation in the highly class-conscious, resource proletariat in western Canada, which he contrasts with the conservative and hopelessly anti-French and racist eastern craftworker movement. The western, resource-based radical labour movement fails only in its inability to harness nationalism "as a political weapon in a colonial context."[78]

Drache's account ignores what is evident to most labour historians of western Canada – that is, the coexistence within the early western, especially the BC white labour movement, of a radical class-consciousness and a virulent nativism and racism directed most strongly against Asians.[79] As Bryan Palmer points out in his critique of Drache's thesis, Drache misunderstands the national ideologies that animated socialist labour politics in western Canada. Although led largely by British workers, socialist politics and the radical labour upheaval in the west got much of their support from other European immigrant workers: "If there was a nationalism they would have embraced, it was the nationalism of radical independence movements endorsed by many Polish, Croatian, Slovak, Ukrainian and Finnish workers – the nationalism of armed revolt in the Old World [rather than] . . . some mystical Canadian nationalism."[80]

Racism and anti-alien sentiment formed highly emotive ideologies in the making of a radical class consciousness among white, western workers, with opposition to Asian and non-British immigration in many cases providing a catalyst for organization by white labour.[81] But several authors repeat Pentland's error in reading the official reports – records, such as the 1885 and 1902 royal commissions on Chinese immigration, of white labour's opposition to Asian labour – as accurate portrayals of the cultural predispositions and behaviour of Asian workers, rather than as accounts of labour relations seen through the prism of anti-Asian and racist ideologies.

Thus, Paul Phillips attributes the lack of success among white Nanaimo miners in organizing into a trade union to two factors – the fanatic opposition of the virulently anti-union employer, Dunsmuir, and the large minority of oriental workers. "Immobile, unacculturated and docile under threats of deportation, they constantly undermined worker solidarity."[82] Similarly, McCormack takes as factual the basis of preference among BC employers for Asian workers that "they remained unassimilated and therefore impossible to organize."[83]

Explanations for the racist oppression and economic and political subordination of Asians in western Canada range from purely psychological and cultural[84] to economic. Peter Li and B. Singh Bolaria analyse the inferior political (non-citizen) status of Asian workers in terms of capital's needs to divide workers and super-exploit weaker sections. Their attempts to apply Marxism to Canadian ethnic oppression and racism are imbued with economistic and functionalistic logic, attributing these phenomena exclusively to "capital's needs" and an instrumentalist state that automatically does capital's bidding.[85] No separate level of effectiveness is conceded to ideology, the practices or experiences of white or Asian subordinate classes, or the mediation of class relations by race and ethnicity.

Ann Sunahara's study of the treatment of Japanese Canadians during the Second World War reveals that the bases for racism toward BC Asians were multi-layered, rooted simultaneously in several, mutually reinforcing historical processes. These included class relations (for example, resentment of white small business and labour at the success of Japanese-Canadian middlemen), international and domestic politics (western fear of Japanese military aggression; the Canadian cabinet's tradition of buying political power at the expense of unpopular minorities which flourished under Mackenzie King), and the ideology of separate and "unassimilable" races, long nourished in Canada's immigration policy.[86]

The stereotype of the "docile Asian worker" is also an exaggeration. Though far less militant in the workplace than white workers, Asians participated in strikes in the BC lumber industry and fisheries as early as the 1860s, with the majority of all strikes involving Vancouver's Asian population occurring at the end of the First World War and in the early years of the Depression. Moreover, although racist, exclusionary practices were the most common outcomes of the perceived threat of "oriental labour," this was not the only response of the white labour movement. Inclusive and solidaristic responses occurred most frequently with the activities of the One Big Union after the First World War and the organizing drive in the lumber industry, canneries, and berry farms launched during the 1930s by the Workers Unity League.[87]

Certain factors underlie the development of an ethnically differentiated and stratified working class in Canada's most western province: the role of the state, racist ideology, and the racial and class consciousness and collective action of both white and Asian labour. As we will show, the challenge of integrating analyses of race ideologies and politics based on both class and race, as well as minority resistance, is replicated in attempts to understand the contemporary experiences of Caribbean and Asian immigrants in Canada.

Immigrants and Resistance

In general, the depiction of the role of non-British, non-French immigrant groups in resistance to class exploitation and the subordinating practices of capital and the state has in Canadian political economy vacillated between two extremes. Immigrant workers from Europe and Asia are seen either as "scabs" and hapless victims of capital and state authorities or as "dangerous foreigners."[88] As Gregory Kealey argues, the images of both the immigrant strike-breaker and the "violent, foreign revolutionary" are racist and xenophobic in origin, though both have had some basis in reality.[89]

The form and strength of resistance, or alternatively submission, to capitalist authority have been for immigrant workers, as for established workers, influenced by a conjuncture of historically specific structural and ideological factors. Thus, the polarized class conditions of many groups of non-British workers both in newly opened staples-producing regions and in sweated industries "often produced more violent and class-conscious responses by ethnic workers than was prevalent among established workers."[90] The explanation for a different pattern of responses may reside in the systematic privileges and disadvantages conferred on groups of workers by the state, employers, and labour organizations based on ideological notions of "race" and legal subjectivities of immigrant status and citizenship.

Labour historians seeking to comprehend the alternately divisive and mobilizing, conservatizing and radicalizing potential of ethnicity/race and immigrant status would do well to incorporate immigration history into their analyses of working-class history.[91] The rich insights produced from this integration are apparent in the nuanced treatment of ethnicity by a younger generation of labour historians such as Franca Iacovetta, Craig Heron, Carmela Patrias, Ian Radforth, Bruno Ramirez, Allan Seager, Robert Storey, and (in his more recent work) Bryan Palmer, in their accounts of Hamilton steelworkers, Italian workers in Toronto and Montreal, northern Ontario Finnish lumberworkers, Albertan coal miners, and the development of a multicultural patchwork of labour markets in different localities.[92]

A fruitful marriage of labour and immigration history places on the research agenda not only consideration of employer, state, and trade union practices but also the internal and frequently contradictory dynamics of ethnic communities themselves. For the first generation of immigrant workers, their communities, kinship ties, traditions, and memories of resistance often served as separate but reinforcing sources of refuge and rebellion against cultural alienation and material trauma. However, successive waves of immigration, corresponding to distinct stages of capital accumulation and incorporating immigrants into historically specific labour markets, have fashioned ethnic communities that are internally divided by class, generation, and, frequently, political ideology. The complex and internally stratified nature of ethnic communities is frequently lost in studies that confine their analysis to the working-class segment of immigrant groups.[93] Similarly, the multidimensional and transformative character of ethnicity will be captured only when ethnicity is treated no longer statically as synonymous with "national origin" but rather as a historical process with both emergent and "traditional" properties.[94]

No matter what their political ideology, ethnic community associations formed important arenas of political activity for immigrants, as well as offering escape from the hostility they frequently encountered in Canada, companionship, gaiety, and mutual aid. The ability to communicate in the immigrants' mother tongues and provide social activities based on ethnic cultures and loyalties was key to the success or failure not only of ethnic associations but also of radical and socialist political organizations that hoped to attract immigrants into their ranks.

The ability of the Socialist Party of Canada and later the Communist Party to draw on Finnish, Ukrainian, Jewish, and other European immigrant communities resided in their establishment of autonomous language locals and the culturally supportive atmosphere these entailed. This ethno-linguistic autonomy, however, which garnered large non-British memberships for socialist organizations, presented problems of communication and integration between British executives and language-based leagues.[95] The multi-dimensional role played by language and ethnicity in these radical organizations suggests that the relationship between class consciousness and ethnic consciousness has been complex and historically variable in the Canadian context, and Canadian political economy is only beginning to explore it adequately.

Over the past twenty years, the large-scale migration of non-white peoples to Canada, and their encounters with and resistance to racism, have placed a new set of analytical and political questions on the agenda, centring on race and racism and their role in defining Canadian culture and institutions. In an emergent body of literature, men and women of colour are giving voice to their experiences of pervasive racism in Canada and documenting their courageous struggles against minority disadvantage and racism. The urgent need to address issues of contemporary racism is apparent.

Racism, Feminism, and Resistance

Although contemporary racism forms the subject of a growing body of research in Canada, most of this work has investigated attitudinal dimen-

sions, thus treating racism in isolation from Canadian capitalist development, class formation, or other central concerns of Canadian political economy.[96] This predominantly survey research has been imbued with liberal
assumptions that treated racism as exceptional or as a deviation, a matter of
individual wrongdoing inflicted by misguided or prejudiced individuals. The
political implications of these studies followed the tenets of official multiculturalism, which saw the sharing of information on cultural differences as the
chief means for reducing ethnic and racial prejudice.

During the 1970s and early 1980s, academic and community studies
appeared on "visible minorities," non-white groups that had grown considerably with the opening up of immigration from Asia, the Caribbean, and
Latin America.[97] These studies were concerned primarily to document
minority perceptions of discrimination and the many forms of racial disadvantage inscribed in the realms of employment, immigration, education, law
enforcement, and housing. Some also chronicled growing politicization,
community development, and often militant resistance in black communities
to racial attacks and disadvantage. A few revealed how for important sections of both black and South Asian communities, radical ties and traditions
formed in the nexus of imperialist development and anti-colonial struggle
were significant resources in challenging Canadian racism.[98]

More recently, books and reports have appeared written by activists at the
forefront of the fight against racism. Dionne Brand and Krisantha Sri Bhaggiyadatta have produced a book, *Rivers Have Sources*, based on interviews
with people from the native, black, Chinese, and South Asian communities
(primarily in Toronto), which documents how non-white peoples themselves
experience and understand racism and its pervasive effects in all aspects of
their lives.[99] The picture of racism that emerges is that of an immensely
supple, variable, and seemingly intractable "common sense," socially and
politically constructed within a range of important locations – education,
social services, private corporations, trade unions, and the mass media. The
book also offers spirited documentation of the many local campaigns and
struggles engaged in by non-whites to fight the endemic racism of the public
educational system, workplace, labour movement, police, and mass media,
as well as the racist scourge of organizations such as the Ku Klux Klan. In
revealing the oppositional elements of minority peoples' cultures, and the
strength and support for resistance within their communities, Brand and Sri
Bhaggiyadatta bring non-white peoples into history outside the categories of
"problem" and "victim," where they have been placed by contemporary
racism.

A recent book by Tania Das Gupta on immigrant women occupying the
lowest rungs of manufacturing and service jobs reclaims a history of resistance against the structures of sexism, racism, and class exploitation among
a group generally neglected by the labour movement and ignored within

political economy.[100] Other recent publications by immigrant women and women of colour convey lived responses to their circumstances, most often in richly evocative experiential forms, inspired by black feminist writings in Britain and the United States.[101]

In addition to these writings by community activists, feminist scholarship is beginning to expose the web of social relations that constitute both the class location and the practices of immigrant and minority women. This work is informed by attempts to bridge the theoretical and political-organizational chasm between white feminism and the struggles of immigrant and ethnic-minority women. Different feminist authors emphasize different moments in the racial/ethnic and gendered reproduction of immigrant and minority women as subordinate or marginal groups and portray resistance to such subordination.

Thus Franca Iacovetta, writing on southern Italian women taking up paid work in the garment trades in post-war Toronto,[102] focuses on the continuities and breaks with their patterns of agricultural and domestic labour, and authority and resistance within the family, established in their home villages. Her study affirms that an immigrant woman or man arrives at Canada's shores not as tabula rasa to be shaped and moulded by capitalist labour practices or, as in Pentland's account, as a bearer of a static set of cultural traits. Rather, these people bring to their labour and to their political involvement in Canada prior traditions of work and resistance which then are circumscribed and shaped by their new workplace and household circumstances. Charlene Gannage's case study of a small, Jewish-owned garment shop, with a gender and ethnic division of labour, illuminates the interplay of work and family in shaping immigrant women's work experience and subordination in the workplace and trade union structures.[103] Roxana Ng's research reveals how the routinized work of employment agencies contributes to the constitution of "immigrant women" as a separate and socially subordinate group in the labour market.[104]

Laura Johnson's study of immigrant women homeworkers discloses the many dimensions of exploitative employer practices and official neglect that trap a large group of southern European, Asian, and black women in sweated, hazardous work and living conditions.[105] Carla Lipsig-Mumme's lively account of feminist organizing in the 1980s in the International Ladies' Garment Union, designed to counter the industry's trend toward homeworking, gives lie to the stereotype of docile immigrant women.[106] These feminist works show how indispensable immigrant women have been, and continue to be, to the survival and settlement of their communities and development of Canadian capitalism. Even during periods of largely male migration, women have performed vital work as paid labourers, unpaid household workers, and contributors to family business.[107]

The burgeoning work by minority community activists and feminist scholars enriches our understanding of the place of class, race, ethnicity, and gender within Canadian political economy. It incorporates analyses of the social relations that traverse sites generally neglected by traditional political economy, such as the home and ethnic community organizations, and indicates how these social relations articulate with workplace and labour market relations. Enlivened by ongoing struggles, this work speaks to the experience of flesh-and-blood immigrant and minority women and thus breathes life into the analysis of class formation and resistance in a way that does not simply "add on" race, ethnicity, and gender, but incorporates them as meaningful and legitimate categories for political economy.

CONCLUSION

We began this essay with the claim that the Canadian political economy tradition has only unevenly absorbed an adequate analysis of race and ethnicity and that too much of the tradition sets aside these issues as irrelevant. Our goal has been to demonstrate that race and ethnicity, along with gender, are constituent features of class formation and potential resistance and that these axes of oppression provide the modalities, conflicts, and contradictions through which class is lived in Canada.

Much of the tradition has incorporated the notion that Canada began as a white settler colony. This concept has interpretive value, but we have argued that its image of Canada is a hegemonic ideological construction that obscures important aspects of reality. Theorists who frame their analyses in these terms cannot speak fully to the experiences of Canada's most oppressed peoples. Further, they unnecessarily limit their own capacity to interpret Canadian history and society.

Seeing Canada as a white settler colony denies, first, the significance of the very long period of Native occupation, before Europeans arrived. It does not provide, either, an accurate description of the early contact period (which lasted at least three hundred years). Few of the first Europeans were settlers. They came with the commercial objective of harnessing Native labour power for profit, and there was a long period of struggle over the terms of this commercial relationship. As Innis and Ryerson recognized, Native labour and Native resistance were crucial for early class and state formation.

As well, the white settler colony construct reinforces a ruling-class and ethnocentric image of immigration, by drawing attention only to the collective action, victories, and defeats of one privileged segment of the Canadian working class. It fails to show how race and ethnicity have contributed both to divisions and unity within the working class and to workers' deference to and defiance of capitalist authority.

The development of one or several analytical frameworks, as alternatives, would require a separate essay. We will conclude, instead, with a series of propositions and considerations that arise from the preceding discussion and suggest an alternative political economy that brings Natives and immigrants into Canadian history while avoiding the categories of historical relic, problem, or victim.

(1) There is a need to beware of Eurocentric models of development in understanding both the historical and the contemporary relations of production among Natives and to replace such models with analyses sensitive to complex relations between capitalist and non-capitalist relations of production. The white settler colony notion is irretrievably a hegemonic, ruling-class construct, successfully hegemonic precisely because it touches real experience and human prejudice at crucial junctures. The concept is dangerous because it carries an image of the "ideal" proletarian: white, mobile, literate, male, independent of family ties and supports (and, for socialists, also organized and class-conscious). Few workers match this image in any society, and certainly in Canada at any period. Actual workers engage in or depend on non-wage domestic labour, live in communities from which they are rarely happy to move, have national, ethnic, or regional identities, and make sense of the world through the ideological constructions available to them. Since this is the reality, it is better to begin here, rather than with a concept that "sees" these qualities as problematic factors or variations that must be explained (and, in political struggle, overcome).

(2) It cannot be assumed that class dynamics and conflict are non-existent just because the language and politics of class are absent, as occurs for many Native and ethnic minority movements. Classes are not predetermined entities and do not exist apart from other forms of subjectivity and domination based on gender, race, and ethnicity. Classes are constructed in struggles, experienced and interpreted through the categories available to gendered, nationally conscious people. An analysis based on class formation may make intelligible the determination of struggles, not solely by objective economic relations, but rather by the structured totality of social relations based on class, gender, racial, and ethnic definition.[108]

(3) For both Native people and immigrants, race and ethnicity are prima facie neither divisive nor facilitative of class mobilization and struggle. Their role in class formation must be explained with reference to the context of social relations and institutional practices (of labour, capital, and the state) largely outside individuals' immediate control and to the character of specific national or communal forms of organization. These latter potentially provide the crucial social foundations for collective action.

(4) Just as the development of Canadian political economy cannot be understood without reference to the international political economy, neither can the development of Canadian Native and immigrant societies be understood outside the context of a wide range of international developments.[109]

This realization implies, for Native societies, use of anthropological research conducted outside Canada and attention to Native peoples' own interpretation of Canadian history. For immigrant groups, researchers ought to link labour with immigration history, so as best to determine the traditional and emergent properties of ethnicity.

Consistent recognition of the salience of gender, race, and ethnicity for class analysis is essential to accurate understanding of Canadian history. Because Canada continues to be a gendered, racially, and ethnically heterogeneous society, the need to comprehend these factors will not disappear. As much work has already demonstrated, political economy can provide nuanced analyses of Canadian class and state formation that take into account a materialist understanding of Native and ethnic cultures and the self-organization of Native peoples and ethnic minorities incorporating notions of "nation" and "community." If these path-breaking analyses tell us anything, they reveal that the survival of the labour movement, and the well-being of the wider working class, depend on our successfully confronting and ameliorating oppression based on gender, ethnicity, and race. In the beginning and minimally, political economy must develop a critical theoretical practice in opposition to hegemonic mystifications that deny the lived experience of so many Canadians. Only through such practices will the struggle be joined in solidarity and strength.

NOTES

We are pleased to acknowledge the contributions to this paper made by Wallace Clement and Glen Williams, editors both thorough and *engagé*. Mel Watkins prodded us into painful but essential reassessment of our own assumptions at crucial junctures. Peter Usher's comradely comments have provided enough questions for at least two more, similar papers. Portions of this work benefited also from discussions with members of the Carleton–University of Ottawa social policy group and with participants in a session at the Canadian Ethnic Studies Conference, Halifax, October 1987. Although their help has greatly improved this paper, none of them, of course, should be held responsible for the analyses that resulted.

1 There are four representative national organizations of Native peoples corresponding to four national political groupings. The Assembly of First Nations represents most status Indians – Native people who are recognized by the federal government to be within the ambit of the Indian Act. Non-status Indians and some people who identify themselves as Métis are represented by the Native Council of Canada. The Métis of the prairies, who are descended from early marriages between settlers and Natives, and who have for at least a century and a half maintained a distinct culture, are represented by the Métis National Coun-

cil. The Inuit of Arctic Canada are represented by the Inuit Tapirisat of Canada, among other more specialized organizations.

Within each of the national political groupings are Native peoples who have developed markedly different traditional cultures with both agrarian and hunter-gatherer bases. Further, the members of all the national groups live in extremely variable material circumstances. Some live in large cities, others on reserves, both poor and prosperous, and still others live in large areas of the country where the legal status of the land is unresolved. Some Native people are waged workers, a few are capitalists, while many others make their living in a "mixed economy," combining cash income (from trapping and waged work) with income in kind (from fishing and hunting).

For an overview of Native people's circumstances nationally, see Ponting, ed., *Arduous Journey*; Morrison and Wilson, eds., *Native Peoples*; and Boldt and Long, *The Quest for Justice*.

2 In this chapter, we address the English-Canadian political economy tradition only as it pertains to the situation of Natives and immigrants. We are thus not treating one other major type of ethnic relations and oppression in Canadian historical development – British domination of the French and the unique position of Quebec and the French collectivity within Confederation. For a treatment of French-English relations in Canada as it pertains to language, see the chapter in this volume by William Coleman.

3 These were not the only motivations behind determination of who might enter (and who must leave) Canada. As Reg Whitaker persuasively argues, "national security" concerns since 1945 have not only competed with but sometimes overrode economic considerations in the selection of immigrants. Whitaker, *Double Standard*.

4 See Gilroy, *There Ain't No Black in the Union Jack*, and, for a different formulation of a similar point which also takes gender into account, Ng, "The Social Construction of Immigrant Women." A roughly parallel argument about the role of the Canadian state in this process appears in Usher, "Are We Defending a Culture or a Mode of Production?" See also Bouchard and La Rusic, *The Shadow of Bureaucracy*.

5 One such colonizer was Edward Gibbon Wakefield, who wrote important sections of Lord Durham's Report on the Affairs of British North America (1839). Wakefield suggested that British society be created in the colonies by manipulating the proportions among land, labour, and capital. He believed that the key to economic growth was the establishment in the colonies of an English community containing wealthy capitalists and entrepreneurs. For a discussion of Wakefield's influence in Canada, see Goodwin, *Canadian Economic Thought*, 20-9.

6 See Glen Williams, "Canada," 28-32; Ehrensaft and Armstrong, "The Formulation of Dominion Capitalism"; Panitch, "Dependency and Class"; Drache, "Formation and Fragmentation"; McNally, "Staple Theory"; and Naylor, *Canada in the European Age*.

7 Ehrensaft and Armstrong, "Formation," 101.

8 Glen Williams, "Canada," 28.

9 Ehrensaft and Armstrong, "Formation," 100.

10 Glen Williams, "Canada," 30.

11 Ehrensaft and Armstrong, "Formation," 141; Glen Williams, "Canada," 31–2.

12 The merits of the white settler colony thesis in situating Canada historically in the global economy are evident in the articles by Williams and by Ehrensaft and Armstrong.

13 Probably the most important lacunae concern (mostly) recent work toward theoretical interpretation of Native political activism and its roots in Native peoples' material circumstances. We do not discuss the very interesting arguments in Dosman, *Indians: The Urban Dilemma*; Frideres, *Native People in Canada*; Ponting, "Relations between Bands and the Department of Indian Affairs"; and Tennant, "Native Indian Political Organization in British Columbia." This strand of work is obviously important to political economy, but it requires an extended treatment that would take us outside the central theme of this chapter. A useful guide to the political economy literature on Native peoples appears in Drache and Clement, *The New Practical Guide*; see chapter 16, by Jennifer Mauro, and chapter 17, by Michael Asch. An excellent recent bibliography, which lists several earlier bibliographies, is Peters, *Aboriginal Self-Government*.

14 Innis, *The Fur Trade in Canada*, 388.

15 Innis's own summary appears in *The Fur Trade*, chap. 6.

16 Ibid., 388.

17 Ibid.

18 Ibid., 392.

19 See Rich, *The Hudson's Bay Company*; RRotstein, "Fur Trade and Empire."

20 Excellent reviews of the literature appear in Ray and Freeman, *"Give Us Good Measure"*; and Thistle, *Indian-European Trade Relations*.

21 See Van Kirk, *"Many Tender Ties."* Ron Bourgeault offers a somewhat different analysis of the role of Native women in the fur trade. His work is discussed later in this chapter.

22 Ibid., 240.

23 See Ray, *Indians in the Fur Trade*; Ray and Freeman, *"Give Us Good Measure"*; and Trigger, *Natives and Newcomers*.

24 See Thistle, *Trade Relations*.

25 Ryerson, *The Founding of Canada*, viii; Ryerson, *Unequal Union*.

26 Ryerson, *Founding*, 18.

27 Ibid., 43.

28 See ibid., chap. 6 and 16.

29 See, for example, Leacock, "The Montagnais-Naskapi," and the references cited therein. More generally, see Sahlins, *Stone-Age Economics*, and Godelier, *Perspectives in Marxist Anthropology*.

30 A partial exception is Zlotkin and Colborne, "Internal Canadian Imperialism,"

which provides an excellent overview of the strategic positioning of the national Native movement during the 1970s.

31 Besides the works discussed below, see *Fireweed* (winter 1986) Special Issue by Native Women; Silmon, ed., *Enough Is Enough*; and Little Bear and Boldt, *Pathways to Self-Determination*.

32 See M. Campbell, *Half-Breed*, and Adams, *Prison of Grass*.

33 See Manuel and Posluns, *The Fourth World*; Cardinal, *The Unjust Society* and *The Rebirth of Canada's Indians*; Peltier and Poole, *No Foreign Land*. See also Robinson and Quinney, *The Infested Blanket*.

34 Adams, *Prison*.

35 An exemplary application of this principle is Clement, *The Struggle to Organize*.

36 Panitch, "Dependency and Class," 14; McNally, "Staple Theory."

37 Ehrensaft and Armstrong, "Formation," 101.

38 Drache, "Formation and Fragmentation," especially 49, 53. Similarly, in P. Phillips and E. Phillips's otherwise very useful synthesis (*Women and Work*) of the literature on Canadian women's participation in the labour market, Native women appear only in a short discussion of the fur trade and then vanish from the remainder of Canadian history.

39 Ehrensaft and Armstrong, "Formation," 140; see also 101.

40 Bourgeault, "The Indian, the Metis and the Fur Trade." See also Bourgeault, "The Development of Capitalism."

41 See Brody, *The People's Land* and *Maps and Dreams*.

42 Usher, "The North," 491. See also Usher, "Evaluating Country Food" (which discusses issues arising in attempts to establish the value of income in kind), "The Class System," and "Staple Production." A similar but less theoretically explicit view is presented in T.R. Berger, *Northern Frontier*.

43 A summary of this analysis and an exploration of its political implications appear in Asch, *Home and Native Land*.

44 Leacock, "Introduction"; Etienne and Leacock, eds. *Women and Colonization*; Leacock, *Myths of Male Dominance*.

45 See Watkins, "From Underdevelopment to Development" and "Dene Nationalism."

46 See Bourgeault, "The Indian, the Metis and the Fur Trade," and "The Development of Capitalism." Contrasting treatments appear in Dyck, ed., *Indigenous Peoples*, and Tanner, ed., *The Politics of Indianness*.

47 See Dobbin, "Prairie Colonialism," and Loxley, "The 'Great Northern Plan' "

48 Speck, *An Error in Judgement*.

49 This scholarly neglect reflected prevailing ethnocentric assumptions (that minorities would assimilate to the official "charter group" cultures), domination of these disciplines by scholars of British and French origins, and a dearth of language skills, scholarly incentive, and archival resources on the "other" ethnic groups. See Howard Palmer, "Canadian Immigration."

50 A. Greer, "Wage Labour," 7.

51 See Phillips, "Introduction," and, for more critical assessments, Greer, 'Wage Labour"; Drache, "Formation and Fragmentation," and B. Palmer, Review.

52 See Pentland, 'The Lachine Strike of 1843."

53 Pentland, *Labour and Capital*, 113.

54 Greer, "Wage Labour," 14.

55 See Pentland, *Labour and Capital*, 55.

56 Ibid.

57 Bleasdale, "Class Conflict."

58 The most authoritative critique of Pentland's treatment of the Irish is Akenson, "Ontario." Akenson takes issue with Pentland's equation of Roman Catholic Irish with subsistence farmers (in Ireland) and his assumption that they were prevented from settling on land and thus forced to take non-agricultural, labouring jobs in Upper Canada.

59 Miles, *Racism and Migrant Labour*, 140.

60 See Gilroy, *There Ain't No Black*, 38–9.

61 Pentland, *Labour and Capital*, 91–2.

62 Greer regards Pentland's inattention to women's roles in production and household subsistence as symptomatic of "his tendency to equate 'labour' with wage labour [which] prevented him from taking account of the household economy of family production for family use." Greer, "Wage Labour," 20. Without the household subsistence activities of those immigrant women who accompanied their menfolk across the Atlantic – tending gardens and livestock, caring for children, and preparing foodstuffs and household necessities – the ability of employers to procure and maintain reserves of cheap labour would have been severely diminished.

    Ruth Bleasdale emphasizes the importance of family migration to Canada of Irish labourers and the fact that many labourers in canaller communities lived with women and children in family units. Bleasdale, "Class Conflict," 19. However, like other historians of the Irish in Upper Canada, Bleasdale treats both the work and the (class and ethnic) violence on the canals as exclusively male activities.

63 See Panitch, "Dependency and Class," 14–17.

64 Ibid., 14.

65 Ibid., 17.

66 Ehrensaft and Armstrong, "Formation," 141–2.

67 G. Laxer, "Foreign Ownership," 311–45.

68 The Alien Labour Act prohibited the importation of foreign workers under contract from a restricted number of countries.

69 Craven, *"An Impartial Umpire"*; Avery, *"Dangerous Foreigners"*.

70 Brodie and Jensen, *Crisis, Challenge and Change*.

71 Craven, *"An Impartial Umpire"*, chap 6.

72 Harney, "Montreal's King of Italian Labour," 63.

73 Panitch, "Dependency and Class, 14.
74 See Harney, "Montreal's King"; Avery, *"Dangerous Foreigners"*.
75 Creese, "Working Class Politics."
76 See ibid., 70, 116. Howard Palmer (*Patterns of Prejudice*) similarly identifies opposition to immigration by white labour unions in Alberta around the turn of the century as stemming from both concern about economic competition and assumptions about the inferiority of central and eastern Europeans and Asians.
77 Drache, "Formation and Fragmentation," 62.
78 Ibid., 62, 71.
79 See Creese, "Working Class Politics"; McCormack, *Reformers, Rebels and Revolutionaries*; Phillips, "The National Policy"; McDonald, "Working Class Vancouver"; Ward, *White Canada Forever*; and H. Palmer, *Patterns of Prejudice*.
80 B. Palmer, "Listening to History," 62.
81 Thus, the Anti-Asiatic Exclusion League was formed in 1921, under the aegis of the Vancouver Trades and Labour Council as well as veterans' organizations and the Retail Merchants' Association. Its objective was to create a "white Canada" through education and political organization. Creese, "Working Class Politics," 133.
82 Phillips, "The National Policy," 57.
83 McCormack, *Reformers*, 10.
84 Ward's *White Canada Forever* dismisses economic factors, arguing that the perceived unassimilability of the Chinese was at the root of the anti-Asian movement.
85 Li, "A Historical Approach"; Li and Bolaria, "Canadian Immigration Policy"; Li and Bolaria, eds., *Racial Minorities*; and Bolaria and Li, *Racial Oppression in Canada*.
   Li has produced some valuable historical research on the political subordination of the Chinese within immigration policy and its debilitating effects on the family lives of male migrants. But Li's explanation for the marginal non-citizen status of Chinese in Canadian immigration policy is incomplete, failing to acknowledge the effects of pressure from white workers and small businessmen in bringing about progressively more stringent head taxes. Creese, "Working Class Politics," 93.
   Bolaria's theorizing on Canadian immigration policy is muddled. He indiscriminately conflates theories of internal colonialism and "class/race exploitation," without examining the development of Canadian immigration policies. Bolaria, "Dominant Perspectives."
86 Sunahara, *The Politics of Racism*.
87 The WUL not only accepted Asians but solicited them as political equals. Creese argues that the ideal circumstance facilitating such inter-racial solidarity was an economic crisis, with high levels of unemployment, thus allowing revolutionary socialism to gain ascendancy over labour reforms. A key factor, then, in mediat-

ing the relationship between the economy and the rise and fall of labour racism was the degree of class consciousness among white workers. Creese, "Working Class Politics," 162.

88 Avery's important book, *"Dangerous Foreigners"*, unproblematically accepts the views of Canadian officials that foreign workers were dangerous and possessed inherent traits of violence that set them apart from British-Canadian society. See Lindstrom-Best, "Review."

89 G. Kealey, "Labour and Working Class History."

90 Ehrensaft and Armstrong, "Formation," 142.

91 This point is made elegantly in Bruno Ramirez's brief consideration ("Ethnic Studies") of the relationship between ethnic studies and working-class history.

92 See the articles by Heron and by Storey and Radforth in Heron and Storey, eds., *On the Job*; Ramirez, "Brief Encounters"; Seager, "Class, Ethnicity and Politics"; and B. Palmer, *Working-Class Experience*. For a superb overview of transformations in the labour process that treats ethnicity as significant in Canadian historical development, see Heron and Storey, "On the Job in Canada."

93 Carmela Patrias challenges the new labour history's tendency to isolate the culture of rank-and-file immigrants from that of other social strata within these groups in her study of Communist and patriotic associations in the Hungarian-Canadian community ("Patriots and Proletarians").

94 See Ramirez, "Ethnic Studies," 48; Yancey, Erickson, and Juliani, "Emergent Ethnicity."

95 See McCormack, *Reformers*; Sangster, "The Communist Party," 31, 48, 52.

96 See Berry, Kalin, and Taylor, *Multiculturalism*; Henry, "The Dynamics of Racism in Toronto"; and Driedger and Mezoff, "Ethnic Prejudice." On the correlation between social class and attitudes toward immigrants and native peoples, see Filson, "Class and Ethnic Differences."

97 See Krauter and Davis, *Minority Canadians*; Tulloch, *Black Canadians*; Case, *Racism and National Consciousness*; Head, *The Black Presence*; Ubale, "Equal Opportunity"; Lazarus, *A Crack in the Mosaic*; Ramcharan, *Racism*; Ujimoto and Hirabayashi, eds., *Visible Minorities*.

98 Forsythe, ed., *Let the Niggers Burn!*; Henry, *Black Politics*.

99 Brand and Bhaggiyadatta, *Rivers Have Sources*.

100 Tania Das Gupta, *Learning from Our History*.

101 See *Fireweed*, Women of Colour Issue, 16 (1983); Silvera, *Silenced*; *Resources for Feminist Research* "Immigrant Women in Canada," 16:1 (March 1987).

102 See Iacovetta, "From *Contadina* to Workers."

103 See Gannage, *Double Day, Double Bind* and "A World of Difference."

104 See Ng, "Social Construction."

105 See L. Johnson, *The Seam Allowance*.

106 Working outside the official strike machinery, the multi-ethnic female Action Committee for Garment Workers faced the wrath of both the employer and the entrenched Jewish male leadership. See Lipsig-Mumme, "Organizing Women."

107 See Burnet, ed. *Looking into My Sister's Eyes*; Adilman, "A Preliminary Sketch."
108 A useful formulation for exploring the reciprocal effects between class and racial
    or ethnic dynamics is Adam Przeworski's broad definition of class struggle
    which encompasses struggles that bring classes into being as well as struggles
    between organized class forces; see "Proletariat into a Class." On the reciprocal
    determination between "race" and class politics in Britain, elaborating on
    Przeworski's concept of class formation, see Gilroy, *There Ain't No Blacks*, 30-1.
109 The massive pool of world refugees, currently estimated at 15 million, and the
    fact that Canada is increasingly sought as a safe haven for refugees make all the
    more pressing the necessity of linking world political and economic develop-
    ments to Canadian immigration and the formation of immigrant communities.
    For interesting examinations of the contradictions and ideological and racial
    biases in Canadian immigration policy, see Malarek, *Haven's Gate*; Whitaker,
    Double Standard; and Abella and Troper, *None Is Too Many*.

CHAPTER TWELVE

Taking Culture Seriously: A Political Economy of Communications

Ted Magder

Most political economists would agree that the manner in which attitudes, ideas, and values are transmitted, elaborated, and consumed within the spheres of culture and communications helps generate social relations and the structures of power and conflict in Canada. Yet the revival of Canadian political economy has not yielded many sustained inquiries into the nature of Canadian cultural production, distribution, and consumption. Canadian political economy tends to focus on economic development and on social and political relations as they relate to, or are derived from, the basic processes of production. It is not so much a bad case of economism, but only that concern over the economy (classically defined to include financial, resource, and manufacturing activities) has been the dominant area of research. No doubt the relative neglect of the cultural sphere stems also from an unstated assumption that the best approach to contemporary cultural practices lies within semiotics and content analysis, which concentrate on the ideological dimensions of cultural practice and try to uncover its various systems of meaning and representation. Analysis of the "text" is indeed vital to the study of culture, but the "context" of culture – its economic, political, and social determinants – must also be probed. This is the task for a political economy of culture.

"Culture," as one of its most astute students has observed, is "the *signifying system* through which necessarily (though among other means) a social order is communicated, reproduced, experienced and explored."[1] The cultural sphere is bounded by the traditional arts, such as theatre, dance, and painting, on the one side and by the cultural industries, such as television, radio, cinema, and the press, on the other.[2] These practices are not the epiphenomena of supposedly more basic social activities nor simply a condition of "leisure" or the experience of "entertainment." Through cultural practices individuals gain a sense of themselves and how they can relate to others – as citizens, as members of a class or social group, as men or women, as natives or blacks, as Québécois or westerners. As vehicles for symbolically representing everyday life and for producing and transforming meaning and information, cultural practices are an integral component of the struggle for, and maintenance of, power, an integral component of politics writ large.

If cultural practices are important ultimately for what they say, why have a political economy of culture? Political economy allows us to analyse the "context" of cultural practices, relating what is produced to how production takes place, how it is organized institutionally and economically, and, increasingly, how it is regulated by the state.[3] Indeed the method of political economy is well suited to the analysis of contemporary cultural practices, which now firmly and increasingly depend on the process of capitalist commodity production. The production of culture has become a big business. Moreover, there is an undeniable affinity between the commercialization of production and the form and content of contemporary cultural products. Increasing concentration and monopolization within the cultural industries have helped standardize and homogenize cultural production. That "Hollywood" refers both to the most dominant film production and distribution companies in the world and to the dominant form of filmmaking itself is proof positive of these trends. And while there is still considerable space for resistance to these trends, the constraints on creative and democratic cultural production must be recognized and analysed.

At one very basic level, the problems inherent in the organization of contemporary cultural production are readily apparent in Canada, where indigenous cultural products occupy a very minor position in their own domestic market. A political economy of culture brings us face to face with the issue of Canada's extreme dependency on foreign – mostly American – cultural products; nowhere is the theme of dependency more firmly in evidence than in the cultural sphere. We need to understand how this dependency has been secured, reproduced, and challenged; specifically, we need a more nuanced appraisal of the somewhat confused manner in which the Canadian state has sought to redress the cultural imbalance through the promotion of Canadian cultural production and the regulation of foreign products. But a political economy of Canadian culture must discuss more than cultural nationalism. To trumpet cultural sovereignty in the context of a free trade deal with the United States is a futile gesture unless we ask ourselves a very basic and difficult question: cultural sovereignty for what? This cannot be a detached academic exercise. If the new political economy is to remain committed to social change, to the development of a more progressive, democratic, and egalitarian social system, we need to establish a cultural sphere radically different from the current commercialized, centralized, and undemocratic structures. A political economy of culture will help us not only to understand the current structure but also to develop a more democratic alternative. Otherwise we have not yet learned to take culture seriously enough.

What follows is a critical review of some of the more important currents in the attempt to establish a political economy of culture in Canada.[4] It is by no means exhaustive, especially since it does not cover the literature in Quebec. Unlike many of the other fields covered by Canadian political economists, the study of culture is still relatively underdeveloped. It is, however, similar in one basic respect: we begin with Harold Innis.

INNIS: THE BIAS OF COMMUNICATION

Although better known, and more widely studied, for his work on the political economy of staples production, Harold Innis was one of Canada's first theorists of communications and culture. His sometimes arcane, often obtuse later works – the Innis of time and space – are concerned principally with the historical relationship between political organizations and the various technologies of communications. Driven by a desire to understand how empires, the very pinnacles of political organization and power, were reproduced, extended, and transformed, Innis increasingly sought the answer in the way political power and social control were mediated through the structures of communication and culture. For Innis, the most impressive imperial systems were those that managed to balance space, or territorial control, and time, or socio-cultural continuity. It was not an easy task; in fact, Innis argued that each empire, for reasons not always made clear, contained a bias toward either space or time; these biases – key to understanding the broadest cyclical dynamics of history – were revealed in the various technologies of communication.[5] In pursuing these themes, Innis's normative stance was never far removed: his overriding concern was to discover the "conditions favourable to creative thought"; his overriding fear was the erosion of those conditions through monopolies of knowledge.[6]

To clarify Innis's schema and ascertain its usefulness for a contemporary political economy of culture, let us briefly examine his discussion of the American empire and its structure of communications. Innis argued that the American empire was biased heavily toward the spatial dimensions of political organization; it was, therefore, unable to maintain continuity or stability without the use of force. Much of its inherent instability stemmed from the character of its communications infrastructure, organized originally around the sanctity of a free press. According to Innis's schema, paper was a medium biased toward space. In the United States this bias was seriously exacerbated by the commercialization of the press, the introduction of advertising, and the development of newspaper monopolies. Instead of being the basis for an informed and democratic sphere of opinion and debate, the

American press had been debased by sensationalism, sentimentalism, and an "obsession with the immediate."[7]

Innis wrote: "The guarantee of freedom of the press under the Bill of Rights ... has meant an unrestricted operation of commercial forces and an impact of technology of communication tempered only by commercialism itself."[8] "Under the pressure of publishers and advertisers the journalist has been compelled to seek the striking rather than the fitting phrase, to emphasize crises rather than developmental patterns."[9] Press barons such as Hearst and Pulitzer had discovered a cynical formula for commercial success: "You cannot aim too low. The story you present cannot be too stupid."[10] Worse still, the tragedy that had befallen the press in the United States was being played elsewhere over and over again in the twentieth century, wherever and whenever "the industrialization of the means of communication [had] become dominant."[11]

Innis's concern with the commercialization, monopolization, and homogenization of cultural practices is in principle quite justified. He is on relatively firm ground when he argues, for instance, that Canadian cultural production must be organized "along lines free from commercialism," if it is to withstand the pressures of Americanization.[12] But while his analysis begins from political economy, it ends in a rather static, resolutely pessimistic and idealist conception of cultural practices. In fact a careful reading of Innis reveals a man increasingly uncomfortable with the politics and culture of his time. Unfortunately, his normative stance led him to develop a blanket critique of "the cruelty of mechanized communication and the tendencies which we have come to note in the modern world."[13]

Innis makes no firm distinction between the industrialization of culture and communications on the one hand and their specific organization as spheres of capitalist accumulation on the other. Like the mass society theorists of his time, Innis argued that the new media of communications were woefully ineffectual in establishing the conditions for creative thought or cultural continuity: "Superficiality became essential to meet the various demands of large numbers of people and was developed as an art by those compelled to meet the demands. The radio accentuated the importance of the ephemeral and of the superficial. In the cinema and the broadcast it became necessary to search for entertainment and amusement."[14] Creative thought could be sustained only through rediscovery of the oral tradition. We must take Innis seriously and deal critically with his assertion that the downfall of Western "culture" began at the "dusk of Grecian civilization."[15]

The "masses" are inert, even non-existent in Innis's framework; at worst, the "illiterate" consumers to whom the new media must pander. And although Innis is keenly aware of the relationship between socio-political power and culture, nowhere does he signal awareness of the particular patterns of social domination that inhere in the current practices of cultural production. For the most part, Innis speaks of nations and of empires, not of classes, genders, races, or ethnicities. Innis's schema is at best too impressionistic, too vague to sustain a rigorous analysis of the multifarious factors that affect the production, distribution, and consumption of culture and communications.

At its worst, Innis's schema is too deterministic. He derives attributes of a given medium from the technological characteristics of the medium itself. Paper is characterized by a bias toward space and decentralization; radio, toward time and centralization. In Innis's work this is at times a rather confusing, if not altogether erroneous, heuristic device. Radio, for instance, seems to have been particularly inappropriate in establishing the conditions for continuity. Because of Innis's sensitivity to other causal factors, his analysis avoids the worst errors of technological determinism, but it seriously vitiates the work of Innis's disciple in communications studies. Marshall McLuhan's dictum that "the medium is the message" seems to isolate the specificity of each medium but is ultimately the basis for a formalistic social theory that removes human agency from the study of communications and maps only the innate technical characteristics of each medium.[16] A social theory of communications becomes an argument that control and content are irrelevant next to the technical attributes of the media themselves. If political economy too readily adopts either Innis's space-time distinction or McLuhan's theory of the media's discrete pyschic functions, it would become little more than a discipline in search of the proper technical balance between media that we may use but never really control.

PORTER, CLEMENT, AND CLARKE: MEDIA OWNERSHIP AND PRODUCTION

John Porter's mammoth study of social class and power in Canada is an important point of departure for political economists of culture and communications. Like Innis, Porter maintained that culture ("the ideological system") was crucial to the maintenance of social cohesion:

The consensus which is necessary for the maintenance of social structure does not come about through some metaphysical entity of a group or social mind, or general will. Rather, the unifying of value themes is achieved through the control of the media, and therefore the structure of the ideological system becomes articulated with other systems of power. The ideological system must provide the justification for the economic system, the political system, and so forth, and this it does by attempting to show that the existing arrangements conform with the traditional value system. But the ideological system in highly developed societies has become specialized in terms of both content and technology so that like other institutions it acquires some degree of autonomy from which it acquires a power of its own.[17]

As he turned his attention to the mass media, in particular to the press and to broadcasting, Porter noticed three things: the mass media were "big business," there was a high degree of "corporate concentration," and there were many cases of "cross-ownership" (either between media or with other sectors of corporate endeavour).[18] To uncover the structure of power and control, Porter examined the pattern of ownership, concentrating on the "media elite," the most important individuals in the largest mass media institutions. Porter discovered highly concentrated businesses, controlled tightly by well-established families of Canadian capital, such as the Siftons, Thompsons, Hunters, and Bassetts: "Inheritance through kinship, rather than social mobility, [was] the principal means of recruitment to that group which owns the major mass media instruments."[19]

It was hardly a surprise then that the ideological orientation of the mass media was "conservative, supporting the *status quo* over a wide range of social and economic policy."[20] This bias was a result not only of owner's direct interference in news production but also of their tacit control of supposedly independent publishers, editors, and journalists. Indeed Porter had few kind words for this group of "professionals"; he described them as a group of badly trained, badly organized middle-class men of British origin who were all too willing to endorse or work within the prevailing structure of values. From Porter's perspective, the mass media were well structured to operate within "the confraternity of power" that ruled Canada. Here, as elsewhere, Canada "has a long way to go to become in any sense a thorough-going democracy."[21]

Using data from the 1970 Special Senate Committee on Mass Media (the Davey Report), Wallace Clement updated and extended Porter's study of the media elite. As the Davey Report noted: "The trend towards fewer and fewer owners of our sources of news and information is already well entrenched. There are only five cities in the country where genuine competition between newspapers exists; and in all of these five cities, some or all of these competing dailies are owned by chains."[22] Clement gave empirical substance to Porter's notion of a "confraternity of power," by uncovering extensive overlap between the economic elite and the media elite (more than two-thirds "simultaneously hold important corporate positions outside the media").[23] Clement concurred with Porter that the media elite functions to maintain the status quo, by operating as "gatekeepers, performing the function of selection and screening alternatives by establishing limits of tolerance."[25] While the "gatekeepers" did not necessarily produce a systematic ideology, through "appointments and active participation in publication and broadcasting" they did ensure that the mass media were "biased in favour of the existing arrangements of power."[25]

Clement and Porter employed what has become known as an instrumentalist approach. As Robert Hackett explains, "Instrumentalism may be defined as the view that social institutions are the instruments of those who occupy elite decision-making positions (corporate owners, state bureaucrats, senior politicians), and who manipulate them in their own narrow interests, often at the expense of subordinate social groups."[26] While there are serious problems with such an approach, it would be inappropriate to dismiss the work adumbrated above. Empirical studies of ownership patterns and concentration in the media are part and parcel of a political economy of culture. Those who own the major media institutions in Canada constitute an important and powerful group whose interests, while not always uniform, affect the dynamics of Canadian culture and communications. Further, such studies undermine common-sense assumptions about the pluralism of the press, one of the fundamental tenets of capitalist democracies. As an American media critic, A.J. Liebling, has wryly noted: "Freedom of the press is guaranteed only to those who own one."[27]

Yet as both the Davey Report and the later Kent Commission demonstrate, it is all to easy to derive palliative and reformist conclusions from evidence about ownership patterns that in and of itself is quite critical of the status quo.[28] These two government-sponsored studies concluded that an independent and pluralist press could be re-established if the Canadian state curtailed the size of chains and forced conglomerates to divest either their media or non-media holdings and if journalists developed higher "professional" standards. While such actions might reduce concentration, the recommendations do not address the underlying problem that led to media concentration and "cheapskate" journalism in the first place. Newspaper publication would still derive most of its revenue from mass consumer advertising. As Clement and Porter fully realized, this fact more than any other has led to media production that hugs the middle of the road and reinforces the status quo.

In other words, media content has less to do with who owns or controls the media than with the atmosphere in which they operate and which they must survive. Indeed, direct interventions by owners are quite rare, and the media do produce items embarrassing to the principal sources of economic, political, and social power. In day-to-day terms, media production is a very complex process; its routines, its limitations, and its constraints require far more detailed analysis than an instrumentalist approach can provide. As Debra Clarke explains, a political economy of media production, and cultural production more generally, must "investigate the total process, from the raw materials to the organization of production and its constraints, to the actual routines of production and the practices of producers, to the actual product which results."[29] As Clarke, among others, demonstrates, the "news" is not the "simple presentation of the real world. It is a *re*-presentation," a "social construction," of basic issues, conflicts, and themes within society.[30] Through detailed study of the process of production in five major television information programs in Canada, Clarke provides evidence to support the following observations:

that television news production is fundamentally a "passive" journalistic mode; that television news is the outcome of a highly regulated and routinized production process; that television news portrays the social world in a fragmented, decontextualized, and ahistorical manner which concentrates upon events, upon formalized institutions, and which depends upon official, institutionalized sources; that power is largely invisible in television news, since the journalistic concept of "politics" equates it with parliamentary procedures of government, rather than power; that journalists, as a professional group, share a range of common traits . . . [and] are structurally denied access to a comprehensive knowledge of the news/current affairs audience . . . , which in turns lends a particular character to the form and content of television information programming.[31]

Clarke's work is emblematic of the type of analysis needed in other areas of cultural practice. More detailed studies of the process of cultural production will not only help uncover the links between production and content but may also serve as the base for developing more democratic forms of cultural practice.

FROM SMYTHE TO LEISS: THE AUDIENCE AS COMMODITY

In the late 1970s, in an attempt to redress what he saw as Western Marxism's serious neglect of the political and economic significance of the mass media, Dallas Smythe introduced a unique theoretical framework for a political economy of mass communications systems in contemporary capitalist societies. For Smythe, "the first question that historical materialists should ask about mass communications systems is *what economic function for capital do they serve*, attempting to understand their role in the reproduction of capitalist relations of production."[32] The answer was remarkably simple: the principal task of the mass media is to "mass produce audiences and sell them to advertisers. These audiences work on, and are consumed in, the marketing of mass-produced consumer goods and services to themselves."[33] Accordingly, the commodity form of mass-produced, advertising-supported communications is not the message, information, or entertainment, but the audience itself. Smythe contends that the "material transmitted to the audience is an inducement (gift, bribe, or 'free lunch') to recruit potential members of the audience and to maintain their loyal attention."[34]

Although Smythe describes one of the ways in which the mass media reproduce capitalist relations, the audience-as-commodity thesis contains serious drawbacks. As Graham Murdock points out, "Smythe's preoccupation with the relations between communications and advertising leads him to underplay the independent role of media content in reproducing dominant ideologies."[35] As we have noted, a political economy of culture can not, in and of itself, deal with the many important questions pertaining to culture as a signifying system or a system of meaning. The content of the mass media is not simply a "free lunch." In his apparent effort to vilify all inquiry into the styles and forms of representation and signification in the media, Smythe has laid the basis for an impoverished theory of cultural production. Further, not all forms of cultural production under monopoly capitalism are driven by the sale of advertising, not only in the traditional arts, but in important sectors of the "cultural industries," such as cinema, popular music, and popular fiction. Further, although Smythe claims that his theory reflects a fundamental reality of monopoly capitalism, it is best applied only to North America. Until very recently, most western European broadcasting systems were not organized around private corporations dependent on advertising revenue.

But there is a much more basic problem in Smythe's analysis. It is simply not the case that the principal commodity produced by the mass media is audiences. You cannot produce what you do not own, and in no sense do the mass media own audiences in the same way that capital owns labour. From a materialist perspective what the mass media produce is their content or programs. As Michael Lebowitz has recently argued, in terms of the sale of advertising space or time, the media function *as part of the process of selling the commodities of industrial capital to consumers*."[36] The audience is a central component in a political economy of culture; however, Smythe's theoretical construction does more to obfuscate than clarify the various relations that can obtain between the audience and the commodities of culture. This is most apparent in his tendency to speak of a "mass-produced audience," which, like the concept of an essential and a priori unified working class, is clearly untenable. The audience is a highly differentiated conglomerate of individuals and groups, and because so much of its work (to use Smythe's phrase) occurs in an isolated and individualized setting, it is a very ineffective "major antagonist" to monopoly capitalism or mass communications systems.[37]

Even so, Smythe makes a valuable case for advertising as an important element in contemporary cultural practices. As William Leiss, Stephen Kline, and Sut Jhally cogently argue, advertising needs to be understood in two basic respects. First, "advertising considerations . . . influence greatly the operations of media, particularly their orientation to content and programming and the organization of audiences in terms of social, spatial, and temporal qualities. The competition for audiences through programming [becomes] the sine qua non of all media."[38] For mass-audience television this competition is a major factor in the "lowest common denominator" approach to programming. For broadcasting firms dependent on advertising revenues, there is a strong bias toward the "tried and true" formula, toward programming that will all but guarantee a large audience. The competition for audiences leads also to a certain uniformity of scheduling among the major networks. There is, or is believed to be, a set time of day for which certain types of programs – news, game shows, sports, and so on – will attract the biggest audience. The routines of mass-audience television are tampered with only rarely.

But second, advertising not only impinges on the production practices of media institutions, it is itself an important cultural form: "National consumer product advertising has become one of the great vehicles of social communication . . . Its creations appropriate and transform a vast range of symbols and ideas; its unsurpassed communicative powers recycle cultural models and references back through the networks of social interactions. This venture is unified by the discourse through and about objects, which bonds together images of persons, products and well-being."[39] Through a penetrating and detailed historical survey of national consumer advertising, Leiss, Line, and Jhally show that advertising has become a powerful form of social communication, that it is "*the privileged discourse for the circulation of messages and social cues about the interplay between persons and objects.*"[40] They are far from sanguine over this development. As they argue elsewhere, advertising has been instrumental in replacing old notions of social solidarity and collectivity with new, ever-changing associations "oriented strongly around products and messages about products."[41] In its most developed form, advertising presents a

magical representation of the social collectivity. It is magical because the product stands in a quite indeterminate relation to the personal activities, interactions, and self-transformations that are portrayed in the advertising messages. In much national television advertising there is no sensible, "causal" relation at all; rather, the product is simply associated with a highly-stylized set of visual images. The product, in other words, simply *represents* a social collectivity as such, which is defined by its style and activities as a distinct social grouping vis-a-vis others.[42]

Finally, as Leiss and his colleagues argue, the pervasiveness of advertising in modern consumer societies only enhances the undemocratic structure of the market-place; open, collective discussion over non-commercial relations between people and objects is non-existent or marginalized.[43] Clearly, the study of advertising has important implications for a political economy of culture.

DEPENDENT CULTURAL DEVELOPMENT

"The State or the United States": so Graham Spry described the two fundamental options facing Canadian policy-makers as they grappled with the first broadcasting legislation in the early 1930s. Spry's argument, repeated in varying forms many times since, was that unless the state protected and facilitated Canadian cultural activities, commercial pressure from the market-place would lead, almost ineluctably, to continental cultural integration. Generally speaking, in television, radio, cinema, book publishing, and the periodical press, it has been cheaper to import cultural products than produce them in Canada. Dependency on foreign products remains a trenchant feature of Canadian cultural life: Canadian films occupy between 3 to 5 per cent of the total annual screen-time in their own domestic market;[44] 71 per cent of the consumer magazines distributed in Canada originate from foreign sources;[45] English Canadians spend 71 per cent of their television viewing time watching foreign programs, and only 2 per cent of all English-language dramatic programming available (including "sitcoms," soap operas, and police shows) is Canadian; and while French Canadians spend a majority of their viewing time watching Canadian programs, in the dramatic category only 20 per cent is Canadian.[46] In 1976, Secretary of State Hugh Faulkner observed: "In all these means of communications, which should be available to Canadians not only to learn about the world, but also to talk to one another about where they have been and where they are going, we have allowed the market forces to prevail over other considerations and the market forces have brought us very near disaster."[47] The ramifications are economic as well as cultural. In 1986, Canada had a net cultural trade deficit of about $1.5 billion vis-à-vis the United States.[48]

If the dilemma is as old as the cultural industries themselves, so too are attempts by the Canadian state to resolve it. Since 1929, when the Royal Commission on Broadcasting (Aird Commission) noted that "Canadian radio listeners want Canadian broadcasting" and recommended complete nationalization of existing private stations and establishment of an autonomous public broadcasting organization to fulfil that need, the Canadian state has tried, in different ways and with varying success, to facilitate, regulate, and protect Canadian cultural activities. What cultural activity there is in Canada exists in large measure because of state support. That dependency on foreign products remains so pervasive indicates both the extent of the problem and the ambivalence with which it has often been addressed.

Students of Canadian culture have long recognized the importance of state activities. Yet, as I have argued elsewhere, much of their work suffers from a somewhat simplistic view of the state itself: of the way it makes decisions, functions, and interacts with society.[49] The Canadian state is neither the bête noir of cultural dependency nor the potential saviour of national cultural development. Bureaucratic optimism is exhibited by Bernard Ostry, who states: "The administration of culture has become a big, beautiful machine"; abject pessimism typifies Susan Crean's otherwise excellent work. Both extremes reflect an unwillingness to consider seriously the social forces that impinge on the policy process and the limits that exist on the actions of the state.[50] If Canadian cultural policy appears awash in contradictions, it is a sign less of bureaucratic and political incompetence than of the contradictory dynamics within Canada as a whole.

My own work on the history of Canadian feature film policy is an attempt to demonstrate the complex and changing interaction between the state and this sector of the cultural industries.[51] As we have noted, Canadian cinemas exhibit almost exclusively foreign – mostly American – feature films. For most of this century, production of Canadian feature films was either sporadic or non-existent. But since the late 1960s, and with the help of both direct and indirect public subsidies, a viable private sector of Canadian feature film production has emerged. We must be able to account for both phenomena. Dependency on foreign films has much to do with Hollywood's export orientation since the early 1920s. Western European countries, such as Britain, France, and Italy, which have sustained domestic film industries have done so in large measure through various mechanisms of public support, including subsidies to production and protective legislation such as exhibition quotas.

Why did the Canadian state not initiate similar measures at the same time? The answer has to do not only with the power of American corporations in Canada but also with the fact that the massive inflow of foreign films was in the interests of Canadian capital involved in the exhibition, distribution, and, quite often, production of feature films. Moreover, outside the industry, there was no systematic, organized opposition to this massive dependency. When criticism of Hollywood's dominance did appear, it was tainted by the bias we have already discussed in Innis: American films were rejected *tout court* as a pernicious and wasteful form of "mass" culture; the idea of producing feature films in Canada was rejected as, culturally speaking, a waste of time and energy (especially if it had to involve public subsidy).[52] Dependency on American films was reproduced, intentionally or otherwise, by a variety of domestic forces.

But things also change. In the late 1960s, the emergence of film-makers from within the National Film Board (NFB) and Canadian Broadcasting Corporation (CBC) who wanted a chance at private feature film production, coupled with a generally more favourable attitude toward popular culture as the basis for economic and cultural development, prompted the Canadian state to introduce a program of loans and grants to encourage private production of feature films. The establishment of the Canadian Film Development Corporation (now Telefilm) did signal an important shift in the state's treatment of cultural dependency in the late 1960s.

Yet there were major limits to the policy. Production was facilitated, but protective measures, such as a quota, were not introduced, more because of domestic concerns than the possibility of American retaliation. Canadian exhibitors argued vehemently that their livelihood would be threatened if they were forced to show Canadian films; most "experts" within the Canadian industry felt that, given a small domestic market and the high cost of feature films, private Canadian production would have to be geared toward the "international" (read: American) market and that quotas would only distort the dynamics of the market-place; and, finally, theatre legislation itself falls within provincial jurisdiction, and while the mechanics of federalism are not necessarily a conservative force, they do make it harder to coordinate and initiate new policies.

Twenty years later, Canada has a domestic feature film industry. It is also Hollywood's most profitable foreign market. Ultimately, the Canadian state found a way to fashion a compromise between those forces that wanted a strong domestic feature film industry and the established interests, Canadian and foreign, within the industry. The success of the industry has come about because Canadian producers have learned, as the "experts" suggested they should, to operate within the circuit of the international film industry. As I have argued elsewhere, "Concerns over the inflow of foreign culture were incorporated within an economic rationale that emphasised the production of commercial feature films for consumption in the world market."[53] Many of the films produced in Canada do not "look" Canadian, and most of the industry's current work is on American films that are made in Canada. The few films that do reflect Canadian sensibilities have sometimes found a respectable if small audience at home and abroad (some have even been commercially successful). While these facts may unnerve Canadian nationalists, they do suggest an important shift in the structure of cultural dependency. In feature films, as in television and popular music, it may perhaps be better to speak of dependent cultural development, in which Canadian cultural production is geared toward an international market-place dominated by American media conglomerates, and begin to analyse the contradictions to which this gives rise.

As the study of film policy reveals, the Canadian state employs various steering mechanisms in its dealings with the cultural sector. For analytical purposes, these modes of intervention may be divided into four general categories, each of which raises specific questions about the relationship between the state and cultural activities. In the case of the CBC, the NFB, and the National Arts Centre the state operates as proprietor: it owns and controls specific production activities. The establishment and continued existence of these institutions break with the principle of market-based cultural production, but their development was not designed to usurp private cultural production in Canada. As Frank Peers, among others, has claimed, the Canadian broadcasting system is a "peculiar hybrid," a public service, fulfilling national objectives, and a private industry, governed by market-based criteria.[54] An understanding of this "balance," and its changes over time, is critical. Equally important is an understanding of the concept of a public service fulfilling national objectives, or of public media. As Liora Salter has argued, public media include not only state-supported broadcasting systems.[55] Non-commercial community radio stations and native communications societies may come closer to the ideal of public media than the CBC.

Aside from its role as proprietor, the state functions also as patron: it provides funds for cultural activities without any rights of ownership or management. Through such institutions as the Canada Council, the Canadian state has become a major provider for the traditional arts.[56] Here, too, critical questions arise. As Susan Crean has observed, through the Canada Council and the major institutions of "official culture," such as the National Ballet, the Canadian Opera Company, the Stratford Festival, and the symphony orchestras, the state has nourished the standard repertoire of international high culture, but it has done far too little to support the development of popular expression in these areas. As she explains: "In most cultures, the artistic underground is the refuge of what is (as yet) unacceptable and unaccountable to the mainstream. Commercially as well as aesthetically, the underground serves as the testing ground for tomorrow's fashions in Official Culture. But, in Canada, the underground does not work that way. It is not the *avant garde*, or the counter-culture, or Bohemia; it is a "minority" culture all on its own, living in the shadow of Official Culture, tied to it economically, but cut off."[57]

Robin Endres makes a similar point: the Canadian state has not only concentrated its direct subsidies on the building of large auditoriums and the funding of elite-dominated "arts" organizations but has also indirectly subsidized these ventures through tax write-offs for private donations. Endres shows that the subsidized "arts" can be extremely remunerative to the state itself (through the payment of rents, taxes, and so on). She comments: "*The artists themselves are the real subsidizers of art in this country.*"[58]

The Canadian state facilitates cultural production in one further way. Primarily through tax incentives (capital cost allowances for Canadian films and tax write-offs for private philanthropy vis-à-vis the arts), the state functions as a catalyst, encouraging private support for cultural activities. Unlike direct subsidies or grants, tax expenditures allow for greater market "flexibility" in the allocation of resources within the cultural sphere; they

also depoliticize the state's involvement, because the major allocative decisions are made by citizens and the total cost of these expenditures are
difficult to quantify.[59]

Finally, the Canadian state is deeply involved in Canadian cultural life
through its powers of regulation. The Canadian Radio-Television and Tele-
communications Commission (CRTC), for instance, licenses and regulates all
Canadian broadcasting, both public and private, in accordance with the
principles established in the Broadcasting Act of 1968. The CRTC possesses
enormous power, but, as a number of studies show, it has not been very
successful in establishing programming "of high standard, using predominantly Canadian creative and other resources."[60] As Robert Babe has noted,
the CRTC has become the victim of a common ailment among regulatory
boards: it has fallen under the spell of the private-sector interests it is
supposed to regulate. Over the years, the CRTC has allowed private broad-
casters to ignore their own promises of performance, to substitute more
costly Canadian productions with cheap, American imports. It has licensed
many new private stations and encouraged the spread of private cable companies across the country. Increased competition for advertising dollars, in
an ever more fragmented market, makes it even more difficult for private
braodcasters to fund high-quality Canadian programming designed for the
domestic market. The licensing decisions on pay-TV have done little to
reverse this trend.

FINAL CONSIDERATIONS

By now it should be clear that the principal task of a political economy of
culture is to uncover the specific economic, political, and social dynamics
that attend the various forms of cultural practice. We need to understand the
"context" within which cultural practices take place. While culture may be
entertaining, it is also always political; indirectly at least, its structures and
forms reveal the relations of power within society as a whole.

Where then do we go from here? Obviously we must continue to analyse
the process and effects of the commercialization of culture. Ownership
structures and levels of concentration remain major areas of concern; so,
too, is the much more ominous trend toward the internationalization of
cultural production in which national production and consumption patterns
become integrated into a world-wide market. The success of Canada's
popular music industry, and the recent boom in television and film production, permit Canadian production companies to operate within world
markets. The federal government's recent policy initiatives must be situated
within this context; more and more, federal cultural policy has been geared
toward development of stable production houses and private entrepreneurs

which can establish ties with the rapidly expanding multinational corporations in the communications and cultural industries; in this sense, Garth Drabinsky and Cineplex-Odeon may be *the* success story of the federal government's feature film policy.[61] Relatedly, the introduction of new cultural technologies, including satellite distribution, videotex, and the "information revolution" which has accompanied the use of computers, must be examined critically.

At the same time, we must ask tough questions about state-supported cultural institutions and practices, including "public" broadcasting. Criticism of private, commercial cultural production is impoverished when existing forms of "public" service are the only alternative presented. A strong, vibrant, popular democratic system of culture and communications will be established only after public and private cultural institutions and practices are transformed.

Finally, we need far more studies of audiences and cultural workers themselves. We must see how audiences sustain cultural practices and make them meaningful. We cannot assume that the audience is an inert mass; neither of course, can we assume that it exercises its full rights as a sovereign consumer. As an integral component of the relations of cultural production, cultural workers must also come under analysis. Through such work, as Clarke herself demonstrates, we may better understand the daily routines under which so much of our culture is produced. One of the strengths of Canadian political economy has been its sustained attention to the process of production itself. The newsroom is just one place where this tradition can be applied; television productions, film shoots, and arts companies require similar treatment. Indeed, such studies might serve as the basis for a more informed alliance of cultural workers dissatisfied with the status quo. In the end, their support is crucial if the mechanisms of communications and culture are to undergo the radical transformation which should be the goal of a political economy of culture.

NOTES

1 Raymond Williams, *Culture*, 13.
2 Drawing useful boundaries for the study of culture is no easy task. Williams's definition obviously applies to more social activities than I have listed; nevertheless, his own analysis covers the same general territory. In Canada, the study of the cultural industries has been undertaken generally under the rubric of communications studies (which itself embraces a wider set of activities). I have found it useful at times to employ the two terms, *culture* and *communications*, as a couplet. I hope that this does not confuse the issue further.

3 See the excellent discussion by Garnham, "Contribution."
4 For a useful overview of communication studies in Canada, see Salter, "Introduction."
5 See Innis, *Empire and Communication* and *The Bias of Communication*.
6 Innis, *Empire and Communication*, 9. See also Whitaker, " 'To Have Insight.' "
7 Innis, *Bias of Communication*, 187.
8 Innis, "The Strategy of Culture," 15.
9 Innis, "The Press," 85.
10 Innis, "Great Britain, the United States, and Canada," 407.
11 Innis, "The Press," 78.
12 Innis, "Strategy of Culture," 20.
13 Innis, *Bias of Communication*, 191.
14 Ibid., 82.
15 Ibid., 3.
16 See McLuhan, *Understanding Media*. For a short, incisive critique of McLuhan's method see Raymond Williams, *Television*, 126–30.
17 John Porter, *The Vertical Mosaic*, 460.
18 Ibid., chap. 15.
19 Ibid., 483–4. Porter's approach followed from his assumption that a study of elites would uncover the basic form and character of social power. For an excellent discussion of Porter's work see Panitch, "Elites," especially 231–3.
20 John Porter, *The Vertical Mosaic*, 484.
21 Ibid., 522, 557.
22 Clement, *The Canadian Corporate Elite*, 288.
23 Ibid., 326.
24 Ibid., 282.
25 Ibid., 27.
26 Hackett, "For a Socialist Perspective," 141–2.
27 In Clement, *The Canadian Corporate Elite*, 343.
28 See Special Senate Committee on Mass Media, and Canada, Royal Commission on Newspapers, Report. The Davey Report was particularly acerbic in its description of the commercial mass media. It also suggested (1, 84) a rather useful and straightforward standard for evaluating the media's performance: "*How Successful is that newspaper, or broadcasting station, in preparing its audience for social change?*" The state's response to these reports was minimalist in the extreme.
29 See Clarke, "The Labour Process," 2. See also Clarke, "Network Television News."
30 Clarke, "Labour Process," 59, 2.
31 Ibid., 7–8.
32 Smythe, "Communications," 1.
33 Smythe, *Dependency Road*, xiv.

34 Smythe, "Communications," 5.

35 Murdock, "Blindspots," 113.

36 Lebowitz, "Too Many Blindspots," 169. It is not clear why Lebowitz links the media to the process of selling the commodities of industrial capital only; surely, the advertising-based media also help the sale of other forms of capital, including the service sector.

37 See Smythe, *Dependency Road*, xv, where he argues that the audience has replaced organized labour as monopoly capitalism's major antagonist.

38 Leiss, Kline, and Jhally, *Social Communication*, 71.

39 Ibid., 3, 7.

40 Ibid., 47.

41 Jhally, Kline, and Leiss, "Magic," 20.

42 Ibid.

43 See Leiss et al., *Social Communication*, 306-10.

44 See Canada, Film Industry Task Force, *Canadian Cinema*, 8.

45 See Audley, *Canada's Cultural Industriess*, 57.

46 See Canada, *Task Force on Broadcaseting Policy*, Report, chap. 5.

47 In Audley, *Canada's Cultural Industries*, xxiv.

48 See Crane, "Battle Lines," A1, 8.

49 See Magder, "A 'Featureless' Film Policy," especially 81-5.

50 Ostry, *The Cultural Connection*, 175. See Crean, *Who's Afraid of Canadian Culture?* and Crean and Rioux, *Two Nations*.

51 Magder, "Film Policy' and "Political Economy."

52 The first full-scale review of federal cultural policy, the Massey Report, codified this bias. Although the report talked of an "American invasion" and observed that "Hollywood refashions us in its own image," it did not recommend protective measures or the establishment of a Canadian feature film industry. The report puts its faith instead in the documentary tradition of the NFB, believing nonfiction films a much more effective way to develop Canadian culture. Canada, Royal Commission on National Development in the Arts, Letters and Sciences, Report, 18, 50, and chap. 4.

53 Magder, "Film Policy," 87.

54 Peers, *The Public Eye*, xiii.

55 Salter, "Inequality," especially 305-12.

56 Unlike the Canada Council, Telefilm provides loans and invests in Canadian television and film productions. It expects to see returns on its capital expenditures.

57 Crean, *Who's Afraid?*, 166 and chap. 4 and 5.

58 Endres, "Art and Accumulations," 437.

59 For a useful discussion of the tax incentives used to promote Canadian film production in the late 1970s see Lyon and Trebilcock, *Public Strategy*, especially chap. 6.

60 Broadcasting Act, 1968, section 3(d). See, for example, Babe, *Canadian Televi-*

sion Broadcasting. For an informative yet polemical discussion of the CRTC see Hardin, *Closed Circuits*.

61 Consider the following statement in a position paper issued by the Department of Communications: "Technological developments are simply one facet of that sweeping, international movement often referred to as the "information revolution". This sea-change in the world economy is enhancing the importance to national economies of information products at the expense of manufactured products. Canadian products – including film and video products – represent a significant subcategory in this broad information field. This new reality has persuaded many states to regard the development of cultural industries as a necessary component of national economic and industrial strategies. Canada's film and video industry is a key growth sector in the context of the information revolution. It must be in a position to seize the opportunities of the new environment." Canada, *National Film and Video Policy*, 25.

Bibliography

Abella, I.M. *Nationalism, Communism and Canadian Labour*. Toronto: University of Toronto Press 1973.

Abella, Irving, and Troper, Harold. *None Is Too Many: Canada and the Jews of Europe, 1933-1948*. Toronto: Lester and Orpen Dennys 1982.

Abercrombie, Nicholas, Hill, Stephen, and Turner, Bryan S. *Sovereign Individuals of Capitalism*. London: Allen and Unwin 1986.

Acheson, T. "The National Policy and Industrialization of the Maritimes." *Acadiensis* 1 (1972).

Adams, H. *Prison of Grass*. Toronto: New Press 1975.

Adilman, T. "A Preliminary Sketch of Chinese Women and Work in British Columbia 1858-1950." In *Not Just Pin Money: Selected Essays on the History of Women's Work in British Columbia*, edited by B.K. Latham and R.J. Padro. Victoria: Camosun College 1984.

Adams, N., Biskin, L., and McPhail, M., eds. *Feminists Organizing for Change: The Contemporary Women's Movement in Canada*. Toronto: Oxford University Press 1988.

Aitken, H.G.J. "Defensive Expansionism: The State and Economic Growth in Canada." In *Approaches to Canadian Economic History*, edited by W.T. Easterbrook and M.H. Watkins. Toronto: McClelland and Stewart 1967.

- "Government and Business in Canada: An Interpretation." *Business History Review* 38:1 (1964).

- "Myth and Measurement: The Innis Tradition in Economic History." *Journal of Canadian Studies* (winter 1977).

Akenson, D. "Ontario: Whatever Happened to the Irish?" *Canadian Papers in Rural History* 3 (1982): 204-56.

Alexander, D. *Atlantic Canada and Confederation*. Toronto: University of Toronto Press 1983.

Amin, S. *Accumulation on a World Scale: A Critique of the Theory of Underdevelopment*, vol. 1. New York: Monthly Review Press 1974

Anderson, K. "A Gendered World: Women, Men and the Political Economy of the Seventeenth Century Huron." In *Feminism and Political Economy: Women's Work, Women's Struggles*, edited by H.J. Maroney and M. Luxton. Toronto: Methuen 1987.

Anderson, Perry. *Arguments within English Marxism*. London: Verso 1980.

- "The Figures of Descent." *New Left Review* 161 (Jan.-Feb. 1987): 35-63.

Andrew, C. "Women and the Welfare State." *Canadian Journal of Political Science* 17:4 (1984).

Antler, Ellen. "Women's Work in Newfoundland Fishing Families." *Atlantis* 2:2 (1977).

Archibald, B. "Atlantic Regional Underdevelopment and Socialism." In *Essays on the Left*, edited by L. LaPierre et al. Toronto: McClelland and Stewart 1971.

Armstrong, Pat. *Labour Pains: Women's Work in Crisis*. Toronto: Women's Education Press 1984.

Armstrong, Pat, and Armstrong, Hugh. "Beyond Numbers: Problems with Quantitative Data." *Alternate Routes* 6 (1983).

- "Beyond Sexless Class and Classless Sex: Towards Feminist Marxism." *Studies in Political Economy* 10 (winter 1983).

- "Women." In *The New Practical Guide to Canadian Political Economy*, edited by D. Drache and W. Clement. Toronto: James Lorimer 1985.

Armstrong, Pat, et al. *Feminist Marxism or Marxist Feminism: A Debate*. Toronto: Garamond Press 1985.

Armstrong, W. "Imperial Incubus: The Diminished Industrial Ambitions of Canada, Australia, and Argentina, 1870-1930." Unpublished conference paper, Feb. 1987.

Arnup, Kathy. "Lesbian Mothers and Child Custody." *Atkinson Review of Canadian Studies* 1:2 (1984): 35-40.

Arthurs, H.W. "Rethinking Administrative Law: A Slightly Dicey Business." *Osgoode Hall Law Journal* 17 (1979): 1-45.

Asch, M. *Home and Native Land*. Toronto: Methuen 1984.

Audley, Paul. *Canada's Cultural Industries*. Toronto: James Lorimer 1983.

Avery, Donald. *"Dangerous Foreigners": European Immigrant Workers and Labour Radicalism in Canada, 1896-1932*. Toronto: McClelland and Stewart 1979.

Babcock, Robert. *Gompers in Canada: A Study in American Continentalism before the First World War*. Toronto: University of Toronto Press 1974.

Babe, Robert. *Canadian Television Broadcasting Structure, Performance and Regulation*. Ottawa: Ministry of Supply and Services 1979.

Bakker, I. "Paradoxes of the Feminization of the Labour Force." In *The Feminization of the Labour Force*, edited by J. Jenson, E. Hagen, and C. Reddy. Oxford: Polity Press/Oxford University Press 1988.

- "Pay Equity in Ontario: More than a Defensive Victory." *Canadian Dimension* (March 1987): 4-5.

- "The Reproduction of the Working Population in Canada, 1945-1983." PHD dissertation, New School for Social Research, Department of Economics, May 1986.

- "Women and Economic Development in Canada: Some Methodological Approaches for Assessing the Impact of Economic Policies on Women." Paper prepared for the OCED Experts' Meeting on the Impact of Economic Policies on Women, Working Party No. 6, Manpower and Social Affairs Directorate, Paris (Jan. 1982).

Banting, Keith, and Simeon, Richard. *And No One Cheered: Federalism, Democracy and the Constitution Act*. Toronto: Methuen 1983.

Barrett, L.G. "Perspectives on Dependency and Underdevelopment in the Atlantic Region." *Canadian Review of Sociology and Anthropology* (Aug. 1980).

Barrett, M. *Women's Oppression Today: Problems in Marxist Feminist Analysis*. London: Verso and New Left Books 1980.

Benston, M. "The Political Economy of Women's Liberation." *Monthly Review* 21 (4 Sept.): 13–27.

Bercuson, D.J. *Fools and Wise Men*. Toronto: McGraw-Hill Ryerson 1978.

Berger, Carl. *The Writing of Canadian History*. Toronto: Oxford University Press 1976.

Berger, T.R. *Northern Frontier, Northern Homeland: The Report of the Mackenzie Valley Pipeline Inquiry*. Ottawa: Department of Supply and Services 1977.

Bernier, Gérald, and Salée, Daniel. "Social Relations and the Exercise of State Power in Lower Canada (1791–1840): Elements for an Analysis." *Studies in Political Economy* 22 (1987): 101–44.

Berry, J., Kalin, R., and Taylor, D. *Multiculturalism and Ethnic Attitudes in Canada*. Ottawa: Supply & Services 1976.

Black, Don, and Myles, John. "Dependent Industrialization and the Canadian Class Structure: A Comparative Analysis of Canada, the United States, and Sweden." Working Paper No. 24, Comparative Projection Class Structure and Class Consciousness, Department of Sociology, University of Wisconsin 1985; also *Canadian Review of Sociology and Anthropology* 23:2 (May 1986): 157–81.

Blais, A. "Industrial Policy in Advanced Capitalist Democracies." In *Industrial Policy*. Research Study 44, Royal Commission on the Economic Union and Development Prospects for Canada. Ottawa: Supply and Services 1986.

Bleasdale, R. "Class Conflict on the Canals of Upper Canada in the 1840s." *Labour/Le Travail* 7 (spring 1981): 9–39.

Boismenu, Gérard, *Le Duplessisme*. Montreal: Les Presses de l'Université de Montréal 1981.

- "L'état fédératif et l'hétérogenéité de l'espace." In *Espace régional et nation: pour un nouveau débat sur le Québec*, by Gérard Boismenu et al. Montreal: Boréal Express 1983.

Bolaria, B.S., "Dominant Perspectives and Non-White Minorities." In *Racial Minorities in Multicultural Canada*, edited by P.S. Li and B.S. Bolaria. Toronto:

Garamond Press 1983.

Bolaria, B.S., and Li, P.S. *Racial Oppression in Canada.* Toronto: Garamond Press 1985.

Boldt, Menno, and Long, Anthony J. *The Quest for Justice: Aboriginal Peoples and Aboriginal Rights.* Toronto: University of Toronto Press 1985.

Bouchard, S. and La Rusic, I. *The Shadow of Bureaucracy: Culture in Indian Affairs.* Dept. of Indian Affairs and Northern Development, 1981

Bourgault, Pierre L. *Innovation and the Structure of Canadian Industry.* Science Council of Canada Special Study No. 23. Ottawa: Information Canada 1972.

Bourgeault, R. "The Development of Capitalism and the Subjugation of Native Women in Northern Canada." *Alternate Routes* 6 (1983): 110-40.

– "The Indian, the Metis and the Fur Trade: Class, Sexism and Racism in the Transition from 'Communism' to Capitalism." *Studies in Political Economy* 12 (fall 1983): 45-80.

Bourque, Gilles. "A propos du mouvement indépendantiste." *Canadian Journal of Political and Social Theory* 10:3 (1986): 153-64.

– "Class, Nation and the Parti Québécois." *Studies in Political Economy* 2 (1979): 129-58.

Bourque, Gilles, and Laurin-Frenette, Nicole. "Les classes et l'idéologie nationaliste au Québec, 1760-1970." *Socialism québécois* 20 (1970)

– "La structure nationale québécois." *Socialism québécois* 21, 22 (1971).

Bourque, Gilles, and Legaré, Anne. *Le Québec: la question nationale.* Paris: Maspero 1979.

Boyd, Neil, ed. *The Social Dimensions of Law.* Toronto: Prentice-Hall 1986.

Boyd, Susan B. "Child Custody and Working Mothers." In *Equality and Judicial Neutrality*, edited by Sheilah L. Martin and Kathleen E. Mahoney. Calgary: Carswell 1987.

Boyle, Christine. "Home Rule for Women: Power-Sharing between Men and Women." *Dalhousie Law Journal* 7 (1983): 790-809.

Bradbury, Bettina. "Women's History and Working-Class History." *Labour/Le Travail* 19 (spring 1987).

Brady, A. "The Constitution and Economic Policy." In *The Canadian Economy and Its Problems*, edited by H.A. Innis and W. Plumptre. Toronto: University of Toronto Press 1934.

– "The State and Economic Life in Canada." *University of Toronto Quarterly* 2:4 (1933).

Brady, A., and Scott, F.R., eds. *Canada after the War.* Toronto: Macmillan 1943.

Brand, Dionne, and Bhaggiyadatta, Krisantha Sri. *Rivers Have Sources, Trees Have Roots: Speaking of Racism.* Toronto: Cross Cultural Communication Centre 1986.

Braverman, Harry. *Labor and Monopoly Capitalism.* New York: Monthly Review Press 1974.

Brenner, J., and Ramas, M. "Rethinking Women's Oppression." *New Left Review*

146 (July–Aug. 1984).

Breton, R. "Regionalism in Canada." In *Regionalism and Supranationalism*, edited by David Cameron. Montreal: Institute for Research on Public Policy 1981.

Brickey, Stephen, and Comack, Elizabeth. "The Role of Law in Social Transformation: Is a Jurisprudence of Insurgency Possible?" *Canadian Journal of Law and Society* 2 (1987): 97-119.

Brickey, Stephen, and Comack, Elizabeth, eds. *The Social Basis of Law*. Toronto: Garamond Press 1986.

Britton, J., and Gilmour, J. *Canada. The Weakest Link: A Technological Perspective on Canadian Industrial Underdevelopment* Background Study No. 43. Ottawa: Science Council of Canada 1978.

Brodie, J. "The Gender Factor and National Leadership Conventions in Canada." In *Party Democracy in Canada: The Politics of National Party Conventions*, edited by G. Perlin. Scarborough: Prentice-Hall Canada Inc. 1987.

– *The Political Economy of Regionalism*. Toronto: Harcourt, Brace, Jovanovich (forthcoming).

– *Women and Politics in Canada*. Toronto: McGraw-Hill Ryerson 1984.

Brodie, J., and Jenson, J. *Crisis, Challenge and Change: Party and Class in Canada Revisted*. Ottawa: Carleton University Press 1988.

– "The Party System." In *Canadian Politics in the 1980s*, edited by M.S. Whittington and G. Williams, 2nd ed. Toronto: Methuen 1984.

Brody, H. *Maps and Dreams*. Harmondsworth: Penguin 1981.

– *The People's Land*. Harmondsworth: Penguin 1975.

Brooks, S., and Tanguay, A.B. "Quebec's Caisse de dépôt et placements: Tool of Nationalism?" *Canadian Public Administration* 28:1 (1985).

Brown, Jennifer S.H. *Strangers in Blood: Fur Trade Company Families in Indian Country*. Vancouver: University of British Columbia Press 1980.

Brunelle, Dorval. *L'état solide: sociologie du fédéralisme au Canada et au Québec*. Montreal: Editions Sélect 1982.

Brym, R. "Anglo-Canadian Sociology." *Current Sociology/La Sociologie contemporaire* 34 (1986): 1-152.

– "The Canadian Capitalist Class, 1965-1985." In *The Structure of the Canadian Capitalist Class*, edited by R.J. Brym. Toronto: Garamond 1985.

– "Variations in the Strength of Democratic Socialism: With Special Reference to North America." In *Marxism and Social Structure: Essays in Honour of T.G. Bottomore*. edited by M. Mulkay and M. Outhwaite. Oxford: Basil Blackwell 1986.

– ed. *The Structure of the Canadian Capitalist Class*. Toronto: Garamond 1985.

Brym, R., and Sacouman, J., eds. *Underdevelopment and Social Movements in Atlantic Canada*. Toronto: New Hogtown Press 1979.

Burnet, J., ed. *Looking into My Sister's Eyes: An Exploration in Women's History*. Toronto: Multicultural History Society of Ontario 1986.

Burrill, G. and McKay, I., eds. *People, Resources and Power. Critical Perspectives on*

Underdevelopment and Primary Industries in the Atlantic Region. Fredericton: Acadiensis Press 1987.

Burstyn, V. "Masculine Dominance and the State." In *The Socialist Register 1983*, edited by R. Miliband and J. Saville. London: Merlin 1983.

– *Women against Censorship*. Toronto: Douglas and MacIntyre 1985.

Burt, S. "Women's Issues and the Women's Movement in Canada since 1970." Macdonald Commission Research Studies 34: 124-6.

Cain, Maureen. "Beyond Formal Justice." *Contemporary Crises* 9 (1985): 335-74.

Campbell, Charles. "The Canadian Left and the Charter of Rights." *Socialist Studies* 2 (1984): 30-45.

Campbell, M. *Half-Breed*. Toronto: McClelland and Stewart 1973.

Campbell, Tom. *The Left and Rights: A Conceptual Analysis of the Idea of Socialist Rights*. London: Routledge and Kegan Paul 1982.

Canada. Film Industry Task Force. *Canadian Cinema: A Solid Base*. Ottawa 1985.

– *National Film and Video Policy*. Ottawa 1984.

– Privy Council Office. Report of the Task Force on the Structure of Canadian Industry. *Foreign Ownership and Canadian Industry*. Ottawa: Queen's Printer 1968.

– Privy Council Office. Report of the Task Force on Labour Relatins. *A Study of the Changing Social, Economic, and Political Background of the Canadian System of Industrial Relations*. Ottawa: Queen's Printer 1968.

– Royal Commission on Newspapers (Tom Kent, Chair). Report. Ottawa 1981.

– Royal Commission on National Development in the Arts, Letters and Sciences. Report. Ottawa 1951.

– Science Council Industrial Policies Committee. *Hard Times, Hard Choices: Technology and the Balance of Payments*. 1981

– Task Force on Broadcasting Policy. Report. Ottawa 1986.

Canadian Review of Sociology and Anthropology. Special edition on Underdevelopment, Dependency and Regionalism (Aug. 1980).

Cardinal, H. *The Rebirth of Canada's Indians*. Edmonton: Hurtig 1977.

– *The Unjust Society*. Edmonton: Hurtig 1969.

Cardoso, F.H., and Faletto, E. *Dependency and Development in Latin America*. Berkeley: University of California Press 1979.

Carroll, W. "The Canadian Corporate Elite: Financiers or Finance Capitalists." *Studies in Political Economy* (summer 1982).

– *Corporate Power and Canadian Capitalism*. Vancouver: University of British Columbia Press 1986.

– "Dependency, Imperialism and the Capitalist Class in Canada." In *The Structure of the Canadian Capitalist Class*, edited by Robert Brym. Toronto: Garamond Press 1985.

Case, F.I. *Racism and National Consciousness*. Toronto: Plowshare Press 1977.

Chouinard, Vera. "Class Formation, Conflict and Housing Policies." Paper presented to the Annual Meeting of the Association of American Geographers, Portland, Oregon, 21–27 April 1987.

Chunn, Dorothy E., and Gavigan, Shelley A.M. "Social Control: Analytical Tool or Analytical Quagmire?" *Contemporary Crisis*, forthcoming.

Clark, Melissa. "The Canadian State and Staples: An Ear to Washington." PHD thesis, McMaster University 1979.

- "Continental Capital Accumulation: The Canadian State and Industrial Resource Development." *Contemporary Crises* 8 (1984): 203–26.

Clark-Jones, Melissa. *A Staple State: Canadian Industrial Resources in Cold War.* Toronto: University of Toronto Press 1987.

Clarke, Debra. "The Labour Process in Television News Information Broadcasting: Intrinsic Constraints and Their Textual Outcomes." Paper presented at the annual meetings of the Canadian Communications Association, Montreal, May 1987.

- "Network Television News and Current Affairs in Canada: The Social Contexts of Production." PHD dissertation, Department of Sociology and Anthropology, Carleton University 1987.

Clarkson, Stephen. *Canada and the Reagan Challenge: Crisis in the Canadian-American Relationship.* Toronto: James Lorimer in association with the Canadian Institute for Economic Policy 1982.

Clement, W. *The Canadian Corporate Elite: An Analysis of Economic Power.* Toronto: McClelland and Stewart 1975.

- "Canadian Political Economy." In *An Introduction to Sociology*, 2nd ed., edited by M. Rosenburg, W. Shaffir, A. Turowetz, and N. Weinfeld. Toronto: Methuen 1987.

- *Class, Power and Property: Essays on Canadian Society.* Toronto: Methuen 1983.

- "Contemporary Developments at Inco and Their Impact on the Sudbury Region." In *Multinational Corporations and Regional Development: Conflicts and Convergences*, edited by L. Michaud. Rome: Herder 1983.

- *Continental Corporate Power: Economic Elite Linkages between Canada and the United States.* Toronto: McClelland and Stewart 1977.

- *Hardrock Mining: Industrial Relations and Technological Change at Inco.* Toronto: McClelland and Stewart 1981.

- "Labour in Exposed Sectors: Canada's Resource Economy." *Fennia* 163 (1985).

- "A Political Economy of Regionalism in Canada." In *Modernization and the Canadian State*, edited by D. Glenday et al. Toronto: Macmillan 1978.

- "Regionalism as Uneven Development: Class and Region in Canada." *Canadian Issues* 5 (1983).

- *The Struggle to Organize: Resistance in Canada's Fishery.* Toronto: McClelland and Stewart 1986.

- "Transformations in Mining. A Critique of H.A. Innis." In *Class, Power and Property: Essays on Canadian Society*, edited by W. Clement. Toronto: Methuen 1983.

Clement, Wallace and Drache, Daniel. *A Practical Guide to Canadian Political Economy*. Toronto: Lorimer 1978.

Clow, Michael. "Politics and Uneven Capitalist Development: The Maritime Challenge to the Study of Canadian Political Economy." *Studies in Political Economy* (summer 1984).

Cohen, G.A. *Karl Marx's Theory of History: A Defence*. Princeton, NJ: Princeton University Press 1978.

Cohen, Marjorie. *Free Trade and the Future of Women's Work: Manufacturing and Service Industries*. Toronto: Garamond Press 1987.

- "The Macdonald Report and Its Implications for Women." *Feminist Action Feministe* 1 (Dec. 1985): 13–15.

Coleman, William. "A Comparative Study of Language Policy in Quebec: A Political Economy Approach." In *The Politics of Canadian Public Policy*, edited by M. Atkinson and M. Chandler. Toronto: University of Toronto Press 1983.

- *Business and Politics: A Study in Collective Action*. Montreal and Kingston: McGill-Queen's University Press 1988.

- "The Capitalist Class and the State: Changing Roles of Business Interest Associations." *Studies in Political Economy* 20 (1986).

- "From Bill 22 to Bill 101: the Politics of Language under the Parti Québécois." *Canadian Journal of Political Science* 14:3 (1981): 459–86.

- *The Independence Movement in Quebec 1945–1980*. Toronto: University of Toronto Press 1984.

Comack, E. " 'We Will Get Some Good Out of This Riot Yet': The Canadian State, Drug Legislation and Class Conflict." In *The Social Basis of Law*, edited by Stephen Brickey and Elizabeth Comack. Toronto: Garamond Press 1986.

Commission of the Yukon Territory. Brief to the Royal Commission on Canada's Economic Prospects presented by F. H. Collins, Commissioner of the Yukon Territory. Exhibit 52 (1955).

Commons, John R. *The Economics of Collective Action*, edited by K.H. Parsons. New York: Macmillan 1950.

Conklin, D.W., and St-Hilaire, F. *Canadian High-Tech in a New World Economy: A Case Study of Information Technology*. Halifax: Institute for Research on Public Policy 1988.

Connelly, Patricia. "On Marxism and Feminism." In *Politics of Diversity: Feminism, Marxism and Nationalism*, edited by R. Hamilton and M. Barrett. Montreal: Book Centre Inc. 1986.

Connelly, Patricia, and MacDonald, Martha. "Women's Work: Domestic and Wage Labour in a Nova Scotia Community." *Studies in Political Economy* 10 (winter 1983); and in *The Politics of Diversity: Feminism, Marxism and Nationalism*, edited by R. Hamilton and M. Barrett. Montreal: Book Centre Inc. 1986.

Corrigan, Philip, and Sayer, Derek. *The Great Arch: English State Formation as Cultural Revolution*. Oxford: Basil Blackwell 1985.

- "How the Law Rules: Variations on Some Themes in Karl Marx." In *Law, State and Society*, edited by Bob Fryer, Alan Hunt, Doreen McBarnet, and Bert Moorhouse. London: Croom Helm 1981.

Corry, J.A. *The Changing Conditions of Politics*. Alan B. Plaunt Memorial Lecture. Toronto: University of Toronto Press 1963.

- *Difficulties of Divided Jurisdictions*. Royal Commission on Dominion-Provincial Relations. Ottawa: King's Printer 1939.

- *Growth of Government Activities since Confederation*. Royal Commission on Dominion-Provincial Relations. Ottawa: King's Printer 1939.

Courchene, T. "Avenues for Adjustment: The Transfer System and Regional Disparities." In *Canadian Confederation at the Crossroads*, edited by M. Walker. Vancouver: Fraser Institute 1978.

Cox, R.W., and Jamieson, S.M. "Canadian Labour in a Continental Perspective." In *Canada and the United States*, edited by A.B. Fox et al. New York: Columbia University Press 1976.

Crane, David. "Battle Lines Drawn for Cabinet Battle over Cultural Future." *Toronto Star*, 5 August 1986.

Craven, P. *"An Impartial Umpire": Industrial Relations and the Canadian State 1900-1911*. Toronto: University of Toronto Press 1980.

- "Law and Ideology: The Toronto Police Court 1850-80." In *Essays in the History of Canadian Law*, Vol. II, edited by David H. Flaherty. Toronto: University of Toronto Press 1983.

- "The Law of Master and Servant in Mid-Nineteenth-Century Ontario." In *Essays in the History of Canadian Law*, Vol. I, edited by David H. Flaherty. Toronto: University of Toronto Press 1981.

Craven, P., and Traves, T. "The Class Politics of the National Policy, 1872-1933." *Journal of Canadian Studies* (autumn 1979): 14-38.

Crean, Susan. *Who's Afraid of Canadian Culture?* Toronto: General Publishing 1976.

Crean, Susan, and Rioux, Marcel. *Two Nations*. Toronto: James Lorimer 1983.

Creese, G. "Working Class Politics, Racism and Sexism: The Making of a Politically Divided Working Class in Vancouver, 1900-1939." PHD dissertation, Department of Sociology, Carleton University 1986.

Creighton, D. *The Commercial Empire of the St. Lawrence*. Toronto: Ryerson 1937.

- *The Empire of the St. Lawrence*. Republication of *Commercial Empire*. Toronto: Macmillan 1956.

Crime and Social Justice. Special Issue on Canada and the U.S.: Criminal Justice Connections. 26 (1986).

Cross, M. and Kealey, G.S. *Modern Canada, 1930-1980*. Toronto: McClelland and Stewart 1984.

Cuff, R.D., and Granatstein, J.L. *Ties That Bind: Canadian-American Relations in Wartime from the Great War to the Cold War*. Toronto: Stevens/Hakkert 1977.

Cuneo, C.J. "Comment: Restoring Class to State Unemployment Insurance." *Canadian Journal of Political Science* 19:1 (1986): 93-8.

- "State, Class and Reserve Labour: The Case of the 1941 Canadian Unemployment Insurance Act." *Canadian Review of Sociology and Anthropology* 16 (1979): 147–70.
- "State Mediation of Class Contradictions in Canadian Unemployment Insurance, 1930–1935." *Studies in Political Economy* 3 (1980):37–65.

Dahl, R. *A Preface to Democratic Theory*. Chicago: University of Chicago Press 1956.

Das Gupta, Tania. *Learning from Our History: Community Development with Immigrant Women, 1958–86, a Tool for Action*. Toronto: Cross Cultural Communication Centre 1986.

Dawson, R.M. *Democratic Government in Canada*. Toronto: University of Toronto Press 1949.

Desmarais, J. *Labour-Management Relations: An Overview*. MR 176. Ottawa: Energy, Mines and Resources Canada (1977).

Devlin, Richard. "Tales of Centaurs and Men: A Preliminary Theoretical Inquiry into the Nature and Relations of Law, State and Violence." *Osgoode Hall Law Journal*, forthcoming.

Dickinson, J., and Russell, B. *Family, Economy and the State: The Social Reproduction Process under Capitalism*. Toronto: Garamond Press 1986.

Dobb, Maurice. *Studies in the Development of Capitalism*, rev. ed. New York: International Publishers 1964.

Dobbin, M. "Prairie Colonialism: The CCF in Northern Saskatchewan, 1944–1964." *Studies in Political Economy* 16 (spring 1985).

Doern, G.B., and Toner, G. *The Politics of Energy: The Development and Implementation of the NEP*. Toronto: Methuen 1985.

Dosman, Edgar I. *Indians: The Urban Dilemma*. Toronto: McClelland and Stewart 1972.

Dow, Alexander. "Prometheus in Canada: The Expansion of Metal Mining, 1900–1950." In *Explorations in Canadian Economic History: Essays in Honour of Irene M. Spry*, edited by Duncan Cameron. Ottawa: University of Ottawa Press 1985.

Drache, Daniel. "The Canadian Bourgeoisie and Its National Consciousness." In *Close the 49th Parallel etc.: The Americanization of Canada*, edited by Ian Lumsden. Toronto: University of Toronto Press 1970.
- "Canadian Capitalism: Sticking with Staples." *This Magazine* (July–Aug. 1975).
- "The Crisis of Canadian Political Economy: Dependency Theory versus the New Orthodoxy." *Canadian Journal of Social and Political Thought* (fall 1983).
- "The Formation and Fragmentation of the Canadian Working Class: 1820–1920." *Studies in Political Economy* 15 (fall 1984).
- "Harold Innis: A Canadian Nationalist." *Journal of Canadian Studies* (May 1969).
- "Harold Innis and Canadian Capitalist Development." *Canadian Journal of Political and Social Theory* 6 (winter/spring 1982).

- "Rediscovering Canadian Political Economy." In *A Practical Guide to Canadian Political Economy*, edited by W. Clement and D. Drache. Toronto: James Lorimer 1978.
- "Staple-ization: A Theory of Canadian Capitalist Development." In *Imperialism, Nationalism, and Canada*, edited by Craig Heron. Toronto: New Hogtown Press 1977.
Drache, Daniel, and Clement, Wallace. "Introduction: The Coming of Age of Canadian Political Economy." In *The New Practical Guide to Canadian Political Economy*, edited by D. Drache and W. Clement. Toronto: James Lorimer 1985.
- *The New Practical Guide to Canadian Political Economy*. Toronto: James Lorimer 1985.
Draimin, T., and Swift, J. "What's Canada Doing in Brazil?" *This Magazine* (Jan.-Feb. 1975).
Driedger, L., and Mezoff, R.A. "Ethnic Prejudice and Discrimination in Winnipeg High Schools." *Canadian Journal of Sociology* 6:1 (1981).
Dunlop, John T. *Industrial Relations Systems*. New York: Henry Holt and Co. 1958.
Durham, Lord. Report on the Affairs of British North America. London 1839.
Dyck, Noel, ed. *Indigenous Peoples and the Nation-State*. St John's: Institute of Social and Economic Research, Memorial University of Newfoundland 1985.
Easterbrook, W.T. "Innis and Economics." *Canadian Journal of Economics and Political Science* 19:3 (1953).
Easterbrook, W.T., and Aitken, H.G.J. *Canadian Economic History*. Toronto: Macmillan 1956.
Economic Council of Canada. *Living Together: A Study of Regional Disparities*. Ottawa: Supply and Services 1977.
Ehrensaft, Philip, and Armstrong, Warwick. "The Formation of Dominion Capitalism: Economic Truncation and Class Structure." In *Inequality: Essays on the Political Economy of Social Welfare*, edited by A. Moscovitch and G. Drover. Toronto: University of Toronto Press 1981.
Elkins, David, and Simeon, Richard. eds. *Small Worlds: Provinces and Parties in Canadian Political Life*. Toronto: Methuen 1980.
Emmanuel, A. *Unequal Exchange: A Study of the Imperialism of Trade*. New York: Monthly Review 1971.
Endres, Robin. "Art and Accumulation: The Canadian State and the Business of Art." In *The Canadian State: Political Economy and Political Power*, edited by L. Panitch. Toronto: University of Toronto Press 1977.
Energy, Mines and Resources Canada. *Mineral Policy: A Discussion Paper*. Ottawa: Supply and Services 1982.
Ericson, Richard V. *The Constitution of Legal Inequality*. John Porter Memorial Lecture. Ottawa: Carleton University Information Services 1983.
- *Reproducing Order: A Study of Police Patrol Work*. Toronto: University of Toronto Press 1982.
Etienne, Mona, and Leacock, E., eds. *Women and Colonization: Anthropological*

Perpsectives. New York: Monthly Review Press 1980.

Falardeau, Jean-Charles. *The Rise of Social Sciences in French Canada*. Quebec: Department of Cultural Affairs 1967.

Filson, G. "Class and Ethnic Differences in Canadians' Attitudes to Native People's Rights and Immigration." *Canadian Review of Sociology and Anthropology* 20:4 (1983): 454-82.

Findlay, S. "Facing the State: The Politics of the Women's Movement Reconsidered." In *Feminism and Political Economy: Women's Work, Women's Struggles*, edited by H.J. Maroney and M. Luxton. Toronto: Methuen 1987.

Finkel, Alvin. *Business and Social Reform in the Thirties*. Toronto: James Lorimer 1979.

- "Origins of the Welfare State in Canada." In *The Canadian State: Political Economy and Political Power*, edited by L. Panitch. Toronto: University of Toronto Press 1977.

Fireweed. Special Issue by Native Women (winter 1986).

- Women of Colour Issue, 16 (1983).

Fitzpatrick, Peter. "Law and Societies." *Osgoode Hall Law Journal* 22 (1984): 115-38.

Fogarty, John. "Staples, Super-Staples and the Limits of Staple Theory: The Experiences of Argentina, Australia and Canada Compared." In *Argentina, Australia and Canada: Studies in Comparative Development 1870-1965*, edited by D.C.M. Platt and Guido di Tella. London: Macmillan Press 1985.

Forbes, E.R. *The Maritime Rights Movement*. Montreal and Kingston: McGill-Queen's University Press 1979.

Forsey, E. *Trade Unions in Canada 1812-1902*. Toronto: University of Toronto Press 1981.

Forsythe, D., ed. *Let the Niggers Burn*. Montreal 1971.

Fournier, Francine. "Les femmes et la vie politique au Québec." In *Travailleuses et féministes: les femmes dans la société québécoise*, by Marie Lavigne and Yolande Pinard. Montreal: Boréal Express 1983.

Fournier, Pierre, "Le Parti québécois et les pouvoirs économiques." In *La chance au coureur*, edited by J.F. Léonard. Montreal: Editions Nouvelle-Optique 1978.

- "The New Parameters of the Quebec Bourgeoisie." *Studies in Political Economy* 3 (1980): 67-91.

- ed. *Capitalisme et politique au Québec*. Montreal: Albert Saint-Martin 1981.

Fowke, V.C. *Canadian Agricultural Policy*. Toronto: University of Toronto Press 1946.

- *The National Policy and the Wheat Economy*. Toronto: University of Toronto Press 1957.

- "The National Policy - Old and New." *Canadian Journal of Economics and Political Science* 18:3 (Aug. 1952).

Fox, B., ed. *Hidden in the Household: Women's Domestic Labour under Capitalism*. Toronto: Women's Press 1980.

Frank, A.G. *Capitalism and Underdevelopment in Latin America*. New York: Monthly Review Press 1967.

Frideses, J. *Native People in Canada: Contemporary Conflicts*. Scarborough: Prentice-Hall 1983.

Gagnon, Alain. "A Tranquil Quebec: The End of Conflictual Relations." In *Contemporary Canadian Politics: Readings and Notes*, edited by R. Jackson, D. Jackson, and N. Baxter-Moore. Toronto: Prentice-Hall 1987.

Gagnon, Mona-Josée. "Les comités syndicaux de condition féminine." In *Travailleuses et féministes: Les femmes dans la société québécoise*, edited by Marie Lavigne and Yoland Pinard. Montreal: Boréal Express 1983.

– "Les femmes dans le mouvement syndical québécois." In *Travailleuses et féministes: Les femmes dans la société québécois*, edited by Marie Lavigne and Yolande Pinard. Montreal: Boréal Express 1983.

Gannage, C. *Double Day, Double Bind*. Toronto: Women's Press 1986.

– "A World of Difference: The Case of Women Workers in a Canadian Garment Factory." In *Feminism and Political Economy: Women's Work, Women's Struggle*, edited by H.J. Maroney and M. Luxton. Toronto: Methuen 1987.

Garnham, Nicholas. "Contributions to a Political Economy of Mass-Communication." *Media, Culture and Society* 1 (1979).

Gavigan, Shelley A.M. "Law, Gender and Ideology." In *Legal Theory Meets Legal Practice*, edited by Anne Bayefsky. Edmonton: Academic Printing and Publishing, forthcoming.

– "Marxist Theories of Law: A Survey of Some Thoughts on Women and the Law." *Canadian Criminology Forum* 4 (1981): 1–12.

– "Women and Abortion in Canada: What's Law Got to Do with It?" In *Feminism and Political Economy: Women's Work, Women's Struggles*, edited by H.J. Maroney and M. Luxton. Toronto: Methuen 1987.

– "Women, Law and Patriarchal Relations: Perspectives within the Sociology of Law." In *The Social Dimensions of Law*, edited by Neil Boyd. Toronto: Prentice-Hall 1986.

Genovese, Eugene D. "The Hegemonic Function of the Law." In *Marxism and Law*, edited by Piers Bierne and Richard Quinney. New York: John Wiley & Sons 1982.

Geras, Norman. "Post-Marxism?" *New Left Review* 163 (1987): 40–82.

Gibbins, Roger. *Prairie Politics and Society: Regionalism in Decline*. Toronto: Butterworths 1980.

Gilroy, Paul. *There Ain't No Black in the Union Jack*. London: Hutchinson 1987.

Glasbeek, Harry. "Why Corporate Deviance Is Not Treated as a Crime – the Need to Make 'Profits' a Dirty Word." *Osgoode Hall Law Journal* 22 (1984): 393–439.

– "Workers of the World Avoid the Charter of Rights." *Canadian Dimension* 21 (April 1987): 12–14.

Glasbeek, Harry, and Mandel, Michael. "Crime and Punishment of Jean-Claude

Parrot." *Canadian Forum* 59 (Aug. 1979): 10–14.

– "The Legalisation of Politics in Advanced Capitalism: The Canadian Charter of Rights and Freedoms." *Socialist Studies* 2 (1984): 84–124.

Godbout, Jacques. *La participation contre la démocratie*. Montreal: Albert Saint-Martin 1983.

Godelier, M. *Perspectives in Marxist Anthropology*. London: Cambridge University Press 1977.

Goff, Colin H., and Reasons, Charles E. *Corporate Crime in Canada: A Critical Analysis of Anti-Combines Legislation*. Scarborough: Prentice-Hall 1978.

Gonick, C.W. "Foreign Ownership and Political Decay." In *Close the 49th Parallel etc.: The Americanization of Canada*, edited by Ian Lumsden. Toronto: University of Toronto Press 1970.

– *The Great Economic Debate*. Toronto: James Lorimer 1987.

Goodwin, C.D.W. *Canadian Economic Thought: The Political Economy of a Developing Nation 1814–1914*. Durham, NC: Duke University Press 1961.

Gordon, D., Edwards, R., and Reich, M. *Segmented Work, Divided Workers*. New York: Cambridge University Press 1982.

Gore, Charles. *Regions in Question*. London: Methuen 1984.

Grayson, J.P. *Plant Closures and De-Skilling: Three Case Studies*. Ottawa: Science Council of Canada 1986.

Greer, Allan. "Wage Labour and the Transition to Capitalism: A Critique of Pentland." *Labour/Le Travail* 15 (spring 1985).

Guindon, Hubert. "Social Unrest, Social Class and Quebec's Bureaucratic Revolution." *Queen's Quarterly* 71 (summer 1964): 150–62.

Gunton, Thomas. "Manitoba's Nickel Industry: The Paradox of a Low-Cost Producer." In *Resource Rents and Public Policy in Western Canada*, edited by Thomas Gunton and John Richards. Halifax: Institute for Research on Public Policy 1987.

Gutman, Herbert. "Interview." In *Visions of History*, edited by Henry Abelove et al. New York: Pantheon 1983.

Hackett, Robert. "For a Socialist Perspective on the Media." *Studies in Political Economy* 19 (spring 1986).

Hall, Stuart. *Drifting into a Law and Order Society*. London: Cobden Trust 1980.

– "The State in Question." In *The Idea of the Modern State*, edited by G. McLennan, D. Held, and S. Hall. Milton Keynes: Open University 1984.

Hall, Stuart, Crichter, Charles, Jefferson, Tony, Clarke, John, and Roberts, Brian. *Policing the Crisis: Mugging, the State and Law and Order*. London: Macmillan 1978.

Hamel, Pierre, and Léonard, Jean-François. *Les organisations populaires, L'état et la démocratie*. Montreal: Nouvelle-Optique 1981.

Hamilton, R., and Barrett, M. "Introduction." In *The Politics of Diversity: Feminism, Marxism and Nationalism*, edited by R. Hamilton and M. Barrett. Montreal: Book Centre Inc. 1986.

- *The Politics of Diversity: Feminism, Marxism and Nationalism*. Montreal: Book Centre Inc. 1986.

Hardin, Herschel. *Closed Circuits: The Sellout of Canadian Television*. Vancouver: Douglas and McIntyre 1985.

Harney, R. "Montreal's King of Italian Labour: A Case Study of Padronism." *Labour/Le Travailleur* 4 (1979).

Hastings, Ross, and Saunders, Ronald P. "Ideology in the Work of the Law Reform Commission of Canada: The Case of the Working Paper on the General Part." *Criminal Law Quarterly* 25 (1983): 206–22.

- "Social Control, State Autonomy, and Legal Reform: The Law Reform Commission of Canada." In *State Control: Criminal Justice Politics in Canada*, edited by R.S. Ratner and John L. McMullan. Vancouver: University of British Columbia Press 1987.

Havemann, Paul. "From Child Saving to Child Blaming: The Political Economy of the Young Offenders Act, 1908–1984." In *The Social Basis of Law*, edited by Stephen Brickey and Elizabeth Comack. Toronto: Garamond Press 1986.

Hay, Douglas. "Property, Authority and the Criminal Law." In *Marxism and Law*, edited by Piers Bierne and Richard Quinney. New York: John Wiley & Sons 1982.

Head, Wilson. *The Black Presence in the Canadian Mosaic*. Toronto: Ontario Human Rights Commission 1975.

Henry, F. "The Dynamics of Racism in Toronto." Mimeo. Toronto: Department of Anthropology, York University 1978.

Henry, K.S. *Black Politics in Toronto since World War I*. Toronto: Multicultural History Society of Ontario 1981.

Heron, Craig, and Storey, Robert. "On the Job in Canada." In *On the Job*, edited by Craig Heron and Robert Storey, Montreal: McGill-Queen's University Press 1985.

- eds. *On the Job*, Montreal: McGill-Queen's University Press 1985.

Himmelweit, S. "The Real Dualism of Sex and Class." *Review of Radical Political Economics* 16:1 (spring 1984): 167–84.

Hirschman, Albert. "A Generalized Linkage Approach to Development with Special Reference to Staples." *Economic Development and Cultural Change* 25. Supplement (1977). Reprinted in *Essays in Trespassing: Economics to Politics and Beyond*, by Albert Hirschman. Cambridge: Cambridge University Press 1981.

- *Essays in Trespassing: Economics to Politics and Beyond*. Cambridge: Cambridge University Press 1981.

- *Strategy of Economic Development*. New Haven, Conn.: Yale University Press 1958.

Hirst, Paul Q. "Socialist Legality, Review of Tom Campbell, *The Left and Rights*." *Economy and Society* 14 (1985): 113–27.

Holland, Stuart. *Capital vs the Regions*. London: Macmillan 1976.

Holmes, J. "The Crisis of Fordism and the Restructuring of the Canadian Auto Industry." In *Frontyard/Backyard*, edited by J. Holmes and C. Leys. Toronto: Between the Lines 1987.

Holmes, J., and Leys, C. *Frontyard/Backyard*. Toronto: Between the Lines 1987.

- "Introduction." In *Frontyard/Backyard*, edited by J. Holmes and C. Leys. Toronto: Between the Lines 1987.

Horowitz, G. *Canadian Labour in Politics*. Toronto: University of Toronto Press 1968.

Horvat, Branko. *The Political Economy of Socialism*. White Planes: Sharpe 1982.

Hosek, C. "Women and the Constitutional Process." In *And No One Cheered*, edited by K. Banting and R. Simeon. Toronto: Methuen 1983.

Houle, F. "Economic Strategy and the Restructuring of the Fordist Wage-Labour Relationship in Canada." *Studies in Political Economy* 11 (Summer 1983).

- "L'état canadien et le capitalisme mondial: strategies d'insertion," *Canadian Journal of Political Science* (Sept. 1987).

House, J.D. "The Mouse That Roars: New Direction in Canadian Political Economy." In *Regionalism in Canada*, edited by R. Brym. Toronto: Irwin 1986.

Hunt, Alan. "The Ideology of Law: Advances and Problems in Recent Applications of the Concept of Ideology to the Analysis of Law." *Law and Society Review* 19 (1985): 11-37.

- "The Politics of Law and Justice." *Law and Politics*, IV. London: Routledge and Kegan Paul 1981.

- "The Radical Critique of Law: An Assessment." *International Journal of the Sociology of Law* 8 (1981): 47-77.

- "The Theory of Critical Legal Studies." *Oxford Journal of Legal Studies* 6 (1986): 1-45.

Hutcheson, J. "The Capitalist State in Canada." In *(Canada) Ltd.: The Political Economy of Dependency*, edited by R. Laxer. Toronto: McClelland and Stewart 1973.

- *Dominance and Dependency: Liberalism and National Policies in the North Atlantic Triangle*. Toronto: McClelland and Stewart 1978.

Hutchinson, Allan. "Part of an Essay on Power and Interpretation (with Suggestions on How to Make Bouillabaisse)." *New York University Law Review* 60 (1985): 850-86.

Hutchinson, Allan, and Monahan, Patrick. "Law, Politics and the Critical Legal Scholars: The Unfolding Drama of American Legal Thought." *Stanford Law Review* 36 (1984): 199-245.

- "Democracy and The Rule of Law." In *The Rule of Law: Ideal or Ideology*, edited by Allan Hutchinson and Patrick Monahan. Toronto: Carswell 1987.

Hyman, Richard. *Industrial Relations*. London: Macmillan 1975.

Iacovetta, F. "From *Contadina* to Worker: Southern Italian Immigrant Working Women in Toronto 1947-62." In *Looking into My Sister's Eyes: An Exploration in Women's History*, edited by Jean Burnet. Toronto: Multicultural History Society of Ontario 1986.

Innis, H.A. *The Bias of Communication*. Toronto: University of Toronto Press 1982.

- "The Canadian Economy and the Depression." *Essays in Canadian Economic History*. Original 1934. Toronto: University of Toronto Press 1956.

- "The Canadian Mining Industry." *Essays in Canadian Economic History*. Original 1934. Toronto: University of Toronto Press 1956.

- *Changing Concepts of Time*. Toronto: University of Toronto Press 1952.

- *The Cod Fisheries*. Toronto: University of Toronto Press 1954; reprinted 1978.

- "Decentralization and Democracy." *Essays in Canadian Economic History*. Toronto: University of Toronto Press 1956.

- "A Defence of the Tariff." Appendix to *A New Theory of Value: The Canadian Economics of H.A. Innis*, by Robin Neill. Toronto: University of Toronto Press 1972.

- "The Economic Development of Canada, 1867–1921: The Maritime Provinces." In *The Cambridge History of the British Empire*, by J.H. Rose et al. Cambridge: Cambridge University Press 1930.

- "Economic Trends in Canadian-American Relations." *Essays in Canadian Economic History*. Toronto: University of Toronto Press 1956.

- *Empire and Communications*, revised by Mary Q. Innis. Original 1950. Toronto: University of Toronto Press 1972.

- *The Fur Trade in Canada: An Introduction to Canadian Economic History*. Original 1930. Toronto: University of Toronto Press 1956.

- "Government Ownership and the Canadian Scene." *Essays in Canadian Economic History*. Toronto: University of Toronto Press 1956.

- "Great Britain, the United States, and Canada." In *Essays in Canadian Economic History*. Toronto: University of Toronto Press 1962.

- *A History of the Canadian Pacific Railway*. London: McClelland 1923.

- "Introduction to Canadian Economic Studies." *Essays in Canadian Economic History*. Toronto: University of Toronto Press 1956.

- "An Introduction to the Economic History of Ontario from Outpost to Empire." *Essays in Canadian Economic History*. Toronto: University of Toronto Press 1956.

- "Labour in Canadian Economic History." In *Essays in Canadian Economic History*, edited by M.Q. Innis. Toronto: University of Toronto Press 1956.

- "Military Implications of the American Constitution." *Changing Concepts of Time*. Toronto: University of Toronto Press 1952.

- "On the Economic Significance of Cultural Factors." In *Political Economy in the Modern State*. Toronto: Ryerson 1946.

- "The Penetrative Powers of the Price System." *Essays in Canadian Economic History*. Toronto: University of Toronto Press 1956.

- "The Political Implications of Unused Capacity." *Essays in Canadian Economic History*. Toronto: University of Toronto Press 1956.

- *Political Economy in the Modern State*. Toronto: Ryerson 1946.
- "The Press, a Neglected Factor in the Economic History of the Twentieth Century." In *Changing Concepts of Time*. Toronto: University of Toronto Press 1952.
- "The Problems of Rehabilitation." In *Political Economy in the Modern State*. Toronto: Ryerson 1946.
- *Problems of Staple Production in Canada*. Toronto: Ryerson 1933.
- "Recent Developments in the Canadian Economy. *Essays in Canadian Economic History*. Toronto: University of Toronto Press 1956.
- "Reflections on Russia." In *Political Economy in the Modern State*. Toronto: Ryerson 1946.
- Review of Report of the Rowell-Sirois Commission. *Canadian Journal of Economics and Political Science* 6 (1940): 562–71.
- "The Role of Intelligence: Some Further Notes." *Canadian Journal of Economics and Political Science* 1:2 (1935): 280–7.
- "Roman Law and the British Empire." In *Changing Concepts of Time*. Toronto: University of Toronto Press 1952.
- "The Strategy of Culture." In *Changing Concepts of Time*. Toronto: University of Toronto Press 1952.
- "The Teaching of Economic History in Canada." In *Essays in Canadian Economic History*, edited by Mary Q. Innis. Toronto: University of Toronto Press 1956.
- "Transportation in Canadian Economic History." *Essays in Canadian Economic History*. Toronto: University of Toronto Press 1956.
- "The Wheat Economy." *Essays in Canadian Economic History*. Toronto: University of Toronto Press 1956.
- "The Work of Thorstein Veblen." In *Essays in Canadian Economic History*, edited by H.A. Innis. Toronto: University of Toronto Press 1956.
Innis, H.A., and Easterbrook, W.T. "Fundamental and Historic Elements." In *The Canadian Economy: Selected Readings*, edited by J. Deutsch et al. Toronto: Macmillan 1962.
Ison, Terence G. "The Sovereignty of the Judiciary." *Adelaide Law Review (1986)*: 1–31.
Jaggar, A., and Rothenberg, P., eds. *Feminist Frameworks: Alternative Theoretical Accounts of the Relations between Women and Men*, 2nd ed. New York: McGraw-Hill 1984.
Jalbert, Lizette. "La question régionale comme enjeu politique." In *Espace régional et nation: pour un nouveau débat sur le Québec*, by Gérard Boismenu et al. Montreal: Boréal Express 1983.
- "Régionalisme et crise de l'état." *Sociologie et société* 12:2 (1980): 65–72.
Jamieson, S.M. *Times of Trouble*. Ottawa: Task Force on Labour Relations 1968.
Jenson, Jane. "Economic Factors in Canadian Political Integration." In *The Integration Question*, edited by J.H. Pammett and B. Tomlin. Toronto: Addison and

Wesley 1984.

- "A False Victory: Women, the State and Abortion." In *Women and the State*, edited by Hugh Armstrong, forthcoming.

- "Gender and Reproduction, or Babies and the State." *Studies in Political Economy* 20 (1986): 9-46.

- "Struggling for Identity: The Women's Movement and the State in Western Europe." *Western European Politics* 8:4 (Oct. 1985).

Jessop, Bob. *The Capitalist State: Marxist Theories and Methods*. Oxford: Martin Robertson 1982.

- "On Recent Marxist Theories of Law, the State, and Juridico-Political Ideology." *International Journal of the Sociology of Law* 8 (1980): 339-68.

Jhally, Sut, Kline, Stephen, and Leiss, William. "Magic in the Marketplace: An Empirical Test for Commodity Fetishism." *Canadian Journal of Political and Social Theory* 9:3 (fall 1985).

Johnson, H.G. *The Canadian Quandary*. Toronto: McClelland and Stewart 1977.

Johnson, L. *The Seam Allowance: Industrial Home Sewing in Canada*. Toronto: Women's Press 1982.

Johnson, Leo. "The Development of Class in Canada in the Twentieth Century." In *Capitalism and the National Question in Canada*, edited by Gary Teeple. Toronto: University of Toronto Press 1972.

Kairys, David. "Freedom of Speech." In *The Politics of Law: A Progressive Critique*, edited by David Kairys. New York: Pantheon Books 1982.

Katzenstein, M. Fainsod. "Feminism and the Meaning of the Vote." *Signs* 10:1 (autumn 1984): 5-9.

Kaye, Harvey. *The British Marxist Historians*. Cambridge: Polity Press 1984.

Kealey, G.S. "Labour and Working Class History in Canada: Prospects in the 1980s." *Labour/Le Travail* 7 (spring 1981): 67-94.

- "1919: The Canadian Labour Revolt." *Labour/Le Travail* 13 (spring 1984).

- "Stanley Bréhaut Ryerson: Canadian Revolutionary Intellectual." *Studies in Political Economy* 9 (fall 1982): 103-72.

- *Toronto Workers Respond to Industrial Capitalism, 1867-1892*. Toronto: University of Toronto Press 1980.

Kealey, G., et al. "Canada's Eastern Question." *Canadian Dimension* 13:2 (1978).

Kealey, L., ed. *A Not Unreasonable Claim: Women and Reform in Canada, 1880s-1920s*. Toronto: Women's Press 1979.

Kierans, Eric. Report on Natural Resource Policy in Manitoba. Winnipeg: Queen's Printer 1973.

Klein, Suzanne Silk. "Individualism, Liberalism and the New Family Law." *University of Toronto Faculty Law Review* 43 (1985): 116-35.

Krauter, J.F., and Davis, M. *Minority Canadians: Ethnic Groups*. Toronto: Methuen 1978.

La Rusic, I. *The Shadow of Bureaucracy: Culture in Indian Affairs*. Ottawa: Department of Indian Affairs and Northern Development 1981.

Laclau, Ernesto, and Mouffe, Chantal. *Hegemony and Socialist Strategy: Towards a Radical Democratic Politics*. London: Verso 1985.

– "Post-Marxism without Apologies." *New Left Review* 166 (1987): 79–106.

Lamoureux, Diane. *Fragments et collages: essai sur le féminisme québécois des années 70*. Montreal: Editions Remue-Ménage 1986.

– "Nationalism and Feminism in Quebec: An Impossible Attraction." In *Feminism and Political Economy: Women's Work, Women's Struggles*, edited by H.J. Maroney and M. Luxton. Toronto: Methuen 1987.

Laurin-Frenette, Nicole, and Bourque, Gilles. "Les classes et l'idéologie nationaliste au Québec, 1760–1970." *Socialisme québécois* 20 (1970).

– "La structure nationale québécois." *Socialisme québécois* 21–2 (1971).

Laux, J.K., and Molot, M.A. *State Capitalism: Public Enterprise in Canada*. Ithaca, NY: Cornell University Press 1987.

Laxer, Gordon. "Class, Nationality and the Roots of the Branch Plant Economy." *Studies in Political Economy* 21 (autumn 1986).

– "Foreign Ownership and Myths about Canadian Development." *Canadian Review of Sociology and Anthropology* 22:3 (Aug. 1985): 311–45.

– "The Political Economy of Aborted Development." In *The Structure of the Canadian Capitalist Class*, edited by Robert Brym. Toronto: Garamond Press 1985.

Laxer, James. "Canadian Manufacturing and U.S. Trade Policy." In *(Canada) Ltd.: The Political Economy of Dependency*, edited by R. Laxer. Toronto: McClelland and Stewart 1973.

– *Leap of Faith: Free Trade and the Future of Canada*. Edmonton: Hurtig Publishers 1986.

– "Manufacturing and U.S. Trade Policy." In *(Canada) Ltd.: The Political Economy of Dependency*, edited by R. Laxer. Toronto: McClelland and Stewart 1973.

– "The Political Economy of Canada." In *(Canada) Ltd.: The Political Economy of Dependency*, edited by R. Laxer. Toronto: McClelland and Stewart 1973.

– *Rethinking the Economy*. Toronto: New Canada Publications 1983.

Laxer, R., ed. *(Canada) Ltd.: The Political Economy of Dependency*. Toronto: McClelland and Stewart 1973.

Lazarus, D. *A Crack in the Mosaic – Canada's Race Relations in Crisis*. Cornwall, Ont.: Vesta 1980.

Leacock, E. "Introduction." In *The Origin of the Family, Private Property and the State*, by E. Engels. New York: International Publishers 1975.

– *Myths of Male Dominance*. New York: Monthly Review Press 1981.

– "The Montagnais-Naskapi of the Labrador Peninsula." In *Native Peoples: The Canadian Experience*, edited by R. Bruce Morrison and R. Roderick Wilson. Toronto: McClelland and Stewart 1986.

League for Social Reconstruction. *Social Planning for Canada*. Reprint. Toronto: University of Toronto Press 1975.

Lebowitz, Michael. "Too Many Blindspots." *Studies in Political Economy* 21 (autumn 1986).

Legaré, Anne. "Towards a Marxian Theory of Canadian Federalism." *Studies in Political Economy* 8 (1982).

Leiss, William, Kline, Stephen, and Jhally, Sut. *Social Communication as Advertising: Persons, Products and Images of Well-Being*. Toronto: Methuen 1986.

Levitt, K. *Silent Surrender: The Multinational Corporation in Canada*. Toronto: Macmillan 1970.

Li, P.S. "A Historical Approach to Ethnic Stratification: The Case of the Chinese in Canada, 1858-1930." *Canadian Review of Sociology and Anthropology* 16:3 (1979): 320-32.

Li, P.S., and Bolaria, B.S. "Canadian Immigration Policy and Assimilation Theory." In *Economy, Class and Social Reality*, edited by J.A. Fry. Toronto: Butterworths 1979.

Li, P.S., and Bolaria, B.S., eds. *Racial Minorities in Multicultural Canada*. Toronto: Garamond Press 1983.

Lindstrom-Best, Varpu. "Review of Avery: *'Dangerous Foreigners': European Immigrant Workers and Labour Radicalism in Canada, 1896-1932*." *Labour/Le Travail* 6 (1980).

Lipsig-Mumme, C. "Organizing Women in the Clothing Trades: Homework and the 1983 Garment Strike in Canada." *Studies in Political Economy* 22 (spring 1987): 41-72.

Lipton, C. *The Trade Union Movement of Canada 1827-1959*. Montreal: Canadian Social Publications 1966.

Lithwick, H. "Is Federalism Good for Regionalism?" *Journal of Canadian Studies* 15:2 (summer 1980).

Little Bear, Leroy, and Boldt, Menno. *Pathways to Self-Determination*. Toronto: Methuen 1985.

Logan, H.A. *Trade Unions in Canada*. Toronto: Macmillan 1948.

Loxley, J. "The 'Great Northern Plan.'" *Studies in Political Economy* 6 (autumn 1981).

Lucas, Rex. *Minetown, Milltown, Railtown: Life in Canadian Communities of a Single Industry*. Toronto: University of Toronto Press 1971.

Lumsden, I. ed. *Close the 49th Parallel etc.: The Americanization of Canada*. Toronto: University of Toronto Press 1970.

Luxton, Meg. "From Ladies Auxiliaries to Wives' Committees: Housewives and the Unions." In *Through the Kitchen Window: The Politics of Home and Family*, edited by M. Luxton and H. Rosenberg. Toronto: Garamond Press 1986.

- "Two Hands for the Clock: Changing Patterns in the Gendered Division of Labour in the Home." *Studies in Political Economy* 12 (fall 1983).

Luxton, M. and Rosenberg, H. *Through the Kitchen Window: The Politics of Home and Family*. Toronto: Garamond Press 1986

Lyon, S.D., and Trebilcock, M. *Public Strategy and Motion Pictures*. Toronto: Ontario Economic Council 1982.

Macaulay, Stewart. "Non-contractual Relationships in Business: A Preliminary Study." *American Sociological Review* 28 (1963): 55–67.

McCalla, Douglass. "Forest Products and Upper Canadian Development, 1815–46." *Canadian Historical Review* (June 1987).

– "The Wheat Staple and Upper Canadian Development." Canadian Historical Association *Historical Papers* (1978): 34–55.

McCalla, Douglass, and George, Peter. "Measurement, Myth and Reality: Reflections on the Economic History of Nineteenth-Century Ontario." *Journal of Canadian Studies* 21:3 (fall 1986): 71–86.

McCallum, J. *Unequal Beginnings: Agriculture and Economic Development in Quebec and Ontario until 1870.* Toronto: University of Toronto Press 1980.

McCay, Bonnie. "Fish Guts, Hair Nets and Unemployment Stamps: Women, Work, and the Fogo Island Cooperative." In *A Question of Survival: The Fisheries and Newfoundland Society*, edited by Peter Sinclair. St John's: Memorial University (forthcoming).

McCormack, A.R. *Reformers, Rebels and Revolutionaries.* Toronto: University of Toronto Press 1977.

MacCormick, Thelma. "Deregulating the Economy and Regulating Morality: The Political Economy of Censorship." *Studies in Political Economy* 18 (1985): 173–85.

McDaniel, Susan. "Implementation of Abortion Policy in Canada as a Women's Issue." *Atlantis.* 10:2 (spring 1985): 74–91.

McDonald, R.A.J. "Working Class Vancouver, 1886–1914: Urbanism and Class in British Columbia." *BC Studies* 69/70 (spring/summer 1986).

MacIver, R.M. *The Modern State.* Oxford: Oxford University Press 1926.

Mackenzie, Suzanne. "Women's Responses to Economic Restructuring: Changing Gender, Changing Space." In *The Politics of Diversity: Feminism, Marxism and Nationalism*, edited by Roberta Hamilton and Michele Barrett. Montreal: Book Centre Inc. 1986.

Mackintosh, W.A. "Canadian Economic Policy from 1945 to 1957 – Origins and Influences." In *The American Economic Impact on Canada*, by Hugh G.J. Aitken et al. Durham, NC: Duke University Press 1959.

– *The Economic Background of Dominion-Provincial Relations.* Toronto: McClelland and Stewart 1964.

– "Economic Factors in Canadian History." In *Approaches to Canadian Economic History*, edited by W.T. Easterbrook and M.H. Watkins. Toronto: McClelland and Stewart 1967.

McLellan, David, ed. *Karl Marx, Selected Writings.* Oxford: Oxford University Press 1977.

McLuhan, Marshall. *Understanding Media.* New York: Signet 1964.

McMullan, John L. "The 'Law and Order' Problem in Socialist Criminology." *Studies in Political Economy* 21 (1986): 175–92.

McNally, D. "Staple Theory as Commodity Fetishism: Marx, Innis and Canadian

Political Economy." *Studies in Political Economy* 6 (autumn 1981): 35–64.
- "Technological Determinism and Canadian Political Economy: Further Contributions to a Debate." *Studies in Political Economy* 20 (summer 1986): 165.
Macpherson, C.B. "Capitalism and the Changing Concept of Property." In *Feudalism, Capitalism and Beyond*, edited by E. Kamenka and R.S. Neale. Canberra: Australian National University Press 1975.
- *Democracy in Alberta: Social Credit and the Party System*. Toronto: University of Toronto Press 1953.
- *Democratic Theory: Essays in Retrieval*. Oxford: Clarendon Press 1973.
- "Human Rights as Property Rights." In *The Rise and Fall of Economic Justice and Other Essays*, by C.B. Macpherson. Oxford and New York: Oxford University Press 1985.
- *The Real World of Democracy*. Toronto: CBC Learning Systems 1965.
- *The Rise and Fall of Economic Justice and Other Essays*. Oxford: Oxford University Press 1985.
McRoberts, Kenneth, and Posgate, Dale. *Quebec: Social Change and Political Crisis*, 2nd ed. Toronto: McClelland and Stewart 1980.
Magder, T. "A 'Featureless' Film Policy: Culture and the Canadian State." *Studies in Political Economy* 16 (1985).
- "The Political Economy of Canadian Cultural Policy: The Canadian State and Feature Films, 1917–84." PHD dissertation, Department of Political Science, York University 1987.
Mahon, R. "Canadian Public Policy: The Unequal Structure of Representation." In *The Canadian State*, edited by L. Panitch. Toronto: University of Toronto Press 1977.
- *The Politics of Industrial Restructuring: Canadian Textiles*. Toronto: University of Toronto Press 1984.
- "Regulatory Agencies: Captive Agents or Hegemonic Apparatuses." *Studies in Political Economy* 1 (1979): 162–200.
Malarek, Victor. *Haven's Gate: Canada's Immigration Fiasco*. Toronto: Macmillan 1987.
Mallory, J.R. *Social Credit and the Federal Power in Canada*. Original 1954. Toronto: University of Toronto Press 1977.
Mandel, Michael. "Democracy, Class and Canadian Sentencing Law." In *The Social Basis of Law*, edited by Stephen Brickey and Elizabeth Comack. Toronto: Garamond Press 1986.
- "Democracy, Class and the National Parole Board." *Criminal Law Quarterly* 27 (1984–5): 159–81.
- Legalization of Prison Discipline." *Crime and Social Justice*. Special Issue on Canada and the U.S.: Criminal Justice Connections. 26 (1986).
- "The Rule of Law and the Legalisation of Politics in Canada." *International Journal of the Sociology of Law* 13 (1985): 273–87.
Manuel, G., and Posluns, Michael. *The Fourth World*. Vancouver: Douglas and

McIntyre 1975.

Marchak, Patricia. "Canadian Political Economy." *Canadian Review of Sociology and Anthropology* 22 (1985): 673-709.

- *Green Gold: The Forestry Industry in British Columbia*. Vancouver: University of British Columbia Press 1983.

- "The Rise and Fall of the Peripheral State: The Case of British Columbia." In *Regionalism in Canada*, edited by R. Brym. Toronto: Irwin 1986.

Marks, E., and deCourtivron, I. *New French Feminisms: An Anthology*. New York: Schocken Books 1980.

Maroney, Heather Jon. "Contemporary Quebec Feminism: The Interrelations of Political and Ideological Development in Women's Organizations, Trade Unions, Political Parties and State Policy, 1960-1980." PHD dissertation, McMaster University 1988.

- "Embracing Motherhood: New Feminist Theory." In *Politics of Diversity: Feminism, Marxism and Nationalism*, edited by R. Hamilton and M. Barrett. Montreal: Book Centre Inc. 1986.

- "Feminism at Work." *New Left Review* 141 (1983).

Maroney, H.J., and Luxton, M. "From Feminism and Political Economy to Feminist Political Economy." In *Feminism and Political Economy: Women's Work, Women's Struggles*, edited by H. J. Maroney and M. Luxton. Toronto: Methuen 1987.

Martin, Robert. "The Judges and the Charter." *Socialist Studies* 2 (1984): 66-83.

Marx, E. *Grundrisse*. London: Penguin Books 1973.

Maslove, A. and M. Prince. *Knocking at the Back Door: The Political Economy of Canada - U.S. Free Trade*. Halifax: Institute for Research on Public Policy 1987.

Massey, Doreen. "Regionalism: Some Issues." *Capital and Class* 6 (1978).

Matthews, Ralph. *The Creation of Regional Dependency*. Toronto: University of Toronto Press 1983.

Melody, W. et al. *Culture, Communication and Dependency*. New Jersey: 1981.

Miles, R. *Racism and Migrant Labour*. London: Routledge and Kegan Paul 1982.

Miliband, Ralph. "Activism and Capitalist Democracy." In *Public Law and Politics*, edited by Carol Harlow. London: Sweet and Maxwell 1986.

- *The State in Capitalist Society*. London: Quartet 1969.

Miliband, Ralph and Saville, J. *The Socialist Register 1983*. London: Merlin 1983.

Mill, J.S. "On the Definition of Political Economy." In *Essays on Some Unsettled Questions of Political Economy*, 2nd ed. London: Longmans 1874.

- *Principles of Political Economy with some of their applications to Social Philosophy*, edited by W. J. Ashley. London: Longmans 1926.

Mills, C.W. *The Power Elite*. New York: Oxford 1956.

Monahan, Patrick J. "At Doctrine's Twilight: The Structure of Canadian Federalism." *University of Toronto Law Journal* 34 (1984): 47-99.

Montgomery, David. "Interview." In *Visions of History*, edited by Henry Abelove et al. New York: Pantheon 1983.

Moore, S., and Wells, D. *Imperialism and the National Question in Canada*. Toronto: privately published 1975.

Morrison, R. Bruce, and Wilson, R. Roderick, eds. *Native Peoples: The Canadian Experience*. Toronto: McClelland and Stewart 1986.

Morse, Bradford W. "Introduction." In *Aboriginal Peoples and the Law: Indian, Metis and Inuit Rights in Canada*, edited by Bradford W. Morse. Ottawa: Carleton University Press 1985.

Morton, Desmond, with Terry Copp. *Working People*. Ottawa: Deneau and Greenberg 1980.

Morton, P. "Women's Work Is Never Done." In *Women Unite*. Toronto: Women's Press 1972.

Morton, W.L. *The Progressive Party in Canada*. Toronto: University of Toronto Press 1950.

Moscovitch, A. "Leonard Marsh and Canadian Social Policy." *Journal of Canadian Studies* 21:2 (1986).

Moscovitch, Allan, and Albert, Jim, eds., *The Benevolent State: The Growth of Welfare in Canada*. Toronto: Garamond Press 1987.

Moscovitch, Allan, and Drover, Glenn, eds. *The Welfare State in Canada*. Waterloo: Wilfrid Laurier University Press 1983.

Murdock, Graham. "Blindspots about Western Marxism: A Reply to Dallas Smythe." *Canadian Journal of Political and Social Theory* 2:2 (spring/summer 1978).

Muszynski, Alicja. "Class Formation and Class Consciousness: The Making of Shoreworkers in the BC Fishing Industry." *Studies in Political Economy* 20 (summer 1986).

Muszynski, L. *The Deindustrialization of Metropolitan Toronto: A Study of Plant Closures, Layoffs and Unemployment*. Toronto: Social Planning Council of Metropolitan Toronto 1985.

Myles, John. "The Aged, the State and the Structure of Inequality." In *Structured Inequality in Canada*, edited by John Harp and John Hofley. Toronto: Prentice-Hall 1980.

Mytelka, L.K. "Knowledge-Intensive Production and the Changing Internationalization Strategies of Multinational Firms." In *A Changing International Division of Labour*, edited by J. Caporaso. Boulder: Rienner 1987.

Naylor, R.T. *Canada in the European Age 1453-1919*. Vancouver: New Star Books 1987.

- "Dominion of Debt." In *Domination*, edited by Alkis Kontos. Toronto: University of Toronto Press 1972.

- *Dominion of Debt: Centre, Periphery and the International Economic Order*. Montreal: Black Rose 1985.

- *The History of Canadian Business 1867-1914*. 2 vols. Toronto: James Lorimer 1975.

- "The Rise and Fall of the Third Commercial Empire of the St. Lawrence." In

Capitalism and the National Question in Canada, edited by G. Teeple. Toronto: University of Toronto Press 1972.

Neil, Robin. "The Passing of Canadian Economic History." *Journal of Canadian Studies* 12:5 (1977).

Neis, Barbara. "Doin' Time on the Protest Line: Women's Political Culture, Politics and Collective Action in Outport Newfoundland." In *A Question of Survival: The Fisheries and Newfoundland Society*, edited by Peter Sinclair. St. John's: Memorial University (forthcoming).

Nelles, H.V. *The Politics of Development: Forest, Mines and Hydro-Electric Power in Ontario, 1840-1941.* Toronto: Macmillan 1974.

Ng, R. "The Social Construction of Immigrant Women in Canada." In *The Politics of Diversity*, edited by R. Hamilton and M. Barrett. Montreal: Book Centre Inc. 1986

Niosi, J. "The Canadian Bourgeoisie: Towards a Synthetical Approach." *Canadian Journal of Political and Social Theory* 7:3 (fall 1983): 128-49.

- "Continental Nationalism: The Strategy of the Canadian Bourgeoisie." In *The Structure of the Canadian Capitalist Class*, edited by Robert Brym. Toronto: Garamond Press 1985.

- "The New French Canadian Bourgeoisie." *Studies in Political Economy* 1 (1979).

Niosi, J., and Faucher, P. "The Decline of North American Industry: The United States and Canada." In *Frontyard/Backyard*, edited by J. Holmes and C. Leys. Toronto: Between the Lines 1987.

O'Brien, Mary, and McIntyre, Sheila. "Patriarchal Hegemony and Legal Education." *Canadian Journal of Women and the Law* 2:1 (1986) 69-95.

OECD Economic Surveys 1984/85: Canada. Paris: OECD 1985.

Olsen, D. *The State Elite.* Toronto: McClelland and Stewart 1980.

Ostry, Bernard. *The Cultural Connection.* Toronto: McClelland and Stewart 1978.

Owram, D. *The Government Generation: Canadian Intellectuals and the State, 1900-1945.* Toronto: University of Toronto Press 1986.

Pal, L.A. "Relative Autonomy Revisited: The Origins of Canadian Unemployment Insurance." *Canadian Journal of Political Science* 19:1 (1986): 71-92.

- "Reply: Restraining Class in Policy Explanations." *Canadian Journal of Political Science* 19:1 (1986): 99-102.

Palmer, Bryan D. *A Culture in Conflict.* Montreal: McGill-Queen's University Press 1979.

- "Listening to History Rather Than Historians: Reflections on Working Class History." *Studies in Political Economy* 20 (1986): 47-84.

- *The Making of E.P. Thompson.* Toronto: New Hogtown Press 1981.

- "Review of Pentland, *Labour and Capital*." *Canadian Historical Review* 63 (1982): 227-30.

- "Working-Class Canada: Recent Historical Writing." *Queen's Quarterly* 86 (1979-80).

- *Working-Class Experience: The Rise and Reconstitution of Canadian Labour.* Toronto: Butterworth 1983.

Palmer, B.D., and Kealey, G.S. *Dreaming of What Might Be: The Knights of Labour in Ontario, 1880-1900.* New York: Cambridge University Press 1982.

Palmer, Howard. "Canadian Immigration and Ethnic History in the 1970s and 1980s." *International Migration Review* 15:3 (1981): 471-501.

- *Patterns of Prejudice: A History of Nativism in Alberta.* Toronto: McClelland and Stewart 1982.

Panitch, L. "Corporatism in Canada." *Studies in Political Economy* 1 (1979).

- "Dependency and Class in Canadian Political Economy." *Studies in Political Economy* 6 (1981) 7-34.

- "Elites, Classes and Power in Canada." In *Canadian Politics in the 1980s*, 2nd ed., edited by Michael S. Whittington and Glen Williams. Toronto: Methuen, 1984.

- "Liberal Democracy and Socialist Democracy: The Antinomies of C.B. Macpherson." In *The Socialist Register 1981*, edited by R. Miliband and J. Saville. London: Merlin 1981: 144-68.

- "The Role and Nature of the Canadian State." In *The Canadian State: Political Economy and Political Power*, edited by L. Panitch. Toronto: University of Toronto Press 1977.

- "The Tripartite Experience." In *The State and Economic Interests*, edited by K. Banting. Toronto: University of Toronto Press 1986.

- "Yesterday's News." *Books in Canada* (May 1987).

- ed. *The Canadian State: Political Economy and Political Power.* Toronto: University of Toronto Press 1977.

- ed. "Capitalist Restructuring and Labour Strategies." *Studies in Political Economy* (autumn 1987).

Panitch, L., and Swartz, D. *From Consent to Coercion: The Assault on Trade Union Freedoms.* Toronto: Garamond Press 1985.

Paquet, Gilles. " 'Le fruit dont l'ombre est la saveur': réflexions aventureuses sur la pensée économique au Québec." *Recherches sociographiques* 26:3 (1985).

Parker, I." 'Commodity Fetishism and 'Vulgar Marxism.' '": On 'Rethinking Canadian Political Economy.' " *Studies in Political Economy* 10 (Winter 1983).

- "Harold Innis, Karl Marx and Canadian Political Economy." *Queen's Quarterly* (winter 1977).

Parrot, Jean-Claude. "An Interview." *Studies in Political Economy* 11 (1983): 49-70.

Patrias, C. "Patriots and Proletarians: The Politicization of Hungarian Immigrants in Canada 1924-1946." PHD dissertation, Department of History, University of Toronto 1985.

Pattern, Howard. *Patterns of Prejudice: A History of Nativism in Alberta.* Toronto: McClelland and Stewart 1982.

Patton, Donald. *Industrial Development and the Atlantic Fishery: Opportunities for*

Manufacturing and Skilled Workers in the 1980s. Ottawa: Canadian Institute for Economic Policy 1981.

Peers, Frank. *The Public Eye: Television and the Politics of Canadian Broadcasting 1952-68*. Toronto: University of Toronto Press 1979.

Pelletier, Michel. *De la sécurité sociale à la sécurité du revenue, essai sur la politique économique et sociale contemporaine*. Montreal: Albert Saint-Martin 1982.

Peltier, Wilfred, and Poole, T. *No Foreign Land*. Toronto: McClelland and Stewart 1973.

Pentland, H. Clare. "The Development of a Capitalist Labour Market in Canada." *Canadian Journal of Economics and Political Science* 25 (November 1959).

– *Labour and Capital in Canada 1650-1860*, edited by P. Phillips. Toronto: James Lorimer 1981.

– "The Lachine Strike of 1843." *Canadian Historical Review* 29 (1984): 255:77.

– *A Study of the Social, Economic and Political Background of the Canadian System of Industrial Relations*. Mimeo. Ottawa: Task Force on Labour Relations 1968.

Peters, Evelyn J. *Aboriginal Self-Government in Canada: A Bibiliography 1986*. Kingston: Institute of Intergovernmental Relations, Queen's University 1986.

Petter, Andrew. "The Politics of the Charter." *Supreme Court Law Review* 8 (1986): 473-505.

Phillips, Paul. "The Hinterland Perspective: The Political Economy of Vernon Fowke." *Canadian Journal of Social and Political Thought* (spring 1978).

– "Introduction." In *Labour and Capital in Canada 1650-1860*, by H. Clare Pentland. Toronto: James Lorimer 1981.

– "The National Policy and the Development of the Western Canadian Labour Movement." In *Prairie Perspectives 2: Selected Papers of the Western Canadian Studies Conferences 1970, 1971*. Toronto: Holt, Rinehart and Winston 1973.

– *No Power Greater*. Vancouver: B.C. Federation of Labour 1967.

– "Review – Retrospection and Revisionism: Dependency and Class in Canadian Political Economy." *Journal of Canadian Studies* (summer 1987): 206-7.

– "Staples, Surplus, and Exchange: The Commerical Industrial Question in the National Policy Period." In *Explorations in Canadian Economic History: Essays in Honour of Irene M. Spry*, edited by Duncan Cameron. Ottawa: University of Ottawa Press 1985.

Phillips, Paul, and Phillips, Erin. *Women and Work*. Toronto: James Lorimer 1983.

Pomfret, Richard. *The Economic Development of Canada*. Toronto: Methuen 1981.

Ponting, J. Rick. "Relations between Bands and the Department of Indian Affairs." In *Arduous Journey*, edited by J. Rick Ponting. Toronto: McClelland and Stewart 1986.

– ed. *Arduous Journey: Canadian Indians and Decolonization*. Toronto: McClelland and Stewart 1986.

Porter, A., and Cameron, B. "The Impact of Free Trade on Women in Manufacturing." Background Paper. Canadian Advisory Council of the Status of Women,

1987.

Porter, J. *The Vertical Mosaic*. Toronto: University of Toronto Press 1965.

Porter, Marilyn. "Peripheral Women: Towards a Feminist Analysis of the Atlantic Region." *Studies in Political Economy* 23 (summer 1987).

- "Skipper of the Shore Crew: The History of the Sexual Division of Labour in Newfoundland." *Labour/Le Travail* 15 (spring 1985).

Possibles 10:2 (1986).

Poulantzas, Nicos. *Political Power and Social Classes*. London: Verso 1975.

- *State, Power, Socialism*. London: New Left Books 1978.

Pratt, Larry. "The State and Province-Building: Alberta's Development Strategy." In *The Canadian State: Political Economy and Political Power*, edited by Leo Panitch. Toronto: University of Toronto Press 1977.

Przeworski, A. "Proletariat into a Class: The Process of Class Formation from Katusky's 'The Class Struggle' to Recent Controversies." *Politics and Society* 7 (1977).

- *Capitalism and Social Democracy*. Cambridge: Cambridge University Press 1985.

Pue, W. Wesley. "The Law Reform Commission of Canada and Lawyers' Approaches to Public Administration." *Canadian Journal of Law and Society* 2 (1987): 165-76.

- "Review of Louis A. Knafla, ed., Law and Justice in a New Land: Essays in Western Canadian Legal History." *McGill Law Journal* 32 (1986): 254-9.

Radforth, Ian. "Logging Pulpwood in Northern Ontario." In *On the Job: Confronting the Labour Process in Canada*. Montreal: McGill-Queen's University Press 1986.

Ramcharan, S. *Racism: Nonwhites in Canada*. Toronto: Butterworths 1982.

Ramirez, Bruno. "Brief Encounters: Italian Immigrant Workers and the CPR, 1900-30." *Labour/Le Travail* 17 (Spring 1986): 9-27.

- "Ethnic Studies and Working Class History." *Labour/Le Travail* 19 (1987): 45-8.

Ratner, R.S. "Inside the Liberal Boot: The Criminological Enterprise in Canada." *Studies in Political Economy* 13 (1984): 145-64.

- "Introduction to a Conjunctural Analysis of Social Control in Canada." *Crime and Social Justice*. Special Issue on Canada and the U.S.: Criminal Justice Connections. 26 (1986): 1-10.

Ratner, R.S., and McMullan, J.L. "Social Control and the Rise of the Exceptional State in Britain, the United States, and Canada." *Crime and Social Justice* 19 (1983): 31-43.

Ratner, R.S., and McMullan, J.L., eds. *State Control: Criminal Justice Politics in Canada*. Vancouver: University of British Columbia Press 1987.

Ray, A. *Indians in the Fur Trade: Their Role as Hunters, Trappers, and Middlemen in the Lands Southwest of Hudson Bay 1660-1870*. Toronto: University of Toronto Press 1974.

Ray, A., and Freeman, D. *"Give Us Good Measure": An Economic Analysis of the Relations between the Indians and the Hudson's Bay Company before 1763*. Toronto: University of Toronto Press 1978.

Raynauld, A., and Vaillancourt, F. *L'appartenance des entreprises: le cas du Québec en 1978*. Quebec: CLF 1984.

Renaud, Gilbert. *A l'ombre du rationalisme: la société québécoise de sa dépendance à sa quotidienneté*. Montreal: Editions coopératives Albert Saint-Martin 1984.

Resnick, P. "The Maturing of Canadian Capitalism." *Our Generation* (fall 1982).

Rich, E.E. *The Hudson's Bay Company 1670–1870*. Toronto: McClelland and Stewart 1960.

Richards, J., and Pratt, L. *Prairie Capitalism: Power and Influence in the New West*. Toronto: McClelland and Stewart 1979.

Richards, John. "The Staple Debates." In *Explorations in Canadian Economic History: Essays in Honour of Irene M. Spry*, edited by Duncan Cameron. Ottawa: University of Ottawa Press 1985.

Rioux, Marcel. "Conscience ethnique et conscience de class au Québec." *Recherches sociographiques* 6:1 (1965).

Rioux, Marcel, and Dofny, Jacques. "Les classes sociales au Canada français." *Revue française de sociologie* 3:3 (1962): 290–300.

Robin, Martin. *Radical Politics and Canadian Labour*. Kingston: Industrial Relations Centre, Queen's University 1968.

Robinson, Eric, and Quinney, H.B. *The Infested Blanket: Canada's Constitution – Genocide of Indian Nations*. Winnipeg: Queenston House 1985.

Rotstein, A. "Fur Trade and Empire: An Institutional Analysis." PHD dissertation, University of Toronto 1967.

– *Rebuilding from Within: Remedies for Canada's Ailing Economy*. Toronto: James Lorimer 1984.

Russell, J. Stuart. "The Critical Legal Studies Challenge to Contemporary Mainstream Legal Philosophy." *Ottawa Law Review* 18 (1986): 1–24.

Russell, Peter. "Overcoming Legal Formalism: The Treatment of the Constitution, the Courts and Judicial Behaviour in Canadian Political Science." *Canadian Journal of Law and Society* 1 (1986): 5–35.

– "The Political Purposes of the Canadian Charter of Rights and Freedoms." *Canadian Bar Review* 61 (1983): 30–54.

Ryerson, Stanley. *The Founding of Canada*. Toronto: Progress Books 1960.

– *Unequal Union: Confederation and the Roots of Conflict in the Canadas, 1815–1873*. Toronto: Progress Books 1968.

Sacouman, R.J. "The 'Peripheral' Maritimes and Canada-wide Marxist Political Economy." *Studies in Political Economy* 6 (autumn 1981).

– "Semi-proletarianization and Rural Underdevelopment in the Maritimes." *Canadian Review of Sociology and Anthropology* (Aug. 1980).

Sahlins, M. *Stone-Age Economics*. New York: Aldine Publishing 1972.

Salée, Daniel. "L'analyse socio-politique de la société québécoise: bilan et perspectives." In *Espace régional et nation: pour un nouveau débat sur le Québec*, by Gérard Boismenu et al. Montreal: Boréal Express 1983.

- "Pour une autopsie de l'imaginaire québécois: regards sur la morosité postmoderne." *Canadian Journal of Political and Social Theory* 10:3 (1986).

Sales, A., and Bélanger, N. *Décideurs et gestionnaires, étude sur la direction et l'encadrement des secteurs privé et public.* Quebec: CLF 1985.

Sales, Arnaud. "La construction sociale de l'économie québécoise." *Recherches sociographiques* 26:3 (1985).

Salter, Liora. "Inequality in the Media: Public Broadcasting and Private Constraints." In *Inequality: Essays on the Political Economy of Social Welfare*, edited by A. Moscovitch and G. Drover. Toronto: University of Toronto Press 1981.

- "Introduction." In *Communication Studies in Canada*, edited by Liora Salter. Toronto: Butterworths 1981.

- ed. *Communication Studies in Canada.* Toronto: Butterworths 1981.

Sanders, Douglas. "The Indian Lobby." In *And No One Cheered: Federalism, Democracy and the Constitution Act*, edited by Keith Banting and Richard Simeon. Toronto: Methuen 1983.

Sangster, J. "The Communist Party and the Woman Question 1922-1929." *Labour/Le Travail* 15 (spring 1985).

Sargent, Neil C. "Law, Ideology and Corporate Crime: A Critique of Instrumentalism." Unpublished manuscript, Department of Law, Carleton University 1988.

Saul, J.R. "The Secret Life of the Branch Plant Executive." *Report on Business Magazine*. (Jan. 1988).

Schmidt, Ray. "Canadian Political Economy: A Critique." *Studies in Political Economy* 6 (1981): 65-92.

Scott, F.R. *Essays on the Constitution.* Toronto: University of Toronto Press 1974.

- "The Future of the Legal Profession." In *A New Endeavour: Selected Political Essays, Letters, and Addresses*, edited by Michiel Horn. Toronto: University of Toronto Press 1986.

- "The P.C. and Mr. Bennett's 'New Deal' Legislation." In *Essays on the Constitution*, by Frank R. Scott. Toronto: University of Toronto Press 1977.

Seager, A. "Class, Ethnicity and Politics in the Alberta Coalfields, 1905-1946." In *Struggle a Hard Battle: Essays on Working Class Immigrants*, edited by D. Hoerder. Dekalb, Ill.: Northern Illinois University Press 1986.

Seccombe, W. "The Housewife and Her Labour under Capitalism." *New Left Review* 83 (Jan.-Feb.): 3-24.

- "Reflections on the Domestic Labour Debate." In *The Politics of Diversity: Feminism, Marxism and Nationalism*, edited by R. Hamilton and M. Barrett. Montreal: Book Centre Inc. 1986.

Silmon, J., ed. *Enough Is Enough: Aboriginal Women Speak Out.* Toronto: Women's Press 1987.

Silvera, M. "Resources for Feminist Research." *Immigrant Women in Canada* 16:1 (March 1987).

- *Silenced*. Toronto: William Wallace Publishers Inc. 1983.

Simard, Jean-Jacques. *La longue marche des technocrates*. Montreal: Editions coopératives Albert Saint-Martin 1979.

Skocpol, T. "Bringing the State Back In: Strategies of Analysis in Current Research." In *Bringing the State Back In*, edited by P. Evans, D. Rueschemeyer, and T. Skocpol. Cambridge: Cambridge University Press 1985.

- "Political Response to Capitalist Crisis: Neo-Marxist Theories of the State and the Case of the New Deal." *Politics and Society* 10:2 (1981).

Slater, J., and Molinan, M. "The Decline of Quebec Nationalism." *Canadian Dimension* (Feb. 1987).

Smandych, Russell. "The Origins of Canadian Anti-Combines Legislation, 1890–1910." In *The Social Basis of Law*, edited by Stephen Brickey and Elizabeth Comack. Toronto: Garamond Press 1986.

Smart, Carol. "Feminism and Law: Some Problems of Analysis and Strategy." *International Journal of the Sociology of Law* 14 (1986): 109-23.

- *The Ties That Bind: Law, Marriage and the Reproduction of Patriarchal Relations*. London: Routledge & Kegan Paul 1984

Smiley, Donald. "Canada and the Quest for a National Policy." *Canadian Journal of Political Science* (March 1975).

- *The Federal Condition in Canada*. Toronto: McGraw-Hill Ryerson 1986.

Smith, A. *An Inquiry into the Nature and Causes of the Wealth of Nations*. edited by E. Cannan, 6th edition. London: Methuen 1961.

Smith, D. "Women, Class and Family." In *The Socialist Register 1983*, edited by R. Miliband and J. Saville. London: Merlin 1983.

- "Women, Class and the Family." In *Women, Class, Family and the State*, edited by V. Burstyn and D. Smith. Toronto: Garamond Press 1985.

Smythe, Dallas. "Communications: Blindspot of Western Marxism." *Canadian Journal of Political and Social Theory* 1:3 (fall 1977).

- *Dependency Road: Communications, Capitalism, Consciousness and Canada*. Norwood, NJ: Ablex 1981.

Snider, Laureen. "Legal Aid, Reform and the Welfare State." In *The Social Basis of Law*, edited by S. Brickey and E. Comack. Toronto: Garamond 1986.

- "Legal Reform and Social Control: The Dangers of Abolishing Rape." *International Journal of the Sociology of Law* 13 (1985): 337–56.

- "Revising the Combines Investigation Act: A Study in Corporate Power." In *Structure, Law, and Power: Essays in the Sociology of Law*, edited by P. Brantigham and J. Kress. Beverly Hills: Sage 1979.

- "Towards a Political Economy of Reform, Regulation and Corporate Crime." *Law and Policy* 9 (1987): 37–68.

- "Traditional and Corporate Theft: A Comparison of Sanctions." In *White-Collar and Economic Crime*, edited by P. Wickman and T. Dailey. Lexington: Lexington Books 1982.

Snider, D. Laureen, and West, W. Gordon. "Canada and the United States: Crimi-

nal Justice Connections." Special Issue on Canada. *Crime and Social Justice* 26 (1986).
- "A Critical Perspective on Law in the Canadian State: Delinquency and Corporate Crime." In *The New Criminologies in Canada: State, Crime and Control*, edited by Thomas Fleming. Toronto: Oxford University Press 1985.
- "Critical Perspectives on the Constitution." *Socialist Studies* 2 (1984).
Solberg, Carl E. *The Prairies and the Pampas: Agrarian Policy in Canada and Argentina, 1880-1930*. Stanford, Calif.: Stanford University Press 1987.
Solow, Robert M. "Economic History and Economics." *American Economic Review*, Papers and Proceedings (May 1985).
Solow, Robert M., and Temin, Peter. "Introduction: The Inputs for Growth." *Cambridge Economic History of Europe*, VII, Part I. Cambridge: Cambridge University Press 1978.
Sparer, Ed. "Fundamental Human Rights, Legal Entitlements, and the Social Struggle: A Friendly Critique of the Critical Legal Studies Movement." *Stanford Law Review* 36 (1984): 509-74.
Special Senate Committee on Mass Media (Keith Davey, Chair). Report. Ottawa 1971.
Speck, Dara Culhane. *An Error in Judgement*. Vancouver: Talonbooks 1987.
Stasiulis, Daiva. "Capitalism, Democracy and the Canadian State." In *Social Issues: Sociological Views of Canada*, 2nd ed., edited by D. Forcese and S. Richer. Scarborough: Prentice-Hall, 1988.
Stevenson, Garth. "Canadian Regionalism in Continental Perspective." *Journal of Canadian Studies* (summer 1980).
- "Federalism and the Political Economy of the Canadian State." In *The Canadian State*, edited by L. Panitch. Toronto: University of Toronto Press 1977.
- "The Political Economy Tradition and Canadian Federalism." *Studies in Political Economy* 6 (1981).
- *Unfulfilled Union*. Toronto: Macmillan 1979.
Stevenson, P. "Capital and the State in Canada: Some Critical Questions on Carroll's Finance Capitalists." *Studies in Political Economy* (fall 1983).
Struthers, James. *No Fault of Their Own: Unemployment and the Canadian Welfare State 1914-1941*. Toronto: University of Toronto Press 1983.
Sugarman, David. "Law, Economy and the State in England, 1750-1914: Some Major Issues." In *Legality, Ideology and the State*, edited by David Sugarman. London: Academic Press 1983.
Sumner, Colin. "The Rule of Law and Civil Rights in Contemporary Marxist Theory." *Kapitalistate* 9 (1981): 63-89.
Sunahara, Ann. *The Politics of Racism: The Uprooting of Japanese Canadians during the Second World War*. Toronto: James Lorimer 1981.
Swartz, D. "The Politics of Reform: Conflict and Accommodation in Canadian Health Policy." In *The Canadian State*, edited by L. Panitch. Toronto: University of Toronto Press 1977.

Tanguay, A.B. "Concerted Action in Quebec, 1976-1983: Dialogue of the Deaf."
    In *Quebec: State and Society*, edited by A. Gagnon. Toronto: Methuen 1984.

Tanner, Adrian, ed. *The Politics of Indianness*. St. John's: Institute of Social and
    Economic Research, Memorial University of Newfoundland 1983.

Task Force on Atlantic Fisheries. *Navigating Troubled Waters: A New Policy for the
    Atlantic Fisheries*. Ottawa: Minister of Supply and Services 1982.

Taylor, Charles. "Nationalism and the Political Intelligentsia: A Case Study."
    Queen's Quarterly 62 (spring 1965): 150-68.

Taylor, Ian. *Crime, Capitalism and Community: Three Essays in Socialist Criminol-
    ogy*. Toronto: Butterworths 1983.

- *Law and Order*. London: Macmillan 1981.

- "Theorizing the Crisis in Canada." In *State Control: Criminal Justice Politics in
    Canada*, edited by R.S. Ratner and J.L. McMullan. Vancouver: University of
    British Columbia Press 1987.

Teeple, G. "Introduction." In *Capitalism and the National Question in Canada*,
    edited by Gary Teeple. Toronto: University of Toronto Press 1972.

- ed. *Capitalism and the National Question in Canada*. Toronto: University of
    Toronto Press 1972.

Tennant, P. "Native Indian Political Organization in British Columbia, 1900-
    1969." *B.C. Studies* 55 (1982).

Thistle, Paul Q. *Indian-European Trade Relations in the Lower Saskatchewan River
    Region to 1840*. Winnipeg: University of Manitoba Press 1986.

Thompson, E.P. *The Poverty of Theory and Other Essays*. New York: Monthly
    Review Press 1978.

- *Whigs and Hunters: The Origin of the Black Act*. New York: Pantheon Books
    1975.

Tomlin, B. *The Integration Question*. Toronto: Addison and Wesley 1984.

Traves, T. "The Staple Model and Nineteenth Century Industrialization." Paper
    presented to the Conference on Innis in the 1980s. University of Toronto 1983.

- *The State and Enterprise: Canadian Manufacturers and the Federal Government,
    1917-1931*. Toronto: University of Toronto Press 1979.

Trigger, Bruce. *Natives and Newcomers*. Montreal and Kingston: McGill-Queen's
    University Press 1985.

Tucker, Eric. "The Determination of Occupational Health and Safety Standards in
    Ontario, 1860-1982: From the Market to Politics to . . . ?" *McGill Law Journal*
    29 (1984): 260-311.

- "The Law of Employers' Liability in Ontario 1861-1900: The Search for a
    Theory." *Osgoode Hall Law Journal* 22 (1984): 213-80.

Tulloch, H. *Black Canadians: A Long Line of Fighters*. Toronto: NC Press 1975.

Turk, Austin T. "Law, Conflict, and Order: From Theorizing toward Theories."
    Canadian Review of Sociology and Anthropology 13 (1976): 282-94.

Ubale, B. "Equal Opportunity and Public Policy." A report by the Toronto South
    Asian Community submitted to the Attorney General of Ontario, 1977.

Ujimoto, K.V., and Hirabayashi, G., eds. *Visible Minorities and Multiculturalism: Asians in Canada*. Toronto: Butterworths 1980.

Underhill, F. "O Canada." *Canadian Forum* (Dec. 1929).

Ursel, Jane. "The State and the Maintenance of Patriarchy: A Case Study of Family, Labour and Welfare Legislation in Canada." In *Family, Economy and State: The Social Reproduction Process under Capitalism*, edited by James Dickinson and Bob Russell. Toronto: Garmond Press 1986.

Usher, Peter J. "Are We Defending a Culture or a Mode of Production?" Paper presented to the Canadian Sociology and Anthropology Association Annual Meetings, University of Ottawa, June 1982.

- "The Class System, Metropolitan Dominance and Northern Development in Canada." *Antipode* 8:3 (1976): 28–32.

- "Evaluating Country Food in the Northern Native Economy." *Arctic* 29:2: 105–20.

- "The North: One Land, Two Ways of Life." In *Heartland and Hinterland: A Geography of Canada*, edited by L.D. McCann. Scarborough: Prentice-Hall 1982.

- "Staple Production and Ideology in Northern Canada." In *Culture, Communications and Dependency*, edited by W.H. Melody, L. Salter, and P. Heyer. Norwood: Ablex Publishing 1982.

Valverde, M. *Sex, Power and Pleasure*. Toronto: Women's Press 1985.

Van Kirk, Sylvia. *"Many Tender Ties": Women in Fur Trade Society 1670-1870*. Winnipeg: Watson and Dwyer 1980.

Veblen, Thorstein. "The Discipline of the Machine." In *The Portable Veblen*, edited by M. Lerner. (New York: Viking Press 1948).

- "Why Is Economics Not an Evolutionary Science?" In *The Portable Veblen*, edited by M. Lerner. (New York: Viking Press 1948).

Veltmeyer, H. "The Capitalist Underdevelopment of Atlantic Canada." In *Underdevelopment and Social Movements in Atlantic Canada*. Toronto: New Hogtown Press 1979.

Walters, Vivienne. "Occupational Health and Safety Legislation in Ontario: An Analysis of Its Origins and Content." *Canadian Review of Sociology and Anthropology* 20 (1983): 413–34.

Ward, P. *White Canada Forever*. Montreal and Kingston: McGill-Queen's University Press 1977.

Warskett, Rosemary. "Bank Worker Unionization and the Law." *Studies in Political Economy* 25 (1988): 41–73.

Watkins, Mel. "The Branch Plant Condition." In *Canadian Confrontations: Hinterland vs. Metropolis*, edited by Arthur K. Davis. Edmonton: Western Association of Sociology and Anthropology 1969.

- "Dene Nationalism." *Canadian Review of Studies in Nationalism* 8:1 (1981) 101–14.

- "The Dismal State of Economics in Canada." In *Close the 49th Parallel etc.: The*

Americanization of Canada, edited by Ian Lumsden. Toronto: University of Toronto Press 1970.

- "Economic Development in Canada." In *World Inequality: Origins and Perspectives on the World System*, edited by I. Wallerstein. Montreal: Black Rose Books 1975.

- "From Underdevelopment to Development" in *Dene Nation: The Colony Within*, edited by Mel Watkins. Toronto: University of Toronto Press 1977.

- "The Innis Tradition in Canadian Political Economy." *Canadian Journal of Political and Social Thought* 6 (winter 1982).

- A New National Policy." In *Agenda 1970: Proposals for a Creative Politics*, edited by T. Lloyd and J. McLeod. Toronto: University of Toronto Press 1968.

- "A Staple Theory of Economic Growth." *Canadian Journal of Economics and Political Science* 29 (May 1963): 141–58. Reprinted in *Approaches to Canadian Economic History*, edited by W.T. Easterbrook and M.H. Watkins. Toronto: McClelland and Stewart 1967.

- "The Staple Theory Revisited." *Journal of Canadian Studies* 12:5 (winter 1977).

Webber, M.J. "Agglomeration and the Regional Question." *Antipode* 17:2 (1984).

Westfall, William. "The Ambivalent Verdict: Harold Innis and Canadian History." In *Culture, Communications and Dependency*, edited by W. Melody et al. New Jersey: 1981.

- "On the Concept of Region in Canadian History and Literature." *Journal of Canadian Studies* (summer 1980).

Whitaker, Reginald. "Democracy and the Canadian Constitution." In *And No One Cheered: Federalism, Democracy and the Constitution Act*, edited by Keith Banting and Richard Simeon. Toronto: Methuen 1983.

- *Double Standard: Secret History of Canadian Immigration*. Toronto: Lester and Orpen Dennys 1987.

- "Neo-Conservatism and the State." In *The Socialist Register 1987*, edited by R. Miliband, L. Panitch, and J. Saville. London: Merlin 1987.

- "The Quebec Cauldron." In *Canadian Politics in the 1980s*, 2nd ed., edited by M. Whittington and G. Williams. Toronto: Methuen 1984.

- "'To Have Insight into Much and Power over Nothing': The Political Ideas of Harold Innis." *Queen's Quarterly* (autumn 1983).

White, R.D. *Law, Capitalism and the Right to Work*. Toronto: Garamond Press 1986.

Whittington, M. and Williams, G., eds. *Canadian Politics in the 1980s*. Second edition. Toronto: Methuen 1984.

Williams, Glen. "Canada – The Case of the Wealthiest Colony." *This Magazine* (Feb.–March 1976): 29–30.

- "Canadian Sovereignty and the Free Trade Debate." In *Knocking at the Back Door: The Political Economy of Canada-U.S. Free Trade*, edited by A. Maslove and M. Prince. Halifax: Institute for Research on Public Policy 1987.

- "Centre-Margin Dependency, and the State in the New Canadian Political Economy." Paper presented to the Canadian Political Science Association Meetings, Winnipeg 1986.

- "The National Policy Tariffs: Industrial Underdevelopment through Import Substitution." *Canadian Journal of Political Science* (June 1979): 333–68.
- *Not for Export: Toward a Political Economy of Canada's Arrested Industrialization.* Updated edition. Toronto: McClelland and Stewart 1986.

Williams, Raymond. *Culture.* Glasgow: Fontana 1981.

- *Television: Technology and Cultural Form.* Glasgow: Fontana 1974.

Wilson, E., with A. Weir. *Hidden Agendas: Theory, Politics, and Experience in the Women's Movement.* New York: Tavistock Publications 1986.

Wolfe, D. "Economic Growth and Foreign Investment: A Perspective on Canadian Economic Policy, 1945–1957." *Journal of Canadian Studies* 13:1 (1978): 15.

- "Mercantilism, Liberalism and Keynesianism: Changing Forms of State Intervention in Capitalist Economies." *Canadian Journal of Political and Social Thought* 5:1–2 (1981).
- "The Rise and Demise of the Keynesian Era in Canada: Economic Policy, 1930–1982." In *Modern Canada, 1930–1980's,* edited by M. Cross and G.S. Kealey.
- "The State and Economic Policy in Canada, 1968–75." In *The Canadian State,* edited by L. Panitch. Toronto: University of Toronto Press 1977.

Women's Research Centre. *Women and the Economy Kit.* Vancouver: Women's Research Centre 1986.

Wood, Ellen Meiksins. "Liberal Democracy and Capitalist Hegemony: A Reply to Leo Panitch on the Task of Socialist Political Theory." In *The Socialist Register 1983,* edited by R. Miliband and J. Saville. London: Merlin 1983.

- *The Retreat from Class: The New "True" Socialism.* London: Verso 1986.
- "The Separation of the Economic and the Political in Capitalism." *New Left Review* 127 (1981): 66–95.

Wright, Barry. "Towards a New Canadian Legal History." *Osgoode Hall Law Journal* 22 (1984): 349–74.

Wright, J.B. *The Ideological Dimensions of Law in Upper Canada: The Treason Proceedings of 1814 and 1838.* Jurisprudence Centre Working Paper. Ottawa: Carleton University 1986.

Yancey, W.L., Erickson, E., and Juliani, R.N. "Emergent Ethnicity: A Review and Reformulation." *American Sociological Review* 41:3 (June 1976): 391–403.

Zlotkin, N., and Colborne, D.R. "Internal Canadian Imperialism and the Native People." In *Imperialism, Nationalism and Canada,* edited by Craig Heron. Toronto: New Hogtown Press 1977.

DATE DUE

LEWIS AND CLARK COLLEGE LIBRARY
PORTLAND, OREGON 97219

Lewis and Clark College - Watzek Library
HB121.A2 N49 1989   wmain
/The New Canadian political economy / ed

3 5209 00358 5482